COMMUNITY HEALTH

contemporary perspectives

JANET H. SHIRREFFS
Arizona State University

Prentice-Hall, Inc., Englewood Cliffs, New Jersey 07632

Library of Congress Cataloging in Publication Data

Shirreffs, Janet H.
  Community health, contemporary perspectives.

  Bibliography: p.
  Includes index.
  1. Public health–United States. 2. Public health.
I. Title.
RA445.S47   362.1'0973   81-21115
ISBN 0-13-153494-7   AACR2

Editorial/production supervision and interior design by Kate Kelly
Cover Design by Tony Ferrara Studio
Manufacturing buyer: Harry P. Baisley

Printed in the United States of America

10 9 8 7 6 5 4 3 2

ISBN 0-13-153494-7

Prentice-Hall International, Inc., *London*
Prentice-Hall of Australia Pty. Limited, *Sydney*
Prentice-Hall of Canada, Ltd., *Toronto*
Prentice-Hall of India Private Limited, *New Delhi*
Prentice-Hall of Japan, Inc., *Tokyo*
Prentice-Hall of Southeast Asia Pte. Ltd., *Singapore*
Whitehall Books Limited, *Wellington, New Zealand*

This book is dedicated
   ... to my parents, who were the best teachers I ever had, and
   ... to my students, for whom this work was created.

CONTENTS

PREFACE

This book is written about the health of people, in the collective or group sense, as opposed to the individual or personal level. It is written about the individuals and processes involved in shaping local, state, and national health policy, and in delivering, utilizing, and planning health services in the United States. It examines health problems which affect groups of people and the way in which those in health-related professions attempt to solve them.

There are virtually millions of workers in the public health field who are concerned about the health and quality of life of others. These individuals comprise the nation's health industry and include among others: sanitarians, nutritionists, health planners, epidemiologists, health educators, physicians, and nurses. The challenge of all health workers is to protect and enhance the health of all people in the United States.

Consumers serve as the focal point in community health. Traditionally, consumers have had little voice in shaping health policy; little power to direct or redirect the health system. However, this situation is changing. Consumers are now involved not only in such things as outreach services, but also in shaping health policy at many levels.

Over the past twenty-five years, technological advance, social change, and the growing complexity of health care has had a significant impact upon public and community health. In essence, these factors have created a need to redefine the meaning and scope of contemporary community health. Although the basic goal of community health continues to involve protecting the public from disease and enhancing health or quality of life, the nature of community health activities have expanded significantly over the years. Fulfilling this mission has required that health professionals initiate activities designed to close the gap between traditional public health activities and the needs of today's rapidly changing society.

Community health must now come to terms with many of the complex problems confronting humankind which have as their roots a blend of psychosocial causes as well as the traditional health problems. Whereas physical survival was the major public health concern in the past, psychological and social survival may well be the challenge of this age. Accordingly, community health has begun to respond to the vast and complex network of sociological, psychological, and environmental factors that affect the health of people.

In addition, developments over the past several decades indicate that public health may no longer be narrowly viewed as consisting of only tax-supported or official health agency activities. The health-care system has grown in complexity over the years and has experienced a blending of involvement in both the private and public sector, due primarily to the way in which health care is now financed and some federal health initiatives. Thus the terms "public" or "official" no longer reflect accurately community health in the United States today.

This text is intended for students enrolled in an introductory community health course. It is designed to acquaint college and university students with the role of community health in contemporary society. It is written both for students who are planning to enter the health-related professions and those who may simply seek a deeper appreciation for the evolving nature of public community health.

The material is presented in such a way as to provide a historical reference point as the basis for understanding present and future community health concerns, issues, and priorities. The book is divided into four major sections, each with a specific emphasis or theme. *Part I, Foundations of Community Health,* traces major historical milestones of public health. It also examines the major social, political, and ethical forces which shape public health policy. Public health organization at the national, state, and local levels is revealed through an examination of both government-supported and voluntary organizations. The importance of understanding and appreciating social and cultural norms, beliefs, and traditions in public health programs is emphasized. Epidemiological principles and methods are discussed since they serve as the foundation of community disease control efforts.

Part II, Contemporary Community Health Challenges, seeks to shed light on the role of public health in promoting and maintaining health by: (1) applying epidemiologic methods to understand and control communicable, chronic-degenerative, and psycho-behavioral diseases; (2) fostering environmental quality and ensuring a safe living environment for the public; and (3) enhancing community and occupational safety and health from the local level through the federal level.

Part III, Health Care Delivery, includes an analysis of the total health care system of the United States. The strengths and weaknesses of the system are identified, especially with regard to financing mechanisms and organization. National health insurance proposals are examined and compared to key points and issues. The focus of this section is utilizing effective health-planning principles to provide quality, comprehensive, accessible, and economical health services to all people.

Part IV, Community Health: Focus On Target Groups, provides an in-depth study into population groups of particular public health significance including: mothers, infants, and children; the aged; impoverished minority groups; and the incarcerated. These groups are examined in relation to their unique life situation, and the response of public health to their health needs through environmental and health care interventions.

The overall emphasis of the text is upon the evolving nature of community health and future health concerns. It's theme is people—those who are in need of assistance in order to attain their health potential and those who have the ability to assist in promoting the realization of health potential.

Janet H. Shirreffs

ACKNOWLEDGMENTS

The completion of this book would not have been possible without the cooperation and encouragement of many people. It would be impossible to thank each person individually at this time. However, I would like to acknowledge those who have been of special significance to me.

I am grateful to my students who helped me see a need for a community health text of this nature, and who continue to support a humanistic approach to community health. My gratitude is especially extended to my first college health teacher, Don Read, Professor of Health Education at Worcester State College, for his encouragement, support, and belief in me and in this project.

To my colleagues who served as reviewers and who critically read this text, many thanks. Suggestions forthcoming were invaluable in preparing the final manuscript. Among the editors, I especially wish to thank Kate Kelly for her patience, cooperation, and skill in managing this project.

I express sincere thanks to Susan Broussard for her resourcefulness, promptness, and accuracy in typing the manuscript. There is no better critic in the world than an expert typist.

And also, I wish to extend grateful appreciation to the various individuals and agencies who contributed to this text. To Gary Krahenbuhl and Pam Barnett for their photographic contributions. To Paul Peterson for his artistic contributions in the form of line drawings, models, and charts. In addition, I would like to acknowledge the Environmental Protection Agency, the Arizona Department of Health Services, General Motors Corporation, the American Cancer Society, the American Heart Association, the National Safety Council, and the U.S. Department of Health and Human Services for their cooperation and assistance in preparing this text.

PART

1

foundations of community health

1

HISTORICAL PERSPECTIVES

So let us on this most auspicious anniversary look backward and learn the lessons of experience which it teaches before we take a step into the uncharted future.

Stephen Smith, 1921, on the 50th anniversary
of the American Public Health Association

DEFINING COMMUNITY HEALTH

The broad concern for well-being and enhancing health of large groups of individuals is the primary goal of community health. The concept of health has changed dramatically through the years, as has the nature of health problems confronting public health professionals. One of the most widely recognized and accepted definitions of health was developed by Dubos. This conception of *health** is one in which health or wellness is identified as a "quality of life" involving social, mental, and biological fitness on the part of an individual, which results from adaptations and responses of the individual to the environment.[1] It is an ecological definition of health that implies that enriching interactions on the part of an individual with both the physical and social environment is a key factor in relative health status. As a consequence of the social nature of human beings, if an obstacle to good health exists, it is very likely that it will affect not just one individual, but groups of individuals. Thus the concept of *community health* has evolved.

    The goal of community health remains one of fostering and preserving well-being and promoting "quality of life" in groups of individuals. In 1948, the House of Delegates of the American Medical Association defined community health as

*Words set in italic in text are defined in glossary located at end of each chapter.

4

The art and science of maintaining, protecting and improving the health of the people through organized community efforts. It includes those arrangements whereby the community provides medical services for special groups of persons and is concerned with prevention or control of disease, with persons requiring hospitalization to protect the community and with the medically indigent.

Although community health continues to focus on health promotion and protection, a trend is evident in contemporary society in which community health activities and private medical practice are more closely aligned in a total system of health care delivery in the United States. The distinction between the role of community health in promoting the nation's health and that of private medicine is not as clear as it has been in the past.

COMMUNITY HEALTH: THE PAST

From the beginnings of time, each society has had specific health concerns, accepted cultural beliefs and mores, and a foundation of scientific knowledge. The blend of these interrelated factors creates a social health policy in any era. During the inception of community health, dated at Egyptian times, and continuing through the modern era of health in the early 1900s, the primary community health problems were the prevalence of *communicable diseases,* poor sanitation, and a general lack of medical knowledge and accompanying technology. Until the *germ theory of disease* was advanced, community health workers were burdened with thousands and sometimes millions of people falling ill and succumbing to a variety of communicable diseases. As can be seen, these health professionals of the past lacked vital knowledge of what caused disease and therefore were, for the most part, ineffective in preventing the spread of mass epidemics and ensuing mass deaths. Although Egyptian, Greek, and Hebrew civilizations all made significant contributions to the evolving field of community health, the Romans are credited with providing the rudimentary beginnings of contemporary community health. The health of the public was a priority in the Roman Empire.

Communicable Disease Control

From the medieval period in history through the early 1900s, community health efforts were aimed primarily at the control of large-scale epidemics. Of the many diseases that were *epidemic* during this era, perhaps bubonic plague—or the "Black Death" as it was commonly known—was the most devastating. A *pandemic* existed throughout most of the world for many years during this period. In England alone, over two million people succumbed to plague. Health officials were ineffective in controlling this killer, for they lacked knowledge of its cause. Although quarantines were utilized to separate diseased persons from the rest of society, they were typically too late to be effective. Poor sanitation was an additional factor in the spread of disease. Rat-infested garbage and filth provided an ideal environment for disease-producing organisms to thrive and reproduce.

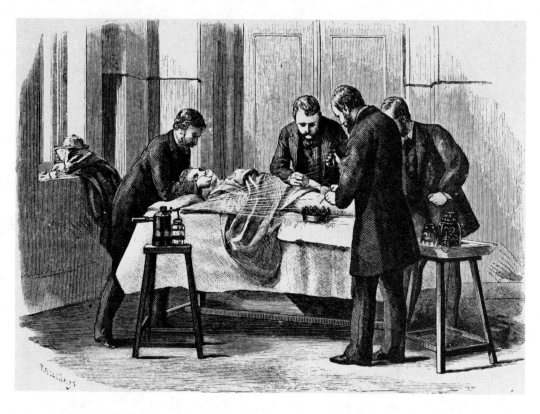

Figure 1-1 Surgery: Operation performed with antiseptic precautions, using Lister carbolic spray. Courtesy National Library of Medicine, Bethesda, Maryland.

In America during early Colonial times, smallpox, yellow fever, and cholera posed major health problems. During the eighteenth and nineteenth centuries, a number of epidemics occurred in the colonies in every major city. (The map in Figure 1-2 offers some indication as to the extent of yellow-fever outbreaks in the United States between 1668 and 1874.) As a consequence of these severe epidemics, the life span of an average citizen in the United States was rarely above 40 years. Although unsophisticated when measured against modern community health practices, some initial steps were taken during these years to control epidemic disease through quarantine and other public health measures were initiated.

The years 1790-1900 can best be characterized by a rapid expansion of medical knowledge and technology. In addition, more effective organization of community health was realized in conjunction with greater humanitarian concern for all people. Many individuals contributed to advanced medical knowledge and to the growing movement of public health. The first major breakthrough in community health came in 1850, when a report written by Lemuel Shattuck dealing with the sanitation and health problems in the

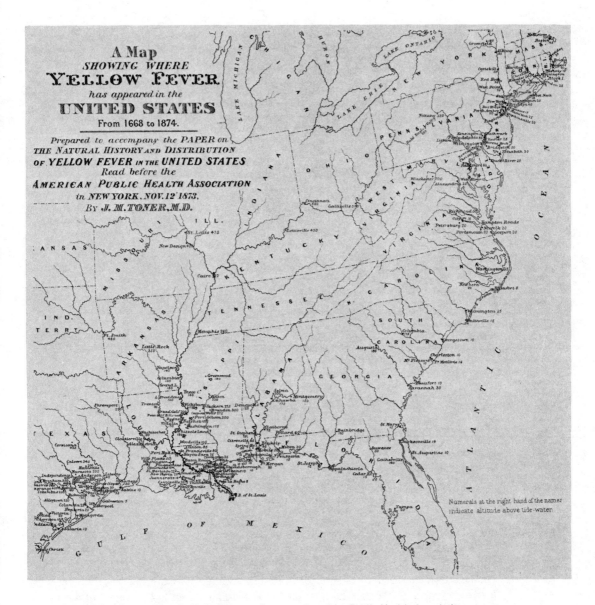

Figure 1-2 Yellow fever outbreak, United States. Courtesy American Public Health Association.

Commonwealth of Massachusetts was made public (Figure 1-3). The Shattuck Report was a significant achievement, for it organized the power of local government around improved sanitation and disease control. It included recommendations for the establishment of state and local boards of health, collection of vital statistics, sanitation programs at the local level, and disease prevention as an integral phase of all medical practice. The implica-

Among the recommendations of this public health document were those for:

the establishment of state and local boards of health

a system of sanitary police or inspectors

the collection and analysis of vital statistics

a routine system for exchanging data and information

sanitation programs for towns and buildings

studies on the health of school children

studies of tuberculosis, the control of alcoholism, the supervision of mental disease

the sanitary supervision and study of problems of immigrants

the erection of model tenements, public bathhouses, and washhouses

the control of smoke nuisances

the control of food adulteration

the exposure of nostrums, the preaching of health from pulpits

the establishment of nurses' training schools

the teaching of sanitary science in medical schools

and the inclusion of preventive medicine in clinical practice, with routine physical examinations and family records of illness.

Figure 1-3 Report of the Sanitary Commission of Massachusetts, Lemuel Shattuck (1793-1859).

tions of this report in the evolution of community health cannot be overestimated. In 1868, nineteen years after the Shattuck Report was presented, the first state public health department in the United States was established in Massachusetts. Another important event in the emergence of community health during these years was the organization of the American Public Health Association in 1872. This organization, which in its founding year elected Dr. Stephen Smith as its first president, continues to provide direction and leadership to public health professionals today.

COMMUNITY HEALTH: THE PRESENT

The health of the nation has never been better. Average life expectancy is 73.3 years—a 2.8-year increase in the past decade (see Table 1-1 and Figure 1-4). The infant mortality rate is the lowest in our history, dropping to a rate of 13 infant deaths per 1,000 live births in 1979. Heart disease and cancer mortality are continuing to decline. But despite the impressive progress, too many of the poor, particularly among the racial and ethnic minorities, lack adequate health care and protection, too many adolescent women become pregnant, too many babies die before their first birthday, too many people die prematurely and suffer needlessly from communicable diseases, chronic diseases, environmental

Table 1-1 Life Expectancy at Birth and at 65 Years of Age, According to Color and Sex: United States, Selected Years 1900–1977[a]

SPECIFIED AGE AND YEAR	TOTAL			WHITE			ALL OTHER		
	Both Sexes	Male	Female	Both Sexes	Male	Female	Both Sexes	Male	Female
At Birth			Remaining Life Expectancy in Years						
1900[b]	47.3	46.3	48.3	47.6	46.6	48.7	33.0	32.5	33.5
1950	68.2	65.6	71.1	69.1	66.5	72.2	60.8	59.1	62.9
1960	69.7	66.6	73.1	70.6	67.4	74.1	63.6	61.1	66.3
1970[c]	70.9	67.1	74.8	71.7	68.0	75.6	65.3	61.3	69.4
1975[c]	72.5	68.7	76.5	73.2	69.4	77.2	67.9	63.6	72.3
1976[c]	72.8	69.0	76.7	73.5	69.7	77.3	68.3	64.1	72.6
1977[c]	73.2	69.3	77.1	73.8	70.0	77.7	68.8	64.6	73.1
At 65 Years									
1900–1902[b]	11.9	11.5	12.2	–	11.5	12.2	–	10.4	11.4
1950	13.9	12.8	15.0	–	12.8	15.1	–	12.5	14.5
1960	14.3	12.8	15.8	14.4	12.9	15.9	13.9	12.7	15.2
1970[c]	15.2	13.1	17.0	15.2	13.1	17.1	14.9	13.3	16.4
1975[c]	16.0	13.7	18.0	16.0	13.7	18.1	15.7	13.7	17.5
1976[c]	16.0	13.7	18.0	16.1	13.7	18.1	15.8	13.8	17.6
1977[c]	16.3	13.9	18.3	16.3	13.9	18.4	16.0	14.0	17.8

[a]Data are based on the national vital registration system.

[b]Death registration area only. The death registration area increased from ten states and the District of Columbia in 1900 to the coterminous United States in 1933.

[c]Excludes deaths of nonresidents of the United States.

Sources: National Center for Health Statistics, *Vital Statistics Rates in the United States 1940-1960,* by R. D. Grove and A. M. Hetzel, DHEW Pub. No. (PHS) 1677, Public Health Service. Washington: U.S. Government Printing Office, 1968. *Vital Statistics of the United States, 1970,* Vol. II, Part A, DHEW Pub. No. (HRA) 75-1101, Health Resources Administration. Washington: U.S. Government Printing Office, 1974. Final mortality statistics, 1975-1977, *Monthly Vital Statistics Report,* Vols. 25, 26, and 28, Nos. 11, 12, and 1, DHEW Pub. Nos. (HRA) 77-1120, (PHS) 78-1120, (PHS) 79-1120, Health Resources Administration and Public Health Service. Washington: U.S. Government Printing Office, Feb. 11, 1977, March 30, 1978, and May 11, 1979. Unpublished data from the Division of Vital Statistics.

hazards, or the effects of tobacco, alcohol, and drugs. And, we continue to know too little about the causes, control, and cure of many diseases that place a significant burden on individuals, on families, and on society.[2]

Contemporary community health concerns are by nature and scope different from those of the past. The rapid development of an industrial nation, with its accompanying technology, rapid pace of life, and competitive spirit has created many new health problems for individuals and groups living in the modern era. In addition, a significant attitudinal change has been evidenced in our society's people and the community health workers of today. Ours is an era of humanitarian concern. Today, a theme of essential

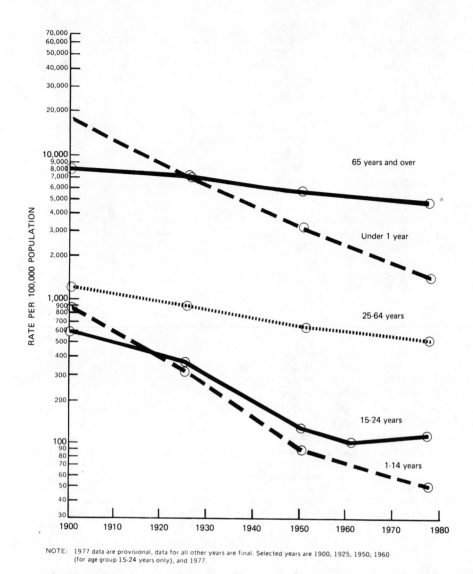

RATE PER 100,000 POPULATION

65 years and over

Under 1 year

25-64 years

15-24 years

1-14 years

NOTE: 1977 data are provisional, data for all other years are final. Selected years are 1900, 1925, 1950, 1960 (for age group 15-24 years only), and 1977.

Figure 1-4 Death rates by age, United States, selected years: 1900-1977. Courtesy National Center for Health Statistics, Division of Vital Statistics.

unity is apparent in the field of health which identifies disease and health as a composite of biological, psychological, social, environmental, and cultural factors. The interplay of all these factors must be assessed in order to understand relative well-being of individuals and groups.

Figure 1-5 Marine Hospital, U.S. Public Health Service Ambulance. Courtesy U.S. Department of Health, Education and Welfare.

Disease Prevention and Health Promotion

Prior to the twentieth century, communicable disease control was the major role and responsibility of public health. The struggle against communicable disease, which spanned the late nineteenth century and the first half of the twentieth century is considered the nation's first public health revolution. Its strategies included major sanitation measures, the development of effective vaccines, and mass immunization. So successful was this first revolution that today, only 1 percent of people who die before age 75 in the United States die from communicable or infectious diseases.

In 1900, the leading causes of death were influenza, pneumonia, diphtheria, tuberculosis, and gastrointestinal infections. In that year, the death rate from these diseases was 580 per 100,000 population. Today, barely 30 people per 100,000 die each year from these diseases.[3]

Although communicable disease prevention and control continue to play an important function in today's community health practices, there has been a general trend of higher *morbidity* and *mortality* rates as a consequence of the *chronic diseases* and degenerative diseases, and greater incidence of the social ailments and accompanying ills of environmental deterioration. Public health activities and practices have expanded and evolved in relation to the changes in the nature of diseases and the sociocultural beliefs of today's society. While the battle to control many of the communicable diseases including sexually transmissible diseases, influenza, and encephalitis has not yet been won (see Table 1-2), community health activities including education and research have been expanded to include prevention and control of such degenerative diseases as heart disease, cancer, and stroke.

The success of the first public health revolution means that the pattern of mortality and disability has shifted dramatically. Death rates for major acute communicable diseases plummeted between 1900 and 1970, while the proportion of major chronic diseases such as heart disease, cancer, and stroke increased more than 250 percent. Today, cardiovascular disease, including both heart disease and stroke, accounts for roughly half of all deaths in the U.S. Cancer accounts for another 20 percent.[4]

To a large extent, heart disease, cancer, and stroke are the indirect consequences of increased *longevity* and lifestyle in a modern technological society. The causes, prevention, and treatment of these diseases are substantially different from those of the communicable nature. But, as was true in the case of communicable disease control, elimination of these diseases will require aggressive and innovative public health intervention.

There is much evidence of a growing national commitment to the thesis that further improvements in the health of American people will not be achieved through greater health expenditures and increased medical care, but through efforts designed to prevent disease and promote health. Richard Schweiker, head of the Department of Health and Human Services in the Reagan Administration, has said he would like to see prevention emphasized in terms of both reimbursement procedures and research.

In 1974, the government of Canada published *A New Perspective on the Health of Canadians.* It introduced a useful concept which views all causes of death and disease as having four contributing elements:

> inadequacies in the existing health care system
> behavioral factors or unhealthy lifestyles
> environmental hazards, and
> human biological factors.

Using that framework, a group of American experts developed a method of assessing the relative contribution of each of the elements to many health problems. Analysis in which the method was applied to the ten leading causes of death in 1976 suggests that perhaps as much as half of U.S. mortality in 1976 was due to unhealthy behaviors; 20 percent to environmental factors; 20 percent to human biological factors, and 10 percent to inadequacies in health care.[5] Increased attention is now being paid to exercise, nutrition, environmental health, and occupational safety. Clearly, prevention is an idea whose time has come.

Table 1-2 Selected Notifiable Disease Rates, According to Disease: United States, Selected Years 1950-1977[a]

DISEASE	YEAR							
	1950	1955	1960	1965	1970	1975	1976	1977
	Number of Cases per 100,000 Population							
Chickenpox	(b)	(b)	(b)	(b)	(b)	78.11	96.06	97.63
Diphtheria	3.83	1.21	0.51	0.08	0.21	0.14	0.06	0.04
Hepatitis A	(b)	19.45	23.15	17.49	27.87	16.82	15.51	14.40
Hepatitis B					4.08	6.30	7.14	7.78
Measles (rubeola)	211.01	337.88	245.42	135.33	23.23	11.44	19.16	26.51
Mumps	(b)	(b)	(b)	(b)	55.55	27.99	17.93	10.02
Pertussis (whooping cough)	79.82	38.21	8.23	3.51	2.08	0.82	0.47	1.02
Poliomyelitis, total	22.02	17.64	1.77	0.04	0.02	0.00	0.01	0.01
Paralytic		8.43	1.40	0.03	0.02	0.00	0.01	0.01
Rubella (German measles)	(b)	(b)	(b)	(b)	27.75	7.81	5.82	9.43
Salmonellosis, excluding typhoid fever	(b)	3.32	3.85	8.87	10.84	10.61	10.74	12.87
Shigellosis	15.45	8.47	6.94	5.70	6.79	7.78	6.15	7.42
Tuberculosis (newly reported active cases)	80.50	46.60	30.83	25.33	18.22	15.95	14.96	13.93
Venereal diseases (newly reported civilian cases):								
Syphilis[c]	146.02	76.15	68.78	58.81	45.46	38.00	33.69	30.10
Primary and secondary	16.73	4.02	9.06	12.16	10.94	12.09	11.14	9.50
Early latent	39.71	12.48	10.11	9.10	8.11	12.57	11.91	9.94
Late and late latent	76.22	53.83	45.91	35.09	25.05	12.81	10.29	10.39
Congenital	8.97	3.33	2.48	1.86	0.97	0.43	0.29	0.22
Gonorrhea	192.45	146.96	145.33	169.36	298.52	472.91	470.47	466.83
Chancroid	3.34	1.65	0.94	0.51	0.70	0.33	0.29	0.21
Granuloma inguinale	1.19	0.30	0.17	0.08	0.06	0.03	0.03	0.03
Lymphogranuloma venereum	0.95	0.47	0.47	0.46	0.30	0.17	0.17	0.16

[a]Data are based on reporting by state health departments.

[b]Not reported nationally.

[c]Includes stage of syphilis not stated.

Note: Rates greater than 0 but less than 0.005 are shown as 0.00. The total resident population was used to calculate all rates except venereal diseases, for which the civilian resident population was used.

Sources: Center for Disease Control, reported morbidity and mortality in the United States, 1978, *Morbidity and Mortality Weekly Report* 27(54), Public Health Service, Atlanta, Ga., Sept. 1979. National Center for Health Statistics, data computed by the Division of Analysis from data compiled by the Center for Disease Control. Veneral Disease Control Division, Center for Disease Control, selected data.

Lifestyle

By applying available prevention techniques coupled with the adoption of healthier lifestyles, it may be possible to eliminate much of the disability and premature death now seen in the U.S. Indeed, a wealth of scientific research reveals that the key to longevity and health can be found in one's personal health habits, particularly smoking and drinking, diet, sleep, exercise, and a few other areas. It appears that health education designed to improve personal health habits will play an important role in the second public health revolution.

There is good evidence now that identifies some of the major risk factors associated with premature death and disability in the U.S. For example, cigarette smoking is the single most important preventable cause of death. Though the actual cause of unprecedented decline in heart disease in the past ten years is not entirely understood, it is noteworthy that the prevalence of cigarette smoking also declined nationally during the same period. Table 1-3 shows that among teenage boys, the incidence of smoking has declined, while among girls it has increased.

Much has been done to educate the public about the risks of smoking. In 1964, the first *Surgeon General's Report on Smoking and Health* was published. Since that time more than 30 million smokers have quit. The 1979 *Surgeon General's Report* presented a comprehensive review of evidence linking smoking with a variety of health problems. School health curricula have been developed to help youth make informed decisions about smoking, and many clinics, techniques, and devices have been developed over the past twenty years to help people quit the smoking habit. Much more can still be done to educate the public about the risks of smoking. But it is less then encouraging to note that at the federal level, the budget of the Office on Smoking and Health experienced drastic budget cuts in 1981.

Misuse of alcohol and drugs exacts a substantial toll of premature illness, death, and disability. Alcohol is a factor in more than 10 percent of all deaths in the U.S. The proportion of heavy drinkers in the population has grown substantially since the 1960s. Of particular concern is the growth of use of both alcohol and drugs among the nation's youth. Alcohol abuse and alcoholism are estimated to cost nearly $43 billion annually.

For the broad range of alcohol and drug problems, strategies for interventions used by community health in the present differ, but there are some common elements. These include prevention through education that starts early and extends throughout life, altering the social climate of acceptability, reducing individual and social stress factors, and law enforcement. Our ability to deal with the alcohol and drug misuse problem as a society depends, in many ways, on our ability to mobilize individuals and groups to work together in schools and communities than on efforts in the health care system.

In addition, lifestyle challenges in the present include improved nutrition and dietary habits, physical fitness and exercise, and stress management. Although evidence is mounting that certain food factors and dietary habits may be linked to health problems as diverse as heart disease, obesity, tooth decay, and some types of cancer, consumers often find it difficult to make informed choices about food. Within the past six years or so there has been a promising resurgence of interest in physical fitness and exercise. Yet,

14

Table 1–3 Teenage Cigarette Smoking, According to Sex and Age: United States, 1968, 1974, and 1979[a]

SEX AND AGE	YEAR		
	1968	1974	1979
	Percent Who Are Current Smokers		
Both Sexes, 12–18 Years	11.5	15.6	11.7
Male			
12–18 years	14.7	15.8	10.7
12–14 years	2.9	4.2	3.2
15–16 years	17.0	18.1	13.5
17–18 years	30.2	31.0	19.3
Female			
12–18 years	8.4	15.3	12.7
12–14 years	0.6	4.9	4.3
15–16 years	9.6	20.2	11.8
17–18 years	18.6	25.9	26.2

[a]Data are based on telephone interviews of samples of the noninstitutionalized population.

Note: A current smoker is a person who smokes at least once a week.

Sources: National Clearinghouse for Smoking and Health, *Patterns and Prevalence of Teenage Cigarette Smoking, 1968, 1970 1972, and 1974,* DHEW Pub. No. (HSM) 74-8701, Health Services and Mental Health Administration, Rockville, Md., July 1974. National Institute of Education, DHEW, unpublished data.

despite a doubling of the percentage of those who exercise, most participants do not exercise often enough or vigorously enough to achieve maximum health benefits. Health professionals continue to ignore the benefit of actively promoting suitable exercise for their patients in spite of national leadership through the President's Council on Physical Fitness and Sports.

Stress is a normal, inevitable part of life. It is experienced in family relationships, school, work, traffic, and in financial and other problems. Everyone develops some means of coping with stress. Of concern is the destructive responses to stress or coping mechanisms such as violence, drug and alcohol abuse, depression, and other forms of mental illness. In a pluralistic society, people meet needs and solve problems in different ways. A neighborhood-based approach with community support systems designed to address diverse individual needs has been essential to the development of individual emotional well-being today.

It appears that contemporary lifestyles—including sedentary habits, affluence, and high levels of stress—may be interwoven as contributory causes in the development of these diseases. As has been the case in pre-modern civilizations, health problems tend to be interrelated with the social, economic, and political parameters of the day.

The Environment

Perhaps one of the most significant changes in the concept of community health is related to fostering "quality of life" for individuals through the preservation of the environment. While sanitation was a major community health problem in the past which contributed to the development of disease, the present concerns are control of air, water, and land and noise pollution, for these detract from the "quality of life" for individuals. Community health is actively involved in bringing about an abatement to environmental destruction. The growth of the United States from an agricultural nation to an industrial giant, with accompanying economic and technological advances, has simultaneously endangered quality of life and health. These adverse side effects of progress can be seen, heard, and felt, although they are often difficult to quantify.

Figure 1–6
Air pollution is a significant cause of death and poor health. Courtesy Arizona Department of Health Services.

Progress has been made, but at a cost to the human environment, with which each individual must interact. The community health field has been responsive to the challenge and threat to environmental health. Operating from the basic philosophical position that the most important index of health is not necessarily how long a person lives, but rather how enriching a person's life has been, community health professionals are exerting effort to promote a clean environment.

The Public Health Service (PHS) has long been committed to delivery of services and funding of research and training in the areas of occupational and environmental health. Building on the efforts of recent years to identify specific hazards in the environment, the PHS is supporting a study to define the role and practice of the primary-care physician in the diagnosis of occupationally and environmentally related diseases.

In a broader context, PHS agencies have stepped up action to protect individual health and the environment. The Food and Drug Administration (FDA) has intensified its efforts to monitor substances that contaminate the food supply and have improved the process by which new products are reviewed for safety and effectiveness. The Bureau of Epidemiology of the Center for Disease Control has been studying the effects of exposure to asbestos, beryllium, radiation, and other agents on the general population.

Certain environmental and occupational health problems are the target of interagency concern. In 1978, the National Toxicology Program was established to strengthen the capacity of the public and private sectors to study chemicals of the public health concern. This effort seeks to develop a long-range comprehensive plan to protect Americans from chemical health hazards. Agencies involved in the project include the FDA, the National Cancer Institute, the National Institute of Environmental Health Sciences, the Center for Disease Control, the Environmental Protection Agency, and the Occupational Safety and Health Administration among others.[6]

It is now estimated that up to 20 percent of total cancer mortality may be associated with occupational hazards. The true dimensions of the asbestos hazard, for example, have become manifest only after a latency period of perhaps thirty years. Rubber and plastic workers, as well as workers in some coke oven jobs, are exhibiting significantly higher cancer rates than the general population (see Table 1-4).

Once occupational hazards are defined, they can be controlled—thus reducing the threat to health. Safer materials may be substituted, manufacturing processes can be changed, hazardous materials can be isolated in enclosures, special clothing and other protective devices may be used, and workers can be educated and motivated to comply with safety procedures.

In addition to industrial and economic development, population growth has contributed to the present environmental crisis. Over-population is viewed as an intensifier to the various forms of pollution and therefore to environmental destruction. At present, it is projected that world population is doubling every thirty-five years.[7] World population has already passed the four-billion mark. The consequence of these enormous increases in population means the necessity for twice as much food, water, resources, houses, and health care services. It also means that the amount of solid wastes and garbage that will have to be handled will double. The implications are incredible, especially when one considers that urban areas in the United States now house two-thirds of the population, where

Table 1-4 BLS Estimates of Occupational Injury and Illness Incidence Rates by Industry, 1976–1977

	INCIDENCE RATES[a]					
	Total Recordable Cases[b]		Lost Workday Cases		Nonfatal Cases Without Lost Workdays	
INDUSTRY DIVISION	1977	1976	1977	1976	1977	1976
Private Sector[c]	9.3	9.2	3.8	3.5	5.5	5.7
Agriculture, forestry, and fishing[c]	11.5	11.0	5.1	4.7	6.3	6.3
Mining	10.9	11.0	6.0	5.8	4.9	5.1
Construction	15.5	15.3	5.9	5.5	9.6	9.8
Manufacturing	13.1	13.2	5.1	4.8	8.0	8.3
Transportation and public utilities	9.7	9.8	5.3	5.0	4.3	4.8
Wholesale and retail trade	7.7	7.5	2.9	2.8	4.8	4.6
Finance, insurance, and real estate	2.0	2.0	0.8	0.7	1.2	1.2
Services	5.5	5.3	2.2	2.0	3.3	3.3

[a]Incidence Rate =

$$\frac{(\text{No. of injuries \& illnesses} \times 200{,}000) \text{ OR } (\text{No. of lost workdays} \times 200{,}000)}{\text{Total hours worked by all employees during period covered}}$$

200,000 = base for 100 full-time equivalent workers (working 40 hours per week, 50 weeks per year).

[b]Includes fatalities. Because of rounding, the difference between the total and sum of the rates for lost workday cases and nonfatal cases without lost workdays may not reflect the fatality rate.

[c]Excludes farms with less than 11 employees.

Source: Bureau of Labor Statistics. U.S. Department of Labor.

overcrowding and poor sanitation already pose serious threats to health. The message of *Global 2000,* a report on the quality of the environment is:

> World population growth, the degradation of the earth's natural resource base and the spread of environmental pollution collectively threatens the welfare of mankind. If these challenges are ignored, they will overwhelm our efforts to improve the quality of life and social opportunities of the world's people, including our own. If they are met and successfully overcome, we will face the twenty-first century with renewed hope and security.[8]

Mental Health

In modern times, increased incidence of both the psychobiological and sociobiological illnesses has been apparent. Survival in a modern society has become a question not simply of physical survival, but of psychological survival as well. Our society, and the lifestyles that are characteristic of our culture, change continually, shifting the balance of factors which govern disease activity. Increased mobility, stress, and rapid change have all contributed to the current disease conditions and community health concerns.

Mental illness is a substantial contributor to disability and suffering for American adults. The President's Commission on Mental Health has reported that at any given time, up to 25 percent of the population is estimated to be suffering from mild to moderate depression, anxiety, or other emotional disorder.

Depression and manic depressive disorders are among the most severe types of mental illness in terms of prevalence, economic cost, and mortality. Of the 29,000 suicides recorded in the U.S. each year, more than 80 percent are believed to be precipitated by depressive illness. Severe depression or manic excitability handicaps manifest themselves in an estimated 2 to 4 of every 100 adults at any given time.

At present, suicide ranks as the ninth leading cause of death for all age groups. Homicide, thought to have its origins in the complexities of life in modern times, ranks tenth. Physicians estimate that 80 percent of the illnesses they treat are *psychosomatic* in origin. These disorders include such things as obesity, drug abuse, tension and migraine headaches, ulcers, colitis, and allergies.

Mental health problems are among the most complex to understand, and many times, the most resistant to treatment. In part, this may result from the absence of a clear definition as to what constitutes mental health or mental illness. It has recently been estimated that 50 percent of the nation's hospital beds are utilized to care for mental patients. Alcoholism and drug dependence are growing national public health concerns which affect ever-increasing numbers of our population from all walks of life and all age groups.

As part of the effort to improve the delivery of mental health services, the U.S. Department of Health and Human Services conducted a careful review of the recommendations of the 1978 President's Commission on Mental Health. As a result, new delivery service programs are now focused on certain high priority groups including children, adolescents, the aged, minorities, American Indians, rural Americans, and those with chronic mental disabilities. Under the Community Support Program of the U.S. Public Health Service, state agencies are developing pilot comprehensive "community support systems" for mentally disabled adults who are capable of living in the community with adequate treatment, rehabilitation, and support services.[9]

There are no easy solutions to these community health problems; the traditional specific-*etiology* concept no longer applies. This has required a response on the part of community health to revise and expand the concept of *epidemiology*. As the incidence of communicable diseases declined, it became increasingly apparent that epidemiological studies would have to reflect the broadened nature of disease by utilizing a multicausation model. Many of the health problems of the present have their origins in an intricate web of psycho- and sociobiological factors. Much additional research will be necessary to sort out the etiology of these conditions. In the meantime, community health must assume the responsibility for education and prevention on the basis of existing knowledge. The ultimate concern of community health is not the disease per se, but rather the choices in lifestyle that individuals make.

Health Care: A Basic Right

In the United States health is considered to be a basic and inalienable right of all citizens. However, access to health care has to a large extent depended upon the individual's economic situation and geographic location. Some have said that we are experi-

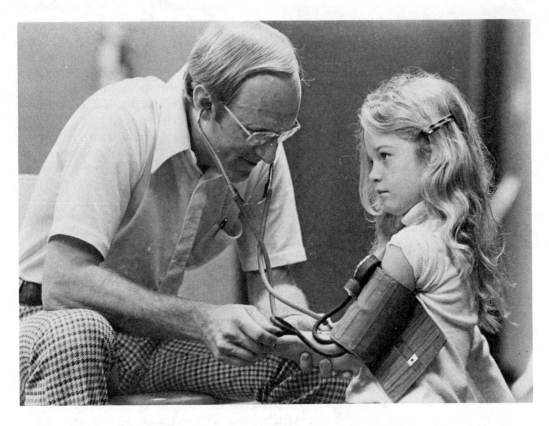

Figure 1-7 Health care is a basic right in the United States. Courtesy Arizona Republic and Phoenix Gazette.

encing a crisis in health care, related to maldistribution and shortage of family-practice physicians, inflated health care costs, and an emphasis on crisis medicine rather than preventive practice. In response, community health is attempting to make provisions for quality health care for all by reducing the disparity between the quality of health care afforded individuals and their socioeconomic station in society. A commitment to this position has been and continues to be reflected by community health program and facility development and maintenance. In summarizing the position of public health, C. Arden Miller, past president of the American Public Health Association has said,

> As advocates of public health, we advocate rights to health services and social supports and safeguards that allow people to enjoy dignity, fulfillment, and well-being . . . . The unique contribution of public health toward its fulfillment may be to establish accountability of public agencies that can secure and protect those rights.[10]

There are many subcultures in the United States that have become the concern of public and community health. These target groups include the elderly, the Appalachian poor, migrant workers, urban ghetto dwellers, and more recently, the imprisoned population.

Despite rapidly growing health care expenditures (see Table 1-5) and increased availability of health services, the public health goal of providing *all* Americans with adequate access to high-quality health services and medical care at a reasonable cost has not been achieved. Premature death rates for all causes and unnecessary disease and disability are higher for the poor, the less-educated, rural residents, and the elderly. Measured in terms of morbidity, mortality, and disability, the differences in health status among different income groups have actually expanded in recent years. Some of this is due to limited socioeconomic options in housing, education, and nutrition caused by lower incomes, but it is also partly the result of inadequate health care. This in turn, is attributable to the system's well-known barriers of (1) rising health care costs, (2) uneven quality, and (3)

Table 1-5 Gross National Product and National Health Expenditures: United States, Selected Years 1929–1978[a]

YEAR	GROSS NATIONAL PRODUCT IN BILLIONS	NATIONAL HEALTH EXPENDITURES		
		Amount in Billions	Percent of Gross National Product	Amount per Capita
1929	$ 103.1	$ 3.6	3.5	$ 29.49
1935	72.2	2.9	4.0	22.65
1940	99.7	4.0	4.0	29.62
1950	284.8	12.7	4.5	81.86
1955	398.0	17.7	4.4	105.38
1960	503.7	26.9	5.3	146.30
1965	688.1	43.0	6.2	217.42
1966	753.0	47.3	6.3	236.51
1967	796.3	52.7	6.6	260.35
1968	868.5	58.9	6.8	288.17
1969	935.5	66.2	7.1	320.70
1970	982.4	74.7	7.6	358.63
1971	1,063.4	82.8	7.8	393.09
1972	1,171.1	92.7	7.9	436.47
1973	1,306.6	102.3	7.8	478.38
1974	1,412.9	115.6	8.2	535.99
1975	1,528.8	131.5	8.6	604.57
1976	1,700.1	148.9	8.8	678.79
1977	1,887.2	170.0	9.0	768.77
1978[b]	2,107.6	192.4	9.1	863.01

[a]Data are compiled by the Health Care Financing Administration.

[b]Preliminary estimates.

Sources: Gibson, R. M., National health expenditures, 1978, *Health Care Financing Review* 1(1) 1–36, Summer 1979. Office of Research, Demonstrations, and Statistics, Health Care Financing Administration, selected data.

unequal access to care.[11] Public programs such as Medicaid and Medicare have been effective in increasing the availability of health services to low-income and elderly populations, yet they are not sufficient to help all those who cannot afford health services. Further, the Reagan Administration is committed to controlling the $600 million the Department of Health and Human Services spends each day. To get this budget under control, cuts are likely in the Medicaid/Medicare programs. If this occurs, the health of poor people may be further jeopardized.

The PHS has recently stepped up efforts to improve the delivery of health care to populations and areas of special need. Family-planning services are available to some 4.5 million women, and a special program to prevent unwanted teenage pregnancy has been initiated. Through the Rural Health Initiative Projects and Health Underserved Rural Areas Projects, some 1.2 million rural Americans now receive health care. Some 557,000 migrant and seasonal workers have access to health care through the 112 centers of the Migrant Health Project. And, 1.9 million people are being served through 190 urban health projects, of which 77 have been recently established.

At the same time, major emphasis has been placed on improving health care delivery systems through planning. Some of the more recent community health efforts designed to provide better care through resource and facility development have included meaningful support for the concept of health maintenance organizations (HMOs), continued support for scholarships to the National Health Services Corps, and the Child Health Initiative Program as a companion to the Child Health Assurance Program.

The signing of the Health Resources, Planning, and Development Act in 1974 by President Gerald Ford, which called for the establishment of Health Systems Agencies throughout the United States, represented an attempt to identify existing problems within the health care delivery system with regard to manpower, facilities, and utilization of services. This was a noteworthy step in the right direction, yet many continue to call for a complete revision of the health care delivery system through the establishment of national health insurance for all citizens. In the Reagan Administration, the national health planning program has found itself battling for both its existence and its authority. Numerous administration officials have identified health planning as a priority for budget cuts, in an attempt to save federal money and reduce federal interference in state and local affairs.

COMMUNITY HEALTH: THE FUTURE

In the future, as in all historical periods, health problems will be unique to the social structures, political atmosphere, and lifestyles of the people. To plan for the future, we can make projections based on our understanding and knowledge of the trends in the past and present. Stress, rapid change, and—although it would seem the two are mutually exclusive—poverty and affluence are characteristics of modern times. Each of these, in combination with other factors, can be seen as contributing to the health concerns of the future.

Disease prevention begins with a threat to health—a disease or environmental hazard—and seeks to protect as many people as possible from the harmful consequences of that threat. Health promotion begins with people who are basically healthy and seeks the development of community and individual strategies that help them to develop life-styles that can maintain and enhance health.[12] The national health strategy of the future will no doubt give greater emphasis to health promotion and disease prevention activities than ever before. The Department of Health and Human Services has identified a number of priority services with potential for substantially reducing death, disease and disability from problems affecting people in the future.

Family planning is one preventive health service recognized as a priority for the future. A child whose birth is planned is far more likely to begin life as a healthy person. Making family-planning information available at the earliest possible age is one aspect of the federal initiative. Thus, a major focus of this area is providing contraceptive information and services to all sexually active adolescents.

Another priority in the future is pregnancy and infant care. Important services during pregnancy include assessment of special risks due to family history or past medical problems, physical exams and basic laboratory tests, amniocentesis where indicated, nutrition, smoking, alcohol, and exercise counseling. Even before they become pregnant, women need to know about the factors that may affect the health of their future babies. Once a baby is born, prospects for good health can be enhanced by a number of preventive services, including immunizations and physical exams. The provision of protection against the seven major childhood diseases through immunization will continue to be a national priority.

As noted earlier, there has been substantial success in minimizing the *infectious diseases* as threats to life. Yet, new diseases appear and familiar diseases may change periodically making existing protective measures ineffective. Legionnaires' disease and toxic shock syndrome are examples of newly identified infections.

The sexually transmissible diseases present a significant public health challenge. In 1977, some ten million cases of these diseases occurred in the U.S., 86 percent of them in 15- to 29-year-olds. Substantial difficulties hinder control of the sexually transmissible diseases, since those infected do not always seek proper care. Genital herpes poses an additional challenge since it can not be cured, nor are immunizations available to protect people from infection. It is estimated that there are two million cases of genital herpes in the U.S. at present. Close monitoring and surveillance of infectious disease incidence will continue to be a national health priority.

Controlling high blood pressure, which affects 1 in 6 Americans is essential if in the future we are to reduce the 500,000 strokes and 1,250,000 heart attacks that occur annually. Since 1972, hypertension screening and control programs have been established by government and voluntary health agencies, health care providers, and industry. Hypertension control in the future will entail continued use of resources and services from a variety of sectors. It also will entail dealing with individual lifestyle changes and motivations for action.

Toxic agents in today's environment present tremendous public health challenges. During a lifetime, people are exposed, often unknowingly, to hazards from many sources. Many of the agents posing new threats to health are industrial and agricultural chemicals. Air pollution and radiation are additional environmental sources of human illness. It takes at least twenty years to determine the full effects of many new compounds on human health—and some in use today may not be known until the twenty-first century. Protection against toxic environmental agents depends on reliable methods of identifying hazards to health. Improving the quality of the environment is a challenge to all sectors of the society—individuals, health professionals, industry, and government. It is clear that in the future the federal government will continue to bear responsibility for setting and enforcing pollution standards and for dealing with health risks related to environmental contamination. Significant environmental reforms have been achieved, but because of the strength of competing interests, health does not always emerge as a top priority.

Occupational safety and health has recently emerged as a priority of the future. Each year 100,000 Americans die from occupational illnesses and almost 400,000 new cases of occupational disease are recognized. Nine of every 10 American industrial workers are not adequately protected from exposure to at least one of the 163 most common hazardous chemicals. Occupational hazards can be controlled by modifying the work environment, patterns of job performance or both. That the work environment can play a major role in compromising health has been known for many decades. In the future, increased emphasis will be placed on efforts to control known hazards, treat affected populations, and develop techniques to identify and prevent harm from materials and processes not now recognized as dangerous.

As discussed earlier, lifestyle influences health more than any other factor including the environmental hazard, health care system, and human biological factors. Community health-education programs, which are rapidly increasing in number, will have a significant role to play in the future of health promotion. Nationally, the target areas for health promotion programs are smoking, alcohol and drug use, nutrition, exercise and fitness, and stress management.

Smoking cessation and related programs designed to educate the public about the risks of smoking will intensify in the future. Improved, cost-effective smoking-cessation techniques will need to be designed as will new anti-smoking literature and advertisements. Special attention will be directed to certain high-risk target groups including women, children and adolescents, and industrial workers in especially hazardous occupational settings.

Preventing alcohol and drug misuse is another major future public health challenge. The social and economic burdens associated with the misuse of these substances on American society is incalculable. Yet, helping people to stop or avoid starting misuse of alcohol or drugs will not be easy, particularly among population groups in which social and economic factors are prominent contributors to alcohol and drug abuse, and therefore complicate potential interventions. Specific target groups that will receive attention in the future include children and adolescents, women, and American Indians.

Improved nutrition is an important health-promotion priority for the nation. Most diet-deficiency diseases that were prevalent early in the century are now rarely seen.

Yet iron deficiency in children and women remains a public health concern. Today's nutrition problems are generally associated with eating too much and with imbalance in the kinds of foods eaten, rather than with eating too little. Obesity is a major problem, especially among women. Americans would clearly be healthier if their diet changed in the future.

In a recent national survey, 82 percent of those polled indicated they need "less *stress* in their lives." There are indications that stress can be related to cardiovascular disease, gastrointestinal disorders, and other physical diseases—as well as mental illness. Whether or not strong, multifaceted community programs dealing with the problems of stress will be developed in the future—and the extent to which they might alleviate the situation—is difficult to predict.[13]

Health-protection and disease-prevention services are considered important for both health and cost-containment reasons. People are accustomed to seeking medical care only when they feel ill and ordinarily perceive no need for preventive health services when they feel well. But evidence suggests that certain key preventive services can do much to both preserve health and reduce health care costs. Major progress has been made toward defining what preventive health services should be delivered to the well population, relative to specific age groups and health risks. Our future challenge will be to make essential services universally available in the United States.

The Health Care System

In the future, efforts will be directed toward identifying ways to change the health care system to meet new requirements, to ensure quality care, and to contain costs. At present, the nation's health care system fails to provide appropriate services to numerous populations of high need for several reasons having to do with inadequate delivery capacity, barriers to accessing available services, and inefficient production of services. In the future, the problems of inadequate access to health care and high cost will be challenged. It is likely that the health care delivery system will undergo a structural change to alleviate the maldistribution of resources that now exists. General directions of the future may involve such things as the development of alternative health care delivery models, changes in the training programs for health professionals, and the targeting of certain health programs toward specific groups.

Improvement of the health care system itself will be a major priority of the future. The HMO concept as a cost-efficient delivery model will continue to be supported. HMO enrollment will be encouraged through employer- and consumer-awareness campaigns and marketing projects. Federal funding will support both the expansion of existing HMOs and the development of new HMOs in certain areas of the U.S. It is estimated that by 1990, there will be some surpluses of physicians and other health professionals. Thus programs and policies will no doubt be adopted to discourage expansion of programs to train these professionals.

Physician specialty imbalance has become a problem, since too many physicians have selected specialties such as surgery and orthopedics, while too few have chosen such primary-care specialties as family medicine, osteopathy, and internal medicine. In an effort to solve the problem, increased financial support will be offered for primary-care and family-medicine training programs. In addition, greater assistance will be offered to qualified minorities and disadvantaged people who enter health-professions education programs. Improving minority students' access to health-professions education will continue to be a social priority.

The effort to hold down the spiraling costs of health care delivery will continue in the future. Research projects that explore ways to reduce costs and improve the quality of health care through more prudent ordering and utilization of such medical procedures as x-ray exams will be supported. Attempts will be made to discontinue inappropriate use of in-patient hospital services, such as surgery that could have appropriately been done on an out-patient basis. Some hospitals will close in the future, and others will be converted for new uses to reduce costly facilities and services duplication.

Financially, health planning faces an uncertain future. The Reagan Administration has asked Congress to cut the funding of health planning by more than 50 percent for 1982. It is impossible to predict what the role of local health systems agencies will be in the future—or for that matter, if they will even exist. It is likely that parts of the health planning structure will be dismantled.

Overall, more efficient utilization of health care resources will be the tenor of the future. In an attempt to reach this goal, hospitals and clinics will have to share their resources with each other to a greater extent than exists today. Less costly forms of care, such as ambulatory, preventive, and home health care will be stressed, and better management techniques will be employed in the entire health care system.

For the categorically poor and other populations residing in medically underserved areas, health care projects in the future will be located and organized so that physical, cultural, and financial barriers to access are minimized. However, it is unlikely that the health resources available in the U.S. will ever be adequate to appropriately serve all shortage areas.[14]

Historically, health has been considered a basic human right, yet there are still outcasts from the present health care delivery system. Community health will have to exert concerted efforts to develop social consciousness on the part of all citizens of the United States. Provision of health care services and manpower will change dramatically in the future. The direction of that change is highly speculative.

Whatever the future holds, a national health policy is certain to be established. It is hoped that this policy will reflect the needs of providers and consumers of health care alike. It will require much thought, cooperation, and dedication to bring equity into health care in the United States, and a dramatic change from crisis-oriented, sick-care system to a preventive-oriented health care system.

Laws and regulations to protect health can be traced back thousands of years in social, religious, and political history. But, whereas the beginnings of public health were to a large extent a question of desperation, hopefully the future of public health will be a question of enlightenment and humanitarian concern.

REVIEW QUESTIONS

1. What are the basic differences in health concerns in the past and present?
2. What kinds of community health concerns may be a part of the future? What will the number-one challenge in the future be? Why?
3. Identify and analyze contemporary community health activities or programs that are responding to a specific current health problem (for example, heart disease, sedentary existence, or environmental deterioration).
4. Discuss the comparative changes in community health as they reflect changes in health problems of the past and present.
5. What are some of the health effects of stress in a modern technological society?
6. Differentiate among medical care, health promotion, and disease prevention activities.

SUGGESTED READINGS

Brieger, Gert H., "The Use and Abuse of Medical Charities in the Late Nineteenth-Century America," *American Journal of Public Health,* 67(3) 264-267, 1977.

Dubos, Rene, *Man, Medicine and Environment.* New York: Praeger, 1968.

Illich, Ivan, *Medical Nemesis: Expropriation of Health.* New York: Bantam, 1976.

Rosen, George, "History and Health Care." *American Journal of Public Health,* 67(4) 326-328, 1977.

Terris, Milton, "Crisis and Change in America's Health System," *American Journal of Public Health,* 63(4) 313-318, 1973.

Wolman, Abel, "A.P.H.A. in Its First Century," *American Journal of Public Health,* 63(4) 319-321, 1973.

NOTES

[1] Rene Dubos, *So Human an Animal.* New York: Scribner's, 1968, p. 15.

[2] U.S. Department of Health, Education and Welfare, *Healthy People.* Washington, D.C.: DHEW (PHS) Publication No. 79-55071, 1979, p. vii.

[3] *Healthy People,* p. vii.

[4] *Healthy People,* p. vii.

[5] *Healthy People,* p. 8.

[6] U.S. Department of Health, Education and Welfare, *Improving Health in America: U.S. Public Health Service Highlights of 1977-80.* Washington, D.C.: DHEW, Pub. No. (PHS) 79-16688, 1979, p. 25.

[7]Paul R. Ehrlich, Anne H. Ehrlich, and John P. Holdren, *Ecoscience: Population, Resources, Environment.* San Francisco: W. H. Freeman and Company, 1977.

[8]Secretary of State Edmund S. Muskie, on the release of the *Global 2000* report to the President of the United States, July 24, 1980. United States Council on Environmental Quality, *The Global 2000 Report to the President: Entering the Twenty-First Century.* Prepared by the Council on Environmental Quality and the Department of State. Washington, D.C.: U.S. Government Printing Office, 1980.

[9]*Improving Health in America,* p. 19.

[10]C. Arden Miller, "Societal Change and Public Health: A Rediscovery," *American Journal of Public Health,* 66(1), 1976, p. 56.

[11]*Improving Health in America,* p. 9.

[12]*Healthy People,* p. 119.

[13]*Healthy People,* pp. 135 and 138.

[14]U.S. Department of Health, Education and Welfare, *Health Services Administration: Forward Plan, FY 1979–1983.* Washington, D.C.: U.S. DHEW Pub. No. (HSA) 79-4328, OPEL, 1979, pp. 7–8.

GLOSSARY

chronic disease   a large number of unrelated, heterogeneous conditions which range in severity, are long-lasting, and are commonly permanent.

communicable disease   a large number of conditions that are usually self-limiting, and are caused by pathogens that can be transmitted directly from person to person or indirectly through an animal, vector, or the environment.

community health   activities designed to promote the relative well-being and enhancement of large groups of individuals.

epidemic   a large number or above average number of cases of a specific disease in a limited geographic area.

epidemiology   the study of the distribution and determinants of disease in man.

etiology   the causative agent(s) or factors which contribute to the development of disease. Etiology refers to a cause-effect relationship.

germ theory of disease   a theory that communicable diseases are the result of specific pathogens that enter the body.

health   "quality of life" involving social, mental, and biological fitness of the individual resulting from adaptation and responses to the environment.

infectious diseases   illnesses easily communicated to others by bacteria.

longevity   length of life

morbidity   the incidence of sickness or illness of an individual as a consequence of specific causes.

mortality   incidence of death as a consequence of a specific illness or sickness.

pandemic   a large number or above-average number of cases of a specific disease in a wide geographic area.

psychosomatic   a physical disorder originating in or aggravated by psychological or emotional processes of the individual.

BIBLIOGRAPHY

Brotman, Herman B., "The Fastest Growing Minority: The Aging," *American Journal of Public Health,* 64(4) 250–256, 1974. (2)

Davis, Kingsley, "The Urbanization of the Human Population," *Scientific American,* 213: 41–53, 1965.

Dubos, Rene, *So Human an Animal*. New York: Scribner's, 1968.

Ehrlich, Paul R., and Anne H. Ehrlich, *Populations, Resources, Environment*. San Francisco: W. H. Freeman and Company, 1972.

Jekel, James, "Communicable Disease Control and Public Policy in the 1970's—Hot War, Cold War, or Peaceful Coexistence?" *American Journal of Public Health,* 64(12) 1578-1585, 1972.

LaLonde, Marc, "Beyond a New Perspective," *American Journal of Public Health,* 67(4) 357-360, 1977.

Rosen, G., "Specialization in Public Health," *American Journal of Public Health,* 62(3) 624-625, 1972.

Tarr, Joel, Terry Yosie, and James McCurley, "Disputes Over Water Quality Policy: Professional Cultures in Conflict, 1900-1917," *American Journal of Public Health,* 70(4) 427-435, 1980.

Terris, Milton, "Evolution of Public Health and Preventive Medicine in the United States," *American Journal of Public Health,* 65(2) 161-168, 1975.

Toffler, Alvin, *Future Shock*. New York: Random House, 1970.

U.S. DHEW, *Healthy People: The Surgeon General's Report on Health Promotion and Disease Prevention*. Washington, D.C.: U.S. DHEW Pub. No. (PHS) 79-55071, 1979.

—— *Health Services Administration: Forward Plan FY 1979-1983*. Washington, D.C.: U.S. DHEW Pub. No. (HSA) OPEL, 1979.

—— *Improving Health in America: U.S. Public Health Services Highlights: 1977-1980*. Washington, D.C.: U.S. DHEW, 1979.

Wardell, Dorothy, "Margaret Sanger: Birth Control's Successful Revolutionary," *American Journal of Public Health,* 70(7) 736-742, 1980.

Waters, William, "State Level Comprehensive Health Planning: A Retrospect," *American Journal of Public Health,* 66(2) 139-144, 1976.

2

SOCIOLOGICAL PERSPECTIVES

Since the beginnings of this century we have witnessed throughout the world an evolution of medicine which has shifted its focus from mere therapeutic concern to prevention first, then to the social aspects of illness.

Dr. Raoul Senault and Monsieur Alphonse d'Houtand, Proceedings of the Seventh International Conference on Health and Health Education, Buenos Aires, 1969 (p. 109).

SOCIOLOGICAL ASPECTS OF HEALTH AND DISEASE

Community health is concerned with the promotion of well-being of individuals in defined *social units,* such as the family, community, nation, and world. Sociological analysis and the utilization of sociological concepts have contributed significantly to a better understanding of health and disease in community health. Illness can accurately be reviewed not only as mental and physical dysfunction, but also as social dysfunction. An individual who is ill is not only less effective in utilizing physical and mental capacities, but is less capable of fulfilling social obligations. As a consequence of the social nature of health and disease, each society has developed a fairly sophisticated array of *norms* and *sanctions* regarding implied appropriate behaviors in health and illness to ensure continuity and normal functioning of the society with regard to health.

The use of a multidisciplinary approach to effectively deal with health problems has become a necessary ingredient to the successful planning and implementation of community health programs. In order to wage a successful campaign against health problems, we must analyze the social and economic conditions of our culture and subcultures. The behavioral patterns and sanctions within groups should be compared with the sanctions of the total society. Social sanctions, norms, and standards—including beliefs and traditions of a community—must be understood and evaluated if health action programs are to achieve the objective of health promotion and preservation.

It is generally agreed that the current approach to health promotion and to an

31

accurate and realistic understanding of the causes of disease should be the application of a *multicausation theory* as opposed to a *single-agent,* cause-and-effect relationship. The importance of using this approach can be better understood by examining the social ailments of our age and how the conditions of social disintegration and disorganization can create personal perceptions of alienation and anxiety. It has been well-documented that internalized anxiety and stress can cause an individual to be more susceptible to physical illness, both communicable and chronic. *Social disorganization,* the absence of meaningful social relationships, and an individual's perception of low social status can contribute to the individual's resistance to disease. In addition, continual and rapid change in modern society may increase both the incidence and amount of generalized stress experienced by individuals in our modern, industrialized nation. The importance of recognizing the social nature of disease and health and of implementing humanistic-sociological approaches to community health programs is receiving widespread acceptance throughout the world. This acceptance is based upon the understanding that an individual lives in a social system in conjunction with his or her physical environment and that the interactions he or she has with a social group and personal subsocial system will to a large extent influence health and disease patterns.

HEALTH ROLES: WELLNESS, AT-RISK, AND ILLNESS

Sociological concepts such as *"sick-role,"* *"well-role"* and *"at-risk role"*, as well as social norms and sanctions related to health-generating or health-negating behaviors are several factors worthy of consideration in community health. Every society has social norms that represent the implicit and expressed values and beliefs of a majority of its members. The health norms represent the values and beliefs of a majority of society's members with regard to health. As is the case with all norms of a society, whether they concern marriage, dress and attire, food, or expected behaviors for specific situations, a person who does not follow established norms and sanctions is classified as a nonconformist. According to medical sociologists, health is valued in our society and is considered to be a norm, while illness is defined as nonconforming and deviant. It has been said that with regard to health, "the internalization of norms is reflected in a person's attitudes, routines and the decisions he or she makes regarding health maintenance, prevention and cure of illness, and is therefore of great importance."[1] However, an important consideration for community health is that not all *subcultures* internalize health norms that are the same as the general society. Therefore, to a large extent, whether a behavior such as narcotic addiction in the ghetto, marijuana usage on a college campus, or absence of a daily fitness program for corporate executives is seen as deviant and nonconforming or conforming and appropriate will depend on the reference point of the individual and the subculture of which he or she is a member. A significant factor is whether the individual has internalized the norms of the subculture or norms of the general society, especially if there is disparity between the two.

Norms: Beliefs and Traditions

In order for community health programs to be effective, the sociological concept of internalization of norms should be considered. The concept can be used constructively to promote health in three ways:

1. If an individual or group possesses internalized norms regarding health behaviors and practices that are detrimental to well-being, such as excessive alcohol consumption in the upper-middle class or rejection of free public health screening opportunities by the Appalachian poor, a modification of internalized values should be effected that are in line with social norms that are constructive to health and foster well-being.
2. If an individual or group possesses internalized norms regarding health that are compatible with those of society and conducive to well-being, these beliefs should be reinforced so that they will be maintained and acted upon.
3. If societal norms regarding health are not health-generating—such as accepting sedentary existence as the "American way of life" and condoning indiscriminate drug taking for symptomatic relief of nearly every problem—community health professionals must aggressively meet the challenge to modify these firmly established beliefs of a majority of Americans.

Beliefs and traditions are powerful forces that demand the respect of community health professionals, for they represent the way in which an individual or group perceives reality. The community health field faces the challenge of creating and fostering the internalization of social norms that are constructive to health and modifying or extinguishing those that are destructive. With the proper approach, well-being can be generated and dignity preserved.

Health Roles

Illness, at-risk, and health are represented by three separate social statuses that can be easily and constructively utilized by community health professionals. Each status has its own role and accompanying set of expectations for behavior. Figure 2-1 illustrates the interrelationship between the social health roles.

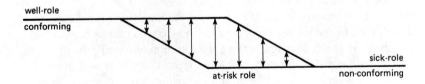

Figure 2-1 Relationships among sick-role, well-role, and at-risk role.

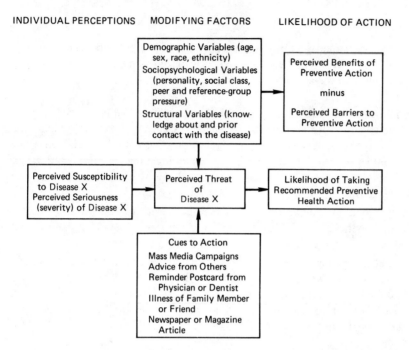

Figure 2-2 The Health Belief Model as a predictor of health behavior. Marshall Becker, Robert Drachman, and John Kirscht, "A New Approach to Explaining Sick-Role Behavior in Low-Income Populations," *American Journal of Public Health,* 64(3) 206, 1974.

The at-risk role implies that the individual is at risk because of a certain health threat or the likelihood of becoming ill. A wide variety of behaviors have been identified and are readily accepted by both the medical profession and society in general that would indicate at-risk status. They include such things as smoking, overeating, a sedentary existence, perfectionism, excessive alcohol consumption, overcommitment to responsibilities, nonparticipation in routine medical check-ups, and indiscriminate self-medication. As is true for the well-role and sick-role, the at-risk role exists on a continuum. For example, the individual who eats a balanced diet daily, exercises regularly, has realistic expectations and goals for life, yet smokes, is at-risk, but at a reduced risk level compared to the individual who has suffered a heart attack and continues to smoke, overeat, and complete thirty-six hours worth of work in a twenty-four-hour day.

The mission of community health is to increase the number of individuals who are fulfilling the well-role, to reduce the number of individuals who assume the sick-role, and promote movement of at-risk individuals along the continuum to well-role. By implication, the at-risk role indicates that the individual is not legitimately ill or well. It implies that at-risk individuals can engage in activities and behaviors that can either improve health status or deteriorate it, or that they live, work, or play in an unsafe environment that may foster illness. It is widely accepted that health is a personal responsibility. Community health can affirm this basic belief by encouraging those at-risk to engage in health-

Figure 2-3 Those who assume the sick-role are expected to behave in a certain way. Courtesy Arizona Republic and Phoenix Gazette.

generating behaviors. This can be accomplished by utilizing health-generating social sanctions, thus increasing social pressure for individual participation. If participation in mass screening programs such as those to detect glaucoma, diabetes, or sickle-cell anemia and adequate physical fitness and emotional well-being are viewed as appropriate behaviors, then the individual who deviates from them can feel both social pressure and cognitive dissonance. This may result in the adoption of constructive health behaviors that push a person from at-risk status to wellness. Health professionals can best accomplish this goal through the use of health education programs that incorporate effective behavior-modifying social sanctions (see Figure 2-2).

In an attempt to alter at-risk behavior, several considerations are virtually important. First it is necessary to identify at-risk *target populations*. These target groups may be hypertensives, migrant workers, corporation executives, or teenage girls utilizing the services of abortion clinics. Second, active and energetic intervention by community health workers who possess the ability to relate to other human beings in their subcultures with genuine concern is a prerequisite for success. Third, it is important that a particular health practice or habit of an individual, such as being sexually promiscuous or abusing drugs, be seen not as a discrete and isolated behavior, but as a representative part of a larger behavior pattern related to the complexities and dynamics of a subcultural system. Community health must respond to the totality of habits or behaviors of the individual, since health behaviors are selections of a complex of internalized social customs of the individual's larger community or subculture.[2] Fourth, it should be remembered that in attempting to alter behavior so that the at-risk role is modified to wellness, changes in behavior from the familiar and comfortable to the unfamiliar and threatening may be required. The need for constancy, continuity, and familiarity are real and cannot be forgotten or neglected by community health workers. Attempts to effect constructive change should be conducted in a nonthreatening way through gradual influence reflecting human sensitivity. Finally, if community health professionals do not have an understanding of and appreciation for the intimate beliefs, values, and shared perceptions of a target group, it will be virtually impossible to predict with any degree of reliability what methods might be most useful in attempting to influence the adoption of constructive health behaviors.

Social Epidemiology

Many of the current health problems have their roots in a complex social-emotional matrix and might appropriately be called the social ailments of our age. In *Future Shock,* Alvin Toffler describes the tremendous impact that rapid technological advance has had on humans living in modern times. Ours is an age of choice and over-choice, of anxiety and stress, of impermanence. Our interpersonal relationships have become increasingly superficial as have many of the other aspects of our physical and social world. Although diseases continue to be classified to some extent according to body system affected (digestive system, respiratory system) and according to the *vector* involved in disease transmission (waterborne, foodborne), an additional classification—*social epidemiology*—is evolving that relates disease to the social condition or situation in which it occurs (poverty-related diseases: TB and parasitic infections; and affluence-related diseases: breast cancer, alcoholism). In addition, social-instability related conditions is seen as a viable classification arrangement for current health problems.[3] A variety of conditions exist today that might accurately be described as social ailments. They range from ulcers, migraine headaches, lung cancer to heart disease, venereal disease, suicide, drug misuse, and obesity. All of these disorders to some extent have their origins in the lifestyles of today. The rapid, dramatic changes in the world have exceeded the limits and capabilities of the human's adaptive range. The result has been increased incidence in a complex variety of diseases. Figure 2-4 illustrates the etiological chain of disease and points out the influence of social situation and physical environment, and vice-versa.

The physical environment is the setting in which social situations develop. The physical environment influences and is influenced by the social situation. The subcultural groups to which an individual belongs will influence the contacts he or she has with vectors and environmental changes, and will influence behavior patterns. In response to an understanding of the social nature of current health problems, the community health field has become concerned not with disease per se, but rather with helping people to make choices regarding lifestyle that will contribute to well-being and self-fulfillment.

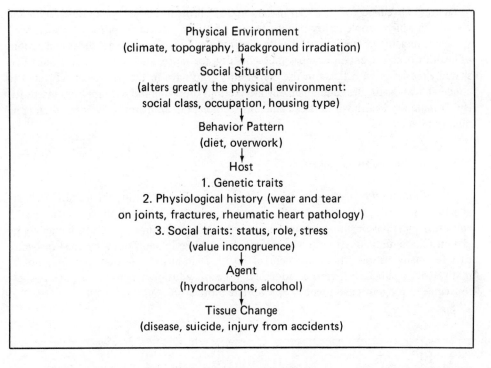

Physical Environment
(climate, topography, background irradiation)
↓
Social Situation
(alters greatly the physical environment:
social class, occupation, housing type)
↓
Behavior Pattern
(diet, overwork)
↓
Host
1. Genetic traits
2. Physiological history (wear and tear
on joints, fractures, rheumatic heart pathology)
3. Social traits: status, role, stress
(value incongruence)
↓
Agent
(hydrocarbons, alcohol)
↓
Tissue Change
(disease, suicide, injury from accidents)

Figure 2-4 The etiological chain. Saxon Graham, "The Sociological Approach to Epidemiology," *American Journal of Public Health,* 64(11) 1046, 1974.

DIALOGUE: A NECESSARY INGREDIENT IN COMMUNITY HEALTH

In order to assist individuals and groups in making choices regarding lifestyles that are health-generating and to help people to deal with rapid social change and restore a sense of permanence, the foundation of community *health education* and community *health services* in the future will be the humanizing of the relationship between the community health professional and the individual. The establishment of real dialogue in social relationships between the community health nurse, physician, health educator, and the individuals in the target populations is of paramount importance in helping people make healthful choices. Real dialogue and genuine relationships between the health worker and the community will reflect the internalized belief that the "person" in the community takes precedence over the "process" of preparing content for public health programs and materials.

Paul Cornely has recently spoken of the hope he has for a new society that is free of the hidden enemies of health. He identified these as "1. addiction to the abundant life, 2. perversion of democracy in favor of vested interest, 3. pollution in the minds of children with advertising programs calling for behavior destructive to their well-being, and

4. racism." He called for "a social metamorphosis brought about by populist fervor and courage in which people rather than technology become the central purpose of society."[4]

Humanizing community health also means humanizing the attitudes and actions of health workers. Genuine compassion, empathy, tolerance, and understanding must be a shared experience with those in the community who have in the past been subjected to condescending attitudes, dehumanizing interactions, bureaucratic red tape, and insensitivity. Community health workers can and must demonstrate humanistic values in their community interactions.

Community Health Education

Community health education is really a social process in which individuals are encouraged to adopt or maintain the behavior patterns discussed above. Again, health educators must have a thorough understanding of the community's culture and an appreciation for the individuals with whom they are working. In addition, they must recognize that for many people, the attainment of health is an abstract notion they may not be motivated to pursue. Therefore, community health educators must anticipate possible resistance to programs and identify appropriate motivators.

Figure 2-5 Dialogue: a necessary ingredient in community health. Courtesy Arizona Department of Health Services.

Communication between the community health educator and citizens has typically occurred in a downward fashion. That is, professionals have created distance from the public by proposing what the needs of the community are in terms of problems and solutions. There has been little evidence of two-way involvement. Soliciting ideas from the people regarding their perceptions of problems, needs, and potential solutions has not been encouraged. Realistically, it is difficult to stimulate communication from the grass-roots level up. In all aspects of modern life, the communication paths often run downward and sometimes horizontally. Although it is difficult, it is essential that dialogue with the community be initiated by community health workers. Gaining acceptance and ultimate program effectiveness requires the involvement of outreach workers from the community to serve as liaisons with the target groups. These outreach workers, as members of the community, have a good understanding of the culture, beliefs, and traditions of the group. They are valuable resources who can facilitate the transmission of health information as well as contributing to the creation of an accepting atmosphere within the community. What is referred to here is not token community participation, but authentic involvement and active participation by the community as a whole.

In the final analysis, community health education will have significant impact on changing health-destroying behavioral patterns and lifestyles to health-generating ones, but *only if* community health educators are able to provide people in the community with access to a variety of *easy* options or alternatives. Some examples might include: presenting easier ways to quit smoking; facilitating the adoption of daily fitness programs through group jogging clubs, publicizing easy isometric fitness programs, and televised exercise programs; and organizing nutrition programs for the aged at senior citizen centers.

COMMUNITY HEALTH PROGRAM PLANNING

Community health planners are committed to dealing with two basic categories of diseases through successful program planning and implementation. First are the diseases associated with modern technological societies, including obesity, hypertension, high intake of refined sugar and carbohydrates, smoking, excessive alcohol intake, sedentary life habits, and the utilization of tranquilizing drugs. Second, there are the diseases associated with developing societies, including acute and communicable diseases, lead poisoning, accidents, parasitic disorders, substandard unsanitary housing, overcrowding, and lack of access to medical care.

Regardless of the target population, be it affluent or poor, community health workers must appreciate the behavioral choices the group sees as alternatives and understand the social factors operating in the form of beliefs and traditions including those related to health. Many, if not all, community health programs are created with the objective of having community members accept and subsequently adopt new health behaviors. But individuals tend to make choices based upon what is easiest and most available to

Figure 2-6
Group fitness programs promote health. Courtesy Arizona Department of Health Services.

them, not what is most healthful. The following examples may serve to illustrate this psychosocial principle:

1. Consuming adequate amounts of protein and fresh vegetables is conducive to health for a poor person, but is difficult to incorporate into his or her lifestyle because of the lack of financial resources to comply.

2. The adoption of socially sanctioned smoking behavior is detrimental to the health of a middle-class adult, but is easily incorporated into his or her lifestyle.

3. If a community health nutritionist attempts to alter completely the diet of a Mexican-American family by virtually eliminating their familiar and culturally accepted foods and types of meals, the nutritionist will surely be doomed to failure. Success is more likely if the nutritionist incorporates essential nutrients by minimal modifications of an established cultural diet, working with existing menus and recommending supplements of certain amounts and types of foods.

Behavior Factors and Program Priorities

As discussed in the previous section, the health choices that people make, like all choices, are related to both personal and societal factors. Personal factors include such things as the subculture, its beliefs and traditions, knowledge about health, financial and economic status, and individual priorities. Societal factors related to public health include such things as the provisions a given society makes for resources for health care, the cost of such care, its availability, types of services offered, and the utilization of outreach workers reflecting subcultural systems.[5] All of these must be considered in health planning if the resulting program development and implementation is to be successful. If mass-immunization programs, screening programs, cancer-education programs, health counseling programs, and well-child clinic programs are to be accepted and utilized by the community, personal behavioral factors must be considered.

In addition to program-development priorities established on the basis of fiscal factors, established need, and effective public dialogue, the location of services and their availability to the target population must receive considerable attention by planners. A family-planning clinic located in the suburbs, created to meet the particular needs of the urban population, is of little value because the target population will have limited accessibility to its services.

In the planning and implementation of all public health services, an attempt should be made to utilize outreach workers who are members of the target population in the community. These individuals, as active participants in the planning and delivery of health services, act as valuable resources of information and can increase public confidence in the programs.

Community health planning in the future will have to alter its perspective and priorities in a number of directions. First, the perspective of community health must begin to concern itself to a greater degree with the behavioral systems or health-destroying habits of the individual, not simply the disease alone. Second, more attention to the preventive and health-promoting aspects of community health will have to assume higher priority over the curative aspects. Third, increased knowledge and understanding of the target community and authentic humanistic concern for whom the programs are being planned must be achieved. Fourth, true and genuine involvement of target population citizens, including assessment of needs and implementation, rather than the professional "looking-in" approach to health planning, is a vital ingredient.

Community health program planning and service implementation in the future will out of necessity involve real dialogue between the community and the health worker. Consumers of health care should be involved in such planning responsibilities as:

1. assessment of health needs, including the collection of data regarding health and sociological aspects of the community
2. identification of goals for intended programs; specific aims
3. decision-making regarding program planning; types of services to be offered and location of these services
4. implementation of health service programs; use of out-reach workers; target population community health educators, and staffing
5. evaluation and follow-up to determine program success (short-term and long-term).

Toward Active Participation

In the downward-communication pattern of the past, the professionals made the assessment of needs, planned and implemented the programs, and told the community what services would be available to them and in what way. The new era of humanistic community health planning will involve both upward and downward communication. The role of community health professionals may well become that of a consultant to the community. Through active participation on the part of the individuals in the community, we may see an end to elitism in public health and a beginning of shared and responsible commitment to improvement and promotion of health by a majority of people in the community. Active participation can result in a more enlightened and knowledgeable public, allowing people to at least partially fulfill their needs for social participation and to assert their human dignity and worth. In affirming the necessity for this approach, Hallanda has said:

> A new attitude has emerged in health policy which recognizes people's capacity to contribute to the solution of their own problems and attempts to provide opportunities for their active participation in the planning and execution of programs.[6]

Whether the concern be for greater participation in mass immunizations and screenings or lead-poisoning and parenthood educational programs, it is the people of the community who can best provide the information, support, and leadership so necessary for successful program participation. These individuals can provide information regarding the most effective medium of communication, provide valuable information about how attendance can be improved by anticipating particular transportation problems individuals might have in getting to the health service, what times of the day might be most conducive to full participation, and what kind of dimensions might be added to achieve participation in the health program, such as a provision for baby-sitters.

The implementation of the above-mentioned ideas could result in more effective, humane, equitable, and better-received programs, especially if they include public accountability. It is hoped that in the future, greater accountability of the health services will be the norm rather than the exception. This means that ultimately, the public must begin to share a greater responsibility in health care services, rather than remain an outside group that is merely on the receiving end of the delivery system.

REVIEW QUESTIONS

1. Describe examples of behaviors and/or which may be a part of sick-role, well-role and at-risk role for the following groups: (1) the affluent, (2) the middle class, and (3) poverty groups.
2. Analyze the beliefs and traditions of the following groups as they may relate to health, health behaviors, and utilization of health care services: (1) Mexican-Americans (low-income), (2) affluent blacks, and (3) American Indians.

3. What are the essential elements of humanistic community health programs?
4. How can community health programs influence health-generating behaviors?
5. Identify areas in contemporary life in which a humanistic approach and attitude would be constructive.
6. Differentiate between upward, downward, and horizontal lines of communication.
7. What factors serve as the basis for the health choices people make?

SUGGESTED READINGS

Bahnson, Claus, "Epistemological Perspectives of Physical Disease from the Psychodynamic Point of View," *American Journal of Public Health,* 64(11) 1034–1040, 1974.

Landy, David (ed.), *Culture, Disease and Healing: Studies in Medical Anthropology.* New York: Macmillan, 1977.

Leininger, Madeleine, *Health Care Dimensions: Transcultural Health Care Issues and Conditions.* Philadelphia: F. A. Davis, 1976.

Miller, Arden C., "Societal Change and Public Health: A Rediscovery," *American Journal of Public Health,* 66(1), 1976, p. 55.

Pratt, Lois, *Family Structure and Effective Health Behavior: The Energized Family.* Boston: Houghton Mifflin, 1976.

NOTES

[1] Leo Baric, "Conformity and Deviance in Health and Illness," *International Journal of Health Education,* 18(1), 1975, p. 3.

[2] Guy Stewart, "Psycho-Sociological Basis of Behavior Change," *Proceedings of the Seventh International Conference on Health and Health Education.* Buenos Aires: International Union of Health Education, 1969, p. 431.

[3] Saxon Graham, "The Sociological Approach to Epidemiology," *American Journal of Public Health,* 64(11), 1974, p. 1046.

[4] C. Arden Miller, "Societal Change and Public Health: A Rediscovery," *American Journal of Public Health,* 66(1), 1976, p. 55.

[5] Nancy Milio, "A Framework for Prevention: Changing Health-Damaging to Health-Generating Life Patterns," *American Journal of Public Health,* 66(5), 1976, p. 437.

[6] Hortensia Hollanda, "We Need to Promote a Real Dialogue with People: Communication and Behavior Change," *Proceedings of the Seventh International Conference on Health and Health Education.* Buenos Aires: International Union of Health Education, 1969, p. 35.

GLOSSARY

at-risk role a social role or identity assumed when others in the group define one as being at-risk of becoming ill or sick.

beliefs the collective sense of what is real to a society.

health education an educational approach designed to improve and maintain health among populations and which exists in the community, the schools, and in health care institutions.

health services any and all services available to a community that are important to health promotion and disease treatment and cure.

multicausation theory a theory of disease holding that two or more factors or agents are involved in disease causation.

norms standards or patterns of acceptable behavior as defined by the social group; rules of conduct that identify what people should do.

sanctions the process by which a society enforces its norms through a system of rewards and punishments.

sick-role a social role or identity assumed when others in the group define one as being ill or sick. The sick-role is seen as deviant or nonconforming to norms.

single-agent theory a theory of disease holding that one agent, factor, or pathogen is responsible for disease causation.

social disorganization instability within a social system, a departure from social order. Riot, violence, crime, and civil war are manifestations of social disorganization.

social epidemiology the practice of incorporating social patterns, the measurement of social structures and identities as they influence disease into traditional epidemiology.

social unit a defined group of people, the point of reference of which may be the family, community, nation, or world.

subculture a cultural subgroup, especially within a nation, differentiated by status, ethnic background, religion, or other factors that functionally unify the group and act collectively on each member.

target population a discrete group of people sharing certain factors or health problems who are isolated for specific public health intervention activities, i.e. hypertensives, adolescent females, and migrant workers.

vector intermediate host of an organism that represents the connecting link between the cause of a disease and a susceptible new host.

well-role a social role or identity assumed when the group defines one as conforming to norms of physical and mental capacity for active participation in social activities.

BIBLIOGRAPHY

Becker, Marshall, Robert Drachman, and John Kirsclt, "A New Approach to Explaining Sick-Role Behavior in Low-Income Populations." *American Journal of Public Health,* 64(3) 205-216, 1974.

Baric, Leo (ed.), "Behavioral Sciences in Health and Disease," *International Journal of Health Education* (Supplement). Geneva: International Union of Health Education, Vol. 18, 1972.

Baric, Leo, "Conformity and Deviance in Health and Illness," *International Journal of Health Education* (Supplement) 18(1) 1-2, 1975.

—— "Communication and Behavior Change," *Proceedings of the Seventh International Conference on Health and Health Education,* Buenos Aires, 1969. Geneva International Union of Health Education, 1969.

Chapman, June and Harry Chapman, *Behavior and Health Care: A Humanistic Helping Process.* St. Louis: C. V. Mosby, 1975.

Christmas, June Jackson, "The Challenge of Change: The 1980 Presidential Address," *American Journal of Public Health,* 71(3) 235-241, 1981.

Coates, Thomas, Robert Jeffery, and Lee Ann Slinkard, "Heart Healthy Eating and Exercise: Introducing and Maintaining Changes in Health Behaviors," *American Journal of Public Health,* 71(1) 15-23, 1981.

Goldsmith, Francis and Godfrey Hochbaum, "Changing People's Behavior Toward the Environment," *Public Health Reports,* 90(30) 231-234, 1975.

Graham, Saxon, "Studies of Behavior Change to Enhance Public Health," *American Journal of Public Health,* 63(4) 327-334, 1973.

Hessler, Richard M. and Andrew C. Twaddle, *Sociology of Health.* St. Louis: C. V. Mosby, 1977.

Kane, Robert L. (ed.), *Behavioral Sciences and Preventive Medicine: Opportunities and Dilemmas.* Washington, D.C.: U.S. DHEW Pub. No. (NIH) 76-878, 1978.

Milio, Nancy, "A Framework for Prevention: Changing Health-Damaging to Health-Generating Life Patterns," *American Journal of Public Health,* 66(5) 435-439, 1976.

Twaddle, Andrew, *Sickness Behavior and Sick-Role.* Boston, Mass.: G. K. Hall, 1979.

3

ORGANIZATION AND ADMINISTRATION OF PUBLIC HEALTH

Community Health
  Health System Model
Health Organization at the Federal Level
  The Department of Health and Human Services
  Public Health Service
  Health Legislation
Health Organization at the State Level
  State Departments of Health Services
Health Organization at the Local Level
  Local Departments of Health Services
Voluntary Agencies
  Functions of Voluntary Agencies
Health Foundations
  Professional Health Organizations
Basis for Community Health Organization

"Public Health administration in a community is as extensive, and the health department is as efficient, as the people want it to be. Health administration can neither exceed to any great extent or lag far behind the wishes of the people."

Public Health Reports, June 12, 1914

COMMUNITY HEALTH

Community health encompasses a wide variety of areas that relate to the *protection* and promotion of health in the United States. In the past, it was appropriate to think of community health in terms of its activities in *disease prevention* and *sanitation.* However, this narrow view of the scope of community health which was true in the past is no longer appropriate in the present. As the nature of health and disease has changed, so has the nature of community health activities and its organization. Individuals and agencies concerned with promoting health in the community have, out of necessity, become involved in such things as reducing chemical and physical dangers in the environment, improving the ability of individuals to employ positive adaptation mechanisms in dealing with stress, and creating an awareness in the public of the ramifications of overpopulation, followed by appropriate action through family planning.

The traditional activities of community health—such as compiling *vital statistics,* preventing the spread of communicable diseases, and ensuring a safe food and water supply for the public—remain key concerns for those involved in community health, but today's professionals are concerned with much more. A variety of services now come under the rubric of public health, dental health services, home health services for the aged, prison health care, new areas in maternal and child-health promotion, such as neonatal

47

care; mental and emotional health services, including suicide prevention and occupational safety and health; and the prevention and management of the addictive diseases, such as drug and alcohol abuse.

Health System Model

A model from which community health organization may be studied was developed by Mary F. Arnold (see Figure 3-1). This model identifies both the functions performed by the health system and the organizations and individuals who perform them. The assumption on which the model is based is that two needs of society are provided for by a health system: "maintenance of a positive biological relationship to the environment and prevention of disruptive behaviors attributed by the society to ill health."[1] Careful examination of the Functional Health System Model will facilitate a better understanding of how people, agencies, and institutions coordinate their efforts through personal care activities, protective activities, education and promotion activities, and social policies planning activities, with the help of support activities, to serve the health needs of the public.

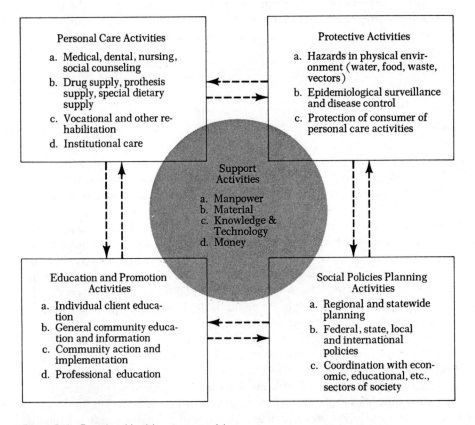

Figure 3-1 Functional health systems model.

Personal care activities This section of the model includes all levels of personal health services. Traditionally, this area has been thought of in terms of cure and treatment of disease. However, it has several levels. Among them are:

1. *Primary prevention:* activities designed to prevent disease from occurring. Immunizations, nutritional services are examples of this level.
2. *Secondary prevention:* activities designed to detect health problems and disease early—to reduce its spread—to increase the likelihood of cure. Diagnostic tests such as the pap smear, laboratory tests and yearly physical exams are examples of secondary prevention activities.
3. *Treatment:* clinical activities in the practice of medicine or self-care designed to effect cure and early recovery from a disease or health problem. The objective of early treatment is to reduce the likelihood of spread of contagious disease and long term disability in certain conditions. Maintenance treatment is applied in conditions such as hypertension and diabetes, where a cure is not possible.
4. *Rehabilitation:* services and activities designed to help the individual recovering from illness or surgery return to the highest level of functioning possible, given individual limitations. Physical therapy for a stroke victim is an example of this level of personal care.

Simply, personal care activities focus on prevention of disease, and the treatment and care of health problems affecting individuals. These services are delivered by a variety of different health professionals, including x-ray technologists, physicians, nurses, physical therapists, and health educators. Many organizations provide personal health services, including hospitals, public health clinics, *voluntary agencies,* and health professionals in private practice.

Protective activities These are gaining increased attention. Their focus is reducing the chances of people becoming exposed to causative agents in the environment, with the goal of reducing the likelihood of disease. The term "environment" is used broadly to refer to the physical and chemical environment, as well as the home, school, and work (social) environment. For example, at both the state and national levels, laws have been enacted regarding water quality, air quality, food handling practices, and management of solid wastes. These public health laws, whether enforced by the Environmental Protection Agency, the Food and Drug Administration, or a State or County Department of Public Health, are designed to reduce and control hazards in the physical environment. Epidemiological surveillance, combined with disease control activities, represent another aspect of protective activities.*

---

*As mentioned earlier, epidemiology is the study of the determinants and distribution of disease among populations. This public health science will be examined in more detail in Chapter 4. Its purpose is to identify the factors that contribute to disease occurrence so that they may be controlled, reduced, or eliminated. The epidemiologist focuses on groups of people, while physicians focus on individual patients.

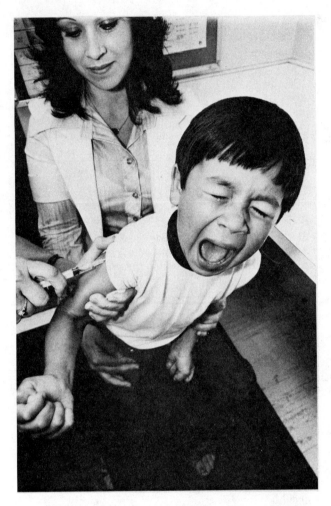

Figure 3-2
Immunization is one type of primary prevention activity. Courtesy Arizona Republic and Phoenix Gazette.

Sanitarians, chemists, epidemiologists, nutritionists, microbiologists, and engineers are all examples of professional groups involved in protective activities within the health system. Each may perform a function that promotes health. An engineer may design a safe landfill site, a chemist may study the potential hazard of food additives, or a microbiologist might attempt to identify the causative agent in a "newly" discovered disease such as Legionnaires' disease and toxic shock syndrome.

Education and promotion activities These are divided into two basic areas: (1) activities that inform and educate the public in matters of health *enhancement* and (2) activities through which health professionals and allied professionals are educated and trained to become members of the health care team. A health system cannot be effectively sustained if it is without trained health manpower or an enlightened public.

Public health education is designed to inform the population about effective utilization of health services and to teach people how they can best promote their own well-being. Health education includes individual client counselling as well as mass education of large groups of people. This process was explained in detail in Chapter 2.

It is obvious that maintaining a sufficient supply of trained health professionals to enter the health system is essential to provide for the needs of the population. These health professionals and allied health professionals are educated and training in medical schools, institutions of higher learning, and specialized training schools throughout the United States. At present, there are over 400 different recognized health professions in the U.S.

Social policies and planning activities This is an area within the functional model of the health system that focuses on effective utilization of resources and coordination of programs, services, and activities carried out by different agencies and which seeks to avoid unnecessary duplication and waste. Health planning encompasses social, cultural, economic, and political considerations. At the national level, planning takes place within the context of a pluralistic social network that is composed of a variety of ethnic, religious, racial, and socioeconomic groups.

Coordinating the programs and services of various groups to provide a comprehensive and quality health care delivery system for the nation is a difficult task. *Official community health agencies* in the United States are organized in an extremely complex manner. The complexity of governmental organization is further complicated as a result of the vast scope of activities engaged in by the voluntary health agencies. In addition, private medicine plays a significant role. Although organization of community health programs has largely been achieved, duplication of services has remained a problem. This is understandable when one considers the large number of agencies, both official and voluntary that are involved in any one health area of concern. But many unmet health needs continue to exist, while the cost of health care is becoming increasingly prohibitive.

Thus, the focus of health planning at present is to develop an organized, effective, accessible, and comprehensive health system that avoids unnecessary duplication, poor utilization of resources—both human and material—and excessive cost. The National Health Planning and Resources Development Act of 1974, which is discussed in greater detail in Chapter 9, is an example of the national initiative to develop a rational approach to planning for health care in the U.S.

Support activities Finally, a health system must have support activities in order to sustain itself. Many resources are essential: human, financial, and material. Human resources include health professionals, volunteers, and other personnel such as administrators, biostatisticians, and technicians. In order to provide the essential material and human resources, adequate financial resources are needed. Indeed, a health system is a complex of people, institutions, and programs initiated and carried out under the auspices of both official and voluntary agencies at levels ranging from the national to local communities. Coordination is the key to its effective functioning. A discussion of the various organizations which comprise the health system in the United States follows.

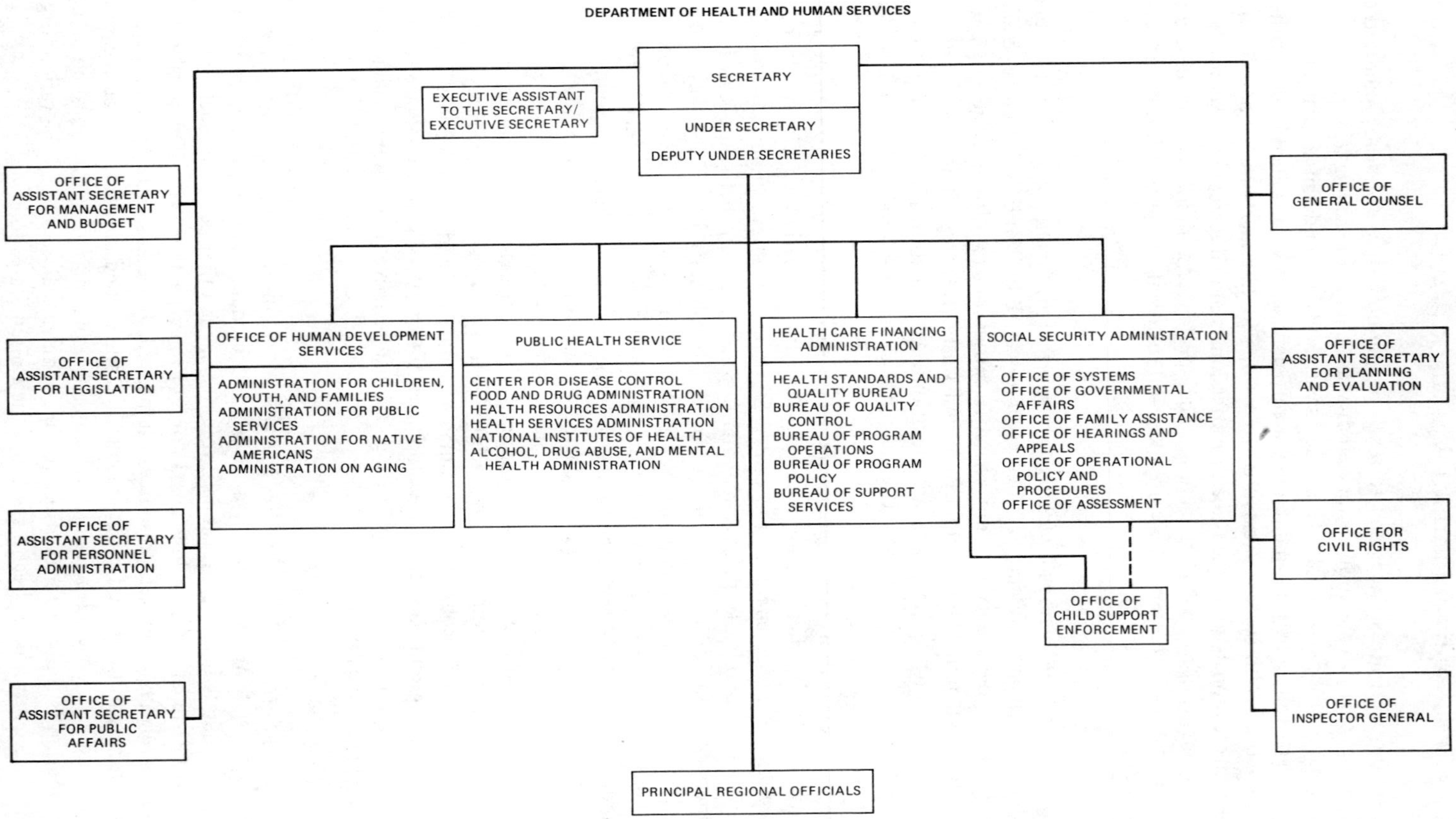

DEPARTMENT OF HEALTH AND HUMAN SERVICES

OFFICE OF GENERAL COUNSEL

OFFICE OF ASSISTANT SECRETARY FOR PLANNING AND EVALUATION

OFFICE FOR CIVIL RIGHTS

OFFICE OF INSPECTOR GENERAL

SECRETARY

UNDER SECRETARY

DEPUTY UNDER SECRETARIES

EXECUTIVE ASSISTANT TO THE SECRETARY/ EXECUTIVE SECRETARY

OFFICE OF ASSISTANT SECRETARY FOR MANAGEMENT AND BUDGET

OFFICE OF ASSISTANT SECRETARY FOR LEGISLATION

OFFICE OF ASSISTANT SECRETARY FOR PERSONNEL ADMINISTRATION

OFFICE OF ASSISTANT SECRETARY FOR PUBLIC AFFAIRS

OFFICE OF HUMAN DEVELOPMENT SERVICES

ADMINISTRATION FOR CHILDREN, YOUTH, AND FAMILIES
ADMINISTRATION FOR PUBLIC SERVICES
ADMINISTRATION FOR NATIVE AMERICANS
ADMINISTRATION ON AGING

PUBLIC HEALTH SERVICE

CENTER FOR DISEASE CONTROL
FOOD AND DRUG ADMINISTRATION
HEALTH RESOURCES ADMINISTRATION
HEALTH SERVICES ADMINISTRATION
NATIONAL INSTITUTES OF HEALTH
ALCOHOL, DRUG ABUSE, AND MENTAL HEALTH ADMINISTRATION

HEALTH CARE FINANCING ADMINISTRATION

HEALTH STANDARDS AND QUALITY BUREAU
BUREAU OF QUALITY CONTROL
BUREAU OF PROGRAM OPERATIONS
BUREAU OF PROGRAM POLICY
BUREAU OF SUPPORT SERVICES

SOCIAL SECURITY ADMINISTRATION

OFFICE OF SYSTEMS
OFFICE OF GOVERNMENTAL AFFAIRS
OFFICE OF FAMILY ASSISTANCE
OFFICE OF HEARINGS AND APPEALS
OFFICE OF OPERATIONAL POLICY AND PROCEDURES
OFFICE OF ASSESSMENT

OFFICE OF CHILD SUPPORT ENFORCEMENT

PRINCIPAL REGIONAL OFFICIALS

Figure 3-3 Organizational chart of the Department of Health and Human Services.

HEALTH ORGANIZATION AT
THE FEDERAL LEVEL

At the federal level, national health policy is shaped. The basis for public health in the United States is derived from the *Preamble of the United States Constitution,* which states a purpose *"to promote the general welfare."* This statement, in addition to others like it throughout the Constitution, have come to mean that promoting health can indirectly mean promoting the "general welfare." Through the years, both the direction and substance of national health policy has changed in response to the evolving needs of the American public.

There are more than fifty different departments, agencies, and bureaus at the federal level that deal with some aspect of the nation's health. For example, the Department of Agriculture is involved in a number of health services including the control of disease in animals, ensuring sanitary methods of handling milk supply, and promoting rural health and sanitation through its Extension Service. The Census Bureau which is housed in the Department of Commerce, is responsible for compiling national population statistics which are of value in health planning. In addition, the Department of the Interior, Department of Labor, and the Department of Defense have certain health responsibilities. In 1953, the Department of Health, Education and Welfare was established, in an attempt to consolidate the most important federal agencies dealing with health in one organization. In 1980, reorganization of this important federal agency took place in which two new departments were created, the Department of Education and the Department of Health and Human Services. The intent of this formal reorganization was to improve further the efficiency of the respective agencies focus in the areas of health and education.

The Department of Health and Human Services

The Department of Health and Human Services is the largest and single most important Federal agency concerned with health in the United States. It has undergone a number of organizational changes over the years to increase its effectiveness. In the present organization of the Department of Health and Human Services, there are six units of the Public Health Service (PHS) (see Figure 3-3). These units contain a large number of bureaus, offices, centers, institutes, and divisions. In addition to the U.S. Public Health Service, the Department of Health and Human Services contains the Office of Human Development Services, the Health Care Financing Administration, and the Social Security Administration. The Department has eleven regional offices, which administer national health program policies at lower levels.

Public Health Service

The Public Health Service (PHS) is primarily responsible for health in the nation. The U.S. Public Health Service evolved from the Marine Hospital which was established in 1798, within the Treasury Department. In 1912, the name of this agency was officially changed. When the Department of Health and Human Services, formerly the Department

of Health, Education and Welfare, was created in 1953, the Public Health Service became
a part of this new department. Under a recently reorganized structure, the Public Health
Service now includes the following divisions:

Food and Drug Administration (FDA)
Health Services Administration (HSA), including:
  Emergency Medical Services
  Community Health Centers
  Federal Health Programs Service
  Indian Health Service
  Maternal-Child Health Service
  National Center for Family Planning Services
  Health Maintenance Organization Service
Health Resources Administration (HRA), including:
  Bureau of Health Manpower
  Health Care Facilities Service
  National Center for Health Services Research
  National Center for Health Statistics
  Bureau of Health Planning and Resources Development
  Nursing Home Improvement
National Institutes of Health (NIH) (Research), including:
  National Cancer Institute
  National Eye Institute
  National Heart, Blood and Lung Institute
  National Institute of Allergy and Infectious Diseases
  National Institute of Arthritis, Metabolism, and Digestive Diseases
  National Institute of Child Health and Human Development
  National Institute of Dental Research
  National Institute of Environmental Health Sciences
  National Institute of General Medical Sciences
  National Institute of Neurological Diseases and Stroke
  National Institute of Aging
Center for Disease Control (CDC), including:
  Bureau of Community Environmental Management
  National Institute for Occupational Safety and Health
Alcohol, Drug Abuse and Mental Health Administration, including:
  National Institute of Mental Health
  National Institite of Drug Abuse
  National Institute of Alcoholism

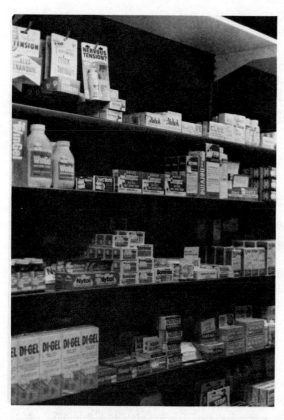

Figure 3-4
The F.D.A. regulates safety and effectiveness of over-the-counter drugs.

Food and Drug Administration Since the creation of the Food and Drug Administration (FDA) in the 1920s, its functions have expanded significantly. This division has both regulatory and enforcement power for the safety and labeling of foods, drugs, and cosmetics, as well as for biological products and medical devices. The FDA serves as a protective agency for consumers, ensuring that food supply that crosses interstate boundaries is safe, and that drugs are safe and effective in treating health problems. The FDA has nineteen district offices in the U.S., as well as field stations and mobile laboratories for the inspection of imported foods, drugs, and cosmetics. Several recent actions of the FDA include (1) prohibiting the use of cyclamates, (2) banning Red Dye No. 2, a coloring agent, and (3) requiring that a toxic-shock warning pamphlet be included in all boxes of tampons sold in the U.S.

Health Services Administration This agency administers various programs designed to provide health services to specific target groups. The Indian Health Service (IHS) provides a variety of health services for American Indians on reservations. Alaska natives come under IHS jurisdiction. In addition, the Health Services Administration (HSA) administers family-planning services for the entire U.S. population, maternal and child-health services, and community health services.

Health Resources Administration   The Health Resources Administration (HRA), established in 1973, conducts programs in health research, planning, and training. The prime responsibility of this agency is the development and maintenance of a quality health care delivery system in the United States that is responsive to the health needs of individual citizens. It is through this division that comprehensive health planning is funded. In addition, the HRA is involved in health services research and health manpower programs and activities. There are two bureaus within the HRA: the Bureau of Health Manpower and the Bureau of Health Planning, Resources, and Development. The enactment of the National Health Planning and Resources Development Act of 1974 (PL 93–641) has had a significant impact on the activities of the Health Resources Administration, and required the development of a national health policy. This legislation will be discussed in more detail in Chapter 9.

National Institutes of Health   This division of the Public Health Service is composed of twelve research institutes. Research sponsored by the National Institutes of Health (NIH) is designed to improve the health of the nation through investigating major prevalent diseases and health problems. Its mission is the control of disease and extension of life. The National Library of Medicine is a part of the NIH and is considered to be the clearinghouse for medical literature and information in the United States.

Center for Disease Control   This center, which is the focus of the government's effort to control disease, is located in Atlanta. Epidemiological studies of disease outbreaks in the United States population are conducted under the direction of the CDC. In recent years, the CDC has undertaken epidemiological investigations of the pneumonia-like Legionnaires' disease, first recognized during 1976 in Philadelphia during a convention of the American Legion, and toxic shock syndrome, associated with tampon use in women, first discovered in 1980. This division also administers all federal programs that are an outgrowth of the Occupational Safety and Health Act of 1970 (OSHA). This Act created a national institute, known as the NIOSH (National Institute for Occupational Safety and Health). OSHA's focus is the provision of safe and healthful working conditions.

Alcohol, Drug Abuse and Mental Health Administration   The focus of this agency is to provide national leadership for the improvement of mental health. It handles problems such as drug abuse and alcoholism as sociomedical consequences of maladjustment and emotional stress. This division provides support to communities to deal with mental health problems, as a consequence of urban sprawl, overcrowding, and increasing dehumanization in modern society.

The PHS, which is headed by the Surgeon General of the United States, has expanded considerably since its inception in 1798. It now includes provisions for comprehensive health planning and delivery, biomedical research, and consumer protection.

Health Legislation

One of the most significant aspects of health at the national level is health legislation. It is important since legislation reflects changes in health organization and

Figure 3-5 The CDC is the focus of disease control efforts in the United States. Courtesy Center for Disease Control.

funding at the national level relating to contemporary local needs and projected future health needs in the United States. The basic thrust of recent health legislation has been the strengthening of lower-level governmental agencies (local and county departments). The objective has been for agencies at the local and county levels to establish integrated health programs and activities that reflect national health policy. In general, the programs that have recently received the greatest amount of federal support have been those that emphasize local initiative. In this way, it is possible to decentralize the federal government by returning federal income-tax money to the states and local geographic units for the improvement of health services and facilities at the grass-roots level.

HEALTH ORGANIZATION AT THE
STATE LEVEL

Each state in the United States is a *sovereign power*. This means that through the vehicle of state constitutions, each state is charged with the responsibility of protecting the health of the people who reside within its boundaries. State governments have the authority and power to generate programs to meet health needs and raise revenue to implement these programs as long as they are compatible with federal constitutional provisions.

Health legislation in the states is almost as significant as national legislation. Legislation is usually introduced in response to a perceived need or problem. It is then acted upon through democratic channels. If the bill is approved, it becomes law and is subsequently implemented and enforced by the state and/or local agency. Briefly, this is how a given state establishes public health law and develops budgets concerning health programs. By way of example, it is through these legislative channels that the state of Arizona elected not to appropriate Medicaid funds over the years for the medically indigent population. Through the same process, all of the other forty-nine states elected to appropriate these funds.

State Departments of Health Services

State health agencies, or the state departments of health services bridge the gap between national health policy and local departments of health. These official state agencies provide resources and guidance to local and county health departments and generally assist the more localized groups in dealing with health problems. No two state health departments, which are coming to be known as State Departments of Health Services, have exactly the same structure and organization, but all have the same goal, complementary to the national goal: promoting and protecting health. Most state departments of health have a Board of Health or Advisory Council. The members of these boards are usually appointed by the governor of the state. The state Boards of Health function within their authority as established by state legislatures. One of the prime functions of the board is to develop health codes for the states, which contain rules and regulations concerned with the state. The executive committee in some states selects and appoints a commissioner or director of the state agency, who in turn is responsible for administering the health program within the state. In some states, the chief administrator of the state health department is appointed by the governor.

Figure 3-6 shows the organizational structure of the Arizona Department of Health Services. The number of administrative divisions indicated in the organizational chart of any given state will reflect the size of the state and the number of health programs which have been established.

State departments of health services are delegated several basic categories of responsibility. The foremost function is to assist local departments in doing an adequate job in health programming. In addition, the state department of health usually is involved in health planning, health policy making, interagency relations, and establishing state standards for health. The following is a list of typical functions of the State Department of Health Services:

1. To represent the public health interests and goals of the state and the elected governing body of the state.
2. To promulgate and enforce public health rules and regulations applicable throughout the state.
3. To determine state public health policy and to provide a statewide coordinated

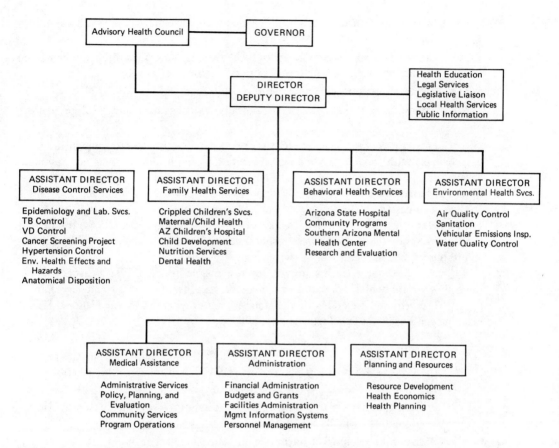

Figure 3-6 Organizational chart of the Arizona Department of Health Services. Courtesy Arizona Department of Health Services.

public health program with clear objectives for the guidance of local health departments.

4. To promote the establishment of full-time local health units.

5. To develop an appropriate plan for the coordination of local health services with related hospital and medical programs which may be developed on a regional basis.

6. To provide financial assistance to supplement the resources of local health departments.

7. To make consultation and other special services available.

8. To assist localities to set up demonstrations on a temporary basis.

9. To establish minimum and stimulate optimum standards of performance.

10. To develop a recruitment and training program for local health department personnel.

11. To delegate certain legal responsibilities of the state health agency, in so far as

feasible and practical to well-organized and adequately staffed local health departments.

12. To carry on all relationships with local citizens and groups through the medium of or in cooperation with local health education.

13. To carry on a statewide program of health education.

14. To evaluate continually or periodically existing state and local programs.[2]

Most state health agencies (SHAs) provide public health programs in the areas of personal health services, environmental sanitation, and health planning and resources development. The diversity and scope of health programs in states vary significantly in response to geographic and population differences as well as financial or budget variations.

The passage of the National Health Planning and Resources Development Act of 1974 created for the first time a network of Health Systems Agencies (HSAs) throughout the United States. These HSAs were responsible for area-wide planning of health services and resources in identified Health Service Areas.

The governor of each state was also responsible for identifying an agency within the state's governmental structure to serve as the state health planning and development agency. The required functions of the state agency as specified by the National Health Planning and Resources Development Act included:

1. Conducting the state's health planning activities and implementing the parts of the state health plan and plans of the HSAs which relate to the government of the state.

2. Preparing a state plan for approval or disapproval by the Statewide Health Coordinating Council.

3. Assisting the Council in reviewing the state medical facilities plan and in performing its functions.

4. Reviewing existing and new institutional health services offered and proposed as to their need and appropriateness.

The full impact of this Act on health planning and the health system in the U.S. is still unknown. However, it does represent the most significant attempt at national health system planning to date and state governments are intricately involved in its implementation.

HEALTH ORGANIZATION AT THE LOCAL LEVEL

Local governments receive delegated authority from the states in matters of health. The local government on the basis of delegated authority develops ordinances and other rules and regulations which are designed to promote health in relatively small geographic areas. A transition has occurred in health organization at the local level. Historically, the city health department was quite visible and county health departments were somewhat rare. Today, county health departments or county departments of health services are increasing in numbers and have become quite significant in the provision of health services to discrete geographic units. This movement away from the establishment of city health departments has occurred largely because it was found that county health departments could better provide for the services needed by people (see Figure 3-7). When groups of small towns pool their resources, financial and professional, the county health department can more efficiently and effectively deliver health services. For both practical and economic considerations it is recommended that a city have a minimum population of 50,000 before attempting to establish a city health department.

Local Departments of Health Services

It is at the local level where most of the direct health services provided to the public are rendered. These services include the items identified below. However, it should be noted that the types of direct health services offered differ significantly both within a given state as well as in different counties and between states.

> *Health education:* the process concerned with the transmission of health knowledge concerning health maintenance and disease, fostering health-constructive behavior changes and the use of appropriate health services.
>
> *Vital statistics:* collecting data and applying statistical methods to identify vital health facts in a given area, such as disease incidence, morbidity and mortality rates.
>
> *Epidemiology:* investigating and establishing disease causation in order to institute effective control measures.
>
> *Disease control:* activities carried out by departments of health that are aimed at the prevention, early diagnosis and treatment of diseases, both communicable and noncommunicable.
>
> *Sanitation:* ensuring a safe living environment through protection of food, water, and milk supplies, regulation of housing, and *rodent control.*
>
> *Laboratory services:* microbiological and serological functions to assist in providing the community with pure food, milk, and water, and to control communicable diseases.
>
> *Operation of health facilities:* the provision of services in adequate and accessible facilities, which include: prevention, health maintenance, diagnostic services, treatment, and rehabilitation.

The type and number of activities included in the basic programs of the local health department varies according to the size of the community, its resources, and health problems. Basically these services and responsibilities include recording and analyzing health data, health education and information, supervision and regulation, administration of personal health services, operation of health facilities, and coordination of activities and resources.[3]

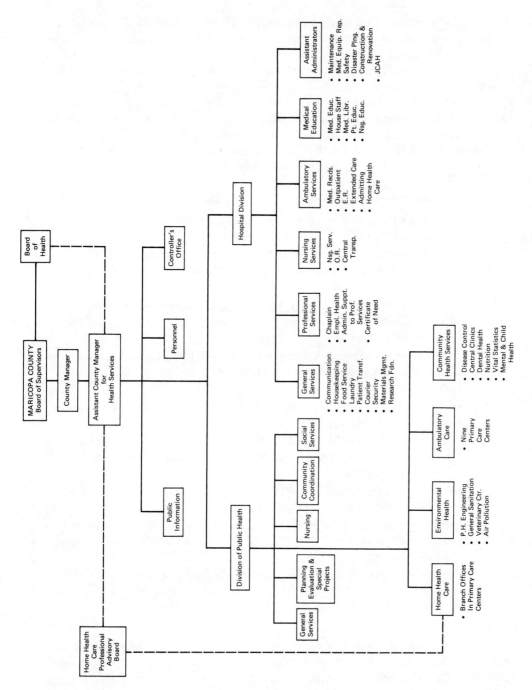

Figure 3-7 Functional chart, Maricopa County Department of Health Services. Courtesy Maricopa County (Arizona) Department of Health Services.

Perhaps a closer examination of each of the basic functions will promote better understanding as to the way in which local health departments provide direct services to the people they serve.

Health education   This function takes place in many different community settings through a variety of techniques. Health fairs, the utilization of the mass media, educational films, presentations and speeches, and conducting classes in such areas as prenatal nutrition are all examples of the methods of community health education. Effective health education programs employ health educators who can communicate well with people in the community and who genuinely care about their well-being. This requires a sound knowledge of the interests, beliefs, culture, and values of the group. In the future, it is likely that health education will occupy a central position in community health programs. And, it will have responsibility for educating the public about the scientific basis for new public health programs as well as to educate people to alter behavior in the interest of disease prevention.

Vital statistics   The collection of health data is more than an exercise in mathematics. The information gained from collecting and analyzing statistics related to human existence in a geographic area can be used to identify strengths and weaknesses in existing health programs. In addition, this information can provide direction to health program planners to develop and implement new services that may be needed by the people in the community. Keeping records of specific data concerning health and disease is also very important nationally. The data collected at the local level is forwarded to the state and then finally to the National Center for Health Statistics. The information compiled provides a basis for identifying national health needs and trends. The role of health statistics in the United States today is to:

1. provide a comprehensive picture of the nature and magnitude of the nation's health problems;
2. assess how well health services are meeting these problems, at what cost and with what gain, and
3. serve basic health research needs.[4]

"Health statistics today encompass health service resources as well as health status and health care utilization in five main areas: population, health status, health manpower, health care facilities, health services utilization and financing."[5] These statistics serve as the basis for understanding the human health needs and problems of people in the United States in addition to measuring the successes of public health programs.

Disease control   This concept has expanded significantly in community health. Programs continue to be deeply involved in the control of communicable diseases such as TB, rubella, and the sexually transmitted diseases. By employing mass-immunization programs, effective treatment techniques, and improving sanitation in general, control of many of the communicable diseases has been quite effective. However, the concept of dis-

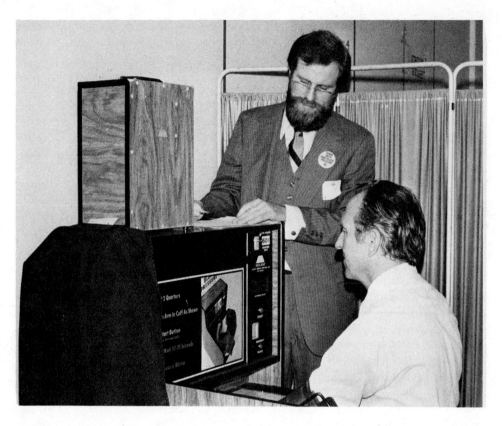

Figure 3–8 The concept of disease control includes hypertension screening. Courtesy Arizona Department of Health Services.

ease control in modern community health must necessarily include programs and services designed to prevent, diagnose, and treat the genetic diseases, chronic diseases, mental-emotional diseases, and the behavioral-addictive diseases, such as alcoholism. In attempting to control these health problems, community health is relying more and more upon the services of community health educators, public health nurses, psychologists and social workers and residents of the community itself (community health aides) who can interact effectively with at-risk individuals and educate for the prevention of these disorders as well as provide support services.

Sanitation Ensuring a safe living environment for the community requires more than the services and expertise provided by a sanitarian. Sanitation today means more than safety and purity of food, water, milk, and the enforcement of housing codes designed to create a safe living environment. The total environment of the community is a key concern to those in community health. The provision of a quality living environment for the residents of the community, an aesthetic environment, free of contamination by

64

pollution or hazardous wastes, and characterized by human social interactions is a futuristic goal of community health.

Laboratory services These are important because they provide the basis for preventing and controlling many kinds of disease and can ensure the safety and purity of the food, water, and milk consumed.

Health facilities With the exception of certain mobile screening or immunization services, health care is provided to those in need through the operation of health facilities established by the local or county health department. These facilities must be accessible. Most community health facilities provide for prevention, diagnostic and treatment services on an *in-patient care* and *ambulatory care* basis, as well as health maintenance programs and *emergency services.* For the diagnostic and treatment phases of services, the individual will usually utilize the professional staff of the facility. Other phases of operation may rely primarily on paraprofessionals or community aide volunteers. Community health facilities in order to be effective should (1) be accessible to those in need, (2) provide a wide range of services to meet community health needs, and (3) provide adequate and quality care comparable to community standards.

Administratively, the local or county health department is guided by a board of health. This local board operates in a similar manner to the state board of health. It has both administrative and legislative functions. In addition, health departments at the local level have a professional staff, including a medical director, public health nurses, sanitarians, and health educators. The professional staff is responsible for providing direct health services to the people of the community. Support staff are important to the effective operation of a community health facility, especially community health volunteer aides. The prime responsibilities of health departments have been and will continue to be the prevention of disease and provision of health care to individuals whose needs have been unmet by private medicine.

VOLUNTARY AGENCIES

Voluntary agencies play a significant role in the health care system of the United States. These organizations are supported by private or nontax funds. They have no legal powers and are usually established in response to a perceived health need to which the federal government has not responded. In attempting to solve health problems, these agencies enlist both human and financial support.

The voluntary health movement originated in 1892, when the Anti-Tuberculosis Society of Philadelphia was founded to combat tuberculosis epidemics. Since that time this organization has changed its name several times. It is now known as the American Lung Association, with the broadened objective of helping to prevent any lung disorder from any of the known causes, including air pollution and smoking.

Once the goal of the organization has been reached or if the federal government establishes programs that can contribute to the solution of the health problem, the group usually changes focus. Rarely does a voluntary agency disband, once its objectives have been reached. Usually, the group revises its objectives and continues to exist. This phenomenon has created tremendous duplication of services and wasted resources in some instances.

Since the beginning of the voluntary health agency movement in 1892, the number and focus of health agencies in the United States has grown tremendously. It is estimated that voluntary organizations in the U.S. today number over 100,000. Generally, voluntary health agencies fall within one of three basic classifications of functions:

1. Emphasis on specific diseases: Alcoholics Anonymous, Guild for Infant Survival, Arthritis Foundation, Cystic Fibrosis Foundation.
2. Emphasis on specific organs or structures in the body: National Society for the Prevention of Blindness, American Heart Association, American Lung Association.
3. Special target group-health concerns or broad health concerns of the entire population: National Safety Council, Planned Parenthood.

Functions of Voluntary Agencies

Of the large number of voluntary agencies operating in the United States today, many continue to assume a vital role in promoting the health of people. Most of these agencies engage in a number of activities in order to carry out their stated mission. The majority of voluntary agencies, are involved, at least to a minimal degree in the following activities:

Research: projects conducted by individuals or institutions that may increase knowledge in a specific area of health concern which are supported by an agency.

Education: educational activities are provided for the public and some agencies provide additional educational services for professionals who may be involved in the area.

Services: a variety of services are offered by voluntary agencies. These services range from such things as providing blood as the National Hemophilia Foundation does, or hospital beds to cancer patients by the American Cancer Society to the dispensing of contraceptives by Planned Parenthood.

Political lobbying: Voluntary health agencies, especially the larger and more influential ones, have established effective lobbies for the purpose of initiating and influencing health legislation of particular concern to the agency. The operating funds acquired by these voluntary agencies by private contributions are used to implement their activities and programs. Most of the operating funds for these organizations come through annual fund raising campaigns. Some of the agencies engage in joint fund-raising projects such as United Fund and Community Chest, while others conduct individual campaigns.

Organizationally, most voluntary agencies operate in a manner similar to official agencies at the national, state, and local level. Staffing usually consists of a board of directors, a professional staff, and volunteers. In voluntary health agencies, paid professionals must usually be supplemented by volunteers. All agencies approved by the National Information Bureau must have evidence of the following eight precepts:

1. *Board:* an active and responsible governing body (must maintain direction of the agency), serving without compensation, holding regular meetings, and operating with effective administrative control.
2. *Purpose:* a legitimate purpose with no avoidable duplication of the work of other sound organizations.
3. *Program:* reasonable efficiency in program management, and reasonable adequacy of resources, both material and personnel.
4. *Cooperation:* evidence of consultation and cooperation with established agencies in the same or related fields.
5. *Ethical promotion:* ethical methods of publicity, promotion, and solicitation of funds.
6. *Fund-raising practice:* in fund-raising:
    a. no payment of commissions for fund-raising.
    b. no mailing of unordered tickets or merchandise with a request for money in return.
    c. no general telephone solicitation of the public.
7. *Audit:* annual audit, prepared by an independent certified public accountant or trust company, showing all income and disbursements, in reasonable detail. New organizations should provide a certified public accountant's statement that a proper financial statement system has been installed.
8. *Budget:* detailed annual budget, translated program plans into financial terms.[6]

Voluntary agencies will continue to play a vital role in promoting and protecting health in the United States. The force of these groups has been very significant in the overall health system in this country. Through them, it has been possible to attack energetically health problems and concerns without encountering the legislative and legal restrictions that are a part of government supported health projects. The voluntary health agencies have come to represent groups of individuals who set out to do something about unmet health needs. They will always have a place in the health care system in the United States.

HEALTH FOUNDATIONS

In the United States, there exist more than 25,000 philanthropic foundations, many of which help to support public health programs. The essential purpose of a philanthropic foundation was described in a report of The Rockefeller Foundation:

> . . . to encourage and stimulate human progress. The accomplishment of this aim depends upon the intelligent distribution of funds. . . . Philanthropy is a

complex process that is both an art and a science, and it must by necessity be creative.[7]

The Rockefeller Foundation This organization was established in 1913 in New York State. The Foundation consists of five divisions, including (1) International Health, (2) Medical Sciences, (3) Natural Sciences, (4) Social Sciences, and (5) Humanities. This foundation over the years has supported research, provided fellowships for postdoctoral work in public health, and funded demonstration projects.

The Commonwealth Fund This organization, founded in 1918, has supported projects designed to improve medical education and medical research studies. It has been instrumental in extending public health activities to rural communities. This philanthropic foundation has also supported the improvement of mental health services.

The W. K. Kellogg Foundation This fund has as its stated purpose "the promotion of health, education, and the welfare of mankind. . . ." Established in 1930, it has aided in the establishment of county health departments and developing health education links between schools and communities.

Philanthropic foundations, unlike the voluntary agencies do not have to rely upon public donations. As a result, they have an advantage in that they can be more flexible and adaptive in their interests and activities, since they are not directly accountable to the public. In addition, they do not have to engage in time-consuming annual fund-raising campaigns. These foundations have clearly and efficiently produced many desirable outcomes in the public interest.

Professional Health Organizations

Professional organizations or societies are established by groups of people who share common training or professional preparation and common career responsibilities. In the health field there are a number of professional organizations that have been created to uphold professional standards of practice and promote the interests of the profession and society.

The American Medical Association (AMA) This organization was created in 1847 "to promote the art of medicine and the betterment of public health." It is actually a federation of state medical societies that informs members of advances in medicine through its publications, notably *The Journal of the American Medical Association,* and its conventions and conferences.

The American Public Health Association (APHA) This important group was founded in 1872. It is comprised of over twenty-two different divisions including radiological health, nutrition, public health nursing, environmental health, public health education, mental health, and epidemiology. The APHA is recognized for its work in promoting the health of the nation. Its publication, *The American Journal of Public Health,* is issued monthly. APHA is regarded as the prime public health professional organization in the U.S.

BASIS FOR COMMUNITY HEALTH ORGANIZATION

Throughout the history of the United States defining the respective responsibilities of federal, state and local governments has been a key issue. At this point in our nation's history, the question is no longer whether the federal government has a responsibility for assuring health care to all citizens, but rather how this responsibility is to be carried out and what role the states and local communities play in sharing this responsibility.

A continued challenge to health organization is developing an effective structure which promotes coordination and avoids duplication in the activities of both the voluntary agencies and official agencies at the local, state and national level.

REVIEW QUESTIONS

1. What are the primary functions of each of the following divisions of the Public Health Service: (1) FDA, (2) HRA, (3) HSA, and (4) NIH?
2. Identify the major problems in the coordination of official and voluntary community health programs in the U.S.
3. Discuss how a bill becomes a law. Analyze the legislative process.
4. Compare the responsibilities of governmental agencies at the federal, state, and local levels in promoting and protecting health.
5. Differentiate between vertical (upward-downward) flows of communication and decision making and horizontal communication, from an organization and administration viewpoint.
6. Describe why the collection and analysis of vital statistics in a community aids health planning. Develop a hypothetical example to describe the process.
7. Differentiate between official and voluntary agencies.
8. What is the basis for community health organization in the United States? What does "to promote the general welfare" imply?

SUGGESTED READINGS

Duncan, Robert C. and others (eds.), *Introductory Biostatistics for the Health Sciences.* New York: John Wiley, 1977.
Gossert, Daniel J., and Arden Miller, "State Boards of Health, Their Members and Commitments," *American Journal of Public Health,* 63:486, 1973.

Lilienfeld, Abraham M., *Foundations of Epidemiology*. New York: Oxford University Press, 1977.

Milio, Nancy, *The Care of Health in Communities: Access for Outcasts*. New York: Macmillan, 1975.

Organizing for Health Care: A Tool for Change, Source Catalog 3. Toronto, Canada: Beacon Press, 1974.

NOTES

[1] Mary F. Arnold, "A Social Systems View of Health Action," in Mary F. Arnold, L. Vaughn Blankenship, and John M. Hess (eds.), *Administering Health Systems: Issues and Perspectives.* Chicago: Aldine Atherton, 1971, p. 20.

[2] American Public Health Association, "The State Public Health Agency," *American Journal of Public Health,* 59, (160), 1969.

[3] ———— "The Local Health Department—Services and Responsibilities," *American Journal of Public Health,* 65:185, 1975.

[4] "Health Statistics: Today and Tomorrow, The Report of the Committee to Evaluate the National Center for Health Statistics, *American Journal of Public Health,* 63(10), 1973, pp. 890-909.

[5] "Health Statistics," p. 910.

[6] John Lear, "The Business of Giving," *Saturday Review,* December 2, 1961.

[7] R. Shaplen, *Toward the Well-Being of Mankind—Fifty Years of the Rockefeller Foundation.* Garden City, N.Y.: Doubleday, 1964.

GLOSSARY

ambulatory care   direct personal health care services to a person seeking treatment or advice on an out-patient, noninstitutionalized basis.

disease prevention   health care activities and services that seek to prevent disease from occurring rather than employ the treatment and/or curative approach; health promotion.

emergency services   those health care services designed to be accessible and effective in treating persons suffering from sudden catastrophic illness and accidents.

enhancement   those public health activities that focus on promoting the health of populations, primarily through education.

epidemiological model   the epidemiologic approach is based upon this model, which illustrates the interaction of three factors in disease: the agent, host, and environment.

in-patient care   services for conditions requiring acute, short-term hospitalization and emergency care as well as long-term chronic and rehabilitative care in special long-term and chronic disease hospitals and skilled-nursing facilities.

official community health agency   agencies and services that are supported by tax dollars and recognized as a governmental agency or service.

protection   those public health activities that focus on reducing the chance of people being exposed to causative disease agents in the environment.

rodent control   rat control, especially through managing the disposal of garbage and sewage, designed to reduce or eliminate this reservoir of infection.

sanitation   environmental control measures directed toward the vehicles of disease transfer. Attempts are designed to insure safe and healthful water, milk, and food supply.

sovereign power each state is delegated the responsibility of protecting the health of the people who reside within its boundaries; "police power."

vital statistics data obtained through statistical methods applied to the vital facts of human existence; birth, death, morbidity rates.

voluntary agency agencies and services that are supported entirely by financial contributions from citizens and private organizations.

BIBLIOGRAPHY

American Public Health Association, *Health is a Community Affair.* Cambridge, Mass.: Harvard University Press, 1971.

———, "The Local Health Department—Services and Responsibilities," An Official Statement adopted Nov. 10, 1963. *American Journal of Public Health,* 41(31) 302-307, 1951.

———, "The State Public Health Agency," An Official Statement. *American Journal of Public Health,* 55(5) 2011, 1965.

Arnold, Mary F., "A Social Systems View of Health in Action," in Mary F. Arnold, Vaughn Blankenship, and John Hess (eds.), *Administering Health Systems: Issues and Perspectives.* Chicago: Aldine Atherton, 1971.

Ducas, Dorothy (ed.), *National Voluntary Health Agencies.* New York: National Health Council, 1969.

Hanlon, John, *Principles of Public Health Administration,* 6th ed. St. Louis: C. V. Mosby, 1969.

Jain, Sagar (ed.), "Role of State and Social Governments in Relation to Personal Health Services," Supplement, *American Journal of Public Health,* 71(1), 1981.

Rogers, Everett, and Rekha Agarwala Rodgers, *Communication in Organizations.* New York: The Free Press, 1976.

Sloane, Robert, and Beverly LeBor Sloane, *A Guide to Health Facilities: Personnel and Management.* St. Louis: C. V. Mosby, 1977.

U.S. DHEW, *1976 Annual Report.* Washington, D.C.: U.S. DHEW, 1977.

Weyman, Myron, "Health Departments: Then and Now," *American Journal of Public Health,* 67(10) 913-914, 1977.

4

EPIDEMIOLOGICAL FOUNDATIONS

". . . we could be free of an infinitude of maladies both of body and mind, and even also possibilities of the infirmities of age, if we had sufficient knowledge of their causes, and all the remedies with which nature has provided us."

René Descartes (1596-1650)

EPIDEMIOLOGY: PRINCIPLES AND PROCESS

Disease has occurred in human populations throughout history. While the nature of prevalent disease may change with time, diseases of many kinds will continue to affect people in the future. Many diseases are currently preventable, others are only manageable, and still others continue to elude public health intervention and medical control.

Epidemiology had its beginnings in the study of the great epidemic diseases such as bubonic plague, cholera, and smallpox. During this time, epidemiologic principles were employed exclusively for the control of infectious and communicable diseases. However, as time passed, the tenets of epidemiology have been applied to a variety of diseases and health problems, including the chronic and degenerative and psychobehavioral diseases. Consequently, we now speak of the epidemiology of heart disease, measles, or accidents, because each disease has the same elements: the disease determinants, the human population in which it occurs, and the distribution of the disease in a population.[1]

The Nature of Epidemiology

Epidemiology is the study of the distribution and determinants of disease and health problems in human population. Through the epidemiologic approach, a disease or health problem is identified in terms of its characteristics, its cause(s)—or *etiology*—and its usual course. The objective of epidemiology is to isolate specific risk factors or precursors to the development of a disease or health problem. In this way, it becomes possible

73

to either prevent or intervene early in the disease course and reduce the likelihood of its spread or progression.

Epidemiology is a discipline that employs specialized methods for investigating disease causation and health problems in individuals and groups. Epidemiologic studies analyze health problems in terms of their occurrence and distribution in population groups and attempt to provide information on how these diseases and problems may be controlled.

Epidemiologic Model

The epidemiologic approach is based upon a model that illustrates the interaction of three factors: the *host,* the causative (etiologic) *agent*(s), and the *environment* in disease (see Figure 4-1). The dynamic interrelationships of the three factors of host, agent, and environment make for a challenging analysis. The agent refers to anything that may directly or indirectly cause health problems. Host represents the person who may be either susceptible or resistant to a health problem. Environment refers to the physical, biological and chemical environment with which the individual has contact.

The *epidemiologic model* is useful both in predicting which persons may develop a certain disease and in controlling the spread of disease by intervening at one of the three points. However, the fact that disease causation is rarely the result of a single factor or agent has complicated disease-control efforts. To illustrate this point, consider the leading cause of death in the U.S. today—heart disease. A variety of factors ranging from heredity to personality, inadequate exercise, smoking, and obesity may all contribute to the development of heart disease and may be accurately considered causative factors. To further complicate matters, each of these so-called causative factors may carry a different weight or relative strength in the production of disease. Thus, with the exception of a small number of diseases specifically communicable in nature, most health problems and diseases in the present are the result of a whole complex of causes that interact in the individual and with the environment in which that individual lives, plays, and works.

Agent   The term agent(s) refers to the true cause(s) of a health problem or disease, without which the disease or health problem cannot occur. In traditional epidemiology causative (etiologic) agents include biological, chemical, and physical agents. A substance or force must satisfy the condition that either its extreme presence or absence is the immediate cause of disease, in order to be classified as a causative agent (see Table 4-1).

Figure 4-1   The epidemiologic model.

Table 4-1 Agent factors

BIOLOGICAL AGENTS	CHEMICAL AGENTS	PHYSICAL AGENTS
Protozoa	Pesticides	Heat
Metazoa	Food additives	Light
Bacteria	Pharmacologics	Radiation
Viruses	Industrial chemicals	Noise
Rickettsia	Air pollutants	Vibration
Fungi	Cigarette smoke	Speeding objects

Source: Agent, Host, Environment: Principles of Epidemiology, Homestudy Course 3030G. Atlanta: Center for Disease Control, 1978.

At present, there are still many diseases and health problems affecting people in which the agents are still unrecognized. This is especially true of the chronic and psychobehavioral diseases, such as hypertension, ulcerative colitis, drug abuse, and schizophrenia. In other diseases, a complex of two or more factors acting in concert may be required to produce the disease or condition. For example, sudden infant death syndrome (SIDS) is believed to be the result of several factors including viral infection and an underdeveloped central nervous system working together to cause death in otherwise healthy infants.

Disease agents may also be classified according to their basic nature. Perkins originally designed this classification scheme which modified, includes:

1. *Nutritive elements:* This category includes not only fats, carbohydrates, and proteins, but specific substances present in food, minerals, and water. Excessive intake or absence of specific nutritive elements may result in disease. For example, obesity is the result of excessive caloric intake, Kwashiorkor results from inadequate protein intake, and scurvy results from vitamin C deficiency.

2. *Exogenous chemical agents:* This includes poisons, irritants, and allergens which arise outside the body and are capable of producing disease if they come in contact with or enter the body of people. Examples include inhaled air pollutants, injected pesticide residue on food products, and poison-ivy skin infections.

3. *Endogenous chemical agents:* This includes improperly regulated bodily functions that result in the production of disease-producing chemicals. Examples include diabetes, resulting from inadequate pancreatic production of insulin and hyperthyroidism, resulting from oversecretion of the hormone thyroxin, and perhaps breast cancer.

4. *Physiologic factors:* Certain physiologic changes and events that occur during the life span are related to specific disease conditions in people. Examples include pregnancy, which may result in abnormal location of the fetus (ectopic pregnancy) and threaten the mother's life, and the aging process, which is accompanied by degenerative changes.

5. *Genetic factors:* This category includes both the concept of genetically determined susceptability to disease and diseases which result directly from a gene or gene combinations. Examples include baldness, diabetes, Tay-Sachs disease, and Down's syndrome.

6. *Psychic factors:* This includes those intangible forces and influences that pertain to the emotions and the conscious and subconscious mental states. There is some controversy over the legitimacy of psychic factors being classified as an agent of disease. Yet there is a strong belief that some psychological element is associated with almost every illness. Examples include headache, diarrhea, and hypertension, as well as depression, phobias, and anxieties.

7. *Physical factors:* This includes such physical properties as sunlight, fire, radiation, as well as mechanical forces including those resulting from gravity and centrifugal force that can exert harmful effects on people.

8. *Living parasites:* This category encompasses the most understood and largest group of disease agents. It includes protozoa, fungi, bacteria, viruses, and other agents that cause the communicable and infectious, as well as the parasitic diseases.[2]

Host The term host refers to people, and more specifically, to a susceptible group of people. There are a number of body defenses that increase resistance of an individual to injury or disease, including skin, hair, and the lymphatic system. Most factors are classified into two types: biologic (age, race, and sex) and behavioral (habits and customs) (see Table 4-2).

The host factors of age, sex, and ethnic group are very important. Determination of the relationship between these factors and disease occurrence is typically the first step in an epidemiological study. However, all host factors and characteristics are important since they affect both the risk of exposure to a source of infection and the individual's resistance or susceptability to disease. For example, without the motor vehicle, an integral part of modern U.S. lifestyle, deaths and disability could not be associated with motor-

Table 4-2   Host factors

BIOLOGIC FACTORS	BEHAVIORAL FACTORS
Age	Habits (smoking, drinking)
Sex	Personal hygiene
Previous disease	Use of water
Ethnicity-race	Occupation
Immunity levels	Lifestyle
Nutritional status	Socioeconomic status
Heredity	Marital status
	Recreation

Source: Agent, Host, Environment: Principles of Epidemiology, Homestudy Course 3030G. Atlanta: Center for Disease Control, 1978.

Figure 4-2 Fast food chains have had an effect on American dietary habits.

vehicle accidents. And, the risk of exposure of a recluse to cold viruses, compared to that of a schoolteacher, is much lower.

Age is considered to be the single most important host factor related to disease occurrence. For example, polio, measles, and chickenpox are most prevalent among children. On the other hand, hypertension, cancer, and stroke affect predominantly older persons. Likewise, the adolescent-young adult years are marked by peak incidence in suicide and motor-vehicle accidents, especially among males.

Environment The environment is an epidemiologic term that refers to conditions that may be favorable or unfavorable to both the agent and host. There are three general classifications in the environment factor including the (1) physical or inanimate, which includes geologic, geographic or climatic features; (2) animate or biological, which includes trees, grasses, flowers, as well as pathogenic parasites; and (3) socioeconomic, which is comprised of a variety of elements, including the relationship of people to other people.

Other environmental factors include, water, milk, food, plants, animals, housing conditions, noise, and other environmental pollutants. The sanitation measures in a community, including the provision of a safe water supply and adequate sewage disposal are important environmental factors as they relate to disease control. In summary, the

Figure 4-3 Stress is an example of a psychic factor in diseases.

agent-host-environment factors interrelate in extremely varied combinations to produce disease in human populations.

EPIDEMIOLOGICAL MEASURES AND METHODS

Rates

Epidemiologists study how and why diseases and other health problems are distributed in a population in order to control them. There are two factors of prime consideration in epidemiology: *population at risk* and *rates*. Rates are fractions that are used by epidemiologists to compare things. The bottom number, called the *base,* is usually expressed in numbers 1,000, 10,000, or 100,000. Thus:

$$\text{Rate} = \frac{\text{Events}}{\text{Population at risk}} \times 1{,}000 \; [10{,}000 \text{ or } 100{,}000]$$

Denominators for rates are comprised of people, called collectively "the population at risk," which may be represented by all the people in a given geographic area, or a specific

Figure 4-4 The environment is an epidemiologic variable. Courtesy EPA-DOCUMERICA, Gene Daniels.

susceptible group within that area.[3] Rarely are factors that result in illness and death randomly distributed among the entire population. Therefore, the epidemiologist must relate these cases and deaths to specific population groups in which they have occurred. This process generally consists of relating cases to subpopulations characterized on the basis of such variables as age, sex, race, occupation, socioeconomic status, and location (see Table 4-3 for an age-adjusted listing of the leading causes of death).

To follow the formula above, epidemiologists identify all the events or cases of a disease, and this number serves as the numerator in the rate fraction. Then they identify the population at risk that might be susceptible to this health problem or disease, and this becomes the denominator. Basically, rates measure the probability of the occurrence of some disease or event in a populaton. By computing rates in given subpopulations, it becomes possible to compare various groups and factors that might contribute to disease occurrence.

There are several rates of particular importance to the epidemiologist—incidence, prevalence, and mortality rates. Both prevalence and incidence are morbidity rates. *Prevalence* refers to the number of people affected by a specific disease at a given time.

Table 4-3 Age-Adjusted Death Rates and Average Annual Percent Change, According to Leading Causes of Death in 1950: United States, Selected Years 1950–1977[a]

YEAR	CAUSE OF DEATH					
	All Causes	Diseases of the Heart	Malignant Neoplasms	Cerebro-vascular Diseases	All Accidents	Tuberculosis
	Deaths per 100,000 Resident Population					
1950	841.5	307.6	125.4	88.8	57.5	21.7
1955	764.6	287.5	125.8	83.0	54.4	8.4
1960	760.9	286.2	125.8	79.7	49.9	5.4
1965	739.0	273.9	127.0	72.7	53.3	3.6
1970[b]	714.3	253.6	129.9	66.3	53.7	2.2
1975[b]	638.3	220.5	130.9	54.5	44.8	1.2
1976[b]	627.5	216.7	132.3	51.4	43.2	1.1
1977[b]	612.3	210.4	133.0	48.2	43.8	1.0
	Average Annual Percent Change					
1950–77	-1.2	-1.4	0.2	-2.2	-1.0	-10.8
1950–55	-1.9	-1.3	0.1	-1.3	-1.1	-17.3
1955–60	-0.1	-0.1	0.0	-0.8	-1.7	-8.5
1960–65	-0.6	-0.9	0.2	-1.8	1.3	-7.8
1965–70	-0.7	-1.5	0.5	-1.8	0.1	-9.4
1970–77	-2.2	-2.6	0.3	-4.5	-2.9	-10.7
1975–77	-2.1	-2.3	0.8	-6.0	-0.5	-0.9

[a]Data are based on the national vital registration system.

[b]Excludes deaths of nonresidents of the United States.

Note: Age-adjusted rates computed by the direct method to the total population of the United States as enumerated in 1940, using 11 age groups.

Source: Division of Vital Statistics, National Center for Health Statistics, selected data.

The prevalence of a disease is determined by two things: how often the disease occurs and how long it lasts. Thus, the prevalence rate in a population is the total of new cases that occur that day plus any cases left over from previous days still affected. In determining prevalence rate, many factors must be taken into account, including seasonal variations.

The computation of *incidence rates* is another way of measuring disease morbidity. This measure represents only newly diagnosed or reported cases. Incidence rates are generally computed monthly or yearly (see Table 4-4 for other common rates). They are the most commonly used method of measuring the extent or frequency with which a disease or health problem is experienced by a population group.

The mortality rate is a measure of the frequency of occurrence of deaths within a defined population during a specified interval of time. Two types of mortality rates are used in epidemiology: crude mortality rates and cause-specific mortality rates. *Crude mortality rates* measure the frequency of occurrence of deaths from all causes. *Cause-specific mortality rates* measure the frequency of deaths attributed to specific causes.

Table 4-4 Commonly used rates in epidemiology

NAME OF RATE AND DEFINITION	EXAMPLES: U.S. 1960 (U.S. 1967)
Birth rate (crude): $$\frac{\text{Number of live births}^a}{\text{Estimated midyear population}^c} \times 1{,}000$$	23.7 live births per 1,000 estimated population per year (17.8/1,000 for 1967)
Fertility rate: $$\frac{\text{Number of live births}^a}{\substack{\text{Estimated number of females} \\ \text{aged 15–44 at midyear}^c}} \times 1{,}000$$	118.0 births per 1,000 females aged 15–44 per year (87.6/1,000 for 1967)
Death rate (crude): $$\frac{\text{Number of deaths}^a}{\text{Estimated midyear population}^c} \times 1{,}000$$	9.5 deaths per 1,000 estimated population per year (9.4/1,000 for 1967)
Age-specific death rate: $$\frac{\substack{\text{Number of deaths of a} \\ \text{specified age group}^a}}{\substack{\text{Estimated midyear population} \\ \text{of that age group}^c}} \times 1{,}000$$	3.0 deaths at ages 35–44 per 1,000 estimated population of that age, per year (3.5/100,000 for 1967)
Cause-specific death rate: $$\frac{\substack{\text{Number of deaths from} \\ \text{a specified cause}^a}}{\text{Estimated midyear population}^c} \times 100{,}000$$	6.1 deaths from tuberculosis per 100,000 estimated population 3.5/100,000 for 1967
Infant mortality rate: $$\frac{\substack{\text{Number of deaths under} \\ \text{one year of age}^a}}{\text{Number of live births}^b} \times 1{,}000$$	26.0 infant deaths per 1,000 live births (22.4/1,000 in 1967)
Neonatal mortality rate: $$\frac{\substack{\text{Number of deaths under} \\ \text{28 days of age}^a}}{\text{Number of live births}^b} \times 1{,}000$$	18.7 neonatal deaths per 1,000 live births (16.5/1,000 in 1967)

[a]Number in a defined population during a given calendar year.
[b]Number in the population in which the events in the numerator occurred.
[c]Refers to the population and year in which the events in the numerator occurred.

Investigation of Disease and Health Problems

The objective of epidemiological investigation is to identify ways of preventing disease or controlling its progress. This objective remains the same for the psychobehavioral health problems, chronic and degenerative disease, and communicable disease outbreaks. In order to accomplish this basic objective it is important to analyze the problem from the perspective of time, place, and personal characteristics.

Time Variations in the frequency of occurrence of a disease in a population over time is commonly referred to as a *temporal disease pattern.* There are three basic time spans used to describe temporal disease patterns: (1) the epidemic period, which is of variable length depending upon the duration of a particular epidemic, (2) a twelve-month period to identify seasonal variations, and (3) an extended period of years in which to identify long-term trends. Seasonal variations and long-term trends of disease incidence are important considerations in confirming or rejecting the existence of a current epidemic and in predicting future epidemic periods.

Changes that occur over a period of years are called *secular changes.* Figure 4-5 illustrates secular change with reference to reported cases of paralytic poliomyelitis over a period of twenty-two years. Medical progress and public health achievements are measured by secular changes. Seasonal and cyclic changes are the terms applied to short-term changes in disease patterns. For example, drownings are high in incidence during the summertime, whereas suicide rates peak during the Christmas season and in spring.

Place Information gathered during a case count provides insight into the population at risk as it relates to place or geographic location. In epidemiological studies, *spot maps* of cases are made to identify patterns that may exist with reference to geographic distribution. The epidemiologist looks for clustering of cases that may appear in conjunction with certain geographic areas such as census tracts, sanitary districts, and school areas. If clustering occurs, associations with possible sources of infection, such as contaminated water, milk, or food supplies may be revealed. Spot mapping may also be applied to place of work or occupation. Generally, investigation of the place variable includes an analysis of such factors as residence, occupation, and events.

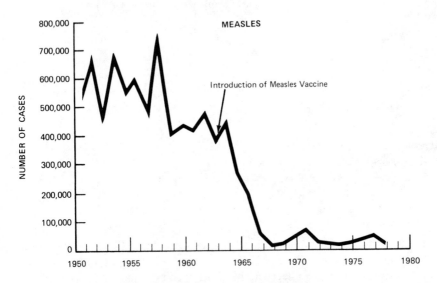

Figure 4-5 Reported cases of measles: United States, 1951–1978.

TABLE 4-5 Relationship between Cancer at Various Sites and the Use of Alcohol and Tobacco

SITES	NUMBER OF CASES	RELATIONSHIP WITH USE OF ALCOHOL	RELATIONSHIP WITH USE OF TOBACCO	SEX RATIO (M:F)
Hypopharynx	4,225	very strong	very strong	28.0
Larynx	5.524	very strong	very strong	27.4
Esophagus	5,007	very strong	strong	16.6
Lung	4,616		very strong	11.8
Oropharynx	3,216	strong	very strong	11.6
Tongue	4,856	very strong	strong	9.3
Oral cavity (other sites)	4,145	strong	very strong	8.6
Lips	3,609		strong	8.1
Bladder and other urinary organs	962		strong	2.6

Source: Flamant, R., O. Lasserre, P. Lazar, R. Leguerinais, P. Denoix, and D. Schwartz, "Differences in sex ratio according to cancer site and possible relationship with use of tobacco and alcohol; Review of 65,000 cases," *Journal of the National Cancer Institute,* 32:1309-1316, 1964. As quoted in *Alcohol and Health: New Knowledge,* DHEW Pub. No. (ADM) 75-212.

Personal Characteristics In epidemiologic investigations, people are identified according to such things as their inherent or acquired characteristics (age, sex, race, and immunization levels), by their activities (occupation, recreational activities, religious practices and customs), and by the circumstances under which they live (social, economic, and environmental conditions) (see Table 4-5).

As has been mentioned previously in this chapter, age is the single most significant host variable because of its association with specific diseases and health problems. Analysis of the cases by age is frequently the most important and productive procedure in the analysis of person variables.

Ethnicity, or race, and sex are also important variables in the attempt to describe a disease pattern. Frequently illness and death rates are significantly different between men and women and between white and nonwhite populations. For example, mortality from coronary heart disease, cirrhosis of the liver, and lung cancer is more likely to occur among men than women. Women generally tend to be more susceptible to diabetes, arthritis, and hypertension. In terms of ethnicity, Tay-Sachs disease affects primarily the offspring of Jews with Eastern ancestry, while cervical cancer is relatively uncommon among Jewish women. The Japanese experience higher rates of gastric cancer than any other racial group. Socioeconomic status is also an important variable since it generally reflects both occupation and income.

In the study of a specific disease or health problem, the first step is an accurate description of its occurrence in the population. In order to do this, the specific disease must be recognized with some reliability. The information collected for each person affected by a disease includes time (day, month, season, year), place (country, urban, or rural residence), and various personal characteristics of affected persons (age, sex, and race or ethnic group).[4]

Figure 4-6 Ethnicity or race is an important person variable in epidemiological studies.

EPIDEMIOLOGICAL RESEARCH

The study of disease requires a logical approach. It demands that all cases in a given population be identified and investigated. Among the benefits of this epidemiological approach to diseases are the following:

1. The *natural course of disease* can often be defined. The existence and importance of an asymptomatic phase can be clarified, as can the relationship between known clinical and inapparent cases.
2. The *importance of a disease in the community* can be determined, and from this,
3. The *effectiveness of control measures* and the *need for more or different types of health services* can be ascertained.
4. Contributory *risk factors* often come to light that provide clues to effective control, for example, cigarette smoking and its association with lung cancer.
5. Often *new syndromes* are identified, or *new symptoms* suggestive of a known disease are uncovered.
6. Some of the time the *cause of the disease* in question can be determined.

Each item on the list provides information of value in the control of a particular disease, and it is the desire to control diseases that motivates us to study them in the first place.[5]

Epidemiological research typically compares two or more groups of people. Research methods vary depending upon the *hypothesis* that is developed. A hypothesis is basically an unproven assumption, used to explain certain observations, which acts as a basis for further study of a question. A hypothesis identifies a causal factor, infers the effect derived from this factor, and suggests the amount or degree of the causal factor necessary to produce the effect. For example, the statement: "The pill causes cancer." is an incomplete hypothesis. The hypothesis would be more correct and complete if it stated: "A female using the birth-control pill for twenty years has an 80% greater risk of developing breast or cervical cancer than a female who never used the pill." The second hypothesis more carefully identifies various characteristics and exposure time than the first.

Most studies are observational in nature. This simply means that the epidemiologist observes circumstances and events which take place in a natural pattern of life.

Descriptive Epidemiology

Epidemiologists conduct both descriptive and analytic studies. *Descriptive studies*, as the name implies, merely describe the population with regard to certain characteristics. Descriptive studies are used to develop rates concerning the occurrence of disease and other characteristics. They describe the frequency and distribution of the disease and the characteristics with which it seems to be associated. Descriptive epidemiology provides public health professionals with information regarding the characteristics that are present in a diseased group and absent in a nonaffected group. Descriptive studies answer the question: "Are there any characteristics present in people who have the disease that are not present in people who do not have the disease?" For example, breast cancer is more common in women who have not given birth nor breast fed than women who have breast fed. Goiter is more common in geographic areas in which soil is deficient in iodine. Chickenpox, measles, and mumps typically affect children, as opposed to adults. Sickle-cell anemia is an uncommon disease among whites when compared with blacks. In descriptive epidemiology variables associated with age, ethnicity, geography, occupation, season, year, marital status, and sex are all important as they relate to the occurrence of a disease.

Analytic Epidemiology

Analytic studies are used to identify association(s) between a disease and possible causative factors or influences. Once it has been determined that a disease seems to be associated with certain characteristics, the task remains to support or discredit that hypothesis.

Prospective approach In order to test the hypothesis in analytic epidemiology, the first step is to identify the population at risk,—for example, women who have given birth—and from this large population, a sample or study group is selected. The sample is then divided into two groups of people who are alike as possible in all respects, except that one group manifests the disease or suspected characteristics, while the other does

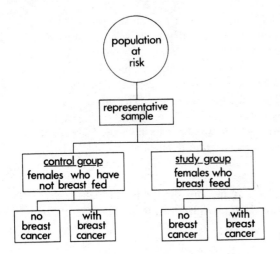

Figure 4-7 Model of a prospective study.

not. Both groups are followed for over a decade or more to determine if there is a difference in disease incidence. This technique is called the *prospective approach* of information gathering (Figure 4-7). It begins with an exposed and unexposed group of people (a *cohort*), categorized according to suspected precursor conditions, and follows these people to establish the frequency of the development of subsequent diseases. The exposed group is the study group, while the unexposed group is the control group.

To continue the earlier example, in a prospective study, a sample of women who have given birth to at least one child would be separated into two groups. The two groups would be as similar as possible except that the study-group would not have breast-fed, while the control group would have breast-fed, since this is the suspected characteristic in developing breast cancer. Once divided, both groups would be followed through the years until the women reached their mid-fifties. At the completion of the study, breast-cancer incidence between the two groups would be compared to assess whether or not breast-feeding is inversely related to breast cancer.

Retrospective approach Another popular approach to gathering epidemiologic information in analytic studies is the *retrospective approach* or case-history study. In this approach, the epidemiologist looks backward in time from the onset of illness to look for possible associations or factors. The retrospective study is easier, cheaper, and faster to conduct than a prospective study.

As is the case in the prospective study, the retrospective study begins with two groups (see Figure 4-8). However, in the retrospective study, the study group has the disease itself, rather than characteristics considered to be associated with the disease. In addition, the retrospective study does not use a reference population. Instead of randomly selecting individuals to comprise an exposed study group and a nonexposed control group from a common population, the retrospective study begins with cases of disease and then compares them with a control of noncases. Retrospective studies examine the past histories of all subjects to see if those in the study group possess a characteristic more often or to a greater extent than those in the nondisease control group.

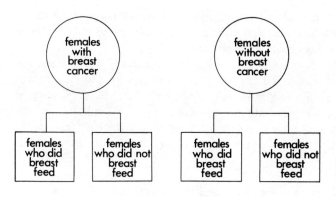

Figure 4-8
Model of a retrospective study.

Retrospective studies only provide information as to whether or not a certain characteristic or condition is more common among persons affected with a given disease than those not affected. Only prospective studies can determine the strength of the association between a given characteristic and a disease. For example, a retrospective study is able to suggest that many people who eat a low-fiber diet develop stomach or intestinal cancer, or that many alcoholics die of cirrhosis of the liver. But this does not mean that the majority of people who ingest low amounts of dietary fiber will develop stomach or intestinal cancer; nor does it mean that the majority of alcoholics will die of cirrhosis. The retrospective study cannot infer to what extent a certain factor or characteristic is associated with a given disease, only whether or not it is associated. This is because the retrospective study is essentially a case history, and as such lacks a reference population.

An example may serve to illustrate the retrospective approach. A group of individuals who have been diagnosed as having lung cancer is identified and selected for study. This group comprises the study group. Another group is selected of equal size that is like the study group in as many ways as possible except that the individuals do not have lung cancer. This nondisease group is the control group. The investigator in this study then examines the past histories of all the subjects who have lung cancer and those who do not. The investigator concludes that a characteristic seen more frequently in the study group, compared to the control group, is cigarette smoking—or, more cigarette smokers developed lung cancer than non-cigarette smokers.

Associations

In epidemiological research, rates are compared in an attempt to identify *associations.* Associations are relationships that exist between the occurrence of risk factors and the occurrence of a disease or health problem. There are three basic types of association in epidemiological analysis: a positive association, a negative association, and no association. A positive association occurs when a factor and a disease or health problem tend to occur together. For example, drinking alcohol and driving are positively associated with motor-vehicle accidents. A negative association occurs when a factor and a disease or health problem tend not to occur together. For example, marathon runners seem to be protected from developing heart disease because of the physiological change resulting from training. No association is said to exist when the factor and disease or health problem occur independently, or at random. For example, a classic Jamaican study on the effects of heavy marijuana use indicated that smoking marijuana is not necessarily associated with development of the "amotivational syndrome."

Determining *causality* between factors and disease is difficult. This is especially true in the chronic and psychobehavioral diseases. It is relatively simple to identify that X disease (tuberculosis) was caused by Y germ (tubercle baccili). But, what is the cause of alcoholism, or drug abuse, or cancer? With the appearance of the chronic and psychobehavioral diseases, the concept of agent has been translated into the larger context of causative factors. There are five basic criteria that epidemiologists currently use in judging causality:

1. *Consistency:* When an association consistently exhibits itself in studies with different designs in the same type of association.
2. *Strength:* When the association shows that a given factor makes some disease more likely (for example, 40 percent).
3. *Specificity:* When the association refers to one specific disease or for two diseases that are logically connected (for example, lung cancer and chronic bronchitis).
4. *Time relationships:* When the association logically occurs before the development of the disease or health problem.
5. *Coherence:* When the supposed causal relationship makes sense in terms of existing biological facts.[6]

As a result of the nature of the prevalent diseases and health problems in modern times, epidemiologists have broadened their perspective to identify multiple causation. The objective of much work in contemporary epidemiology is to isolate specific risk factors or precursors to the development of disease. In this way it becomes more likely that prevention of these diseases, such as heart disease and emphysema, is possible.

A CLASSIC EPIDEMIOLOGICAL STUDY

John Snow on Cholera

The foundations of epidemiology were laid in the nineteenth century, when a few classic studies made major contributions to saving lives. One of the major contributors to early epidemiology was John Snow, an influential London surgeon who in 1853 showed that cholera was spread through ingestion of excreta of cholera patients. The following is a description of the work of John Snow on cholera, which provided the ground work of current knowledge about the nature and transmission of this disease.

Several serious epidemics of cholera occurred in the United Kingdom between 1832 and 1854. The cause of the disease was unknown. Dr. Snow suggested,

. . . . that the poison of cholera is swallowed, and acts directly on the mucous membrane of the intestines, is at the same time reproduced in the intestinal canal, and passes out, much increased, with the discharges; and that these discharges become mixed with the drinking water in rivers or wells, reach the alimentary canals of other persons, and produce the like disease in them.

The most terrible outbreak of cholera which ever occurred in this kingdom is probably that which took place in Broad Street, Golden Square, and the adjoining streets, a few weeks ago. Within two hundred and fifty yards of the spot where Cambridge Street joins Broad Street, there were upwards of five hundred fatal attacks of cholera in ten days. The mortality in this limited area probably equals any that was ever caused in this country, even by the plague; and it was much more sudden, as the greater number of cases terminated in a few hours. The mortality would undoubtedly have been much greater had it not been for the flight of the population. Persons in furnished lodgings left first, then other lodgers went away, leaving their furniture to be sent for when they could meet with a place to put it in.

There were a few cases of cholera in the neighbourhood of Broad Street, Golden Square, in the latter part of August; and the so-called outbreak, which commenced in the night between the 31st August and the 1st September, was, as in all similar instances, only a violent increase of the malady. As soon as I became acquainted with the situation and extent of this irruption of cholera, I suspected some contamination of the water of the much frequented street-pump in Broad Street, near the end of Cambridge Street; but on examining the water, on the evening of the 3rd September, I found so little impurity in it of an organic nature, that I hesitated to come to a conclusion. Further inquiry, however, showed me that there was no other circumstance or agent common to the circumscribed locality in which this sudden increase of cholera occurred, and not extending beyond it, except the water of the above mentioned pump. I found, moreover, that the water varied, during the next two days, in the amount of organic impurity, visible to the naked eye, on close inspection, in the form of small white, flocculent particles; and I concluded that, at the commencement of the outbreak, it might possibly have been still more impure. I requested permission, therefore, to take a list, at the General Register Office, of the deaths from cholera, registered during the week ending 2nd September, in the subdistricts of Golden Square, Berwick Street, and St. Ann's Soho, which was kindly granted. Eighty-nine deaths from cholera were registered, during the week, in the three sub-districts. Of these, only six occurred in the four first days of the week; four occurred on Thursday, the 31st August; and the remaining seventy-nine on Friday and Saturday. I considered, therefore, that the outbreak commenced on the Thursday; and I made inquiry, in detail, respecting the eighty-three deaths registered as having taken place during the last three days of the week.

On proceeding to the spot, I found that nearly all the deaths had taken place within a short distance of the pump. There were only ten deaths in houses situated decidedly nearer to another street pump. In five of these cases the families of the deceased persons informed me that they always sent to the pump in Broad Street, as they preferred the water to that of the pump which was nearer. In three other cases, the deceased were children who went to school near the pump in Broad Street.

With regard to the deaths occurring in the locality belonging to the pump, there were sixty-one instances in which I was informed that the deceased persons used to drink the pump-water from Broad Street, either constantly or occasionally. In six instances I could get no information, owing to the death or departure of everyone connected with the deceased individuals; and in six cases I was informed that the deceased persons did not drink the pump-water before their illness.

The result of the inquiry then was, that there had been no particular outbreak or increase of cholera, in this part of London, except among the persons who were in the habit of drinking water of the above-mentioned pump-well.

I had an interview with the Board of Guardians of St. James' parish, on the evening of Thursday, 7th September, and represented the above circumstances to them. In consequence of what I said, the handle of the pump was removed on the following day. . . .

The additional facts that I have been able to ascertain are in accordance with those above related; and as regards the small number of those attacked, who were believed not to have drank the water from Broad Street pump, it must be obvious that there are various ways in which the deceased persons may have taken it without the knowledge of their friends. The water was used for mixing with spirits in all the public houses around. It was used likewise at dining-rooms and coffee-shops. The keeper of a coffee-shop in the neighbourhood, which was frequented by mechanics, and where the pump-water was supplied at dinner time, informed me (on 6th September) that she was already aware of nine of her customers who were dead. The pump-water was also sold in various little shops, with a teaspoonful of effervescing powder in it, under the name of aherbet; and it may have been distributed in various other ways with which I am unacquainted. The pump was frequented much more than is usual, even for a London pump in a populous neighbourhood.

There are certain circumstances bearing on the subject of this outbreak of cholera which require to be mentioned. The workhouse in Poland Street is more than three-fourths surrounded by houses in which deaths from cholera occurred, yet out of five hundred and thirty-five inmates only five died of cholera, the other deaths which took place being those of persons admitted after they were attacked. The workhouse has a pump-well on the premises, in addition to the supply from the Grand Junction Water Works, and the inmates never sent to Broad Street for water.

There is a Brewery in Broad Street near to the pump, and on perceiving that no brewer's men were registered as having died of cholera, I called on Mr. Huggins, the proprietor. He informed me that there were above seventy workmen employed in the brewery, and that none of them had suffered from cholera,—at least in a severe form,—only two having been indisposed, and that not seriously, at the time the disease prevailed. The men are allowed a certain quantity of malt liquor, and Mr. Huggins believes they do not drink water at all; and he is quite certain that the workmen never obtained water from the pump in the street. There is a deep well in the brewery, in addition to the new River water. . . .

I am indebted to Mr. Marshall for the following cases, which are interesting as showing the period of incubation, which in these three cases was from thirty-six to forty-eight hours. Mrs. ___, of 13 Bentinck Street, Berwick Street, aged 28, in the eighth month of pregnancy, went herself (although they were not usually water drinkers), on Sunday, 3rd September, to Broad Street pump for water. The family removed to Gravesend on the following day; and she was attacked with cholera on Tuesday morning at seven o'clock, and died of consecutive fever on 15th September, having been delivered. Two of her children drank also of the water, and were attacked on the same day as the mother, but recovered.

Dr. Fraser also first called my attention to the following circumstances, which are perhaps the most conclusive of all in proving the connexion between the Broad Street pump and the outbreak of cholera. In the "Weekly Return of Births and Deaths" of September 9th, the following death is recorded as occurring in the Hampstead district: "At West End, on 2nd September, the widow of a percussion-cap maker, aged 59 years,—diarrhoea two hours, cholera epidemica sixteen hours."

I was informed by this lady's son that she had not been in the neighbourhood of Broad Street for many months. A cart went from Broad Street to West End every day, and it was the custom to take out a large bottle of the water from the pump in Broad Street, as she preferred it. The water was taken on Thursday, 31st August, and she drank of it in the evening, and also on Friday. She was seized with cholera on the evening of the latter day, and died on Saturday, as the above quotation from the register shows. A niece, who was on a visit to this lady, also drank of the water; she returned to her residence, a high and healthy part of Islington, was attacked with cholera, and died also. There was no cholera at the time, either at West End or in the neighbourhood where the niece died. Besides these two persons, only one servant partook of the water at Hampstead West End, and she did not suffer, or, at least, not severely. There were many persons who drank the water from Broad Street pump about the time of the outbreak, without being attacked with cholera; but this does not diminish the evidence respecting the influence of the water, for reasons that will be fully stated in another part of this work. . . .

[Table I] exhibits the chronological features of this terrible outbreak of cholera. It is pretty certain that very few of the fifty-six attacks placed in the table to the 31st August occurred till late in the evening of that day. The irruption was extremely sudden, as I learn from the medical men living in the midst of the district, and commenced in the night between the 31st August and 1st September. There was hardly any premonitory diarrhoea in the cases which occurred during the first three days of the outbreak; and I have been informed by several medical men, that very few of the cases which they attended on those days ended in recovery.

Table I

Date	No. of Fatal Attacks	Deaths
August 19	1	1
" 20	1	0
" 21	1	2
" 22	0	0
" 23	1	0
" 24	1	2
" 25	0	0
" 26	1	0
" 27	1	1
" 28	1	0
" 29	1	1
" 30	8	2
" 31	56	3
Sept. 1	143	70
" 2	116	127
" 3	54	76
" 4	46	71
" 5	36	45
" 6	20	37
" 7	28	32
" 8	12	30
" 9	11	24
" 10	5	18
" 11	5	15
" 12	1	6
" 13	3	13
" 14	0	6
" 15	1	8
" 16	4	6
" 17	2	5
" 18	3	2
" 19	0	3
" 20	0	0
" 21	2	0
" 22	1	2
" 23	1	3
" 24	1	0
" 25	1	0
" 26	1	2
" 27	1	0
" 28	0	2
" 29	0	1
" 30	0	0
Date unknown	45	0
Total	616	616

The greatest number of attacks in any one day occurred on the 1st of September, immediately after the outbreak commenced. The following day the attacks fell from one hundred and forty-three to one hundred and sixteen, and the day afterwards to fifty-four. A glance at the above table will show that the fresh attacks continued to become less numerous every day. On September the 8th—the day when the handle of the pump was removed—there were twelve attacks; on the 9th, eleven; on the 10th, five; on the 11th, five; on the 12th only one; and after this time, there were never more than four attacks on one day. During the decline of the epidemic the deaths were more numerous than the attacks, owing to the decrease of many persons who had lingered for several days in consecutive fever.

There is no doubt the mortality was much diminished, as I said before, by the flight of the population, which commenced soon after the outbreak; but the attacks had so far diminished before the use of the water was stopped, that it is impossible to decide whether the well still contained the cholera poison in an active state or whether, from some cause, the water had become free from it. The pump-well has been opened, and I was informed by Mr. Farrell, the superintendent of the works, that there was no hole or crevice in the brickwork of the well, by which any impurity might enter; consequently in this respect the contamination of the water is not made out by the kind of physical evidence detailed in some of the instances previously related. I understand that the well is from twenty-eight to thirty feet in depth, and goes through the gravel to the surface of the clay beneath. The sewer, which passes within a few yards of the well, is twenty-two feet below the surface. The water at the time of the cholera contained impurities of an organic nature, in the form of minute whitish flocculi visible on close inspection to the naked eye, as I before stated. Dr. Hassell, who was good enough to examine some of this water with the microscope, informed me that these particles had no organized structure, and that he thought they probably resulted from decomposition of other matter. He found a great number of very minute oval animalcules in the water, which are of no importance, except as an additional proof that the water contained organic matter on which they lived. The water also contained a large quantity of chlorides, indicating, no doubt, the impure sources from which the spring is supplied. Mr. Eley, the percussion-cap manufacturer of 37 Broad Street, informed me that he had long noticed that the water became offensive, both to the smell and taste, after it had been kept about two days. This, as I noticed before, is a character of water contaminated with sewage. Another person had noticed for months that a film formed on the surface of the water when it had been kept a few hours.

Whether the impurities of the water were derived from the sewers, the drains, or the cesspools, of which latter there are a number in the neighbourhood, I cannot tell. I have been informed by an eminent engineer, that whilst a cesspool in a clay soil requires to be emptied every six or eight months, one sunk in the gravel will often go for twenty years without being emptied, owing to the soluble matters passing away in to the land-springs by percolation. As there had been deaths from cholera just before the great outbreak not far from this pump-well, and in a situation elevated a few feet above it, the evacuations from the patients might of course be amongst the impurities finding their way into the water, and judging the matter by the light derived from other facts and considerations previously detailed, we must conclude that such was the case. A very important point in respect to this pump-well is that the water passed with almost everybody as being perfectly pure, and it did in fact contain a less quantity of impurity that the water of some other pumps in the same parish, which had no share in the propagation of cholera. We must conclude from this outbreak that the quantity of morbid matter which is sufficient to produce cholera is inconceivably small, and that the shallow pump-wells in a town cannot be looked on with too much suspicion, whatever their local reputation may be.

Whilst the presumed contamination of the water of the Broad Street pump with the evacuations of cholera patients affords an exact explanation of the fearful outbreak of cholera in St. James' parish, there is no other circumstance which offers any explanation at all, whatever hypothesis of the nature and cause of the malady be adopted. . . .[7]

REVIEW QUESTIONS

1. Define epidemiology and explain the epidemiologic model.
2. Identify possible agents for the following: (1) alcoholism, (2) lung cancer, (3) emphysema, (4) genital herpes, (5) drowning, and (6) schizophrenia.
3. List five biologic host factors and five behavioral host factors. Explain how these might relate to (1) motor-vehicle accidents, (2) hypertension, and (3) the common cold.
4. What is a *rate*? What is meant by the term *population at risk*? Differentiate between prevalence and incidence.
5. Compare prospective and retrospective study techniques and uses.
6. Explain what is meant by associations. Distinguish among positive association, negative association, and no association. Give examples of each.

SUGGESTED READINGS

Austin, Donald and Benson Werner, *Epidemiology for the Health Sciences.* Springfield, Ill.: Charles C Thomas, 1977.

Higgonson, John, "A Hazardous Society? Individual versus Community Responsibility in Cancer Prevention," Rosenhaus lecture, *American Journal of Public Health,* 66(4) 359–366, 1976.

Terris, Milton, "The Epidemiologic Revolution, National Health Insurance and the Role of Health Departments," *American Journal of Public Health,* 66(12) 1155–1164, 1976.

Yeracaris, Constantine and Jay Kim, "Socioeconomic Differentials in Selected Causes of Death," *American Journal of Public Health,* 68(4) 342–351, 1978.

NOTES

[1] *Agent, Host, Environment: Principles of Epidemiology,* Homestudy Course 3030G, Lesson 1. Atlanta: Center for Disease Control, 1978, p. 1.

[2] John Fox, Carried Hall, and Lila Elveback, *Epidemiology: Man and Disease.* New York: Macmillan, 1972, pp. 36-38.

[3] Donald Austin and Benson Werner, *Epidemiology for the Health Sciences.* Springfield, Ill.: Charles C Thomas, 1977, p. 6.

[4] John Fox, Carrie Hall, and Lila Elveback, p. 6.

[5] Carter Marshall, *Dynamics of Health and Disease.* Englewood Cliffs, N.J.: Prentice-Hall, 1972, p. 64.

[6] Donald Austin and Benson Werner, pp. 44-45.

[7] John Snow, *On the Mode of Communication of Cholera,* 2nd ed. London: Churchill, 1855. Reproduced in "The Broad Street Pump Outbreak (August-September, 1849)," *Snow on Cholera.* New York: Commonwealth Fund, 1936.

GLOSSARY

agent refers to the cause(s) of a health problem or disease; includes biological, chemical, and physical agents.

analytic study the type of study employed in epidemiology to identify associations between a disease and possible causative factors.

associations relationships that exist between the occurrence of risk factors and the occurrence of a disease or health problem.

causality attempts to determine the agent(s) responsible for disease occurrence.

cause-specific mortality rate a measure of the frequency of deaths attributed to specific causes.

chain of infection the process in which a pathogen in a reservoir or carrier of a disease, leaves the host and infects a new susceptible host.

cohort a group of people identified as a sample population for a study and who are categorized according to a suspected precursor condition.

crude mortality rate measures the frequency of occurrence of deaths from all causes.

descriptive study epidemiological investigation that describes the population with regard to certain characteristics as it relates to disease occurrence.

environment the place variable in the epidemiologic model; refers to the physical, biological, and chemical environment with which the individual has contact.

epidemiologic model the epidemiological approach is based upon this model, which illustrates the interaction of three factors in disease: agent, host, and environment.

epidemiology the study of the distribution and determinants of disease in human populations.

etiology the cause(s) of a disease or health problem; agent of disease including biological, chemical, and physical agents.

host refers to people or, more specifically, to a susceptible group of people in the epidemiologic model. Host factors are classified into two types: biologic and behavioral.

hypothesis an unproven assumption used to explain certain observations and which serves as a basis for further study of a question; identifies a factor and infers the effects of the factor.

incidence rate represents rates that measure only newly diagnosed or reported cases of a disease or health problem.

population at risk denominators for rates; may be represented by all the people in a given geographic area or a specific susceptible subgroup within that area.

prevalence represents rates that measure the number of people affected by a specific disease at a given time.

prospective approach type of epidemiological study that begins with a group of people (cohort) categorized according to a suspected precursor condition, and then follows them to some future time to establish frequency of the disease occurring.

rates measures of the probability of the occurrence of some disease or event in a population; fractions used by epidemiologists in comparisons.

retrospective approach a type of epidemiological study in which the investigator begins by identifying cases of a disease and then looks backward in time to identify suspected precursor conditions.

secular changes changes in the occurrence of a disease in a population that occur over a period of years.

spot maps used to identify geographic patterns that may exist with reference to distribution of cases according to place.

temporal disease pattern variations in the frequency of occurrence of a disease in a population over time.

BIBLIOGRAPHY

Austin, Donald and Benson Werner, *Epidemiology for the Health Sciences.* Springfield, Ill.: Charles C Thomas, 1977.

Dawber, T. R., F. E. Moore, and G. V. Mann, "Coronary Heart Disease in the Framingham Study," *American Journal of Public Health,* 47 Supplement, 4–24, 1957.

Fox, John, Carrie Hall, and Lila Elveback, *Epidemiology: Man and Disease.* New York: Macmillan, 1972.

Johnson, D., "Epidemiology," in Kilbourne, E. D. and W. G. Smillie (eds.), *Human Ecology and Public Health,* New York: Macmillan, 1969.

"Landmarks in American Epidemiology 1929–79—A Special Section," *Public Health Reports,* 95(5), 1980.

Lowe, C. R. and J. Kostrzewski (eds.), *Epidemiology: A Guide to Teaching Methods.* London: The International Epidemiological Association, 1973.

MacMahon, B., "Epidemiologic Methods," in Clark, D. W., and B. MacMahon (eds.), *Preventive Medicine.* Boston: Little, Brown, 1967.

MacMahon, B. and T. F. Pugh (eds.), *Epidemiology: Principles and Methods.* Boston: Little, Brown, 1970.

Marshall, Carter, *Dynamics of Health and Disease.* Englewood Cliffs, N.J.: Prentice-Hall, 1972.

Mausner, Judith and Anita Bohn, *Epidemiology: An Introductory Text.* Philadelphia: W. B. Saunders, 1974.

Morris, R. J., *Cholera 1832: The Social Response to an Epidemic.* New York: Holmes & Meir, 1976.

Principles of Epidemiology, Homestudy Course 3030G. Atlanta: Center for Disease Control, 1978.

Sinnecher, Herbert, *General Epidemiology.* New York: John Wiley, 1977.

U.S. DHEW, *Health: United States 1976–77 Chartbook.* Washington, D.C.: U.S. DHEW, Publ. No. (HRA) 77-1233, 1978.

PART

II

contemporary community health challenges

5

EPIDEMIOLOGY AND DISEASE CONTROL

Control of Community Diseases
Communicable Disease Control
  Chain of Infection
  Epidemiologic Analysis of Communicable Disease Control
  Prevention and Control
Chronic and Degenerative Disease Control
  Causative Factors
  Epidemiologic Analysis of Chronic Disease
  Control of Chronic Diseases
  Cancer
  Cardiovascular Disease
Psychobehavioral Disease Control
  Causative Factors
  Epidemiologic Analysis of Psychobehavioral Disease
  Mental Illness
  Substance Abuse
Disease Control

> The past 100 years have seen the virtual completion of this first epidemiologic revolution—the conquest of the infectious diseases. . . . The second epidemiologic revolution—the control of noninfectious disease has already begun.

Milton Terris, "Public Health in the U.S.:
The Next 100 Years," Public Health Reports,
93, No. 6 (November–December 1978), 603.

CONTROL OF COMMUNITY DISEASES

Public health disease control measures are designed to alter any link involved in the chain of infection in the communicable diseases and to effect primary and secondary prevention of the chronic and psychobehavioral diseases. Much progress has been made in the control of communicable disease. An examination of Figure 5-1, which compares selected causes of death in 1900 and in 1977, will support the extent of control public health has gained over this classification of disease. However, equally important is the fact that many communicable diseases still exist at epidemic, pandemic, and endemic levels. These include hepatitis, encephalitis, tuberculosis, and genital herpes, to mention a few.

      Public health measures designed to control communicable diseases focus on (1) prevention of spread and (2) increasing the resistance of potential hosts to reduce likelihood of a new infection. A number of public health activities aim to prevent spread of

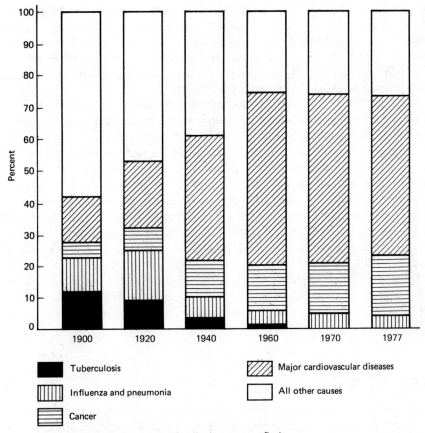

Percent

| | 1900 | 1920 | 1940 | 1960 | 1970 | 1977 |

■ Tuberculosis   ▨ Major cardiovascular diseases

▥ Influenza and pneumonia   □ All other causes

▤ Cancer

Note: 1977 data provisional; data for all other years are final.

Figure 5-1 Deaths for selected causes as a percent of all deaths: United States, selected years, 1900–1977. Courtesy National Center for Health Statistics, Division of Vital Statistics.

communicable diseases by destroying the organism or pathogen that causes the disease, eradicating the source of an infection, such as an animal reservoir in the case of rabies; or by reducing the degree of communicability of those infected. Reducing communicability is achieved by limiting human activity. *Isolation*, in which an infected person is prevented from coming into contact with nondiseased persons, and *quarantine*, in which persons suspected to have been exposed are restricted in their human contacts until favorable laboratory tests are obtained, are two methods of reducing communicability.

Control measures that increase the resistance of potential hosts include passive immunization, active immunization, and public health activities that generally promote health and nutrition. Specific immunizations will be discussed in greater detail later in this chapter.

In order to ensure communicable disease surveillance and control, certain laws are considered vital. Most legislation regarding this important aspect of public health delegates the states the power of promulgating and enforcing communicable disease laws. Perhaps the two most important of communicable disease laws relate to mandatory reporting of all cases of certain communicable diseases listed in a communicable disease code to the official health agency and compulsory immunization against certain communicable diseases as was once the case with smallpox vaccinations.

While the chronic and psychobehavioral diseases have by no means been controlled to the same extent as the communicable diseases, it is predicted that major declines in the prevalence of these diseases will be achieved in the next 100 years. Public health measures designed to control the chronic diseases include effective health education, early detection, screening and treatment programs, and environmental controls that reduce specific carcinogens and other risk factors in the community and in the workplace. By and large, control of the chronic and psychobehavioral diseases requires an informed public who are able to protect themselves from health hazards in the physical and social environment. Control of many communicable diseases can be directed against a specific cause, yet this is not possible for the chronic diseases, since the causative agent is usually unknown and usually considered to be nonliving. Thus chronic disease control is not a simple public health task. It requires that all risk factors associated with chronic diseases be identified. Subsequently, measures that prevent contact between risk factors and the population at large must be effected. A more detailed discussion of the various control measures in chronic disease appears later in this chapter.

COMMUNICABLE DISEASE CONTROL

During the first half of the twentieth century tremendous strides were made in controlling many of the communicable and infectious diseases. But one notable exception in the United States is the sexually transmitted diseases, including gonorrhea and genital herpes, which continue to increase in incidence. In other countries, diseases such as cholera, yaws, typhoid fever and the amoebic dysenteries still exert a considerable toll on human life. And, malaria remains the leading cause of death in the world. Simply, a *communicable disease* is a disease caused by organisms that can be transmitted directly from person to person or indirectly through an animal or the environment. Figure 5-3 shows the stage in communicable disease progression.

Chain of Infection

Communicable diseases result from the interaction of the agent, host, and environment in an orderly process which involves six steps or components. Included in this sequence, commonly called the *chain of infection,* are:

1. causative agent (pathogen)
2. reservoir of the agent (case or carrier)
3. portal of exit (a body opening, natural or artificial)

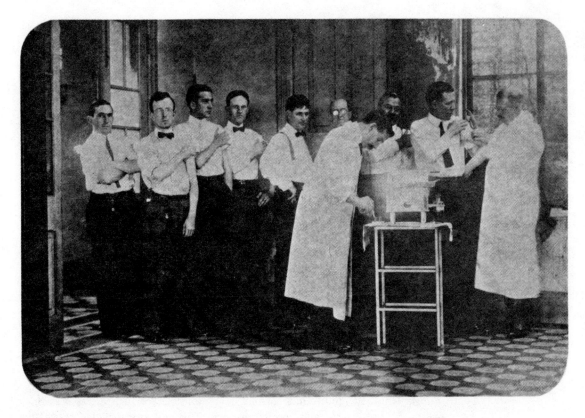

Figure 5-2 Administration of the first typhoid vaccination, 1909. Courtesy American Public Health Association.

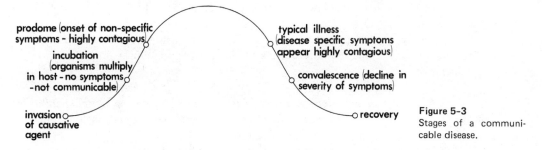

prodome (onset of non-specific symptoms - highly contagious)

incubation (organisms multiply in host - no symptoms -not communicable)

invasion of causative agent

typical illness (disease specific symptoms appear highly contagious)

convalescence (decline in severity of symptoms)

recovery

Figure 5-3
Stages of a communicable disease.

4. means of transmission (direct or indirect contact)
5. entry into new host (a body opening, natural or artificial)
6. host susceptibility (see Figure 5-4).

From an epidemiologic standpoint, knowledge of the infectious disease process is important in order to identify the most appropriate control measures. In addition, it is

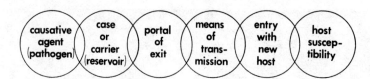

Figure 5-4
The chain of infection.

important to understand the nature and characteristics of disease producing organisms called *pathogens*.

Etiologic Agents There are six basic categories of etiologic (causative) agents or pathogens capable of producing infectious disease in humans. These include:

1. *Protozoa:* Unicellular animals that cause diseases such as malaria and amoebic dysentery. Protozoa are usually vector-borne.
2. *Metazoa:* Multicellular animal parasites that cause such diseases as trichinosis, hookworm, and schistosomiasis.
3. *Bacteria:* Unicellular plant-like organisms that cause a variety of diseases including tuberculosis, meningitis, and salmonellosis. Many bacteria that cause human disease reproduce in humans and the environment.
4. *Viruses:* Life-like organisms that contain either DNA or RNA. These are the smallest of pathogens, and they produce diseases including smallpox, measles, influenza, encephalitis, and rabies. These diseases are usually directly transmittable from person to person.
5. *Fungi:* Uni- and multicellular plants are responsible for such diseases as ringworm, histoplasmosis, and coccidiomycosis. This category includes yeasts and molds.
6. *Rickettsia:* Intracellular parasites that are intermediate in size between bacteria and viruses and share the characteristics of both categories. Some diseases caused by rickettsia include louse- and tick-borne typhus and Q-fever.

The recognized pathogens are the direct cause of infectious disease in humans. Their ability to live and multiply outside the human body improves their likelihood of producing disease.

Reservoirs of infection A *reservoir* is considered to be the normal habitat in which a pathogen or infectious agent lives and multiplies. These habitats include humans, animals, and various aspects of the environment.

The two major categories of human sources of infection include clinical cases and carriers. *Clinical cases* refer to those individuals who are infected with a specific disease. When an infectious disease occurs, there is a period between host acquisition of the causative agent and the onset of symptoms of the disease. This period is known as the prodromal stage of the illness and is usually when the individual is likely to spread the pathogens unconsciously about. *Carriers* refer to individuals who harbor an infectious disease, yet who have no overt symptoms or signs. These people are capable of spreading their infection to others and are particularly dangerous from a public health standpoint, since neither they, nor their contacts, are aware of the presence of infection, and therefore take no special precautions to prevent spread of the disease to unaffected people. Plants, soils, and water in the environment all serve as a reservoir of infection for a variety of diseases including histoplasmosis and coccidiomycosis.

Exit of agent from the host The way in which a pathogen or infectious agent leaves its host is called the *portal of exit*. The organism must escape from a natural or artificial body opening. The respiratory tract is a common portal to many diseases including the common cold, tuberculosis and influenza. The urinary and intestinal tracts also serve as portals of exit and are associated with such diseases as typhoid, cholera, and the bacillary dysenteries, among others. In addition, the mouth and skin may serve as a portal of exit for a variety of diseases. Open lesions are responsible for spread of the sexually transmitted diseases.

Transmission of the agent to new host Once the pathogen has left the reservoir, the communicable disease organisms are transmitted from one host to another by direct or indirect transmission. *Direct* implies immediate transmission, as in the case of either contact or droplet spread. The sexually transmitted and enteric diseases exemplify the role of contact in direct transmission. Many respiratory diseases are communicable by means of droplet spread in which infectious aerosols are produced by talking, sneezing, and coughing. Through droplet spread, infection may be transmitted to susceptible individuals within a 3-foot distance.

The *indirect mode* of disease transmission is accomplished through either living or inanimate mechanisms. Living (animate) mechanisms involve such vectors as mosquitoes, fleas, and ticks. Inanimate mechanisms of indirect transmission involve spread by means of air or other vehicles. Any substance, including food, water, milk or biological products, can be considered a vehicle if it is capable of transporting an infectious agent and introducing it to a suitable host (see Figure 5-5).

Entry into new host The portals of entry for a pathogen into the host are essentially the same as the exit portals from reservoirs of infection. Susceptibility or

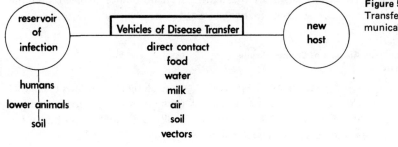

Figure 5-5
Transfer vehicles of communicable diseases.

Figure 5-6 Water testing is done to ensure a safe drinking water supply. Courtesy Arizona Department of Health Services.

resistance to disease depends on both genetic factors and the general factors of resistance and specific acquired immunity. General factors that provide some degree of resistance to infection include the skin, mucous membranes, gastric acidity, and cilia. Factors that increase susceptibility include malnutrition and pre-existing ill health. Host resistance can be increased to the greatest extent by specific *acquired immunity*. Acquired immunity may be obtained naturally by having had a specific disease (natural), or artifically through vaccination. *Passive immunity* is obtained by means of transplacental transfer from mother to newborn. Artificial mechanisms of acquiring such antibodies involve the administration of either vaccines or toxoids (active) or antitoxins. This will be discussed in greater detail later in this chapter.

Epidemiologic Analysis of Communicable Disease Control

The methods and techniques of epidemiology are designed to detect a causal association between a disease and a characteristic of the person or the environment in which the disease is found. Epidemiological data are usually organized according to the variables of time, place, and personal characteristics.

106

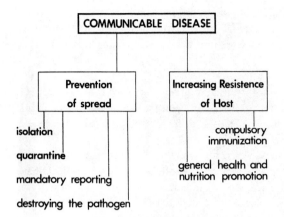

```
          ┌─────────────────────────┐
          │  COMMUNICABLE  DISEASE  │
          └─────────────────────────┘
```

| Prevention of spread | Increasing Resistence of Host |

isolation

quarantine

mandatory reporting

destroying the pathogen

compulsory immunization

general health and nutrition promotion

Figure 5-7
Communicable disease control measures.

Prevention and Control

Control of the communicable diseases takes place by attacking the chain of infection through altering either the host, the environment or the disease agent. Although communicable diseases have not been eliminated, they have largely been controlled. Indeed, public health and medicine have had far greater success in controlling infectious diseases than chronic and psychobehavioral diseases (see Figure 5-7).

Reservoirs A community may be protected from disease spread by preventing the transfer of pathogens from an infected host (reservoir) to other noninfected persons. One way in which this is accomplished is the isolation of an infected person or animal from noninfected persons until the danger of disease spread has passed. Quarantine, another reservoir control method, is imposed on individuals who have been exposed to a disease and are suspected to be infected, yet who have not developed the symptoms. These individuals are segregated from the rest of the community. The period of time set for either isolation or quarantine is usually based on laboratory findings.

The most desirable method of communicable disease control which attempts to alter the reservoir of infection would be total elimination of the reservoirs of infection. However, this in most instances is impossible. Generally a community may be protected by preventing transfer of infection from a known reservoir to other potential hosts, once the reservoir is identified. Another method used to effect communicable disease control is treatment of infected persons. Thus, infected persons (reservoirs), are treated so their disease is rendered noncommunicable.

Portal of exit Concern with the reservoir alone is insufficient from a disease-control standpoint. For example, a person with malaria usually does not transmit the disease to others. The pathogen, or causative agent of malaria, endangers others via the female Anopheles mosquito. Thus, public health professionals must also be concerned with *how* a specific pathogen escapes from the reservoir and transfers infection. Escape may be in the form of coughing, sneezing, or other secretions from the respiratory tract. It may result from open lesions with which an uninfected person has contact, or from animal bites or sucking insects.

Transmission   As was stated earlier, transmission may be either direct or indirect. Direct transmission implies direct contact with an infected reservoir or person, while indirect transmission implies that some vehicle of transfer or vector passes the disease from the reservoir to a susceptible host.

Vectors include lice, mosquitoes, ticks, and rodents. They represent the intermediate link between a case and a susceptible new host. Public health control efforts have been largely successful in blocking the transfer of infection via vectors by destroying the breeding places of vectors and using pesticides such as DDT in the war against the Anopheles.

A major transfer medium responsible for disease spread in the past was milk. However, through dairy sanitation and with the advent and utilization of pasteurization, spread of diseases such as typhoid, dysentery, and bovine tuberculosis has been virtually eradicated in the United States.

Foods also can become contaminated and serve as a medium of transfer for disease. Generally, the best method of disease control in foods is proper heating and cooling of food so that pathogens will be destroyed. This has required that the public be educated in proper methods of food handling, preparation, and cooking.

Entry in portal of new host   Entry into the new host usually takes the same form as did the exit from the reservoir of infection. However, the mere entry and presence of pathogens in the body of a new host is not synonomous with disease spread. In order for a new host to become infected he or she must be susceptible to, or lacking resistance to the infection, Thus, the host with no specific resistance against a disease is termed susceptible.

Public health disease control efforts are aimed at increasing the resistance of the new host. This is accomplished primarily through immunizations. For example, artificial active immunity can be produced through vaccinations against such diseases as diphtheria, tetanus, smallpox, polio, and cholera. *Active immunity* is said to exist when an individual's own body produced antibodies necessary to protect itself from contracting a specific disease. In the immunizations mentioned earlier, and in many others, antigens are injected into the body which cause the formation of antibodies. Acquired immunity refers to protection from a disease such as measles, because one has already had one attack of the disease.

Disease control methods also employ immunizations that provide passive immunity. This especially is true during a disease outbreak because the duration of passive immunity is relatively short, usually a few weeks. Passive immunity exists when antibodies produced in some other individual or animal are introduced into a person. This procedure is employed only when it has been conclusively determined that an individual

has been exposed to and is susceptible to a specific disease. This is an emergency procedure which has serious limitations.

CHRONIC AND DEGENERATIVE DISEASE CONTROL

In the United States today, *chronic disease* accounts for as much as 75 percent of all
deaths. These diseases have emerged as the leading causes of death and major causes
of disability in most developed countries. Heart disease continues to rank as the leading
cause of death in developed areas, accounting for nearly 51 percent of all deaths. During
the past 25 years, death rates for strokes, arteriosclerosis, and kidney disease have shown
marked reductions. However, cancer, which ranks second as a cause of death, has increased
over the past twenty years. For example, in 1978, the *age-adjusted* cancer mortality rate
was 133 deaths per 100,000 population; 6 percent higher than in 1950.[1] Accidents
remain the fourth leading cause of death in the U.S.

As public health and medicine gained control over the communicable diseases,
life expectancy increased. Consequently, a greater proportion of the population now
lives beyond 64 years of age, compared to that of 1900. Life expectancy for men and
women is 69 and 76.7, respectively. People who are middle-aged and older are generally
more susceptible to developing chronic and degenerative diseases.

The chronic diseases category includes a large number of usually unrelated
conditions which are long-lasting and generally permanent. At present, these diseases
constitute a major public health challenge. The leading causes of death are indicative of
major health problems, as well as economic loss which results from death during the later
working years. Mortality data alone fail to describe the full impact of the chronic diseases.
Over eighty-five million Americans are affected by one or more of the chronic conditions.
In 1977, about one-eighth of the U.S. population reported a limitation of activity resulting
from a chronic condition. Between 1972 and 1977, there was a 38 percent rise in the
proportion of people 45-to-64 years old and a 20 percent rise in the 17-to-44 age group
who were unable to carry out their major activity due to chronic disease disability.[2]

Unlike the communicable diseases, heart disease, cancer, emphysema, arthritis,
and diabetes cannot be controlled by applying the chain-of-infection model. Epidemiologists and others concerned with control of the chronic diseases are presented with a
difficult challenge, for these diseases present special problems for investigating causality.
The absence of a known causative agent in many chronic diseases makes diagnosis difficult. In addition, multiple factors operate in causation, and the way in which these
factors combine to cause disease is complex. The interaction of factors may be additive
or synergistic (multiplicative) in producing disease. Further, because many chronic
diseases have inordinately long latent periods, comparable to the incubation period of
communicable disease, it becomes difficult to identify factors which may have preceded
the disease. For example, eating patterns in youth may have some bearing on the occurrence of coronary heart disease in middle life. Finally, epidemiologists have difficulty in

TABLE 5-1 Selected Notifiable Disease Rates, According to Disease: United States, Selected Years 1950–1977[a]

DISEASE	YEAR							
	1950	1955	1960	1965	1970	1975	1976	1977
	Number of Cases per 100,000 Population							
Chickenpox	(b)	(b)	(b)	(b)	(b)	78.11	96.06	97.63
Diphtheria	3.83	1.21	0.51	0.08	0.21	0.14	0.06	0.04
Hepatitis A	(b)	19.45	23.15	17.49	27.87	16.82	15.51	14.40
Hepatitis B					4.08	6.30	7.14	7.78
Measles (rubeola)	211.01	337.88	245.42	135.33	23.23	11.44	19.16	26.51
Mumps	(b)	(b)	(b)	(b)	55.5	27.99	17.93	10.02
Pertussis (whooping cough)	79.82	38.21	8.23	3.51	2.08	0.82	0.47	1.02
Poliomyelitis, total	22.02	17.64	1.77	0.04	0.02	0.00	0.01	0.01
Paralytic	(b)	8.43	1.40	0.03	0.02	0.00	0.01	0.01
Rubella (German measles)	(b)	(b)	(b)	(b)	27.75	7.81	5.82	9.43
Salmonellosis, excluding typhoid fever	(b)	3.32	3.85	8.87	10.84	10.61	10.74	12.87
Shigellosis	15.45	8.47	6.94	5.70	6.79	7.78	6.15	7.42
Tuberculosis (newly reported active cases)	80.50	46.60	30.83	25.33	18.22	15.95	14.96	13.93
Venereal diseases (newly reported civilian cases):								
Syphilis[c]	146.02	76.15	68.78	58.81	45.46	38.00	33.69	30.10
Primary and secondary	16.73	4.02	9.06	12.16	10.94	12.09	11.14	9.50
Early latent	39.71	12.48	10.11	9.10	8.11	12.57	11.91	9.94
Late and late latent	76.22	53.83	45.91	35.09	25.05	12.81	10.29	10.39
Congenital	8.97	3.33	2.48	1.86	0.97	0.43	0.29	0.22
Gonorrhea	192.45	146.96	145.33	169.36	298.52	472.91	470.47	466.83
Chancroid	3.34	1.65	0.94	0.51	0.70	0.33	0.29	0.21
Granuloma inguinale	1.19	0.30	0.17	0.08	0.06	0.03	0.03	0.03
Lymphogranuloma venereum	0.95	0.47	0.47	0.46	0.30	0.17	0.17	0.16

[a]Data are based on reporting by State health departments

[b]Not reported nationally.

[c]Includes stage of syphilis not stated.

Note: Rates greater than 0 but less than 0.005 are shown as 0.00. The total resident population was used to calculate all rates except venereal disease, for which the civilian resident population was used.

Sources: Center for Disease Control, reported morbidity and mortality in the United States, 1978, *Morbidity and Mortality Weekly Report* 27(54), Public Health Service, Atlanta, Ga., Sept. 1979. National Center for Health Statistics, data computed by the Division of Analysis from data compiled by the Center for Disease Control. Veneral Disease Control Division, Center for Disease Control, selected data.

compiling accurate incidence data since many chronic conditions are characterized by an indefinite onset.[3]

Causative Factors

In an epidemiological analysis of specific chronic or degenerative disease, one begins by identifying causative factors. As is the case when considering the infectious diseases, each disease is considered unique and therefore must be analyzed individually. However several categories of potential causative factors can be classified. These include:

Nutritional This may include overeating or overnutrition, which may lead to obesity, or undernutrition which leads to malnutrition, as well as excessive or insufficient intake of specific nutrients and food substances. For example, high intake of animal fat is considered by some to be associated with the development of heart disease, while low dietary fiber or roughage intake is related to the development of gastrointestinal cancer.

Lifestyle An individual's lifestyle may increase the likelihood of developing one or more chronic conditions, or it may serve as some protection from developing them. Personal habits, including smoking, physical fitness, sleep and relaxation time, alcohol consumption, recreational pursuits, and personal hygiene are all included in this category. It is well established that lifestyle does exert a tremendous impact upon health status. The 1980 Surgeon General's Report, *Healthy People,* emphasizes the value of certain behaviors in promoting health and preventing disease. Tables 5-2 and 5-3 show American alcohol consumption levels and self-assessed weight levels.

Personality This category includes such things as anxiety levels of the individual, general temperament, competitiveness and drive, and ego development. For example, *"Type-A" personality* has been correlated with heart disease. Researchers are now hypothesizing that there may be a "cancer personality." Accident proneness as a personality type is suggested as a way of explaining the fact that certain people are frequently involved in accidents.

Heredity The role of genetics or familial make-up in the subsequent development of the chronic and degenerative diseases has been well established. Cancer, heart disease, diabetes, and arthritis, to name a few, have some hereditary factors. Schizophrenia is likewise believed to be related to genetics.

Occupation In several instances, place of work and type of occupation is a factor in the development of chronic disease. For example, asbestos workers have a greater risk of developing cancer than the rest of the population. Occupation may also contribute to disease by virtue of the stresses placed upon the individual in the workplace and/or work habits. In a famous study in London of bus workers, it was found that the sedentary, highly stressed bus drivers had a statistically significant higher rate of heart attack than

TABLE 5-2 Consumption of Alcohol by Persons 18 Years of Age and Over, According to Selected Characteristics: United States, January 1975[a]

CHARACTERISTIC	DRINKING LEVEL			Drinkers, Average Daily Consumption of Absolute Alcohol			
	All Levels	Abstainers or Less Than 1 Drink per Year	Infrequent Drinkers (1-6 Drinks per Year)	0.100 Oz. or Less	0.101-0.200 Oz.	0.201-0.550 Oz.	0.551 Oz. or More
				Percent Distribution			
Total	100	34	10	21	7	11	16
Sex							
Male	100	25	8	18	7	14	25
Female	100	43	11	25	6	8	7
Race							
White	100	33	10	22	7	11	16
Black	100	47	10	19	3	7	9
Family Income							
Less than $5,000	100	53	10	16	3	5	11
$5,000-$9,999	100	39	11	15	4	11	16
$10,000-$14,999	100	28	10	25	9	12	15
$15,000 or more	100	16	8	27	10	16	21
Marital Status							
Single	100	19	11	22	8	13	28
Married	100	33	9	22	8	11	15
Separated, divorced, or widowed	100	51	11	19	2	6	9
Education							
Less than high school graduate	100	50	9	16	3	6	13
High school graduate	100	27	10	23	8	13	18
Some college	100	22	13	26	8	12	18
College graduate	100	21	6	28	11	16	16

[a]Data are based on household interviews of a sample of the civilian noninstitutionalized population.

Source: Calculated from tables in Rappeport, M., P. Labaw, and J. Williams, *The Public Evaluates the NIAAA Public Education Campaign: A Study for the U.S. Department of Health, Education, and Welfare*, Vols. I and II. Princeton, N.J.: Opinion Research Corporation, July 1975.

TABLE 5-3 Self-Assessed Weight Status among Persons 17 Years of Age and Over, According to Sex and Age: United States, 1974[a]

SEX AND AGE	SELF-ASSESSED WEIGHT STATUS				
	Total	Under-weight	About Right	Over-weight	No Rating
	Percent Distribution				
Male					
All ages 17 years and over	100.0	9.6	51.0	30.5	8.9
17–44 years	100.0	10.8	50.9	28.1	10.2
45–64 years	100.0	6.2	49.9	37.9	8.9
65 years and over	100.0	12.1	60.7	23.8	3.3
Female					
All ages 17 years and over	100.0	6.2	41.9	48.9	3.1
17–44 years	100.0	6.0	42.5	48.4	3.1
45–64 years	100.0	4.6	36.0	56.1	3.3
65 years and over	100.0	9.6	51.1	36.9	2.4

[a]Data are based on household interviews of a sample of the civilian noninstitutionalized population.

Source: Division of Health Interview Statistics, National Center for Health Statistics, data from the Health Interview Survey.

the ticket-takers on the buses who were in constant motion up and down the aisles and stairs of the double-decker buses.

In applying the epidemiologic model to chronic diseases, a multicausational model is used (see Figure 5-9). While the causative agent in the communicable diseases is nearly always *one* agent, in the chronic and psychobehavioral diseases, *many* factors must be considered. In addition, as was mentioned previously, there is a relative lack of a known disease agent in many of the chronic diseases which makes identification difficult. As might be supposed, today's health problems are infinitely more complex to prevent and control.

Epidemiological Analysis of Chronic Disease

When applied to chronic diseases, the methods and techniques of epidemiology are designed to identify associations between *risk-factors,* which are represented by characteristics of people and their environment as they relate to the development of disease. In this way, it is possible to develop a profile of those attributable risk-factors a person might possess that would increase the likelihood of developing a specific disease. Developing a profile which includes previous chronic disease victims age, race, and personal lifestyle habits, makes it theoretically possible to prevent the disease from occurring by eliminating all contact between the risk-factor and the general population. For example, it has been established that victims of heart disease are more frequently men than wo-

Figure 5–8
Occupation is a factor in the development of chronic disease. Courtesy Center for Disease Control, Atlanta, Georgia.

Causative Factors

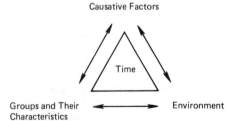

Groups and Their Characteristics   ←→   Environment

Figure 5-9 Multicausational model.

men; that cigarette smoking greatly increases the risk of heart disease; and that these individuals are generally sedentary, overweight, and in poor physical condition. This type of profile offers insight for those involved in instituting public health control and prevention measures as they relate to heart disease. *Primary prevention* is possible by altering susceptibility or reducing exposure for susceptible individuals to a known risk-factor(s).

In the foregoing example, this would require stopping smoking, thereby reducing the exposure to a risk-factor; or exercising on a regular basis, thereby reducing the exposure to sedentary life.

Control of Chronic Diseases

Control and particularly prevention, of the chronic diseases, is extremely difficult.

Protecting a man against smallpox by vaccination is quick, simple, effective. Asking this same man to protect himself from heart disease by losing 25 pounds and jogging several miles a week is a complex request which demands a change in his entire style of living. It offers less certain protection than vaccination in that it deals not with a necessary cause but with a risk factor whose elimination may still leave the individual exposed to a number of risks, some or most of which have yet to be identified.[4]

Prevention While primary prevention is the best way to control the chronic diseases, they are generally controlled at the secondary prevention and tertiary prevention levels. *Secondary prevention* refers to early detection and treatment. It is designed to slow the progression of disease and reduce complications. The role of secondary prevention in many of the chronic diseases including cancer, heart and vessel diseases, and lung diseases cannot be underestimated. *Tertiary prevention* has the objective of restoring functioning and reducing further deterioration or disability resulting from disease. Effective control of many chronic diseases involves controlling the symptoms, but not successfully reversing the pathological damage to the body as a result of the disease process. Figure 5–10 illustrates priorities for controlling the diseases that cause the most disability and death in two main age groups.

Cancer

This disease is the second-leading cause of death in the United States, affecting about 1 of every 4 persons. *Cancer* actually includes several hundred diseases, each characterized by abnormal uncontrolled cell growth. It is said to be *malignant* because of its ability to spread to distant parts of the body (*metastasis*), or to invade nearby body

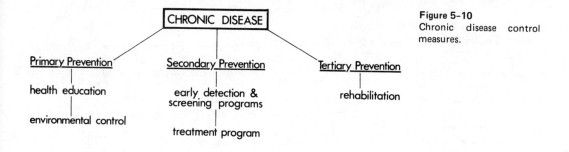

Figure 5-10
Chronic disease control measures.

organs and cause debility. Cancer mortality has been increasing for some sites—such as the respiratory system and the breast, colon, pancreas, and bladder—and has been decreased for others, such as the stomach, rectum, cervix, and uterus. The age-adjusted death rate for cancer for all sites combined rose more rapidly for the black population than for whites between 1950 and 1973. Racial differences in cigarette-smoking patterns and the increased exposure to carcinogenic hazards of urban environments are being investigated as a possible explanation of these trends. The known causes or agents which can transform normal cells into cancer cells are numerous, but as yet no single agent or cause has been identified that has been found common to all forms. Table 5-4, based on epidemiological studies, lists some major risk factors for common cancers.

Many epidemiologic factors are associated with the occurrence of cancer, including radiation, sunlight, chronic irritation, aging, genetics, inhalation and injection of toxic and irritating chemicals. However, the basic cause of cancer remains unknown. At present, nucleic acids are prime targets of cancer research. Investigators are seeking to identify the complex chemistry through which radiation, chemicals, viruses, and other

TABLE 5-4   High-Risk Groups[a]

Colon–Rectum:
- History of rectal polyps.
- Rectal polyps run in family.
- History of ulcerative colitis.
- Blood in stool.
- Over age 40.

Lung:
- Heavy cigarette smoker over age 50.
- Started cigarette smoking age 15 or before.
- Smoker working with or near asbestos.

Uterine–Endometrial:
- Unusual bleeding or discharge.
- Late menopause (after age 55).
- Diabetes, high blood pressure and overweight.
- Aged 50+.

Uterine–Cervical:
- Unusual bleeding or discharge.
- Frequent sex in early teens or with many partners.
- Low socioeconomic background.
- Poor care during or following pregnancy.

Oral:
- Heavy smoker and drinker.
- Poor oral hygiene.

Breast:
- Lump or nipple discharge.
- History of breast cancer.
- Close relatives with history of breast cancer.
- Over age 35; especially over 50.
- Never had children; first child after age 30.

Skin:
- Excessive exposure to sun.
- Fair complexion.
- Work with coal tar, pitch or creosote.

Ovary:
- History of ovarian cancer among close relatives.
- Aged 50+.
- Never had children.

Prostate:
- Aged 60+.
- Difficulty in urinating.

Stomach:
- History of stomach cancer among close relatives.
- Diet heavy in smoked, pickled or salted foods.

[a]Age-adjusted: a method used to make valid statistical comparisons by assuming the same age distribution among different groups being compared.

Source: Courtesy the American Cancer Society, *Cancer Facts and Figures, 1980.*

unknown factors incite cancer. If certain viruses are identified as causes of cancer, preventive vaccines will become theoretically possible.

At present, public health cancer-control measures include public education campaigns designed to inform the public of the importance of avoiding or limiting their exposure to known carcinogenic agents; mass-screening programs designed to detect various forms of cancer early in the disease process; and treatment and rehabilitation programs for persons affected with cancer designed to reduce disability and increase the likelihood of survival. Cancer management is becoming increasingly individualized, both with respect to diagnostic procedures and treatment. Early detection is followed by a precise staging of the disease, and the use of more than one kind of therapy, often in combinations.

Leukemia This disease is cancer of the blood-forming bone marrow. It is customary to categorize leukemia as either acute or chronic. Acute leukemia occurs most frequently (90 percent of cases) in children, reaching a peak incidence during the third year and then dropping off sharply. The five-year survival rate for patients with optimum treatment is now between 50 and 75 percent. Chronic leukemia, on the other hand, usually has a slow onset, and occurs most frequently in middle or later life. This disease may either go into a *remission* (temporary stop) or progress very slowly over a period of months or years without typical symptoms. The survival rate for chronic leukemia for men is 30 percent and 34 percent for women. As yet, it is not known what causes disturbances in the equilibrium in the white blood cells of leukemia victims. However, research is leading closer to identifying those factors which either cause these changes or lower the individual's resistance to them.

Breast cancer This form of cancer strikes women most frequently between the ages of 40 and 60. It exists in higher incidence among childless women, among those who have fewer than two children, and among those who have never breast-fed a baby. The use of the oral contraceptive may increase the likelihood of developing breast cancer, although this claim has not yet been substantiated. The disease is more common among whites than blacks.

Breast cancer strikes 90,000 American women every year. It kills almost 34,000 women annually. Breast cancer is the leading cause of death in women from 40 to 44 years. The five-year survival rate for breast cancer increased from 53 percent for cases diagnosed in 1940 to 65 percent for cases diagnosed in the 1970s. However, there is no real difference in mortality rates over the past 50 years.

Since prevention of breast cancer is not possible in the present, early detection is the best hope for survival. The American Cancer Society is very visible in educating both men and women in breast self-examination, a simple three-step procedure which should be performed monthly to detect an unusual lump or dimpling early. Some 95 percent of women with breast cancer discover a lump themselves. Yet most wait, on average, fifteen months before seeking a physician's diagnosis.[5]

One program designed to facilitate the rehabilitation of women who have had a mastectomy, or breast removed because of cancer, is the American Cancer Society's

Reach to Recovery. This program is designed to help the post-mastectomy patient—cosmetically, psychologically, and physiologically.

Since 1950, cancer treatment has included radiation, chemotherapy, and/or hormones in addition to surgery. Newer drug combinations can sharply reduce the recurrence rate of breast cancer in some patients after surgery. Drug combinations can also provide prolonged control for a number of advanced breast cancers.

Lung cancer This form of cancer has the highest mortality rate of all the cancers. It is the most common form of cancer in men, and its incidence in women is rising. It has the highest number of new cases for any cancer for 1980, excluding skin cancers. In 1977, for the first time, the female age-adjusted lung-cancer death rate per 100,000 people exceeded that for colon-rectum cancer, with the rates at 14.9 for lung and 14.3 for colon-rectum. Only about 10 percent of lung-cancer patients are saved. In 1980 about 101,300 died, the equivalent of about 278 per day.[6]

The earliest symptoms appear to be a cough, expectoration, and wheezing. Risk-factors associated with the subsequent development of lung cancer include cigarette smoking, air pollution, and inhaling noxious chemicals, such as asbestos and uranium ores. The smoker's risk of developing the disease increases as his or her daily intake of cigarettes increases. The typical victim of lung cancer is a male, in the middle years of life, lives in an urban area, and has smoked for a number of years. The 1979 Surgeon General's Report—issued fifteen years after the first one that officially linked cigarette smoking with lung cancer—declared that smoking "is far more dangerous than was supposed in 1964."[7] The Report is a compendium of twenty-two scientific papers on smoking and health compiled by twelve agencies of the former Department of Health, Education and Welfare. Of the 100,000 Americans who have lung cancer today, smoking is responsible for about 83 percent of cases among men and 43 percent among women—more than 70 percent overall.

Metastatic malignancies in the lungs transferred from other sites are more common than primary cancer of the lung. In fact, about half of cancers of the breast metastasize to the lungs if untreated. Primary cancers of the stomach, uterus, prostate gland, and pancreas often metastasize to the lungs. Chest x-ray is the only technique currently available for screening potential lung cancers. And this technique is quite imprecise. Since the five-year survival rate in this disease is only 8 percent for males and 12 percent for females, the only real hope lies in preventing its onset.

Based upon 1978 data, it appears that campaigns against cigarette smoking have had some effect, especially among males 20 years old and up. During the period 1976 to 1978, the percent of male smokers decreased to 38 percent, an average annual decrease of 2 percent for the eleven-year period 1965 to 1976. Between 1965 and 1976, the increase in former smokers accounted for 80 percent of the reduction in the proportion of cigarette smokers. Between 1976 and 1978, only 31 percent of the reduction was attributed to former smokers.

Patterns for women are not as encouraging. In 1978, 31 percent of women 20 years of age or older smoked cigarettes, decreasing at less than 2 percent per year for the previous two years. Between 1976 to 1978, there was no change in the proportion of people who have never smoked.

Teenage smoking which showed increase substantially between 1968 and 1974, showed signs of a decrease by 1979. Among both males and females, current smoking decreased from 16 percent in 1974 to 12 percent in 1979.[8]

Although per-capita cigarette smoking and the percentage of smokers in the U.S. have begun to decline, levels of lung cancer and other diseases continue to rise. This is because these disorders usually take decades to appear. Cancers are now appearing that began in the 1940s, 1950s, and early 1960s, but if the smoking decline continues, we can look forward to a leveling off and eventually a decline in smoking-related lung disease.

According to the American Cancer Society, the prevention of cancer at present involves avoidance or removal of known environmental causes of cancer. This means (1) avoidance of unnecessary and avoidable exposure to radiation, (2) avoidance of exposure to known cancer-producing chemicals and dusts in the work and living environment, and (3) avoidance of exposure to tobacco, particularly cigarette smoke and alcohol. Short of prevention, early diagnosis and treatment provides the best hope for survival.

Cardiovascular Disease

Cardiovascular disease includes those diseases that affect the heart and/or blood vessels. These diseases are responsible for one million deaths annually and untold disability.

Atherosclerosis A common underlying problem associated with most cardiovascular diseases is *atherosclerosis,* which is characterized by a narrowing and thickening of blood vessel walls, as well as reduced elasticity of the vessel. As an underlying cause, atherosclerosis contributes directly to heart attack and stroke that claim 850,000 lives annually. There are a number of diseases that can accurately be classified as cardiovascular, including hypertension, stroke, congestive heart failure, rheumatic heart disease, and congenital defects.

Recently, decreases in death rates from cardiovascular diseases have been evident. The age-adjusted death rate decreased by 18 percent in the twenty years from 1950 to 1970. Among white females, heart disease mortality decreased 25 percent during the period, compared to a 9 percent decrease among males. Among black females and males, the decreases were 28 and 10 percent, respectively.

Some of the suggested explanations for the decline in heart disease mortality are: 1. decreased smoking in general and in smoking of high tar and nicotine cigarettes among adult males, 2. improved management of hypertension, 3. decreased dietary intake of saturated fats, 4. more widespread physical activity, and 6. more widespread use and increased efficacy of coronary care units. Unfortunately, there is no definitive evidence to determine which of these explanations alone or in combination can account for the decline.[9]

Coronary heart disease (CHD) This disease could more accurately be called coronary artery disease, since the heart muscle is usually normal except that circulation to it has been reduced or cut off by narrowing or blocked branches of the coronary arteries. A major question in the control of this disease concerns whether or not the tendency to develop it is hereditary or dependent on the individual's lifestyle and environment. The evidence that coronary heart disease has a hereditary basis is impressive. Especially for those under the age of 40, coronary atherosclerosis is almost entirely a male disease. Only after menopause does its occurrence become nearly equal in men and women. Women's hormonal nature before menopause seems to provide considerable protection from the disease. Likewise, it has been established that in general, young men under 40 with slender statures and poorly developed musculature are significantly more protected against heart disease than the mesomorphic (athletic) young man.

There are also families with a high incidence of coronary attacks and early death, and some families exhibit a tendency toward high levels of cholesterol and *triglycerides* in the blood. In addition, it has been found that diabetes increases the likelihood of coronary disease in families. And, hypertension, or high blood pressure, especially in women, is known to contribute to coronary disease.

There are other nongenetic factors that may be responsible for what has been called an "epidemic" of heart disease in the United States. For example, affluent, developed nations have higher incidences of coronary disease in the population than do less technologically advanced nations. The usual explanation is that people who live in technologically advanced nations tend to be overweight, less physically active, consume richer diets, smoke more cigarettes, and live more competitive lives. Some research even suggests that heavy users of coffee are, as a group, more susceptible to coronary disease.

Heart disease is etiologically complex. Prevention of coronary disease is extremely difficult, since there is no valid screening test, and control efforts must be directed toward known risk-factors. The prediction of who is likely to suffer from coronary disease is best made by a analysis of family history, weight gain after age 25, presence of elevated blood pressure or *hypertension,* elevated levels of *serum cholesterol* and triglycerides, cigarette smoking, and amount of exercise. However, it should be noted that although there is some evidence that elimination of these risk factors may reduce the likelihood of coronary disease development, there is no guarantee of protection. And, since a change in human habits and lifestyles are frequently required in order to reduce the risk-factors associated with heart disease, control efforts are very difficult.

In summary, heart disease is the prime cause of both death and disability in the United States today. Its prevalence increases with age. It is far more common in men than in women. There appears to be little racial difference associated with incidence of this disease. The best hope in the future lies in prevention and in providing early diagnosis and treatment to prevent further progression and complications.

Hypertension This is a common disorder in the United States, affecting at least 23.2 million adults aged 18 to 74. Hypertension, or high blood pressure, refers to an elevation in blood pressure with a systolic pressure of at least 160 or diastolic pressure of at least 95. For people aged 18 to 54, hypertension is more prevalent among men than women. Between ages 55 and 74, it is more prevalent among women.[10] In 1978, the prevalence rate of hypertension was 18 percent among those 18 to 74 years old. Hypertension is substantially more prevalent among black adults than among white adults in the United States. For example, in data compiled during the HANES-I in 1978, the age-adjusted rate of elevated blood pressure for the white population 18 to 74 years old was 16.8 per 100, compared to 30.5 per 100 for black adults. The racial differences appear to be greater among women than men.

Hypertension is a universal disease found in all societies. It occurs most frequently after age 35. And, it is a significant risk-factor in the subsequent development of *stroke* or cerebrovascular accident, renal failure, and congestive heart failure. The cause of blood pressure elevation remains unknown. In most cases, however, several factors have been identified which may contribute to the development of hypertension. These include hereditary predisposition, emotional stress, *obesity,* high salt intake, and excessive smoking. Obesity seems to aggravate hypertension, but the exact relationship is unknown. A sodium-restricted diet along with drug therapy is an accepted treatment to lower blood pressure. However, whether or not high salt consumption is a causal factor in hypertension is unknown.

By far, genetic predisposition is believed to be the most important factor in hypertension. It has been found that if one parent has hypertension, there is a 50 percent chance that the offspring will develop hypertension sometime during its life. If both parents suffer hypertension, the likelihood for hypertension development in the offspring increases to 90 percent.

Overall death rates from hypertension have fallen slightly in the past twenty years. However, the life span of uncontrolled and untreated hypertension is considerably shortened. Death may result from heart attack, heart failure, kidney failure, or stroke.

Two types of high blood pressure mass-screening programs are conducted by the American Heart Association throughout the U.S. One type concentrates on blood pressure readings to identify people with elevated blood pressure. The other adopts a multiphasic approach by also taking a blood test to determine cholesterol and blood-sugar tolerance levels and by administering an electrocardiogram (ECG) to detect abnormal heart rhythms. Many drugs are now available to successfully treat hypertensive patients and maintain control over the elevated blood pressure, thus reducing the likelihood of premature deaths.

It is encouraging that an increasing number of hypertensives are now aware that they have high blood pressure and are currently receiving treatment. Less encouraging is the fact that many hypertensives have stopped taking their medication, which is an effective treatment for the disease.

Stroke   This condition is the third-leading killer in the United States today. In recent years, cerebrovascular death rates have continued to decrease at a greater pace than have heart disease death rates. Possible factors related to the decline include lowered incidence, improved management and rehabilitation of the stroke victim, and effective hypertension therapy (hypertension is a major risk factor for stroke).

Although the stroke victim is usually middle-aged or older, younger men and women are by no means immune. Strokes or cerebrovascular accidents (CVAs) are rare before the age of 45. They affect women more frequently than men and blacks more fre-

Figure 5-11 Reducing the risk of heart attack and stroke. Courtesy Arizona Department of Health Services.

quently than whites. Risk-factors for stroke are similar to coronary disease and include obesity, hypertension, smoking, and heredity.

The American Heart Association Council on Stroke defines a candidate for stroke as a person with high blood pressure and a history of brief, intermittent stroke episodes or Transient Ischemic Attacks (TIAs). Examinations often show evidence of atherosclerosis and indications of diabetes. Tests may reveal increased cholesterol levels in the blood. Stroke occurs when there is interference with the blood supply to the brain.

The major control for CVAs is prevention. This can be achieved primarily by controlling hypertension. For those who have suffered a stroke, early treatment and rehabilitation can reduce and/or prevent chronic disability including paralysis, speech disorders, and impaired thinking. Rehabilitation ideally begins in the acute treatment stage for the stroke victim in the hospital. Controlling high blood pressure is of primary importance in preventing the recurrence of stroke.

PSYCHOBEHAVIORAL DISEASE CONTROL

The *psychobehavioral diseases* include such conditions as mental illness, drug dependence and abuse, *alcoholism*, smoking, and obesity. These diseases are directly related to the society in which one lives. They are nebulous in nature.

Psychobehavioral disorders are very prevalent in the United States. In 1978, almost 23 percent of all women aged 20 to 74 and 13 percent of all men 20 to 74 were classified as obese. The prevalence of obesity increases with age. More black women are obese than white women, while rates for white men and black men are similar. It has been estimated that there are currently nine million alcoholics in the United States and an additional four million persons are said to have a serious drinking problem. Drug use and abuse of both the illicit and prescription drugs is nearly epidemic among young and old people alike. And, although proportionately fewer people in the adult years are smoking now in comparison to 1965, two-fifths of young men aged 21 to 24, and one-third of women in the same age group, smoke. Mental illness in varying forms affects millions of Americans annually.

The psychobehavioral diseases present special problems for epidemiologists and others involved in disease control in the public health field. They exact a toll not only on the quality of human life, but frequently contribute to the development of other physical diseases as well. For example, smoking and lung cancer contribute to heart disease, and alcoholism and cirrhosis of the liver are related to stomach cancer and heart disease. In general, they increase morbidity, mortality, and social pathology among populations. The identification of causative factors of psychobehavioral diseases is nearly impossible, and at best difficult. In addition, the compilation of incidence and prevalence statistics on psychobehavioral disorders like neuroses, barbiturate abuse, and obesity in noninstitutionalized (general) populations is virtually impossible. Profiles, as they relate to age, sex, race, place of residence, and other demographic variables can be feasibly compiled only on outpatient or resident populations seeking treatment. Further difficulties are presented when carrying out epidemiologic investigations in the psychobehavioral diseases, since no method is available for accurately assessing dates of onset of the illness or problem and termination. In some instances, even diagnosis of a problem is difficult.

Causative Factors

Each disorder or disease is considered unique and is therefore analyzed individually. However, several categories of factors can be identified to illustrate potential causative factors for this disease category.

Personality This includes a variety of personality traits and disorders, such as self-concept, ability to adjust to changing demands, compulsivity, aggressiveness, guilt, and worry patterns. Personality is believed to be a major factor in the psychobehavioral diseases, and some have suggested the existence of an *addictive personality*.[11]

Lifestyle   This category is related to both social class and occupation. It includes the lifestyle choices people make, including forms of recreation, and leisure-time activity. Recent evidence suggests that some individuals pursue a risk-taking lifestyle, which includes driving too fast, drinking too much, smoking, and generally pushing oneself to the limits.

Social contacts   The type of people with whom an individual associates and the type of relationships enjoyed by the individual is believed to have some bearing on the development of psychosocial disorders. The influence of peer pressure on drug experimentation has been well documented. Likewise, the loner who is unable to engage in any warm human relationship is a likely candidate for mental illness.

Life-stresses and adaptability   The number and type of outside stresses placed upon an individual is considered to be a potential factor in this category. Social loss, loss of loved ones, marriage, a new job, are all life-stressors. In addition, stresses placed upon the individual in the growth and development years is significant. An additional factor is the adaptability and resilience of the individual to adjust to stressors and regain equilibrium.

Heredity   Although the role of genetics as a causative agent in producing psychobehavioral diseases is not entirely clear, it is believed that familial make-up may predispose certain individuals to develop diseases. This is suspected in schizophrenia and perhaps alcoholism.

In investigating the psychobehavioral diseases, the multicausational model is used, since there is no single causative agent responsible for any of these diseases.

Epidemiological Analysis of Psychobehavioral Disease

Application of epidemiological techniques to the psychobehavioral diseases and disorders are designed to identify associations between risk-factors and given diseases. Profiles are developed that identify those characteristics which might predispose or increase the likelihood of an individual developing a specific disease or problem. For example, although firm evidence is still lacking, experts suggest that adolescent drug abusers are usually males, with higher than average school absenteeism rates, who lack in communication and decision-making skills, and have a lower self-concept than nonabusers. This type of profile offers some information to those responsible for developing prevention and control measures as they relate to drug abuse among adolescents. Primary prevention activities might include such things as classes that promote the development of communication and decision skills and providing school and community counseling that promotes self-esteem.

Many definitions of mental health have been proposed, including adaptive behavior, conformity, and competence to function. However, none is completely satisfactory nor generally agreed upon. Based on mental-health facility utilization rates, it seems clear that mental illness is quite prevalent in the United States. And a variety of studies have demonstrated that the age-specific mortality rates among mentally ill in all settings, are considerably higher than those in corresponding age groups of the general population.[12]

There are few connections which can be offered to explain the development of the most important "functional" mental illnesses, including schizophrenia, neurosis, personality and character disorders, and *affective disorders.* Epidemiological analysis of mental illness has revealed recognized ways of thinking and feeling that can be identified as symptoms, but not causes, of mental illness.

Generally, mental illness is more prevalent among lower socioeconomic levels. In addition, more severe forms of mental illness affect lower socioeconomic groups compared to the middle class. Age is another variable that seems to relate to the occurrence of mental illness. For example, schizophrenia generally occurs before the mid-twenties, while "agitated depression" reaches a peak in middle age. Illnesses characterized by antisocial behavior and aggression are much more common among men, but the affective disorders are twice as common among women.[13] Among alcoholics and drug abusers, the male-to-female ratio is about 5 to 1.

In mental health, primary prevention activities are of two basic types. "*Specific protection activities* refers to those activities and measures, both proven and presumed, which aim to avoid the onset of mental illness. *Health promotion activities* are generally identified and focus on improving the quality of life and well-being, not merely averting pathology."[14] In mental health, parent education, premarital counseling, and more effective use of leisure time are examples of primary prevention. "The key concerns in mental health promotion are social competence, coping skills, and ego-strengthening activities, rather than psychiatric symptomology."[15]

Suicide This is a serious public health problem that claims the lives of an estimated 25,000 lives annually. It ranks as the third-leading cause of death among adolescents, and tenth among adults. Suicidal behavior is classified as risk-taking, self-destructive behavior. No one group of people by race, sex, or occupation fails to be represented by those who have succeeded in committing suicide.

Epidemiologic investigations have identified the following factors about suicide. Suicidal behavior appears to increase in frequency with age. Mid-life crises appear to be precursors to many suicide attempts, yet suicide incidence is highest among older persons. Suicide rates are higher among individuals suffering economic instability. And, while women outnumber men in suicide attempts by a ratio of 3 to 1, men outnumber women in successfully completed suicides by that same ratio.

Studies indicate that geographic, temporal, and religious factors may play a role in suicide. Urban suicides are higher than rural. And the Christmas holiday season and springtime show temporal peaks in suicide. In addition, religious differences seem to affect suicide, as Jews and Catholics have lower suicide rates than Protestants.[16]

Substance Abuse

Substance abuse refers to "repeated implicative use of alcoholic beverages, tobacco, drugs or food as to cause injury to the user's health or to his social or economic functioning."[17] The likelihood of social or economic malfunctioning is the greatest when the substance of abuse is either drugs or alcohol. However, injury to health and well-being may result from abuse of any of the substances.

Alcohol Approximately 70 percent of adult Americans drink alcoholic beverages. And, two-thirds of high school boys and one-half of high school girls were classified as moderate-to-heavy drinkers of alcoholic beverages in 1978. During the past twenty years, the proportion of female drinkers has increased to three-fifths, while male-drinking rates have remained somewhat constant at four-fifths over that same period.

Drinking behavior is inversely related to age and directly related to social class. That is, the higher social classes exhibit greater consumption of alcohol, compared to lower social classes. Younger people tend to consume less alcohol than older people. By color, white and black men vary little in the proportion of drinkers, while white women are more likely to drink than are black women.[18]

Approximately 1 out of every 10 Americans is estimated to be an alcoholic or have a serious drinking problem. In terms of sex, men are three to four times more likely to have drinking-related problems than are women. However, this sex difference has been diminishing over the past fifteen years. Alcoholism rates among racial and religious groups vary tremendously. Jews have lower rates than do either Catholics or Protestants. Blacks, with the exception of black women, have lower rates than their white counterparts. By social class, lower-class drinkers have a slightly higher rate of alcoholism than other classes.

Drugs The most-used illegal drug in the United States is marijuana. Smaller proportions of both adults and adolescents have used other both illegal and legal drugs nonmedically. A recent study indicated that no more than 1 percent had used such drugs as LSD, amphetamines, barbiturates, and tranquilizers.[19] It should be noted that the reliability of these statistics is questionable, since it is virtually impossible to obtain accurate information on drug use.

Epidemiological studies have obtained the following profile information concerning drug abuse. Men are more likely than women to have used both illicit drugs and prescription medications nonmedically. Drug use varies directly with social class, including education level and income. Excluding the use of opiate drugs (heroin), whites are more likely than blacks to use drugs. Prescribed use of the psychoactive drugs is highest among upper-social class women.[20]

Tobacco Proportionately fewer people in practically every adult age group smoked in 1979, compared to the rate of ten years earlier. The most significant drop

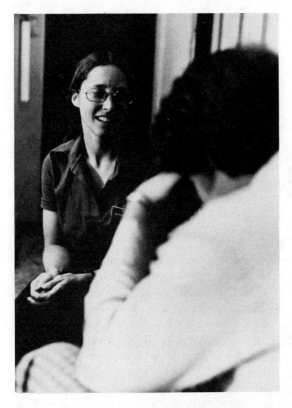

Figure 5-12
Drug counseling session. Courtesy Arizona Department of Health Services.

occurred among men. Based on 1978 data, there appears to be an appreciable change in the social norms governing cigarette smoking among young people. Fewer people are starting to smoke than was true a decade ago. Racial differences among men 25 years and older have remained fairly constant from 1965 to 1978, with the prevalence of smoking about 20 percent higher for blacks than whites.

Smoking levels among teenagers, which increased substantially from 1968 to 1974, showed signs of a decrease by 1979. Among both men and women, smoking has decreased from 16 percent in 1974 to 12 percent in 1979. The sex differential in teenage cigarette smoking (men per 100 women) reversed itself between 1968 to 1979. By 1979, a greater percent of women were smoking than men. Among men, smoking appears to be inversely related to social class, but there is no apparent relationship between social class and women who smoke.[21]

Food The most important epidemiological variable in obesity appears to be gender, though age, color, and class differences have also been noted. In all age groups, a higher proportion of women are obese than men. The index of obesity is defined as 20 percent above ideal weight for one's age, or by a triceps skinfold measurement.

In general, men above poverty level are more likely to be obese than men below poverty level, compared to women, who are more likely to be obese below poverty level. However, black women are more likely to be obese than white women, regardless of age or social class. The differences for men are in the same direction, but less obvious. There is some evidence that up to four-fifths of overweight girls and boys retain this condition as adults, and that diet during infancy is important in establishing adult metabolic patterns.

DISEASE CONTROL

Over the past fifty years tremendous gains have been made in life expectancy through disease control activities in the U.S. Strategies employed included such things as mass immunization campaigns, improved sanitation measures, and improved techniques for treatment and cure in medicine. The net result of these activities is that the communicable diseases have largely been controlled.

Disease control in the future will need to develop new strategies to effectively manage the modern killers and psychobehavioral diseases. A significant amount of research supports the notion that an individual's lifestyle and the habits he or she engages in is the key to whether that individual will be healthy or sick. Yet, we remain a long way away from a national commitment to health-generating habits. A controversy which no doubt will appear as we begin to develop new strategies in disease control is what role should government or health professionals play in attempting to get citizens to give up their pleasurable, but health-damaging habits.

The adverse health effects of a polluted environment and of a society with harmful social conditions such as poverty and ignorance will also need to be addressed if disease control efforts in the future are to be successful.

REVIEW QUESTIONS

1. Identify possible agents for the following: (1) measles, (2) motor-vehicle accidents, (3) cigarette smoking, (4) Rocky Mountain Spotted Fever, (5) skin cancer, (6) homicidal death, (7) hearing loss, and (8) drug abuse.
2. List five biologic host factors and five behavioral factors. Explain how these might relate to (1) heart disease, (2) suicide, and (3) influenza.
3. Identify and describe the chain of infection. Give examples of each link or stage in the chain.
4. How is prevention and control handled when dealing with reservoirs of infection?
5. How is the epidemiologic model applied to control the chronic diseases?
6. What special problems do the psychobehavioral disease present to those concerned with disease prevention and control?

SUGGESTED READINGS

Higgonson, John, "A Hazardous Society? Individual versus Community Responsibility in Cancer Prevention," Rosenhaus lecture. *American Journal of Public Health,* 66(4) 359-366, 1976.

Lavenhar, Marvin, "The Drug Abuse Numbers Game," *American Journal of Public Health,* 63(9) 807-809, 1973.

Macoby, Nathan and others, "Reducing the Risk of Cardiovascular Disease: Effects of a Community-Based Campaign on Knowledge and Behavior," *Journal of Community Health,* 3(2) 100-114, 1977.

Terris, Milton, "The Epidemiologic Revolution, National Health Insurance and the Role of Health Departments." *American Journal of Public Health,* 66(12) 1155-1164, 1976.

Yeracaris, Constantine and Jay Kim, "Socioeconomic Differentials in Selected Causes of Death," *American Journal of Public Health,* 68(4) 342-351, 1978.

NOTES

[1] U.S. DHEW, *Health: United States, 1979.* Washington, D.C.: U.S. DHEW Pub. No. (PHS) 80-1232, p. 163.

[2] *Health: United States, 1979,* p. 53.

[3] Judith Mausner and Anita Bahn, *Epidemiology: An Introductory Text.* Philadelphia: W. B. Saunders, 1974, pp. 310-311.

[4] Carter Marshall, *Dynamics of Health and Disease.* Englewood Cliffs, N.J.: Prentice-Hall, 1972, p. 129.

[5] *Cancer Facts and Figures, 1979.* New York: American Cancer Society, 1979.

[6] *Heart Facts, 1979.* New York: American Heart Association, 1979, p. 16.

[7] U.S. DHEW, *Healthy People: The Surgeon General's Report on Health Promotion and Disease Prevention.* Washington, D.C.: U.S. DHEW Pub. No. (PHS) 79-55071, 1979.

[8] *Health: United States, 1979.*

[9] *Health: United States, 1979.*

[10] U.S. DHEW, *Health: United States, 1976-1977: Chartbook.* Hyattsville, Md.: U.S. DHEW Pub. No. (HRA) 77-1233, p. 14.

[11] James Lieberman (ed.), *Mental Health: The Public Health Challenge.* Washington, D.C.: American Public Health Association, 1977, p. 26.

[12] James Lieberman, p. 41.

[13] James Lieberman, p. 52.

[14] James Lieberman, p. 53.

[15] James Lieberman, p. 146.

[16] James Lieberman, p. 148.

[17] M. Keller, "Definition of Alcoholism," *Quarterly Journal of Studies on Alcohol,* 21: 125-134. Adapted in James Lieberman, *Mental Health,* 1977, p. 148.

[18] James Lieberman, p. 149.

[19] James Lieberman, p. 149.

[20] James Lieberman, p. 149.

[21] *Health: United States, 1976-1977: Chartbook,* pp. 17-18.

GLOSSARY

acquired immunity immunity obtained artificially by vaccination, or naturally by having had a specific disease.

active immunity immunity in which the body produces its own antibodies; may be acquired through innoculation, or in response to having had a specific disease.

addictive personality a personality profile or type that could more easily become dependent on or addicted to substances such as tobacco, alcohol, and drugs.

affective disorders disorders in the feelings or emotions.

age-adjusted a method used to make valid statistical comparisons by assuming the same age distribution among different groups being compared.

alcoholism a disease or disorder of behavior characterized by the compulsive, repeated, and excessive drinking of alcoholic beverages.

atherosclerosis common underlying problem in most cardiovascular diseases, characterized by a narrowing and thickening of blood-vessel walls causing restricted blood flow.

cancer a disease of the cells, characterized by change in cell appearance and uncontrolled growth and spread of malignant cells.

cardiovascular disease disease that involves the heart and the blood vessels.

carriers individuals who harbor an infectious disease yet who show no overt signs or symptoms of the disease.

chain of infection the six-stage process in which an infectious or communicable disease is spread from one host to a susceptible new host.

chronic disease includes a large number of usually unrelated conditions that are long-lasting and generally permanent.

clinical case an individual infected with a given communicable disease.

communicable disease a category of diseases caused by pathogens that can be transmitted directly from person to person or indirectly through an animal or the environment.

direct transmission immediate spread of infection from a case or carrier to a new susceptible host; usually occurs through contact or droplet spread.

health promotion activities public health activities that focus on improving the quality of life and well-being, not merely on averting pathology.

hypertension elevated or high blood pressure.

indirect mode disease spread that is accomplished through either a living or nonliving intermediate host.

isolation public health control measure in which an infected person is prevented from coming into contact with nondiseased persons.

malignant cancerous.

metastasis the spread of cancerous cells from their place of origin to other parts of the body to establish new colonies.

obesity excessive overweight, 20 percent or more above desirable weight range.

passive immunity natural passive immunity is obtained through transplacental transfer of immunity to specific diseases from mother to newborn; also exists when antibodies produced in one person are introduced into an exposed or susceptible person.

pathogen disease-producing organism.

portal of exit the way in which a pathogen leaves its host, through a natural or artificial body opening.

primary prevention chronic disease control measures which attempt to alter susceptibility of an individual or reduce exposure of susceptible persons to known risk-factors.

psychobehavioral disease a category of health problems and diseases which are a result of disturbances in the mind or are characterized by destructive behavior; related to the society in which one lives.

quarantine public health control measure in which persons suspected to have been exposed to a disease are restricted until lab tests determine whether or not the person is infected.

remission the temporary disappearance of cancer symptoms.

reservoir the normal habitat in which a pathogen or infectious agent lives and multiplies.

risk-factors factors that precede chronic disease development and that are highly correlated with the disease; causative factors.

secondary prevention chronic disease control measures related to early detection and treatment, designed to slow disease progression and reduce complications.

serum cholesterol a fatty substance manufac-

tured by the body and present in certain animal foods and products.

specific protection activities activities and measures that aim to avoid the onset of mental illness.

stroke (cerebrovascular accident; CVA) a disease in which part of the brain receives insufficient blood; also called apoplexy.

tertiary prevention chronic disease control measures that attempt to reduce further deterioration or disability from chronic disease and to restore functioning.

triglycerides fat particles that are stored in the body that provide means for fat to be transported in the blood.

"Type-A" personality competitive, hard-driving individual with a great sense of time urgency; personality type is correlated with heart disease.

BIBLIOGRAPHY

Anthony, Nicholas and others, "Immunization: Public Health Programming through Law Enforcement," *American Journal of Public Health,* 67(8) 763-764, 1977.

Austin, Donald and Benson Werner, *Epidemiology for the Health Sciences.* Springfield, Ill.: Charles C Thomas, 1977.

Bachman, Jerals, Lloyd Johnston, and Patrick O'Malley, "Smoking, Drinking, and Drug Use Among American High School Students: Correlates and Trends, 1975-1979," *American Journal of Public Health,* 71(1) 59-69, 1981.

Berkson, David and others, "Changing Trends in Hypertension Detection and Control: The Chicago Experience," *American Journal of Public Health,* 70(4) 389-393, 1980.

Berenson, Abram (ed.), *Control of Communicable Diseases in Man.* Washington, D.C.: American Public Health Association, 1975.

Boyd, William and Huntington Sheldon, *Introduction to the Study of Disease,* 8th ed. Philadelphia: Lea & Febiger, 1980.

Fox, John, Carrie Hall, and Lila Elveback, *Epidemiology: Man and Disease.* New York: Macmillan, 1972.

Jones, Harden and Helen Jones, *Sensual Drugs: Deprivation and Rehabilitation of the Mind.* New York: Cambridge University Press, 1977.

Kagey, Robert, Joyce Vivace, and Walter Lutz, "Mental Health Primary Prevention: The Role of Parent Mutual Support Groups," *American Journal of Public Health,* 71(2) 166-167, 1981.

Lieberman, James (ed.), *Mental Health: The Public Health Challenge.* Washington, D.C.: American Public Health Association, 1977.

Marshall, Carter, *Dynamics of Health and Disease.* Englewood Cliffs, N.J.: Prentice-Hall, 1972.

Mausner, Judith and Anita Bahn, *Epidemiology: An Introductory Text.* Philadelphia: W. B. Saunders, 1974.

Principles of Epidemiology, Homestudy Course 3030G. Atlanta: Center for Disease Control, 1978.

Rouche, B., *Annals of Epidemiology.* Boston, Mass.: Little, Brown, 1967.

Sinnecker, Herbert, *General Epidemiology.* New York: John Wiley, 1977.

U.S. DHEW, *Health: United States, 1976–1977: Chartbook.* Washington, D.C.: U.S. DHEW Pub. No. (HRA) 77-1233.

———, *Health in American 1776–1976.* Washington, D.C.: U.S. DHEW Pub. No. (HRA) 76-616.

6

THE ENVIRONMENT AND COMMUNITY HEALTH

There is no way for society to avoid paying for pollution. If we do not pay for prevention, we pay in other ways in lost recreational uses of rivers and beaches, in higher treatment costs for drinking water, in damage to crops, forests and buildings and, most importantly, through higher medical bills, time lost because of illness, human suffering and premature deaths.

Russell E. Train, former Administrator,
U.S. Environmental Protection Agency

TECHNOLOGY, THE ENVIRONMENT, AND HEALTH

In the United States, a philosophy has emerged that equates quantity with quality of life and progress. Since the Industrial Revolution, the *Gross National Product (GNP)* has increased each year—but so has the intensity of the environmental crisis. All segments of society are becoming increasingly aware of the environmental problems that have come about as a by-product of technological progress. All Americans live in danger—of polluted air that is breathed, poisonous pesticides in the food that is consumed, and contaminated drinking water supplies. Americans have begun to realize that natural resources including air, water, oil, and minerals cannot continue to be wasted or indiscriminately used without increasing the likelihood of causing potential harm to generations in the future. Some even suggest that survival of the human species will require that humans learn to coexist with nature, rather than dominate it.

In 1970, environmental concern reached its historical peak in the form of what became known as *Earth Day*. On Earth Day, people throughout the U.S. spoke out and showed their concern about deteriorating environmental conditions and their support for restoring a balance with nature. This important event in the movement to bring an end to indiscriminate use of resources also was significant to community health because it emphasized the health hazards of a polluted environment.

In the early history of public health in the United States, environmental sanitation was a prime concern. And, the tremendous progress that has been achieved in terms of increased life expectancy and reduced infant and early-childhood mortality rates in the United States is largely a result of energetic public health sanitation measures. Today, environmental health has evolved into a diverse field as technological advances, and increased population have intensified the work that must be accomplished by those whose responsibility it is to "ensure a safe living environment."

Contemporary community health must concern itself not only with providing safe and wholesome food that is not contaminated by rodents or other vectors which may carry disease, but also with setting allowable limits on pesticide residue on food products. Modern foods are largely processed with preservatives and additives. These precooked, instant processed foods constitute an added responsibility for community health professionals, who have traditionally encountered problems associated with improper food-handling practices that could spread food-borne diseases.

In the past, community health concern in the area of providing a safe water supply was largely a question of establishing and enforcing health codes related to septic tank location, well depth, and limits for contaminated *organic wastes* in drinking-water supplies following sewage treatment. Today, the preservation of water quality is a national concern. One major problem is the handling of *inorganic chemicals* added to water supplies that cannot be broken down by waste-water treatment processes (see Figure 6-1). Every day, millions of tons of chemicals and detergents are pumped into U.S. lakes, streams, and rivers. These are the waste products of industrial agricultural processes. And, the entire nation faces the question of whether or not there will be enough water to supply the ever-increasing needs of Americans fifty years from now. One can hardly wonder what our drinking-water supply and recreational water facilities will be like in the future if current trends continue.

In the past, community health was not concerned with air quality per se. Today and in the future, the provision of a safe air supply has become a real challenge that faces the community health field. Because of air pollution, we live in danger of becoming ill. If pre-existing conditions are present, such as emphysema or heart disease, we run the risk of premature death as a result of breathing polluted, poisonous air. The experience in

Figure 6-1 Inorganic chemicals in community water supplies cannot be broken down.

Donora, Pennsylvania in 1948, in which 20 people died and 6,000 people fell ill during a major air-pollution disaster lends credence to this concern. A similar smog resulting from *thermal inversion* (see Figure 6-2) occurred in London in 1952. During this episode, 4,000 deaths were directly attributable to the London smog. No one knows when the next air-pollution disaster will come.

Identifying ways in which *solid wastes* can be disposed of in a healthful way has been a traditional concern of community health. At present, the concern includes not only the design and maintenance of sanitary landfills to manage solid wastes and the development and management of sophisticated incinerators for these purposes, but also finding enough space for establishing these facilities. As the United States has become

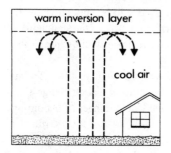

Figure 6-2 Thermal inversion.

136

more urbanized, as its population has grown, and as its people have become a "disposable" society, the enormity of the solid-waste problem increases. The consequence of this phenomenon is that we no longer have the space needed to manage demands efficiently.

The public health field has expanded its involvement in fostering environmental quality and sanitation in order to promote health in the United States. It now must manage its traditional responsibilities of disease prevention and control by energetically attacking the sources of food-borne, water-borne, and milk-borne disease. In addition, it must now manage the problems of air pollution from power generation, auto emissions, and industrial processes; the purification of waste water containing inorganic chemicals; radiological and nuclear hazards posed by both natural and human-made sources; and the assaults waged by noise on humans in both industry and urban life. Whereas the environmental priority of public health in the past was largely a question of disease prevention through sanitation and control, today it has come to mean disease control as well as improvement in the quality of life for people and in the future.

Ecology

Ecology is defined as the study of interactions between living things and their environment. Thus, any discussion of the environment and its relationship to health must necessarily include a brief analysis of ecology. When living organisms and the nonliving matter with which they interact are considered together, they constitute an *ecosystem*. No living thing can exist as an isolated entity. All things are dependent upon one another and the environment in which they live.

Through technological progress, humans have inadvertently disrupted the delicate nature of the ecosystem. Our industrial progress has meant, however unintentional, the exploitation and domination of nature. The result has been disruption of stability of the earth's ecological support system. An example may serve to illustrate this delicate balance and how it can be disturbed. The survival of humans is dependent upon the survival of hundreds of thousands of species of plants and animals. In the past, spraying swamps and bogs with the pesticide DDT was systematically conducted to eradicate the malaria-carrying Anopheles mosquito. Yet, in doing this, the Anopheles has become resistant to DDT. In addition, it became apparent that this pesticide was extremely persistent and could be passed through the food chain as one species of animal feeds on another (see Figure 6-3). Persistent and repeated exposures to pesticides can result in what is termed *bioaccumulation*. These chemicals can be transported great distances by air and water. Some pesticides do not break down easily, and, as a result, they remain in the environment for extended time periods. Thus, quantities of the chemicals absorbed by insects can be transferred to birds, fish, and higher animals—including humans. By the early 1970s, the average American was carrying a potentially dangerous 8 parts per million of DDT in his or her fatty tissues.

People have literally changed the structure, appearance, and balance of the earth. The *Global 2000 Report to the President* found that the world faces an urgent problem of plant and animal resources. It is estimated that by the year 2000, some 15 to 20 percent of all species on earth may be extinct, largely due to clearing or degradation of

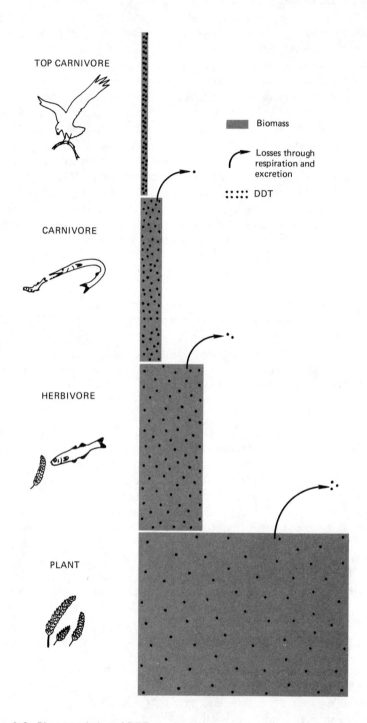

Figure 6-3 Bioaccumulation of DDT.

138

tropical forests. It is significant to note that 80 percent of the world's food supplies are derived from less than two dozen plant and animal species.

Another example of environmental alteration resulting from human activities is the tragic story of Lake Erie. All bodies of water age naturally. This process is called *eutrophication,* and is characterized by increased levels of nitrogen and decreasing levels of oxygen. In the past 50 years, Lake Erie has aged the equivalent of 15,000 years by natural processes, because industrial and agricultural dumping have accelerated the aging of this previously beautiful body of water. The lake had been known for its good fishing, swimming, and high-quality water. Now fishing in a large portion of the lake is non-existent, and swimming and recreational areas have been closed, due to contamination of the water.

The preservation of our environment and the restoration of environmental destruction has become a vital ingredient in national health programs and priorities. Community health is now challenging diseases that result from polluted air and water, contaminated food and disposable commodities, crowded and noisy living conditions, and from natural and human-made sources of radiation. Protecting the environment from further destruction is clearly a community health goal.

Pollutants in the Environment

The primary advantage of environmental quality is that it serves to promote and protect human health. In addition, environmental quality contributes to "quality of life" by providing pleasant living conditions for the people in a society. Controlling pollution is a means to maintaining ecological balance between humans and life-support systems. Yet there are many other dividends that accrue from working towards environmental quality, ranging from aesthetic to economic.

It is difficult, at best, to assess the health dangers that environmental pollution poses. Yet whether delayed or immediate, the adverse effects of environmental pollution are recognized as significant enough to merit prompt and energetic action. In some instances, the toll that pollution wages on human health remains unknown for many years. Scientists and environmentalists suggest that an accurate assessment of the dangers posed by certain pollutants such as pesticides and inorganic chemicals in drinking water may not occur for generations. Determining the adverse health effects of pollution is further complicated due to the variabilities in physical and chemical properties of a specific pollutant, duration of exposure, intensity and type of exposure, and the individual's ability to tolerate the pollutant. It is tragic that some aspects of environmental deterioration are recognized so late that correction is not always possible.

The delay period between the introduction of a pollutant as an environmental agent and the appearance of illness or other adverse health effects sometimes makes it difficult to comprehend the total impact of poor environmental quality on health and human life. This factor, along with the economic factors of controlling pollution and political considerations of setting and enforcing pollution standards, all combine to create an enormous challenge for protecting human health. Environmental pollutants do not affect all people in the same ways. Yet virtually all forms of pollution adversely affect all people in some way or another. Although it is impossible to assess the general effects of pollutants on the health of the entire population, it is reasonable to conclude that in general, they have a deleterious effect on both physical and mental health.

Environmental Protection Agency: Federal Initiative

All residents of the United States have an obligation to take part in improving the environment where pollution has reduced its quality and to preserve that which has not yet deteriorated. The community health field has a vital role to play, since the environment is so closely linked to health and disease. The federal government has provided both initiative and support for the development of environmental protection programs at regional, state, and local levels. Two federal agencies exist that assess and administer environmental programs: the Council on Environmental Quality and the Environmental Protection Agency. In addition, Congress has enacted a wide range of stringent environmental laws and most sovereign states have established departments to deal with environmental quality.

The United States Environmental Protection Agency (EPA) was created in December 1970 "to consolidate, strengthen and coordinate Federal efforts to enhance human health and well-being through environmental rehabilitation and protection."[1] The Environmental Protection Agency operates ten regional offices and four major research centers (see Figure 6-4). It is an independent regulatory agency that reports directly to the President of the United States. Since 1970, existing laws concerning pollution have been considerably strengthened and new legislation has been enacted that has provided the EPA with the means to enforce standards for environmental quality and to facilitate the accomplishment of national goals.

The Environmental Protection Agency has authority in a number of areas, including establishment of noise standards, water and environmental regulation, motor-vehicle and industrial emmissions, regulation of pesticides, and solid-waste management. The EPA sets standards and has the power to enforce these standards. State and local governments have the power to set more stringent standards if they so desire. A major responsibility of the EPA is providing local and state governments with grants for environmental programs including sewage treatment, solid waste management, and noise abatement. In addition, the EPA supports research concerned with the effects of various pollutants on human health, materials, and on controlling sources of pollution.

Another function of the EPA is monitoring programs that may effect the environment. As set forth in the National Environmental Policy Act (NEPA), all federal agencies must prepare a statement of environmental impact in advance of each major action, recommendation, or report on legislation that may significantly effect the quality of the human environment. These impact statements designed to disclose the environmental consequences of proposed action are reviewed by the Environmental Protection Agency.

At the state level, standards for air and water quality as set forth by the EPA are enforced. Since its creation, the agency has initiated a total of over 20,000 formal enforcement actions in the air, pesticides, and water-pollution program areas.

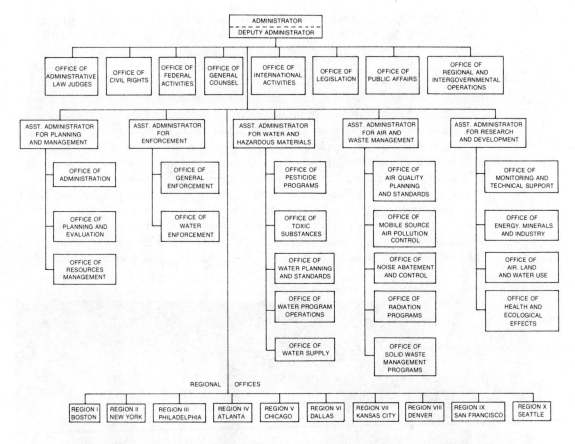

Figure 6-4 Organizational chart, Environmental Protection Agency. Courtesy United States Environmental Protection Agency, Washington, D.C.

AIR QUALITY

Air is an essential ingredient to human life, composed primarily of nitrogen and oxygen. Humans need oxygen in order to carry out essential metabolic processes that sustain life. Each day the average person breathes about 35 pounds of air. Polluted air creates a number of significant health hazards, including burning eyes and throats, irritated respiratory systems, and impaired respiratory functioning. Although air pollution began many years ago, the quality of air has rapidly deteriorated during the past twenty-five years, worldwide.

Air Pollution

The major air pollutants include (1) carbon monoxide, (2) sulfur oxides, (3) nitrogen oxides, (4) hydrocarbons, (5) particulates, and (6) photochemical smog. The

141

Environmental Protection Agency has established air-quality standards that identify maximum tolerable limits in an effort to improve the quality of air throughout the United States. The major source of air pollution is fossil-fuel combustion processes. Fossil fuels include such things as coal, natural gas, and various petroleum products (see Table 6-1).

Air pollution costs the United States over $16 billion per year. It ruins vegetation, flowers, and crops. It can rust steel and causes paint to discolor and peel. Of greater significance, it contributes to the development of respiratory diseases in human beings and premature death. There has been a significant rise in the number of deaths caused each year in the U.S. by emphysema, and air pollution contributes to its development. Air pollution and smoking are the primary causes of chronic bronchitis. And, lung cancer occurs twice as often in cities that have significantly higher air-pollution levels than in rural areas in America. A group of economists studying the cost of air pollution concluded that "more than 100,000 deaths per year can be prevented if air pollution is reduced as much as the Environmental Protection Agency projects."[2] These economists predicted that improved air quality could increase life expectancy by about one year. In addition, they suggest that, the health benefits alone that would accrue from an increase in air

Figure 6-5 Industrial towns have additional threats to human health due to air pollution. Courtesy EPA-DOCUMERICA, LeRoy Woodson.

TABLE 6-1 Air Pollution, According to Source and Type of Pollutant: United States, Selected Years 1970–1977[a]

TYPE OF POLLUTANT AND YEAR	All Sources	Transpor- tation	Stationary Fuel Combustion	Industrial Processes	Solid Waste	Other
SOURCE						
Particulate Matter	*Emissions in 10^6 Metric Tons per Year*					
1970	22.2	1.2	7.1	11.9	1.1	0.9
1972	19.6	1.2	6.4	10.6	0.7	0.7
1974	17.0	1.2	5.6	8.9	0.6	0.7
1975	13.7	1.1	5.0	6.5	0.5	0.6
1976	13.2	1.1	4.6	6.2	0.5	0.8
1977	12.4	1.1	4.8	5.4	0.4	0.7
Sulfur Oxides						
1970	29.8	0.7	22.6	6.3	0.1	0.1
1972	29.6	0.7	22.0	6.7	0.1	0.1
1974	28.4	0.7	22.1	5.6	(b)	(b)
1975	26.1	0.7	20.8	4.6	(b)	(b)
1976	27.2	0.8	21.9	4.5	(b)	(b)
1977	27.4	0.8	22.4	4.2	(b)	(b)
Nitrogen Oxides						
1970	19.6	7.4	11.1	0.6	0.3	0.2
1972	21.6	8.7	11.9	0.7	0.2	0.1
1974	21.7	8.6	12.1	0.7	0.2	0.1
1975	21.0	8.6	11.5	0.7	0.1	0.1
1976	22.8	9.4	12.4	0.7	0.1	0.1
1977	23.1	9.2	13.0	0.7	0.1	0.1
Hydrocarbons						
1970	29.5	12.2	1.5	8.6	1.7	5.5
1972	29.6	12.5	1.5	9.3	1.1	5.2
1974	28.6	11.5	1.5	9.6	0.9	5.1
1975	26.9	11.3	1.4	9.2	0.8	4.2
1976	28.7	11.6	1.5	10.1	0.8	4.7
1977	28.3	11.5	1.5	10.1	0.7	4.5
Carbon Monoxide						
1970	102.2	80.5	1.3	8.0	6.2	6.2
1972	103.8	85.4	1.3	7.9	4.0	5.2
1974	99.7	81.7	1.3	8.2	3.2	5.3
1975	96.9	82.0	1.1	7.3	2.9	3.6
1976	102.9	85.1	1.2	7.8	2.9	5.9
1977	102.7	85.7	1.2	8.3	2.6	4.9

[a]Data are based on reporting by air quality monitoring stations.

[b]Emissions of less than 50,000 metric tons per year.

Note: Because of modifications in methodology and use of more refined emission factors, data from this table should not be compared with data in *Health, United States, 1978.*

Source: Air Quality Planning and Standards Division, *National Air Quality Emission Trends Report, 1977,* EPA-450/2-78-052. Research Triangle Park, N.C.: Environmental Protection Agency, December, 1978.

quality would be \$14.5 billion per year. With the present cost of health care, the health benefits of improved air quality have profound implications for public health policies.

By 1970, over 200 million tons of waste products were being released annually into the air in the U.S. However, air quality is now showing definite signs of improvement. Since 1970, sulfur-dioxide concentrations have been reduced by roughly 30 percent. The national average for particulate matter has dropped about 17 percent. And, carbon-monoxide levels have decreased by about 10 percent. The *Global 2000* report projected that air quality in industrialized nations is likely to worsen in the future as increased amounts of fossil fuels, especially coal, are burned. Emissions of sulfur and nitrogen oxides may be particularly troubling in the future, since they combine with water vapor in the atmosphere and produce acid rain.

Air-Quality Legislation

In 1955, the first federal control act concerning air pollution in the United States was passed. It served to determine the extent of the air-pollution problem in the country. In 1963, the Clean Air Act was passed. It authorized grants to state and local agencies to assist them in their own control programs. In addition, it gave limited authority to the federal government to take the initiative in interstate air pollution abatement. This basic federal authority was strengthened and expanded with the enactment of the Air Quality Act in 1967. This act enabled individual citizens to participate actively in the control process through public hearings. In 1970, the passage of the Clean Air amendments provided even stronger legal tools for air-pollution control and greater citizen participation. Although the primary responsibility for air-pollution control lies with the states, the EPA has the authority to enforce standards when the states do not meet their responsibility.

Relatively strong federal legislation now exists that assists state and local agencies in air-quality control.

> The air quality control process provides an opportunity to bring emissions from point and mobile sources under control; to firmly establish enforcement procedures; to assist effective citizen participation in policy-making and to stimulate changes in other important aspects of society such as land-use patterns, population density, and transportation systems.[3]

Standards imposed by federal and state agencies for permissible degrees of air pollution by contaminants fall into two basic categories. *Ambient air-quality* standards specify the concentration of various pollutants permissible to exist in the lower level of the atmosphere. *Emission standards* specify what quantities of different contaminants may be released per unit of time or per unit of activity by various polluting sources.

Ambient air-quality standards in force as of 1980 in the U.S. are summarized in Table 6-2. Emission standards are presented in Table 6-3. In 1977, the amendments to the Clean Air Act were signed into law. They strengthened emission and stationary-air standards. In addition, one of the provisions of the law prohibits "significant deterio-

TABLE 6-2 National Ambient Air Quality Standards[a]

POLLUTANT	PRIMARY	SECONDARY
Particular Matter		
Annual geometric mean	75	60
Maximum 24-hour concentration[b]	260	150
Sulfur Oxides		
Annual arithmetic mean	80 (.03 ppm)	60 (.02 ppm)
Maximum 24-hour concentration[b]	365 (.14 ppm)	260 (.1 ppm)
Maximum 3-hour concentration[b]		1,300 (.5 ppm)
Carbon Monoxide		
Maximum 8-hour concentration[b]	10 (9 ppm)	
Maximum 1-hour concentration[b]	40 (35 ppm)	same as primary
Photochemical Oxidants		
Maximum 1-hour concentration[b]	160 (.08 ppm)	same as primary
Hydrocarbons		
Maximum 3-hour (6-9 am) concentration[b]	160 (.24 ppm)	same as primary
Nitrogen Oxides		
Annual arithmetic mean	100 (.05 ppm)	same as primary

[a]All measurements are expressed in micrograms per cubic meter ($\mu g/m^3$) except for those for carbon monoxide, which are expressed in milligrams per cubic meter (mg/m^3). Equivalent measurements in parts per million (ppm) are given for the gaseous pollutants.

[b]Not to be exceeded more than once a year.

Source: A Citizen's Guide to Clean Air. Washington, D.C.: Environmental Protection Agency.

ration" of the air in clean-air areas, which includes national parks and wilderness regions. The legislation allows "non-attainment" areas until 1982 to reach standards on most pollutants.

With all this: Will we get clean air and can we keep it clean? It all depends:

on appointed government officials at all levels, on their integrity and their commitment to the goals;

on elected federal and state legislators and city councilmen, on their grasp of the problem and their willingness to serve the public interest;

on society generally, the people as a whole, on their values and system of ethics and priorities, and their willingness to sacrifice certain short-term conveniences for the long-term public good.[4]

Today, the quality of our air has made a small but important reversal toward healthiness. Whether or not this trend will continue is impossible to predict, especially in view of federal budget cuts and the continuing presence of an energy crisis that shows no sign of resolution.

TABLE 6-3 Emissions of Air Pollutants in the U.S., by source (million tons/yr, 1974)

SOURCE	SULFUR OXIDES	NITROGEN OXIDES	HYDRO-CARBONS	CARBON MONOXIDE	PARTICULATES
Transportation	0.8	10.7	12.8	73.5	1.3
Stationary fuel combustion	24.3	11.0	1.7	0.9	5.9
Industrial processes	6.2	0.6	3.1	12.7	11.0
Solid waste disposal	0.0	0.1	0.6	2.4	0.5
Miscellaneous[a]	0.1	0.1	12.2	5.1	0.9
Total	31.4	22.5	30.4	94.6	19.5

[a]Includes oil and gasoline production.

Source: Environmental Protection Agency, in Council on Environmental Quality, Environmental quality, 1975, p. 440.

WATER QUALITY

In the past, the United States experienced numerous water-borne disease epidemics such as cholera, typhoid, and dysentery. Mass epidemics of such diseases have largely been eliminated due to better sewage-treatment facilities and the introduction of other public health procedures designed to provide Americans with safe drinking water. However, contaminated water still poses a threat to many Americans. And, in addition the supply of water is not limitless, and water does not have a built in protection against pollution.

Each year, with a few isolated exceptions, bodies of water in the U.S. become more polluted. A 1975 EPA survey of drinking-water supplies in eighty cities indicated that small quantities of organic chemicals were present in public water systems throughout the United States. It is suspected that some of these chemicals are cancer-producing agents, if consumed in large amounts. Between 1961 and 1973, more than 200 disease outbreaks and poisonings occurred as a result of contaminated drinking water.[5] Some EPA authorities suggest that the incidence of water-borne disease and death is probably ten times higher than reports of such incidents, but for a variety of reasons go unreported. Water-treatment plants comprise the largest financial program under the EPA, yet a recent study revealed that 50 to 87 percent of the plants are not treating water to the levels they are supposed to achieve. The problems are due to facility deficiencies such as equipment design, construction, or operation and maintenance.

Water is an indispensible resource for human beings. It is required for the maintenance of life, since the human body itself is 60 percent water. At present, each person in the U.S. uses on the average about 125 gallons of water per day. And, it is estimated that by "the year 2000 this per capita consumption will be between 300–350 gallons per day."[6] The fact that Americans will be using more water per capita daily is further complicated by the fact that population has increased, which places greater demands on a stable existing water supply.

Water is also an essential ingredient in industry and agriculture (see Table 6-4). Industrial use has increased six times since 1900. Today American industry uses over 56 billion gallons per day. Agricultural water use has also increased six times since 1900.

TABLE 6-4 Some Water Requirements

USE	AMOUNT OF WATER USED (m^3)
Drinking water (adult, daily)	0.001
Toilet (1 flush)	0.02
Clothes washer (1 load)	0.17
Refine a ton of petroleum	2–50
Produce a ton of finished steel	6–270
Grow a ton of wheat	300–500
Grow a ton of rice	1,500–2,000
Produce a ton of milk	10,000
Produce a ton of beef	20,000–50,000

Note: 1 m^3 = 1000 liters = 264 gal. Tons are metric tons (1 ton = 1000 kg).

Source: As adapted by John R. Ehrlich, Anne H. Ehrlich, and John P. Holdren in *Ecoscience: Population, Resources, Environment* (San Francisco: W. H. Freeman and Company, 1977, p. 265.)

Approximately 120 billion gallons per day are used for irrigation. Fresh-water usage of the world's water supplies is expected to increase at least 200 to 300 percent between 1975 and 2000. The bulk of this increase will be for irrigation.

In 1980, the U.S. used over 443 billion gallons of water per day for all functions. Since new water supplies cannot be created, the only practical long-range solution is reusing the same water, utilizing sewage-treatment plants to purify existing supplies.

Pollution of water supplies presents a major problem to public health. Major sources of water pollution can be found in nearly every type of industrial, municipal or agricultural operation. Thousands of chemicals are used today, many of which are toxic, and new ones are being developed for both industry and agriculture. Chemical pollutants such as nitrates, detergents, mercury, phosphates, and radioactive substances are all products of our technological society which pose serious potential threats to water supplies and, subsequently, health.

The widespread use of high-nitrate fertilizers in agriculture and extensive feedlot operations has resulted in increased contamination of both *surface water* and *ground water* supplies. The most commonly used index of water pollution is *biological oxygen demand* (BOD) which refers to the quantity of oxygen required by bacteria to oxidize organic waste aerobically to carbon dioxide and water. If ground water supplies are high in nitrates, it is virtually impossible to purify the water for human consumption. If they consume water high in nitrates, infants up to three months old are especially at risk of developing a blood disease that can be fatal if not properly treated.

Industrial waste accounts for over 50 percent of water pollution in the U.S. Some industrial wastes are toxic; others are not. Both mercury and lead pose serious threats to human health. These, along with many older chemicals represent the waste products of industrial processes.

Figure 6–6 Water treatment plant, sedimentation phase.

Sewage Treatment

Sewage discharges containing harmful bacteria and viruses contaminate water supplies when introduced back into surface waters. Even today, water-borne viruses and bacteria are responsible for outbreaks of a variety of diseases. Sewage-treatment plants are designed to improve the safety of public drinking-water supplies by removing harmful pathogens and contaminents. Sewage treatment is a process by which organic wastes are removed from water, so that the supply can be used again safely. Sewage treatment can include as many as four steps (see Figure 6–8):

1. *Preliminary Treatment* is designed to remove solids such as paper, sticks, and other objects such as metals and plastics.
2. *Primary Treatment* is a process that involves sedimentation to settle suspended solids and particles and provides an environment free of oxygen that anaerobic bacteria can consume organic matter settling to the bottom of the tank. This "anaerobic" or sedimentation phase removes about 35 percent of organic pollutants from sewage water.
3. *Secondary Treatment* is a process which involves coagulation in which small particles are joined together so they may be filtered out and provides an environment in which organic wastes come in contact with oxygen so that aerobic bac-

Figure 6-7 Computerized control board for a modern sewage treatment plant.

teria can oxidize putrescible material. This "aerobic" phase employs aerobic bacteria, air, and sunlight to oxidize and purify the water. After this phase, about 90 percent of organic pollutants have been removed.

4. *Chlorination* is designed to disinfect any remaining microorganisms, before the water is returned to the streams and rivers. Chlorine is added in small amounts.

In the United States, about 50 percent of sewage is treated in all phases and about one-third of recycled water receives chlorination before final discharge. According to the Environmental Protection Agency, eight million Americans receive impure drinking water from community water systems. An estimated thirty million additional people obtain water from wells and springs. According to a recent study of twenty-two communities with a population of greater than 100,000, only 36 percent satisfied surveillance criteria.[7]

Water-Quality Legislation

In 1948, the original Federal Water Pollution Control Act (FWPCA) was passed. This act and its various amendments are often referred to as the Clean Water Act (CWA). It provided loans for treatment plant construction and temporary authority for the fed-

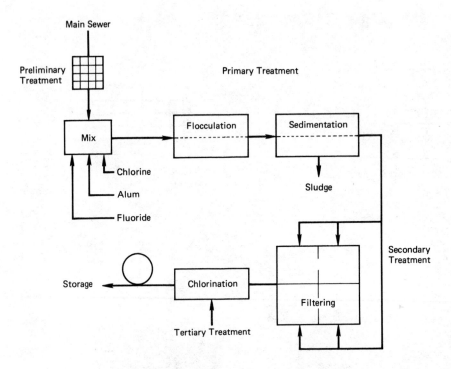

Figure 6-8 Model of water treatment. After preliminary phase, sewage goes through primary (anerobic) treatment, secondary (aerobic) treatment, and tertiary (chlorination) treatment.

eral control of interstate water pollution. The enforcement powers were so heavily dependent on the states that the Act was almost unworkable. In 1956, several amendments to the FWPCA were passed that made the federal enforcement procedures less cumbersome. The 1961 amendments also extended federal authority to include all navigable waters in the United States.

In 1965, the Water Quality Act established a new trend in water-pollution control. It provided that the states set water-quality standards in accordance with federal guidelines. If the states failed to do so, the standards would be set by HHS, subject to a review hearing. In 1966, the Clean Water Restoration Act transferred the federal Water Pollution Control Administration from the Department of Health, Education and Welfare to the Department of the Interior. It also gave Interior the responsibility for the Oil Pollution Act.

After the creation of the EPA in 1970, the present system of water-pollution control was formulated. The EPA was given the responsibility previously held by the Department of the Interior with respect to water-pollution control. In subsequent amendments to the FWPCA in 1973, 1974, 1975, 1976, and 1977, additional federal programs were established. The goals of these programs were to make waterways of the United States fishable and swimmable by 1983 and to achieve zero discharge of pollutants by

1985. The National Pollutant Discharge System was established as the basic regulatory mechanism for water-pollution control. Under this program, the states were given the authority to issue permits to "point-source" dischargers, provided the dischargers assured that the following standards would be met:[8]

1. Source-specific *effluent* limitations (including New Source Performance Standards)
2. Toxic-pollutant regulations (for specific substances regardless of source)
3. Regulations applicable to oil and hazardous-substance liability.

Water quality to be achieved by 1983   In order to achieve the stated water-quality goal of fishable and swimmable waters by 1983, each state was required by the EPA to adopt water-quality standards that meet or exceed the federal water-quality criteria. After each state submitted its own water-quality standards, which were subsequently approved by the EPA, the federal criteria were removed from the Code of Federal Regulations.

Source-based effluent limitations   Under the FWPCA, the EPA is responsible for establishing point-source effluent limitations for municipal dischargers, industrial dischargers, industrial users of municipal treatment works, and effluent limitations for toxic substances (applicable to all dischargers). Standards promulgated or proposed by the EPA prescribe effluent limitation guidelines for existing sources, standards of performance for new sources, and pretreatment standards for new and existing sources. Effluent limitations and New Source Performance Standards apply to discharges made directly into receiving bodies of water.

Toxic-pollutant effluent standards   The EPA is required to publish a list of designated toxic pollutants and is authorized to promulgate effluent standards for those pollutants. Such effluent standards take into account, among other things, the toxicity of the pollutant, its persistence, degradability, and the usual or potential presence of affected organisms. Effluent standards under this section are designed to provide "an ample margin of safety." Source categories to which such standards apply are also specified.

Safe Drinking Water Act   The Safe Drinking Water Act of 1974 amends the Public Health Service Act and is established to assure that the public is provided with safe drinking water. The Safe Drinking Water Act provides the legislative initiative under which Primary and Secondary Drinking Water Regulations are promulgated by the EPA. These regulations apply to water after treatment by all public drinking-water systems. This Act also (1) provides for the protection of underground sources of drinking water, (2) assures that there will be adequate supplies of chemicals needed to treat public water systems, and (3) establishes the National Drinking Water Advisory Council to make recommendations to the EPA about matters relating to this act. The National Drinking Water Advisory Council consists of fifteen members, appointed for three-year rotating terms.

Government involvement   Various levels of government are involved in the protection of water resources. The federal government has the following functions:

1. Provide funds to help communities build adequate sewage treatment plants
2. Provide grants to state water-pollution control programs
3. Conduct research and support research projects designed to identify better ways of purifying sewage water
4. Enforce federal laws concerned with water pollution
5. Cooperate with the states to establish and enforce water-quality standards and prevent pollution
6. Prepare long-range comprehensive programs for water-pollution control
7. Provide technical assistance to states in pollution problems.

State governments have the primary responsibility for water-pollution control. The state agency functions include:

1. Establish and administer water-quality standards
2. Collect and analyze data on water supply and pollution within the boundaries of the state
3. Offer technical assistance to communities and industries that lie within the boundaries in waste-water treatment
4. Provide funds for treatment plant construction to local communities.

It is of some significance to note that some states have formed interstate compacts to challenge regional water-pollution problems.

Local governments are vital to improving water quality and reducing water pollution. The safety and purity of public water supplies is a responsibility of the local government. At the local level the following conditions should be evident:

1. Adequate sewage system
2. Sewage treatment plant that provides secondary sewage treatment
3. Qualified and adequately trained staff to maintain the plant
4. Preplanning for new sewers and treatment plants as the community grows
5. Industries that are cooperative and responsive in controlling water pollution.

LAND QUALITY

Ours is an era of disposability—cans filled with soda pop and beer, plastic yogurt containers, cars, dolls—everything eventually gets thrown away. This has contributed to an intensifying environmental problem. Increasing amounts of solid wastes—including trash, *garbage,* and *rubbish*—are being produced each year in the United States. A mounting

Figure 6-9 Everything eventually gets thrown away, to the tune of 4.5 billion tons annually. Courtesy EPA-DOCUMERICA, Gene Daniels.

problem is the management of this result of a throw-away society. It is estimated that over 4.5 billion tons of solid wastes must be managed in the U.S. annually. Each person in the nation disposes on the average of 5 to 6 pounds of solid waste daily. Further, the volume of wastes increases year by year.

There are only three entities that can absorb and control solid wastes—the earth, bodies of water, and the atmosphere. It is obvious that if any one of these media for solid-waste disposal is misused or overused it will result in overburdening the media. Improper management of solid wastes on land creates health hazards that result both in air and water pollution. Management of solid wastes is clearly a complex environmental problem that has far-reaching public health implications. The most obvious threats to human health are posed by radioactive, poisonous, or flammable wastes. The improper disposal of wastes that are not toxic, flammable, or radioactive also have the potential for creating human health problems.

The dangers associated with improper management of solid wastes have always been a concern of community health. With a land area of 9.16 million square kilometers and a population in 1980 of around 220 million people, the U.S. has an average population density slightly less than that of the world as a whole—24 people per square kilome-

Figure 6-10 Improper management of solid wastes is a public health concern.

ter. Most of these people are concentrated in urban areas, which intensifies problems related to solid-waste management. Improperly disposed of and managed solid waste increases the likelihood of many diseases. Flies, insects, rodents, and other disease-carrying vectors thrive in open dumps and in other areas where management of *refuse* is less than acceptable. In addition, many fires begin and are spread because trash is stored improperly.

Open Dumps

Disposal of wastes is handled by a variety of procedures. Open dumps are the oldest and most traditional method of disposal. In managing solid wastes in this manner, sites are selected for the location of the dump. Waste material is brought to the site via refuse collection vehicles. No effort is made to cover the refuse. Serious health problems can result from this method of handling solid wastes. Not only do dumps endanger the aesthetic appearance of a community, but handling wastes in this manner can result in odor, dust, fires. Open dumps provide a good breeding ground for various vectors including flies, insects, rodents, and mosquitos. Clearly, open dumps as a method of handling solid wastes is less than desirable, yet approximately 82 percent of all collected solid waste in the U.S. is disposed of in this manner.[9]

TABLE 6-5 Uses of Land in the United States

USE	LAND AREA (MILLION HECTARES)	PERCENTAGE OF TOTAL
Pasture and rangeland	360	39.3
Ungrazed forest	192	20.9
Cropland	155	16.9
Desert, swamp, barren tundra (limited use)	110	12.0
Urban and transportation	27	2.9
Military	12	1.3
National wildlife refuges	12	1.3
National parks	12	1.3
Farm buildings and farm roads	11	1.2
Withdrawn from other uses by surface mining	2	0.2
Transmission-line rights of way	1	0.1
Other	24	2.6

Note: The table, which includes Alaska and Hawaii, does not include lakes and reservoirs.

Sources: United States Department of Commerce, *Statistical Abstract of the United States,* 1974, p. 600; National Commission on Materials Policy, *Material Needs and the Environment Today and Tomorrow,* Government Printing Office, Washington, D.C. 1973. As adapted by John R. Ehrlich, Anne E. Ehrlich and John P. Holdren in *Ecoscience: Population, Resources, Environment* (San Francisco: W. H. Freeman and Company) 1977, p. 252.

Sanitary Landfills

A more satisfactory procedure for the management of solid wastes is utilizing a *sanitary landfill.* This is an area selected for disposing of solid wastes that is well designed and engineered. In this method, solid wastes are dumped, compacted, and systemically covered by about 6 inches of dirt. Once the solid wastes in a given area of the landfill are covered with dirt the area is compressed by bulldozers. Compared to the open dump, the sanitary landfill has many advantages. This procedure generally minimizes the likelihood of fire and odor. In addition, well-supervised and well-designed landfills eliminate the health hazards posed by breeding insects and rodents. If properly maintained, sanitary landfills can be reclaimed to provide recreational areas, parks, and golf courses to communities.

However, the sanitary landfill is not without problems. First, the site that is to serve as the landfill must be carefully selected. Consideration must be given to such things as available soil, drainage patterns, hauling distance as well as general land confirmation. Finding suitable land for the development of sanitary landfills can be difficult, especially in large urban areas where land is expensive and demands are great. Once the site is selected, the landfill must be adequately engineered and maintained or it can become little more than an open dump. The adverse health effects and aesthetic problems that are attributed to open dumps can become problems of inadequately managed landfills. In addition, improperly managed sanitary landfills can contaminate public water supplies. The EPA reported that less than 6 percent of sanitary landfills in the U.S. meet minimum standards established by the federal government regarding engineering, operation, and area management.

Incineration

The most widely used method of refuse disposal involves burning or the incineration process. *Incineration* is expensive, both in terms of initial outlay of funds to purchase incinerators and operating costs. Incinerators cost about twice as much to manage solid wastes as do landfills. But, less land is required for the operation of incinerators and a more central location for solid-waste management can be selected. The volume of all types of refuse can be significantly reduced in bulk. Weather changes do not alter performance in incinerators. However, as a result of the cost factor, the use of incinerators is not realistic for communities with less than 55,000 people.[10]

In the future, it may be possible to generate energy from the incineration process. However, this alternate energy source has not yet been tapped. Incineration requires skill in both engineering and operation. Basically, the incineration process includes a charging mechanism, a furnace or primary chamber, a secondary chamber for combustion, and a chimney or release stack to discharge gases.

Solid-Waste Legislation

The Resource Conservation and Recovery Act (RCRA) of 1976 is the legislation that is the basis for the regulation of solid waste. It provides for the protection of the public health and welfare by supplying guidelines to protect the quality of ground water, surface water, and the ambient air from contamination by solid waste. The EPA has established that the problem of disposal of nonhazardous solid waste is primarily a state and local problem and has proposed criteria to assist the states in making regulations to assure the environmentally safe disposal of solid waste. The problem of hazardous wastes is viewed as a more severe problem and one that requires more stringent federal regulations.

In 1979, the EPA proposed criteria for the disposal of nonhazardous solid waste. The conditions enumerated in the proposal are designed to protect ground-water quality, surface-water quality, environmentally sensitive areas, air quality, food chain crops, disease vectors, and safety. According to the regulations, states are to use these standards to identify disposal facilities that need to be upgraded or closed because of the adverse effects they might have on health or the environment.

Hazardous-waste regulation The Love Canal disaster in New York made the hazardous-waste program clear to everyone. In 1979, an estimated 90 percent of hazardous wastes were being disposed of in ways that did not adequately protect public health or the environment.

The Office of Solid Waste promulgated new hazardous waste regulations in 1979

Figure 6-11
The disposal of nonhazardous solid waste is primarily a local problem.

and 1980. These regulations control hazardous waste from the point of generation through transportation, storage, and ultimate disposal of the substance determined to be hazardous. The regulations are waste-specific, rather than industry-specific. Wastes that are ignitable, corrosive, reactive, or toxic are to be considered hazardous. The EPA proposes to add radioactivity, infectiousness, phytotoxicity, teratogenicity, and mutagenicity to the list of characteristics to be considered in determining hazardous wastes.

The states are required to promulgate regulations to implement the federal guidelines for hazardous wastes. These regulations must then be approved by the EPA. However, if a state fails to make or enforce its own acceptable regulations, the responsibility for the control of hazardous waste will revert to the EPA. Working with the State and the Justice Departments, the EPA has investigated over 300 hazardous waste-disposal sites. On the grounds of noncompliance, legal actions have been initiated.

Resource Conservation and Recovery RCRA also provides for the encouragement of conservation by the recycling of many resources by municipalities and commercial establishments. The specific resources identified as suitable for recycling are paper, beverage containers, corrugated boxes, tires, and energy from solid waste. The EPA has conducted seminars for local officials to help them in establishing recycling programs for these resources. EPA grants have aided over seventy communities in planning and developing projects to recover materials and energy from municipal solid waste. By 1980, over 220 cities had programs for separate collection of recyclables. Federal procurement policy gives preference to products making the greatest use of recycled materials, provided the cost is not significantly higher than the product for which it is to be substituted.

In 1970, the Resource Recovery Act was legislated. This Act shifted emphasis from solid-waste disposal to overall problems of control, recovery, and recycling of wastes. It is generally recognized that methods of recycling wastes must be identified in order to safely and effectively reuse what is thrown away. Plastic and glass containers as well as

Figure 6-12
Recycling is profitable for both citizens and the environment.

metal containers such as aluminum are potential sources of reuse. Paper is a resource that can be recycled. At present, millions of tons of paper are recycled, but this represents only about 20 percent of the total paper used in the U.S. The EPA estimates that over seven million automobiles, trucks, and other motor vehicles are discarded each year. These vehicles represent a threat to the aesthetic environment as well as a challenge to those involved in solid-waste management who must deal constructively with literally tons of disposed of steel. Americans must begin to adopt a different philosophy regarding disposability—from discarding to reusing an item, sometimes even in a different form. Nowhere in the world is the litter problem so great as it is in America. Paper, empty cans, broken glass, and abandoned automobiles have become a part of the typical American road and park. Our throw-away society has marred the beauty of the land—of its parks, beaches, and its neighborhoods. To fight back, National Keep America Beautiful, Inc. (KAB) is one voluntary organization that citizens have established for the prevention of litter in the United States.

Clearly, proper and efficient management of over 125 million tons of solid wastes collected annually in U.S. communities is an awesome project. This figure excludes industrial, demolition, and construction wastes. The annual throw-away includes 30 million tons of paper, 4 million tons of plastics, and 55 billion beverage containers.

A variety of things can be done to improve our management of solid wastes, including:

1. Increase public awareness of the magnitude of the problem
2. Heighten public appreciation of a quality, aesthetic environment, free of litter and the appropriate behavioral considerations

3. Institute proper and adequately managed solid-waste programs in communities
4. Research creative methods of recycling solid wastes
5. Adopt better and more efficient management techniques for recycling.

In summary, it is the responsibility of community health and public and government officials to identify better methods for disposal, management, and recycling of solid wastes. In recent years, the United States has consumed roughly 190 million tons of paper, major metals, glass, textiles, and rubber annually. Of the 190 million tons, roughly 48 million tons—about one-fourth—were acquired through recycling programs. Unfortunately, reuse requires that the wastes be separated into basic categories such as paper, iron and steel, aluminum, and glass. Once separated, the wastes are purified and processed to make them suitable for reuse in manufacturing.[11] Today, resource recovery is still in its infancy. However, this approach may be the only answer to the critical problems of solid-waste management in the future.

NOISE

Of all the forms of pollution, noise has been perhaps the least understood. Noise has been traditionally viewed as an inevitable by-product of technological advancement. Most people have accepted increasing noise levels in their communities believing that they have more or less adapted to the unwanted sounds. However, recent research indicates that whether or not an individual perceives noise as a stressor, it is a stimulus which detracts from health as well as quality of life. And, exposure to noise elicits the typical stress response in humans.

It is well documented that continued exposure to high levels of noise can result in permanent hearing loss. This is true for workers exposed to high levels of noise in industry, for rock-and-roll musicians, and for aircraft mechanics. In fact, some sixteen million Americans suffer hearing loss as a result of noise exposure.[12] Too much noise for long periods of time and certain types of noise for even short periods of time can cause hearing loss. Exposure to noise can result in decreased work efficiency, can contribute to accidents, and can detract from learning ability. Noise is a significant health-threatening environmental stressor in modern society.

In addition to the physiological consequences of noise exposure, the psychological ramifications of noise pollution represent a serious community health concern. Noise is more than an annoyance. It has been implicated in higher mental hospital admission rates, irritability, and homicidal crimes. Aside from the outdoor noise of jackhammers, heavy equipment, traffic, and construction, most of our homes are replete with noise sources, including the televisions, stereos, garbage disposals, trash compactors, vacuum cleaners, and power lawnmowers that are a part of American life. Not only does noise disturb sleep and interrupt conversations, it interferes with concentration, and can create stress reactions which have been implicated in the development of such disorders as colitis, heart disease, and gastroenteritis. Dr. Aram Glorig, a noted researcher on the effects of noise on humans, coined the term *sociocussis* to describe the hearing loss which occurs

Figure 6-13
Noise is an everpresent stressor in modern society. Courtesy EPA-DOCUMERICA, Erik Calonius.

in people who live in modern noisy technological societies.[13] In today's mechanized, industrial world almost everybody may be exposed to excessive noise at home, at work, and at play.

Noise Legislation

In 1968, the federal government passed the Aircraft Noise Abatement Act. This Act was an amendment to the Federal Aviation Act and was the first governmental effort designed to deal with the hazards associated with noise. It is under the Noise Control Act of 1972 that the regulations on noise are promulgated (see Table 6-6). It specifies that noise limitations be set for major noise sources in the following categories:

1. construction equipment
2. transportation equipment (airplanes, railroads, and trucks)

TABLE 6-6 Noise Regulations Promulgated or Proposed

NOISE SOURCE	NOISE LEVEL IN dBA	DATE EFFECTIVE
Locomotive		
Stationary		
In gear	87	12/31/76
Idle	70	
Moving	90	
Railroad car		
Under 72 km/hr	88	12/31/76
Over 72 km/hr	92	12/31/76
Motor carriers in interstate commerce		
Under	86	10/15/75
Over	90	
Full-throttle stationary	88	
Medium and heavy trucks	83	1/1/78
	80	1/1/82
Exemptions for fire trucks and mobile homes		
Portable air compressors		
< 250 ft^3/min	76	1/1/78
> 250 ft^3/min	76	7/1/78
Crawler tractors[a]		
20–199 HP[b]	77	3/1/81
	74	1984
20–450 HP	83	1981
	80	1984
Wheel loaders[a]		
20–249 HP	79	1981
	76	1984
250–500 HP	84	1981
	80	1984
Wheel tractors[a]		
20+ HP	74	3/1/81
New truck-mounted solid-waste compactors[a]	78	1/1/79
	75	1982
Exterior bus noise[a]	83	1/1/79
	80	1983
	77	1985
Interior bus noise[a]	86	1979
	83	1983
	80	1985
Street motorcycles[a]	83	1/1/80
	80	1982
	78	1985

TABLE 6–6 *(cont.)* Noise Regulations Promulgated or Proposed

NOISE SOURCE	NOISE LEVEL IN dBA	DATE EFFECTIVE
Moped-type[a]	70	1980
Offroad above 170 cc[a]	83	1980
	80	1982
	78	1985
Offroad above 170 cc[a]	86	1980
	82	1983

[a]Proposed.

[b]HP = horsepower

Source: U.S. Environmental Protection Agency.

3. any motor or engine
4. electrical or electronic equipment.

The Act encourages the development of low-noise emission products by providing that they will have priority in government procurement policies provided their cost does not exceed 125 percent of the cost of the least-expensive product for which they would substitute. Regulations limiting noise levels (in dBA) emitted from a variety of sources have been promulgated.

Originally, the problem of noise control was addressed by the Noise Pollution and Abatement Act of 1970. This act which was a section of the Clean Air Act directed the EPA to investigate and classify the major causes and sources of noise and to determine its effect on humans and the environment. The Noise Control Act of 1972 was the result of this study. This Act authorized broad federal programs to coordinate noise research and control activities as well as to establish noise standards and improve public information. It is designed to eliminate noises at their source and to stimulate the use of noise-control technology.

The Environmental Protection Agency's Noise Enforcement Division is responsible for the development and subsequent implementation of enforcement regulations that are necessary to ensure compliance with the new products standards and labeling requirements. For example, the first level of truck noise-emission standards became effective in January 1978. In addition, this Division provides assistance to states and communities to develop and implement noise-enforcement programs. This is an important process since the 1972 Noise Control Abatement Act places major responsibility for noise control with state and local governments. The EPA has published a Model Community Noise Ordinance and workbook to assist the states and communities in noise abatement and reduction efforts. In summary, the EPA is responsible for:

1. Developing and publishing information on limits of noise that will protect public health and welfare

2. Identifying products that are major sources of noise and providing information on how to control noise from such products

3. Setting standards for noise emissions for construction equipment and all motors, engines, and electrical-electronic equipment

4. Working with the Federal Aviation Administration, will propose standards for aircraft noise, which the FAA will enforce.

Noise Control

In the past decade, the number of local noise-control ordinances has increased dramatically. Today, more than 50 percent of the U.S. municipal population lives in localities having some degree of noise legislation.

There are many sources of noise that are of public health concern at the local level, including (1) aircraft and airport noise, (2) motor vehicle or traffic-related noise, (3) industrial noise, and (4) railway-transit noise. In communities, two types of public health laws are used to control urban noise-nuisance laws and performance zoning codes. *Nuisance laws* are intended to restrict annoying or unpleasant noise sources which are neither measured nor controlled by physical means. *Performance zoning codes* specify maximum allowable limits for noise emitted from various sources or activities. These laws are designed to promote community safety, health, and general welfare while conserving property values and encouraging appropriate land use.[14]

At the federal level, the EPA's Office of Noise Abatement and Control operates a Noise Enforcement Facility (NEF) in Sandusky, Ohio. This facility, dedicated in 1976, is used to conduct enforcement testing, to monitor manufacturers' compliance testing, and to train regional, state, and local enforcement personnel as well as to monitor the effectiveness of federal noise enforcement programs. The Environmental Protection Agency is using its overall authority to achieve a significant reduction in the adverse health and welfare effects of environmental noise. However, in many areas, reducing noise will mean replacement of old equipment with new, quieter products required by EPA regulations.

In order to solve the noise-pollution problem in the United States, stringent noise abatement standards will need to be imposed from the federal level down to the local level. All facets of society—government agencies, industry, and individual citizens—will need to cooperate in creating a quieter, more healthful country. As is true with many other community health activities, prevention is the best and most viable solution to overcoming noise pollution. The best method of reducing community noise levels is altering the facilities processes and equipment that serve as the source of noise. Noise-pollution control is an extremely complicated endeavor. All segments of society—private, industrial, governmental and technical—will need to assume greater responsibility if noise-abatement is to be realized in our communities.

PESTICIDES

In contrast to most other pollutants present in the environment, *pesticides* are deliberately introduced as agents designed to perform many beneficial functions. Pesticides, fungicides, and herbicides have been used successfully to prevent certain vector-borne and insect-borne diseases, to control insect pests, and to increase the quantity and quality of certain foods. However, widespread pesticide use has resulted in serious potential threats to human health as well as environmental problems. Pesticide residues have been found in human tissue and other life forms, and in food, clothing, air, and water.

Recent evidence suggests that the unintentional effects of pesticide use pose a threat to human health so significant that future use of these substances will need to be considered in the context of potential risks as well as benefits. It is presently known that many pesticides at various exposure levels will cause illness. Some highly toxic chemicals can contribute to serious illness in humans and even death. Clearly, there is tremendous variability in the potential for adverse side effects in different pesticides. And, reactions to pesticide exposure among individuals vary greatly. However, each year in the United States, a number of people die and larger numbers experience serious illness as a result of pesticide poisoning. Pesticides can damage the central nervous system, the respiratory system, as well as the digestive system. They have the potential for damaging the skin, eyes, and mucous membranes. Many of the acute health problems associated with pesticides result from individual carelessness in pesticide use, including improper application of the chemicals because of failure to follow instructions. In addition, run-off from farm-

Figure 6-14 In contrast to other pollutants, pesticides are deliberately introduced into the environment to perform many functions. Courtesy EPA-DOCUMERICA, Charles O'Rear.

TABLE 6-7 Pesticides to be Considered for Restricted Classification

Carbofuran	Fenthion
Carbon disulfide	Fonofos
Chlorfenvinphos	Formaldehyde
Chloropicrin	Hexachlorobenzene
Clonitralid	Methamidophos
Cyclohexamide	Methidathion
Dicrotophos	Monocrotophos
Dimethoate	Nicotine (alkaloid)
Dioxathion	O,O-bis (p-chlorophenyl)
Diquat	acetimidoylphosphoramidothioate
Disulfoton	Oxamyl
Endosulfan	Oxydemeton methyl
Endothall	Phorate
EPN	Phosphamidon
Ethoprop	Phosphorus
Ethyl 3-methyl-4-(methylthio) phenyl	Temephos
(1-methyl-ethyl) phosophoramidate	Terbufos
Ethylene dibromide	Toxaphene
Ethylene dichloride	Xylene (aquatic uses)
Fensulfothion	Zinc phosphide

Source: U.S. Environmental Protection Agency.

lands carrying toxic pesticides into most waterways is an increasingly difficult health problem to solve. Proponents of organic farming suggest that *biological controls* can be used as a substitute for chemical pesticides. This, in fact would reduce chemical pollution and contamination of drinking water. However, many scientists predict that food production would decline sharply if manures were used instead of chemical fertilizers, and biological controls used in lieu of pesticides. The federal pesticide law authorizes the EPA to help promote the development and use of these biological controls. A number of these agents have already received EPA approval for either regular or experimental use.

Although research has generally provided information about the immediate hazards of pesticide exposure, little is known about the long-range effects of pesticides on human health. This is particularly significant since people are now increasingly exposed to pesticides since their use is more widespread. Pesticides possess several characteristics that contribute to increased human exposure. Persistent and repeated exposures to pesticides can result in what is termed bioaccumulation. Ironically, the widespread use of pesticides to control various insects and pests has resulted in increased levels of immunity or resistance of a variety of pests. Some pests are thriving again in spite of widespread use of the pesticides designed to control them.

Pesticide Legislation

The hazards and risks of pesticide use have increased in recent years as people have begun to use them more widely. Not only has their use become more widespread in agriculture, but individuals have also begun to use these products routinely to help plants grow, to disinfect houses, and to eliminate unwanted insects and animal pests. In 1972, Congress acted on the growing problems associated with pesticide use by amending the Federal Insecticide, Fungicide, and Rodenticide Act (FIFRA) of 1947.

According to this Act, a pesticide is any substance intended for preventing, destroying, repelling, or mitigating any pest. A pest is defined as any insect, rodent, nematode, fungus, weed, or any other form of terrestrial or aquatic plant or animal life or virus, bacterial organism, or other microorganism (except viruses, bacteria, or other microorganisms on or living in man or other living animals) that is declared by the EPA as injurious to health and environment. All pesticides meeting this definition must be registered with the EPA. Registration is for a limited period of five years. Registered pesticides are classified for either general or restricted use. Certain chemicals may be further restricted in that they must be applied either by or under the direct supervision of a certified applicator. All pesticides must be labeled clearly to specify ingredients, uses, warnings, registration number, and any use restrictions. There are also regulations specifying tolerance levels for certain pesticide chemicals in or on agricultural commodities.

The amendment substantially strengthened the federal government's control to actual application of pesticides by the user and regulation of both intrastate and interstate marketing of pesticide products. As a result of this legislation, all pesticides sold in the United States are registered by the Environmental Protection Agency and must carry an EPA regulation number on the label indicating that the product is safe and effective when used according to the label directions. Today over 34,000 pesticide products are registered by the EPA. Older products may have U.S. Department of Agriculture (USDA) numbers on the label.

The 1972 and 1975 Amendments to the FIFRA gave broad responsibilities to the EPA to protect humans and the environment from the adverse effects of pesticides.[15] The Environmental Protection Agency's objective in pesticide regulation is "to promote an economically and environmentally sound agriculture."[16] Since 1979, the EPA has been reviewing new chemical substances before they are manufactured for commercial purposes to evaluate any risks they may pose to human health or to the environment.

The Environment Protection Agency has initiated efforts to strenghten cooperation between the federal and state authorities. Federal training grants are made available to the states to improve their effectiveness in pesticide regulatory activities. It is hoped that this will improve the quality of the national pesticides enforcement program.

Pesticide Control

Pesticide-enforcement responsibilities of the federal government have increased significantly since the consolidation within the EPA of all federal pesticide regulatory functions. Current national efforts include:

1. Determining pesticide-use patterns most advantageous to humans and the environment
2. Determining the effects of prolonged exposure to low-level doses of pesticides
3. Regulating and controlling selection, use, transportation, and storage of pesti-

cides, and disposal of pesticide wastes, to minimize or eliminate direct effects of humans or indirect pollution of the environment

4. Creating a knowledgeable public, who as consumers will be aware of the use of proper methods for handling, storing, using, and disposing of pesticides.[17]

It is certain that some method of pest control will be needed in the future, for without this there is no viable method of controlling vector-borne disease or of providing an adequate food supply to a growing world population.

RADIATION

Radiation is both beneficial to health and health-endangering. There are many beneficial uses of radiation, including the application of x-rays and radioactive isotopes in medical-dental diagnosis and treatment, use of radioisotopes and lasers in industry for measuring, testing, and processing goods; and electric-power generation and microwave cooking.

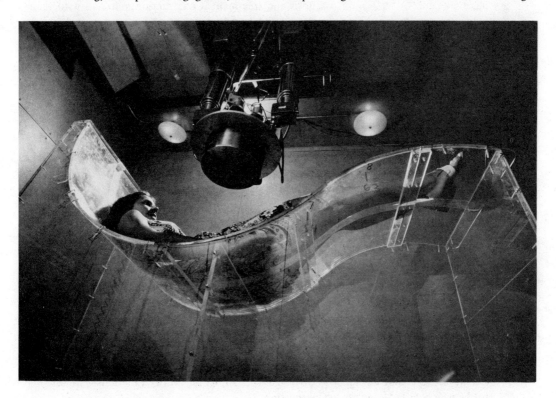

Figure 6-15 Although most of the sources of man-made radiation provide some benefit to humans, we must continually evaluate the risks versus benefits of any radiation we add to the environment. Courtesy EPA-DOCUMERICA, Charles O'Rear.

However, radiation also has the potential for threatening human health. The principal adverse health effects of radiation include genetic disturbances, fertility impairment, acceleration of the aging process, and cancer production. These damaging effects of radiation on some body tissues and organs have been recognized for many years. The blood-forming organs, the thyroid gland, bone marrow, the breast, and the respiratory and reproductive organs are particularly vulnerable to irradiation.

There are two basic types of radiation to which humans are exposed. *Natural background radiation* refers to that which is emitted from natural sources such as air, sunlight, soil, stars, and water. On the average, people receive between .08 to .15 *rads* per year. The second category of radiation is *man-made radiation,* which at present is primarily the result of medical and dental x-rays, scanners, and so forth. Other sources of man-made radiation include fall-out from nuclear weapons testing, uranium mining, nuclear-power generating and fuel reprocessing, and various electronic devices including microwave ovens. Many health experts view the increasing amounts of man-made radiation as a serious health concern.

Many U.S. hospitals and laboratories routinely use radioactive isotopes in basic research as well as in diagnosis and treatment. Construction materials with radioactive properties have been used to build homes, schools, and factories. In buildings constructed of these materials, radioactive gases seep and accumulate in ambient air. The increased use of nuclear reactors for the production of energy has created an additional public health concern. Stringent government regulations govern the testing of atomic weapons and nuclear devices, since these threaten the population with radioactive elements through fall-out.

Although humans are exposed to a variety of sources of both natural and man-made radiation, the level of exposure has remained quite low. The average level of natural radiation to which people are exposed on an annual basis is between 100 and 250 millirems per year.[18]

Radiation Legislation

Since World War II, several agencies have been responsible for various aspects of the regulations, use, and effects of radioactivity. Advisory agencies whose recommendations are recognized by the various agencies include the National Council on Radiation Protection and Measurements (NCRPM), the International Commission on Radiological Protection (ICRP), the Department of Energy (DOE), and the American National Standards Institution (ANSI).

The Atomic Energy Act of 1954 established the basis for the regulation of radiation. It created the Atomic Energy Commission, the Federal Radiation Council, and the Bureau of Radiological Health. With the creation of the Environmental Protection Agency, the FRC was dissolved, and its functions were assigned to the EPA. When the Atomic Energy Commission was dissolved in 1975, its regulatory functions were assigned to the new Nuclear Regulatory Commission.

Since the Atomic Energy Act was written, regulations and recommendations addressing radiation have proliferated to a confusing degree. In 1977, the Committee on Energy and the Environment of the National Academy of Sciences wrote that

> . . . . the regulations are unnecessarily fragmented because of overlaps among regulatory agencies. Some overlap of responsibility may be unavoidable, but regulations should still be better coordinated so as to be reasonably consistent and free of confusing duplications.[19]

There are three major sets of regulations dealing with radiation protection. These regulations and recommendations are set forth in documents. Each of these documents deals with a set of issues related to protection from radiation exposure.

Standards for Protection Against Radiation   Comprehensive standards for protection against radiation were adopted in 1960 to control radiation-exposure levels for a wide variety of operations. Since the Act was set forth by the now-defunct Atomic Energy Commission, its provisions are currently governed by the Nuclear Regulatory Commission. The regulations address both restricted and nonrestricted areas and prescribe limiting dosages to individuals as well as concentrations allowable in air and water.

Other issues regulated by the Standards for Protection Against Radiation include medical treatments (no limits are placed on exposures of patient for diagnosis or therapy), bioassay services, personnel monitoring, caution signs and labels for radioactive materials and radiation areas, instruction of personnel, record-keeping and reports on personnel monitoring, loss or theft of material, incidents involving overexposure or property damage, and dosages received by present and former employees; applications for exemptions; and enforcement.

Environmental radiation protection standards for nuclear power operations   These EPA standards set limits on radiation dosage to members of the public and on release of radioactive materials into the environment, resulting from nuclear power generation with light-water reactors. Provisions mainly involve the "uranium fuel cycle," which refers to the operations of milling of uranium ore, chemical conversion of uranium, isotopic enrichment of uranium, fabrication of uranium fuel, generation of electricity by a light-water-cooled nuclear power plant using uranium fuel. The regulations are applicable to these operations to the extent that they directly support the production of electrical power for public use that employs nuclear energy. Excluded are mining operations, operations at waste-disposal sites, transportation of any radioactive material in support of these operations, and the reuse of recovered nonuranium special nuclear material and byproduct materials from the cycle. Recent EPA involvement in the area of radiation has included monitoring radiation levels in the wake of Chinese nuclear testing and assisting in the development of a radiation-monitoring program at the Three Mile Island nuclear power site.

REVIEW QUESTIONS

1. How does the "American way of life" contribute to deterioration of the environment?

2. What is meant by the term *ecology*? What are the major factors which have contributed to ecological disharmony in industrial countries?

3. What authority does the Environmental Protection Agency have in the following areas: (1) noise abatement, (2) pesticide regulation, (3) water quality, and (4) air quality.

4. Identify and describe the four phases of sewage treatment. Why should communities regulate water supplies?

5. What factors must be taken into consideration when a community selects a site for and method of solid-waste-disposal management?

6. Identify and describe the immediate and potential long-term health hazards of the following pollutants: (1) noise, (2) pesticides, and (3) radiation.

SUGGESTED READINGS

Carson, Rachel, *Silent Spring.* Boston: Houghton Mifflin, 1962.

Fitzpatrick, Malcom, *Environmental Health Planning.* Boston, Mass.: Ballinger, 1978.

Hinkle, Lawrence E. and William C. Loring (eds.), *Effect of Man-Made Environment on Health and Behavior,* U.S. DHEW Pub. No. (CDC) 77-8318. Atlanta: Center for Disease Control, 1977.

——, "Annual Environmental Quality Index," *National Wildlife,* January 1978, 16 pp.

U.S. Environmental Protection Agency, *In Productive Harmony,* Office of Public Affairs (A-107). Washington, D.C.: Environment Protection Agency, 1974.

Olson, McKinely C., *Unacceptable Risk: The Nuclear Power Controversy.* New York: Bantam Books, 1976.

Train, Russell E. and Stanley W. Legro, *EPA Enforcement: A Progress Report, 1976,* U.S. Environmental Protection Agency (EN-329). Washington, D.C.: Environmental Protection Agency, 1977.

NOTES

[1] The Environmental Protection Agency Act of 1970, *United States Statutes at Large,* 91st Congress, 2nd Session, 1970-1971. Vol 84, pt 2, pp. 2086-2089.

[2] *The Nation's Health.* Washington, D.C.: American Public Health Association, April 1976, p. 4.

[3] "Enforcement: A Progress Report." Washington, D.C.: Environmental Protection Agency, 1977, p. 8.

[4]*A Citizen's Guide to Clean Air.* Washington, D.C.: The Conservation Foundation, 1972, p. 79.

[5]"Pollution and Your Health," Washington, D.C.: Environmental Protection Agency, 1976, p. 8.

[6]J.W. MacNeill, *Environment Management: Constitutional Study Prepared for the Government of Canada.* Ottawa: Information Canada, 1971, p. 100. Reproduced by permission of the Minister of Supply and Services Canada.

[7]EPA, "A Drop to Drink: A Report on the Quality of Drinking Water." Washington, D.C.: Environmental Protection Agency, 1973, pp. 2-8.

[8]"Enforcement: A Progress Report," pp. 83-84.

[9]"Solid Waste—It Won't Go Away." Washington, D.C.: League of Women Voters, 1971, p. 5.

[10]J.W. MacNeill, p. 98.

[11]"Solid Waste Management: Recycling and the Consumer." Washington, D.C.: Environmental Protection Agency, 1974, p. 2.

[12]"Pollution and Your Health," p. 12.

[13]Aram Glorig, *Noise and Your Ear.* New York: Grune & Stratton, 1958, p. 28.

[14]Brent Hafen, *Man, Health and Environment.* Minneapolis: Burgess, 1972, p. 113.

[15]"Enforcement: A Progress Report," p. 48.

[16]*Southeast Farm Press,* Wednesday, November 23, 1977, p. 1.

[17]Brent Hafen, pp. 164-165.

[18]Paul R. Ehrlich, Anne H. Ehrlich, and John P. Holdren, *Ecoscience: Population, Resources, Environment.* San Francisco: W.H. Freeman, 1977, p. 583.

[19]National Academy of Sciences, The Committee on Energy and the Environment, 1977.

GLOSSARY

ambient air-quality specify the concentration of various pollutants permissible to exist in the lower level of the atmosphere.

bioaccumulation or biological magnification; refers to the phenomenon in which certain biocides are highly soluble in fatty tissue and will accumulate in cells in higher concentrations up the food chain, ending in humans.

biological controls techniques for controlling insects and pests which do not utilize hazardous chemicals and pesticides.

biological oxygen demand (BOD) the quantity of oxygen required by bacteria to oxidize organic waste aerobically to carbon dioxide and water.

Earth Day In 1970, activities were undertaken throughout the U.S. to verbalize and symbolize concern about deteriorating envrionmental

conditions and to urge support for restoring balance with nature.

ecology the study of interactions between living things and their environment.

ecosystem the network of interactions of living organisms and nonliving matter in the environment.

effluent a contaminated discharge.

emission standards these specify what quantities of different contaminants may be released per unit of time or per unit of activity by various polluting sources.

eutrophication the natural process of aging in bodies of water.

garbage putrescible wastes resulting from the growing, handling, preparation, cooking, and consumption of food.

Gross National Product (GNP) the total market

value of all goods and services provided by a nation during a specific period.

ground water water that percolates into soil, passes through a zone of aeration to a zone of saturation, the upper surface of which is an impervious formation "under ground."

incineration the most widely used method of refuse disposal which involves high-intensity burning of solid wastes.

inorganic chemicals waste products that do not contain life nor do they arise from normal growth.

man-made radiation is primarily the result of medical and dental x-rays, and scanners.

natural background radiation radiation emitted from natural sources such as air, sunlight, soil, stars, and water.

nuisance laws enacted to restrict annoying or unpleasant noise sources that are neither measured nor controlled by physical means.

organic wastes waste products derived from living organisms.

performance zoning codes these specify maximum allowable limits for noise emitted from various sources of activities.

pesticides insecticides, fungicides, rodenticides, and herbicides, as defined in the Federal Insecticide, Fungicide, and Rodenticide Act.

rad the radiation dose absorbed in tissue itself, equal to 100 ERGs per gram.

refuse all putrescible and nonputrescible solid wastes, with the exception of body wastes. This includes garbage, rubbish, street sweepings, dead animals, and industrial wastes.

rubbish all nonputrescible wastes except ashes. This includes both combustible and noncombustible substances such as cans, paper, scrap metal and wood, and so on.

sanitary landfill an area selected for disposing of solid wastes that is well designed and engineered.

sociocussis permanent hearing loss that occurs in people who live in modern noisy technologically advanced societies.

solid wastes the generic term used to describe garbage and refuse combined as waste products, which a community must collect and dispose of.

surface water water in the form of streams, lakes, rivers, and other visible bodies of water.

thermal invasion a phenomenon that occurs when a warm air mass moves over cooler air below. The cool air is trapped, along with whatever air pollutants it contains over the areas.

BIBLIOGRAPHY

Batik, Odetee and others, "An Epidemiological Study of the Relationship Between Hepatitis A and Water Supply Characteristics and Treatment," *American Journal of Public Health,* 70(2) 167-168, 1980.

Carter, Luther, "Pollution and Public Health: Taconite Case Poses Major Test," *Science,* 186 31-36, 1974.

Curran, William, "A Constitutional Right to a Healthy Environment," *American Journal of Public Health,* 67(3) 262-264, 1977.

Ehrlich, Paul R., Anne H. Ehrlich, and John P. Holdren, *Esoscience: Population, Resources, Environment.* San Francisco: W. H. Freeman, 1977.

Environmental Quality. Washington, D.C.: Council on Environmental Quality, 1975.

Finsterbausch, Gail, *Man and Earth: Their Changing Relationship.* Indianapolis: Bobbs-Merrill, 1977.

Ibrahim, Michel A., and Russell F. Christman, "Drinking Water and Carcinogenesis: The Dilemmas," *American Journal of Public Health,* 67(8) 719-720, 1977.

Murdock, William (ed.), *Environment.* Sunderland, Mass.: Sinauer, 1975.

Quarles, John R., "National Water Quality: Assessing the Mid-Course Correction," *Sierra Club Bulletin,* February 14-17, 1977.

Wands, Ralph C., "Solid Waste Disposal—A Long-Standing Public Health Problem Comes of Age," *American Journal of Public Health,* 67(5) 419-422, 1977.

U.S. Council on Environmental Quality, *The Global 2000 Report to the President: Entering the Twenty-First Century*, Vols. I & II. Washington, D.C.: U.S. Government Printing Office, 1980.

U.S. Department of Commerce, *Annual Statistical Abstracts of the United States*. Washington, D.C.: U.S. Department of Commerce, 1977.

U.S. Environmental Protection Agency, *Effects of Noise on People*, NTID 300.7. Springfield, Va.: National Technical Information Service, 1971.

———, *The Economics of Clean Water, Summary*. Washington, D.C.: Environmental Protection Agency, 1972.

———, *Compilation of Air Pollutant Emission Factors*, 2nd ed. Washington, D.C.: Environmental Protection Agency, 1973.

———, *Solid Waste Management: Recycling and the Consumer*, (SW-117), Solid Waste Management Series, 3rd ed. Washington, D.C.: Environmental Protection Agency, 1974.

———, *Pollution and Your Health*, Office of Public Affairs (A-107), Washington, D.C.: Environmental Protection Agency, 1976.

———, *Protecting Our Environment*, Office of Public Affairs (A-107). Washington, D.C.: Environmental Protection Agency, 1977.

7

COMMUNITY AND OCCUPATIONAL SAFETY AND HEALTH

Home Safety
Motor Vehicle Safety
  Driver
  Roadway
  Vehicle
  Highway Safety
  Public Safety
  Community Safety
Occupational Safety and Health
  The Federal Law
  Employer-Employee Duties
  OSHA, NIOSH, and OSHRC
  Current Occupational Health Concerns

> . . . . from existing data, a conservative estimate would place the accident toll in the United States for the first 70 years of the century as at least 6,000,000,000 deaths, 600 million injuries, and an economic loss of well over 300 billion dollars.
>
> *The National Safety Council, 1971*

In a complex, technologically advanced society, accident prevention poses a continuing social problem. *Accidents* touch the lives of more Americans than almost any other single trauma, disease or health problem. For all age groups combined, accidents are the fourth-leading cause of death in the U.S. Every year in this country, approximately 115,000 accidental deaths are reported by the National Safety Council. This averages out to one death every five minutes. In addition, over eleven million injuries are reported every year. Accidents rank as the leading cause of death among both men and women through 38 years of age. Among children up to the age of 14, accidents claim more lives than all the five leading causes of death combined. Indeed, the human suffering and financial loss from preventable accidental death and disability constitute a serious public health challenge.

Accident prevention and environmental safety—be it in the home, at school, at the workplace, or on the road—requires constant surveillance and monitoring. The national bill derived from accidents in 1978 was $68.7 billion. This economic loss to our society includes such things as loss of wages, medical expenses, settlement costs, property damage, and so on. The human cost in suffering, lives lost, broken homes, and long disability is incalculable. A simple sequence of facts illustrates the dimensions of the accident problem. In the time it takes to deliver a ten-minute speech on safety, 2 people will die in accidents, and approximately 200 others will be disabled; the costs involved will be about $1.3 million.[1] In 1978, 104,500 people died as a result of accidents and 10.2 million *disabling injuries* were incurred. Accidents cause more deaths each year than all the infectious diseases combined (see Tables 7-1 and 7-2).

Table 7-1 Accidents and Other Leading Causes of Death, by Age and Sex

CAUSE	NUMBER OF DEATHS			DEATH RATES[a]		
	Total	Male	Female	Total	Male	Female
			All Ages			
All Causes	1,899,597	1,046,243	853,354	877.9	993.9	768.0
Heart disease	718,850	396,482	322,368	332.2	376.6	290.1
Cancer	386,686	210,459	176,227	178.7	199.9	158.6
Stroke (cerebrovascular disease)	181,934	77,351	104,583	84.1	73.5	94.1
Accidents	103,202	71,935	31,267	47.7	68.3	28.1
Motor-vehicle	49,510	35,804	13,706	22.9	34.0	12.3
Falls	13,773	7,226	6,547	6.4	6.9	5.9
Drowning	7,126	6,006	1,120	3.3	5.7	1.0
Fires, burns	6,357	3,866	2,491	2.9	3.7	2.2
Poison (solid, liquid)	3,374	2,024	1,350	1.6	1.9	1.2
Pneumonia	49,889	27,109	22,780	23.1	25.8	20.5
Diabetes mellitus	32,989	13,632	19,357	15.2	12.9	17.4
Cirrhosis of liver	30,848	20,167	10,681	14.3	19.2	9.6
Arteriosclerosis	28,754	11,648	17,106	13.3	11.1	15.4
Suicide	28,681	21,109	7,572	13.3	20.1	6.8
Homicide	19,968	15,355	4,613	9.2	14.6	4.2
Emphysema	16,376	12,594	3,782	7.6	12.0	3.4
			1 to 14 Years			
All Causes	20,886	12,620	8,266	43.1	51.0	34.8
Accidents	9,602	6,275	3,327	19.8	25.4	14.0
Motor-vehicle	4,361	2,677	1,684	9.0	10.8	7.1
Drowning	1,760	1,330	430	3.6	5.4	1.8
Fires, burns	1,158	642	516	2.4	2.6	2.2
Firearms	391	308	83	0.8	1.2	0.3
Cancer	2,364	1,407	957	4.9	5.7	4.0
Congenital anomalies	1,742	902	840	3.6	3.6	3.5
Homicide	766	421	345	1.6	1.7	1.5
Pneumonia	687	365	322	1.4	1.5	1.4
Heart disease	545	282	253	1.1	1.1	1.1
Meningitis	294	181	113	0.6	0.7	0.5
			15 to 24 Years			
All Causes	47,986	35,620	12,366	117.1	172.7	60.7
Accidents	25,619	20,101	5,518	62.5	97.5	27.1
Motor-vehicle	18,092	13,794	4,298	44.1	66.9	21.1
Drowning	2,150	1,950	200	5.2	9.5	1.0
Poison (solid, liquid)	709	505	204	1.7	2.4	1.0
Firearms	665	592	73	1.6	2.9	0.4
Suicide	5,565	4,492	1,073	13.6	21.8	5.3
Homicide	5,196	3,992	1,204	12.7	19.4	5.9
Cancer	2,672	1,665	1,007	6.5	8.1	4.9
Heart disease	1,035	646	389	2.5	3.1	1.9
			75 Years and Over			
All Causes	797,318	355,616	441,702	8,904.5	10,982.6	7,776.4
Heart disease	366,141	158,068	208,073	4,105.6	4,881.7	3,663.3
Stroke (cerebrovascular diasease)	116,753	43,075	73,678	1,309.2	1,330.3	1,297.1
Cancer	116,675	60,435	56,240	1,308.3	1,866.4	990.1
Pneumonia	30,487	14,754	15,733	341.9	455.7	277.0

Table 7-1 *(cont.)* Accidents and Other Leading Causes of Death, by Age and Sex

CAUSE	NUMBER OF DEATHS			DEATH RATES[a]		
	Total	*Male*	*Female*	*Total*	*Male*	*Female*
Arteriosclerosis	23,683	8.728	14,955	265.6	269.5	263.3
Accidents	15,175	7,023	8,152	170.2	216.9	143.5
Falls	7,762	2,980	4,782	87.0	92.0	84.2
Motor-vehicle	2,713	1,622	1,091	30.4	50.1	19.2
Surg complications	1,030	532	498	11.5	16.4	8.8
Fires, burns	1,023	503	520	11.5	15.5	9.2
Diabetes mellitus	13,993	4,732	9,261	156.9	146.1	163.0
Emphysema	6,190	4,891	1,299	69.4	151.1	22.9

[a]Deaths per 100,000 population.

Source: National Center for Health Statistics.

Figure 7-1 Safety education programs have been established in schools and in industry as part of driver education programs. Courtesy Aetna Life and Casualty.

Table 7-2 Accidental Deaths and Injuries by Type, 1978

TYPE	DEATHS	CHANGE FROM 1977	DISABLING INJURIES[b]
	104,500[a]	+1%	10,200,000[a]
Motor-Vehicle	51,500	+4%	2,000,000
Public nonwork	46,900		1,800,000
Work	4,400		200,000
Home	200		10,000
Work	13,000	+1%	2,200,000
Nonmotor-vehicle	8,600		2,000,000
Motor-vehicle	4,400		200,000
Home	23,000	−1%	3,500,000
Nonmotor-vehicle	22,800		3,500,000
Motor-vehicle	200		10,000
Public[c]	21,500	−3%	2,700,000

Disabling Injuries[b] by Severity of Injury, 1978

SEVERITY OF DISABLING INJURY	TOTAL[a]	MOTOR-VEHICLE	WORK	HOME	PUBLIC[c]
All Disabling Injuries[b]	10,200,000	2,000,000	2,200,000	3,500,000	2,700,000
Permanent impairments[d]	360,000	150,000	80,000	90,000	60,000
Temporary total disabilities	9,800,000	1,850,000	2,100,000	3,400,000	2,600,000

[a]Deaths and injuries above for the four separate classes total more than national figures due to rounding and because some deaths and injuries are included in more than one class. For example, 4,400 work deaths involved motor vehicles and are in both the work and motor-vehicle totals; and 200 motor-vehicle deaths occurred on home premises and are in both home and motor-vehicle. The total of such duplication amounted to about 4,600 deaths and more than 200,000 injuries in 1978.

[b]Disabling beyond the day of accident. Injuries are not reported on a national basis, so the totals shown are approximations based on ratios of disabling injuries to deaths developed from special studies. The totals are the best estimates for the current year; however, they should not be compared with totals shown in previous editions of ACCIDENT FACTS to indicate year-to-year changes or trends.

[c]Excludes motor-vehicle and work accidents in public places. Includes recreation (swimming, hunting, etc.), transportation except motor-vehicle, public building accidents, etc.

[d]The term "premanent impairments" includes both permanent partial and permanent total disability. The above estimates thus include impairments ranging from the permanent stiffening of a joint or a finger amputation, to permanent, complete crippling.

Source: NSC estimates (rounded) based on data from the National Center for Health Statistics, state industrial commissions, state traffic authorities, state departments of health, insurance companies, industrial establishments and other sources. Courtesy of the National Safety Council.

Tremendous advances in accident prevention have occurred over the past five decades. *Safety-education programs* have been established in the schools, in industry, and as a part of driver-education programs. More recently, attention has been paid to consumer-products safety. Yet we still need a comprehensive safety-education program for all Americans.

The home has traditionally been considered a refuge from harm and injury. Yet each year, approximately 25,000 people lose their lives as a result of an accident in the home, and about 3.5 million more suffer disabling injuries. Some 22 percent of all deaths occur either in the home or on the premises surrounding the home. The cost of *home accidents* in 1978 was a staggering $7.1 billion.[2]

The majority of those who become injured in home accidents are fall victims. Falls are responsible for about one-third of all home fatalities. It is often not realized that falls represent the most serious threat to loss of life around the home. The very young and the very old seem to be the age groups most frequently involved in fall accidents at home. Fires also contribute to a large number of home fatalities. In 1978, some 5,100 people died in fire-related home accidents. Other *fatal* home *accidents* involve drowning, electrocution, poisoning, and accidental shootings.

Each year more people are injured in home accidents than in *motor-vehicle accidents,* yet few communities have developed programs in home safety. Those most likely to become a victim in home accidents are those under the age of 5 and over the age of 65. While older people are more commonly injured due to falls, young children are more commonly poison victims.[3]

Home accidents most commonly result from a combination of both unsafe practices and unsafe conditions. Thus, home safety education programs should be designed toward both improving the practices of people in homes and the safety of the home environment itself. Since education is a key to home safety and accident prevention, the health education division or office of a public health department can provide direction to a community program in home safety. Home accident prevention is a systematic process. "Such a process holds that education can provide 1. the knowledge that will assist an individual to assume risks in full awareness of potential hazards, 2. judgment of which risks are necessary for those activities worth having within the society one lives in, and 3. the experience to carry out such activities in the most competent way."[4] As mentioned earlier, improper home maintenance and disorder is a significant factor in home accidents. Many simple measures can be adopted by family members to enhance a safe home environment. For example, since fire represents a serious threat to the lives of all family members, each family should attempt to eliminate the causes of home-fire deaths and injuries. An effective means of fire prevention is a voluntary program of home inspection conducted by many local fire departments. Firefighters conduct a free inspection through the home and note any hazards that exist in and about the home. A good emergency plan is an important part of any home-safety program. To prevent loss of lives in home fires, every family member should follow the recommendations of the National Fire Protection Association, which include the following steps:

1. Carefully figure out at least *two* routes to the outside from every room in the house. Remember, fire may block usual stairway or hall exits.

2. From upper floors, use porch and garage roofs, ladders, or trees as ways to safety.

3. Instruct each person how to reach the planned exit. Provide special help for invalids and infants.

Figure 7-2
The majority of those who become injured in home accidents are older people who are fall victims. Courtesy Arizona Republic and Phoenix Gazette.

4. Be sure to sleep with hall or bedroom doors closed to help hold back fire.
5. Agree on a signal (whistle, horn, etc.) which may be needed to alert people in other rooms.
6. Pick an outside meeting place where the family will gather. Establish a rule: "once out—stay out!"

7. Plan to notify fire department quickly after entire family is out of the house.

8. THEN PRACTICE! Avoid a panic tragedy by having everyone familiar with your emergency fire-escape plan.

A Nationwide Network of Poison Control Centers was established in 1956. The primary goal of these centers is the elimination of poisoning accidents. Most communities throughout the U.S. have at least one poison center. These centers answer thousands of calls annually concerning poisoning from drugs, plants, pesticides, household cleaners, and other substances. Staff at the centers advise callers as to how to handle the emergency at home or recommend getting the victim to the nearest hospital. All families should obtain the telephone number of the nearest poison-control center and place it with other emergency numbers for ready reference. Proper storage of medicines, cleaning substances, and other poisonous materials can reduce the likelihood of accidental poisonings.

In recent years, improving the quality and safety of consumer products has gained increased attention. The National Commission on Product Safety recommended the creation of a new federal agency to establish and enforce product safety standards for the protection of the general public. The U.S. Consumer Product Safety Commission conducts the National Electronic Injury Surveillance System, which is a continuous survey of injuries treated in hospital emergency rooms. The list in Table 7-3 contains items which are found in and around the home which were selected from the Commissions total list based on general interest or important trends in product injuries.

Table 7-3 Frequency of Injury for Selected Consumer Products, 1975–1977

ITEM	ESTIMATED NUMBER OF CASES		
	1977	*1976*	*1975*
Bicycles	493,234	447,279	476,813
Knives	202,328	196,661	172,803
Skateboards	140,070	71,438	27,522
Ladders	61,735	54,390	45,588
Lawn mowers	42,609	40,206	41,788
Hammers	39,106	38,413	36,136
Hypodermic needles	17,196	8,914	1,178
Sun lamps	8,869	9,987	12,719
Fireworks	7,555	9,502	4,524
Garden tractors	5,745	4,097	2,617
Propane and butane gas tanks[a]	4,100	1,487	1,544
Two-way radios	1,225	505	315
Hair spray, men's and women's	558	777	1,016

[a]Includes fittings.

Source: Consumer Product Safety Commission National Electronic Injury Surveillance System.

Since the invention of the automobile a century ago, motor-vehicle accidents have claimed the lives of some two million people in the United States. In 1979, more Americans died on the highways in motor-vehicle accidents than the total number of Americans who lost their lives in battle during World War I, the Korean War, or during the Vietnam conflict. Clearly, the motor vehicle has created a very real physical threat to the lives and well-being of all Americans. It is unquestionably an essential—yet dangerous—aspect of modern life in a mobile society. For all people under the age of 75, motor-vehicle accidents rank as the leading cause of death. In the 15-to-24-year age group they are the leading cause of death for both men and women combined. In this age group, men have especially high death rates due to motor-vehicle accidents. It is worth noting that an unusually high number of motor-vehicle accidents that occur in this age group are ones that do not involve another vehicle. In 1978, there were 51,500 fatalities due to motor-vehicle acci-

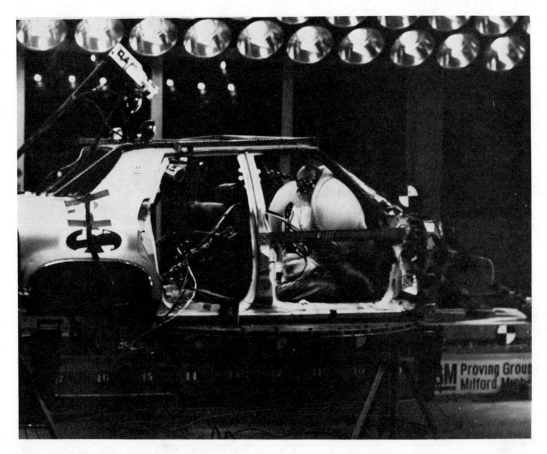

Figure 7-3 The motor vehicle is unquestionably an essential yet dangerous aspect of modern life in a mobile society. Courtesy General Motors Corporation.

dents. About 2 out of 3 deaths in 1978 occurred in places classified as rural. Over half of all deaths occurred in night accidents.[5]

There are a number of factors involved in motor-vehicle accidents including the driver, the vehicle, and the road itself. It is believed to be the interaction of these factors that often sets up the series of events which culminate in the mishap or motor-vehicle accident.

Driver

Experts suggest that the driver is the single most important factor in traffic safety. It is the driver who sees, guides, and makes judgments regarding the control of the vehicle. Drivers indeed have a strong responsibility to perform the driving task properly. The National Safety Council reports that "speeds too fast for conditions" is a contributing factor in nearly 30 percent of all fatal accidents. In most cases, drivers involved in these accidents were violating a speed law (see Table 7-4). However, in order to determine safe speeds, the driver must consider the conditions such as other drivers, other vehicles, the roadway, and environmental factors in addition to posted speed limit.

Driver attitude, knowledge, and skill are all considered important to traffic safety. A person may have adequate knowledge of traffic laws and auto operation and the skill to respond to a variety of complex or unusual traffic conditions, but if these are not applied with the proper attitude, the person can become a menace on the highway.

Figure 7-4
The driver is the single most important factor in traffic safety. Courtesy General Motors Corporation.

Table 7-4 Improper Driving Reported in Accidents, 1978

(KIND OF IMPROPER DRIVING)	FATAL ACCIDENTS			INJURY ACCIDENTS			ALL ACCIDENTS[a]		
	Total	Urban	Rural	Total	Urban	Rural	Total	Urban	Rural
Total	100.0%	100.0%	100.0%	100.0%	100.0%	100.0%	100.0%	100.0%	100.0%
Improper driving	72.8	76.2	72.2	80.5	84.8	77.1	83.4	86.6	79.8
Speed too fast[b]	32.3	16.8	34.5	20.8	6.9	32.5	16.9	6.1	29.8
Right of way	12.3	20.8	11.0	21.7	28.6	16.1	20.4	22.4	18.3
Failed to yield	8.2	14.1	7.3	15.7	19.4	12.7	15.7	16.1	15.2
Passed stop sign	3.2	2.6	3.2	2.6	2.7	2.5	2.0	2.0	2.1
Disregarded signal	0.9	4.1	0.5	3.4	6.5	0.9	2.7	4.3	1.0
Drove left of center	15.1	5.2	16.6	5.6	2.5	8.3	4.8	2.6	7.6
Improper overtaking	2.1	0.8	2.3	2.1	1.8	2.3	3.6	3.9	3.2
Made improper turn	1.1	1.7	1.0	2.4	3.1	1.7	3.9	4.6	3.0
Followed too closely	0.8	0.9	0.7	7.8	11.0	5.2	8.4	10.3	6.2
Other improper driving	9.1	30.0	6.1	20.1	30.9	11.1	25.4	36.7	11.7
No improper driving stated	27.2	23.8	27.8	19.5	15.2	22.9	16.6	13.4	20.2

[a]Principally property damage accidents, but also includes fatal and injury accidents.
[b]Includes "speed too fast for conditions."

Source: Reports of state and city traffic authorities, as follows: Urban—40 cities; Rural—11 states; Total—NSC estimates based on Urban and Rural reports.

Courtesy of the National Safety Council.

Some suggest that driver attitude can largely explain why young drivers' accident rates are so significantly higher than those for middle-aged drivers.

Perhaps the most important human factor known to be associated with all types of accidents including motor-vehicle accidents is alcohol consumption. The National Safety Council estimates that over one-half of all fatal motor-vehicle accidents involved alcohol. This does not mean that the drivers were necessarily drunk, but evidence most often suggests that alcohol was present in the system of either one driver or both in the fatal accidents studied.

Studies have shown that blood-alcohol concentrations of 0.05 percent impair the driving ability of most people to some degree. Even one drink affects a person's responsiveness behind the wheel. In conjunction with the recommendations of the American Medical Association and other organizations, many states have lowered the legal definition of driving "under the influence" of alcohol to 0.10 percent blood-alcohol concentration. Other conditions that appear to be associated with motor-vehicle accidents include limited or poor visibility, distractions, and recklessness.

Roadway

Physical deficiencies in the roadway itself are an important contributing factor in about 10 percent of all traffic accidents. Unsafe road design or a roadway that has deteriorated to an unsafe condition over the years are two major deficiencies. Roadway surface conditions may be influenced by such things as snow, ice, or rain, which can make the operation of a motor vehicle unsafe.

In recent years, considerable emphasis has been placed on building safer roads. Breakaway road signs, removal of fixed objects near the roadway, and the installation of energy-absorbing devices on potentially hazardous poles or abutments are some of the many highway engineering devices being used to make roadways safer.

Vehicle

The National Safety Council estimates that approximately 20 percent of all traffic accidents are related to vehicle condition. As a result the National Highway and Traffic Safety Administration (NHTSA) has issued numerous safety standards that must be met for new automobiles sold in the U.S. These standards include vehicles equipped with shatter-resistant safety glass, energy-absorbing dashboards, seat belts, and, perhaps some day in the future, air bags that inflate upon impact. Most drivers pay little attention to the fact that their only means of controlling a vehicle is four small rubber tires, the steering system, and braking system. A motor vehicle must be in good working condition if it is to be operated safely. The NHTSA has established a standard requiring each state to have a program of periodic inspection for all motor vehicles.

Considering the volume of research into various aspects of vehicle safety and the increasing number of government standards, motor vehicles in the future undoubtedly will be safer.

Highway Safety

If considered only from an economic standpoint, motor-vehicle accidents would still be classified as a major national health problem. Motor-vehicle accidents cost the nation almost half of the $62 billion accident-loss bill. Given the cost of motor-vehicle-accident-related property damage, medical costs, and absenteeism from work due to injury sustained, this category of accidents is economically draining to the nation. Combined with the human toll including loss of life, permanent disability, and traumatic injury, the cost of motor-vehicle accidents is undeterminable.

Considering the ever-increasing size and complexity of the national highway system, the problem of highway safety will continue to be a major social and economic problem in our nation. One means of controlling the traffic-death toll is implementing traffic-safety education programs. Some of these programs are offered by the schools, while others are community-based endeavors.

The National Highway and Traffic Safety Administration has established standards for the construction of motor vehicles and highways, as well as the Highway Safety Program Standards in the following areas:

1. periodic motor-vehicle inspection
2. motorcycle safety
3. driver education and licensure
4. traffic courts
5. alcohol in relation to highway safety
6. surveillance of accident locations
7. highway design, construction, and maintenance
8. pedestrian safety
9. public transportation safety
10. accident investigation and reporting.

Public Safety

Public accidents include those which occur in recreational pursuits, transportation (except motor vehicle) and in other places used in a public way. Public accidents claim about 22,000 lives each year (see Figure 7-5). Falls from public places and drownings are responsible for the largest number of fatalities recorded in this category of accidents.[6]

An important contributing factor in public accidents is lack of supervision in off-the-job, or leisure, activities. In addition, safety experts suggest that many people fail to prepare properly for participation in hazardous recreational activities. Such failure can manifest itself in the use of unsafe equipment, such as improper ski bindings; a lack of adequate training in the task; or lack of physical conditioning necessary for safe participation.[7]

PUBLIC ACCIDENTS, 1978
(For accidental deaths in all places see pages 6 and 7.)

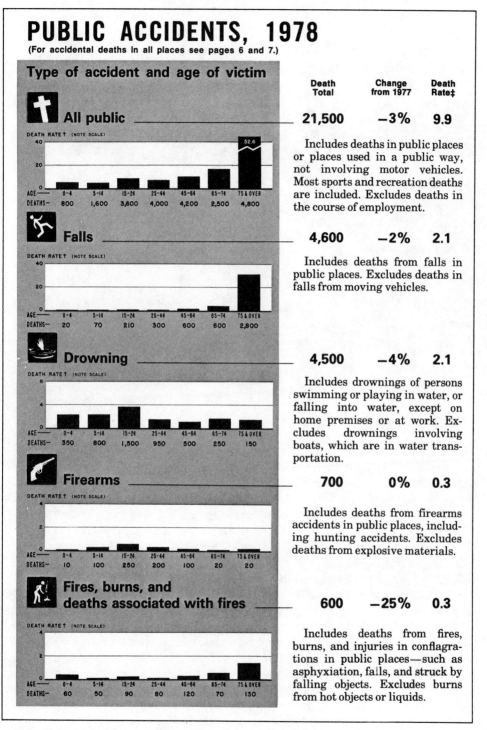

	Death Total	Change from 1977	Death Rate‡
All public	**21,500**	**−3%**	**9.9**

Includes deaths in public places or places used in a public way, not involving motor vehicles. Most sports and recreation deaths are included. Excludes deaths in the course of employment.

	Death Total	Change from 1977	Death Rate‡
Falls	**4,600**	**−2%**	**2.1**

Includes deaths from falls in public places. Excludes deaths in falls from moving vehicles.

	Death Total	Change from 1977	Death Rate‡
Drowning	**4,500**	**−4%**	**2.1**

Includes drownings of persons swimming or playing in water, or falling into water, except on home premises or at work. Excludes drownings involving boats, which are in water transportation.

	Death Total	Change from 1977	Death Rate‡
Firearms	**700**	**0%**	**0.3**

Includes deaths from firearms accidents in public places, including hunting accidents. Excludes deaths from explosive materials.

	Death Total	Change from 1977	Death Rate‡
Fires, burns, and deaths associated with fires	**600**	**−25%**	**0.3**

Includes deaths from fires, burns, and injuries in conflagrations in public places—such as asphyxiation, falls, and struck by falling objects. Excludes burns from hot objects or liquids.

Figure 7-5 Public accidents, 1978. Courtesy National Safety Council.

Figure 7-6 Recreational accidents are on the rise.

The increase in public accidental death and injuries has shown a gradual increase over the years. This trend is no doubt related to a decrease in working hours that has increased the amount of leisure-time for large numbers of people. In addition, the U.S. population has moved into an era of general affluence, which has made it possible for more people to purchase surfboards, guns, camping and skiing equipment, and other types of recreational apparatus. And growing numbers of Americans are engaging in new and often hazardous activities such as snowmobiling, hang gliding, roller skating, skateboarding, and scuba diving.

The public accident problem is very complex. Most of the U.S. population is to some extent exposed to various types of public accident hazards. Approximately 4,500 people drown each year in the U.S. As a result, methods have been designed to reduce the likelihood of drowning. Swimming and "drown-proofing" techniques are taught in water-safety courses throughout the U.S. Boating activities claim the lives of nearly 1,400 people annually. The Federal Boat Safety Act of 1971 was passed to promote recreational boating safety and reduce the growing numbers of injuries. Camping is one of the most rapidly growing recreational activities today. Unfortunately, accidents are an accompanying element of the expanding interest in camping. The American Camping Association has established standards for the conduct of camp programs to make camps as safe as possible. Many states have established fundamental safety regulations and standards for state parks.

Since so much of the activity in the area of public safety is unsupervised, it is the responsibility of each individual to exercise a high degree of self-enforcement in the interest of safety. Clearly public education programs have value in the overall effort to prevent public accidents.

If the four-day work week becomes a reality, people will have one more day of leisure-time a week than in the present. This could mean that more people than ever before will spend more time in recreational pursuits.

> People engaged in recreational activities have accidents because of unsafe behavior, lack of supervision, misuse of environment, and lack of knowledge of rules, regulations and safe practices. To stem the tide of such disasters, public and private organizations are engrossed in the development of educational programs that are relevant to safe living. All programs being offered by schools and other agencies will, of necessity, have to be accelerated to keep abreast of the increasing numbers of participants.[8]

Community Safety

Most safety-education programs are either formal or informal. Formal programs occur in the elementary or secondary schools. These programs, which deal with general safety and accident prevention, fill a valuable need for children and adolescents, but are inaccessible to the adult population. As a result, informal community programs have been designed and implemented to reach the public. These programs disseminate safety information, detail the extent of the safety problem, and encourage people to act in a safe manner. They typically utilize the mass media, since people are often reluctant to attend safety meetings and courses.

OCCUPATIONAL SAFETY AND HEALTH

Throughout history, there has been a certain amount of limited activity designed to improve safety and health in the workplace. However, until recently these efforts were quite inadequate in meeting the needs of American workers. In the late 1930s, large industrial unions were organized in steel, auto, and electrical plants and in mines throughout the U.S. Working conditions were a major concern of these large trade unions. Upton Sinclair's book *The Jungle* brought public attention to the fact that losing limbs to a meat ax in the meatpacking factory was unfortunately a common occurrence among workers in this setting. *The Jungle* is credited with influencing the passage of the first worker's compensation laws for loss of limb to U.S. food-production workers.

While a system of economic compensation for workers injured or disabled on the job existed during these times, no mechanism operated which was designed to improve the safety of the workplace itself. As a result, thousands of American workers continued to be needlessly injured and disabled for life.

During World War II, the Walsh-Healy Act was passed. This Act addressed itself to correct unsafe and unhealthy working conditions of those workers employed by private contractors doing work for the federal government. The regulations contained in Walsh-Healy did not protect other private sector workers or other government employees. State legislative systems designed to protect workers safety and health began in 1914, and by 1935, each state had enacted its own safety and health law as well as an agency to enforce the law. In 1970, Congress passed the Occupational Safety and Health Act. Under the provisions of this Act, private-sector workers were protected against hazards in the work environment for the first time. This Act places all federal and state occupational safety and health enforcement under federal control, with the objective to establish more uniform codes, standards, and regulations and to provide more vigorous enforcement.

In the past decade, the term OSHA has become a new word in the dictionary. It can mean (1) safety and health conditions in the workplace, (2) the federal agency charged with enforcing the law, or (3) the law itself—the 1970 Occupational Safety and Health Act.

Many believed prior to the passage of OSHA (the Act) that workers constitute the healthiest segment of the American population. However, under close scrutiny it becomes clear that this Act was essential to improve the safety and health outlook of American workers. It is reported in the 1977 Report of Workman's Compensation records for New York State that only 1 percent of monies paid out to employees came as a result of a job-related illness. The remainder of compensable cases were from job-related injuries. OSHA activists maintain that more than 100,000 workers die prematurely each year from job-related illnesses, and 14,000 from job-related injuries. According to these sources, an additional 2.3 million workers are either permanently or temporarily disabled by work accidents annually (see Table 7-5). Of the 1 million current and former asbestos workers in the U.S., between 300,000 and 400,000 can expect to die of cancer.

Table 7-5 Work Accidents, 1978

INDUSTRY GROUP	WORKERS[a] (000)	DEATHS 1978	DEATHS Change from 1977	DEATH RATES[b] 1978	DEATH RATES[b] 1968	% Change	DISABLING INJURIES[c] 1978
All Industries	94,800	13,000[d]	+100	14	19	−26%	2,200,000[d]
Trade	22,200	1,300	0	6	7	−14%	400,000
Service	22,900	1,700	−100	7	12	−42%	360,000
Manufacturing	20,300	1,800	0	9	9	0%	490,000
Government	15,400	1,700	0	11	13	−15%	310,000
Transportation and public utilities	5,100	1,500	−100	29	38	−24%	170,000
Agriculture	3,500	1,900	+100	54	65	−17%	190,000
Construction	4,600	2,600	+200	57	74	−23%	240,000
Mining, quarrying	800	500	0	63	117	−46%	40,000

[a]Workers are all persons gainfully employed, including owners, managers, other paid employees, the self-employed, and unpaid family workers, but excluding domestic servants.

[b]Deaths per 100,000 workers in each group.

[c]Disabling beyond the day of the accident.

[d]About 4,400 of the deaths and 200,000 of the injuries involved motor vehicles.

Source: NSC estimates (rounded) based on data from the National Center for Health Statistics, state departments of health, and state industrial commissions; numbers of workers are based on Bureau of Labor Statistics data. Courtesy of the National Safety Council.

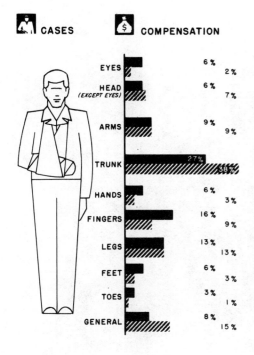

CASES		COMPENSATION
EYES	6%	2%
HEAD (EXCEPT EYES)	6%	7%
ARMS	9%	9%
TRUNK	27%	38%
HANDS	6%	3%
FINGERS	16%	9%
LEGS	13%	13%
FEET	6%	3%
TOES	3%	1%
GENERAL	8%	15%

Disabling work injuries in the entire nation totalled approximately 2,200,000 in 1978. Of these, about 13,000 were fatal and 80,000 resulted in some permanent impairment.

Injuries to the trunk occurred most frequently, with thumb and finger injuries next, according to State Labor Department reports.

Eyes	130,000
Head (except eyes)	130,000
Arms	200,000
Trunk	590,000
Hands	130,000
Fingers	350,000
Legs	290,000
Feet	130,000
Toes	70,000
General	180,000

The chart shows for each body part, per cent *in black* of all injuries, and per cent *in stripes* of all compensation paid.

Source: State Labor Departments, 1972-1973; cases — 19 States, compensation — 9 States.

Figure 7-7 Part of the body injured in work accidents. Courtesy National Safety Council.

The National Safety Council (NSC) reports that *occupational illnesses* and *injuries* cost $23 billion in 1978, with an additional $4 billion in wage lost, $4 billion in insurance administration costs, and $2.5 billion in medical costs. In 1978, 13,000 workers died of work-related causes, and 2.2 million more experienced disabling injuries. Production time lost due to occupational accidents was 245 million days in 1978. Fatalities that occur at the workplace comprise about 12.5 percent of all accidental deaths. Injuries to specific body parts constitute a major occupational hazard (see Figure 7-7).

The Federal Law

The Williams-Steiger Occupational Safety Health Act (PL 91-596) was signed into law on December 31, 1969. OSHA legislation established a strong federal role in industrial health and safety. This Act, administered under the Department of Labor, establishes safety and health standards for the workplace and enforces these standards. OSHA hires federal compliance officers and grants them legal powers to enter any private-property workplace to conduct an inspection. No advance warning is allowed. Under OSHA law, any worker can file a complaint about a safety health aspect of working conditions and request an inspection by OSHA, which must respond within a short period of

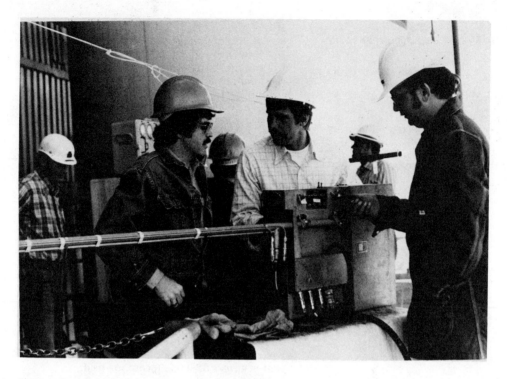

Figure 7-8 A system now operated to improve safety on the job.

time by inspecting the workplace. Under OSHA, the complaining worker, a representative of the workers (generally a union representative), and a representative of management accompany the OSHA compliance officer on the inspection.

Should infringements of OSHA be found, citations are written on the first inspection and fines and abatement (correction-time) periods assigned. Periodic follow-up inspections do occur, but in 1976 the follow-up provision was modified and is now mandatory only in plants found to have eleven or more violations of standards.

Prior to 1970, each state had its own legal statutes regarding occupational safety and health. These laws generally tended to be voluntary in nature with few penalty systems. Under Section 18 of the 1970 OSHA law, states are granted the option of writing their own mandates and standards to supercede federal law if they are "as effective as" federal law. Initially, a number of states sought to retain the state control option. However, some are now reversing this decision and opting to return to federal OSHA coverage. As it now stands, public employees are covered only in states with "state plans." In states with federal coverage through OSHA, and these represent the majority of public employees, special legislation passed by their state legislature is needed to obtain protection. It is likely that much of the authority concerning occupational safety and health will be returned to the states.

Employer-Employee Duties

OSHA sets out two duties for employers, one of which is specific and the other so general in nature that an employer can be cited for most any condition which, in the opinion of the compliance health and safety officer (inspector), may be a hazard. These so-called "general duty" provisions are the following:

1. Furnish to each of his employees employment and a place of employment which are free from recognized hazards that are causing or are likely to cause death or serious physical harm to his employees.
2. Comply with occupational safety and health standards under the Act.

The greatest potential impact of the first of the two above provisions will likely be in the area of health matters. Frequently, health hazards cannot always be determined by visual observation. Such a determination requires tests with proper instrumentation and evaluation of the test data by a qualified expert in the field of industrial hygiene.

OSHA, NIOSH, and OSHRC

The Act created three new governmental agencies:

1. the Occupational Safety and Health Administration (OSHA) within the Department of Labor, which sets and enforces health and safety standards in the nation's workplaces
2. the National Institute for Occupational Safety and Health (NIOSH) in the Department of Health and Human Services, a research agency that might be called the scientific conscience of the federal occupational health and safety program
3. the Occupational Safety and Health Review Commission (OSHRC), which settles disputes arising from enforcement of the Act.

NIOSH is headquartered in Rockville, Maryland, just outside the nation's capital. Its research facilities are located in Cincinnati, Ohio, and Morgantown, West Virginia. The institute also has Regional Offices in ten major cities throughout the country.

Occupational Safety and Health Administration (OSHA) The main responsibility for administering the Act rests within OSHA. It is empowered to inspect the facilities of any employer, to promulgate safety and health standards, to issue citations and to assess penalties for violations of the standards. The administrative officer is an Assistant Secretary of Labor, established under the Act. The organization chart of OSHA is shown in Figure 7-9.

The National Insititute for Occupational Safety and Health (NIOSH) The NIOSH is the federal agency in charge of medical and scientific research under the OSHA

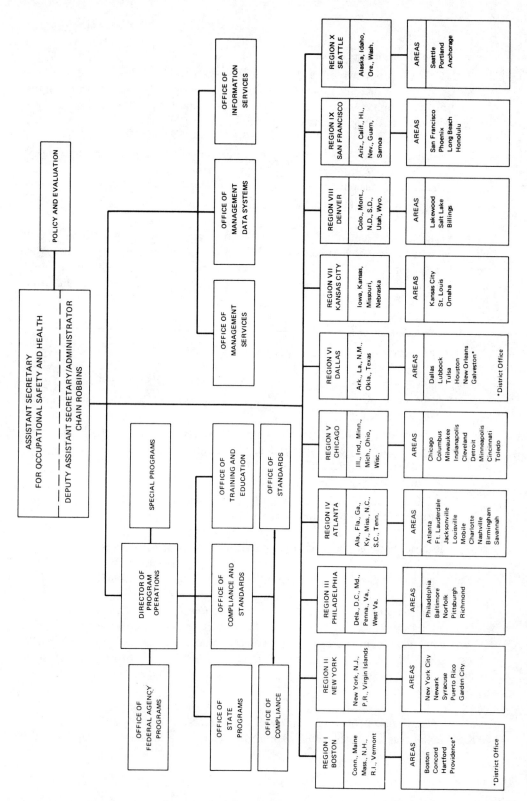

Figure 7-9 Organization of Occupational Safety and Health Administration.

Act. This institute is administered by the Center for Disease Control in the U.S. Public Health Service of the Department of Health and Human Services. The goal of NIOSH is to conduct all of the research necessary to determine appropriate levels of exposure a worker may have to a given substance without getting sick. The purpose of these studies, in the words of the Act, is to determine "the effect of chronic or low-level exposure to industrial materials, processes, and stresses on the potential for illness, disease, or loss of functional capacity in aging adults." This *Threshold Limit Values* (TLV) concept was developed by NIOSH and is viewed by the development of OSHA as a precedent for action in their enforcement programs and the formal establishment of standards.

The information provided by NIOSH is used by the OSHA administration, which subsequently conducts its own investigation, primarily through the use of public hearings before it puts forth a final federal standard. Generally, the process involved in standard setting consumes a good deal of time. However, there are exceptions to this rule. An example is the final standard set on vinyl chloride in September 1974. The association between exposure to vinyl chloride and liver cancer was first noted at the B.F. Goodrich plant in Louisville, Kentucky in January 1974. An emergency standard was established on February 15, 1974. Seven months later the final standard was set to go into effect in April 1975 for the entire plastics industry. The original standard for vinyl chloride was 500 ppm (parts per million); the final standard was 1 ppm.

This speedy enactment is recognized as an exception to the norm in standard promulgations. For, while such hazards as noise, carbon monoxide, silica, lead, and job stress are well recognized, no concrete standards have as yet been set forth.

A major way in which NIOSH determines what is happening in the workplace is through industry-wide studies specifically authorized by the Occupational Safety and Health Act. NIOSH conducts some forty industry-wide studies annually on a wide range of occupational groups. Recent investigations have explored the effects of anesthetic gases on hospital operating-room employees, of grain dusts on grain-elevator workers, of yeast and flour dust on bakery and confectionary workers, and of a host of other substances—asbestos, silica, talc, and solvents.

A number of current industry-wide studies are focusing on two major areas of concern—occupational cancer and hazards to the reproductive systems of workers. Scientists are investigating the possible cancer-causing effects of everything from antimony, which is suspected of causing lung cancer among smelter workers, to wood dust, which appears to be related to nose and throat cancer among woodworkers. NIOSH has also studied the effects of chloroprene, a chemical used in manufacturing synthetic rubber which may cause skin and lung cancer.

Much of the NIOSH research falls within one of the following categories: animal toxicology studies, physical stress, and psychological stress. *Toxicology* is the study of the effects of poisons, or unwanted substances in the body. NIOSH conducted studies in which rats and monkeys were exposed to methyl butyl ketone (MBK), an industrial solvent that was believed to have caused nerve damage to workers at an Ohio coated-fabrics plant several years ago. The studies confirmed that exposure to MBK at the then-current federal standard could cause damage to the nervous system and lungs. This research led to a recommendation that the MBK standard be lowered from 100 parts per million of air (ppm) to 25 ppm.

In other work, NIOSH scientists found damage to the offspring of rats exposed to anesthetic gases like those used in hospital operating rooms, lung obstruction among animals who regularly inhaled polyurethane foam plastic dust and bituminous coal dust, and lung tumors among rats and mice exposed to coal tar mixtures like those found in coke oven emissions. At present, workers may be risking exposure to excess amounts of at least 22,000 toxic chemicals—and those are just the ones we know about. This means engineers and chemists must work constantly to develop more sensitive devices for monitoring worker exposures and for analyzing air samples.[9]

The average worker also encounters a host of physical stressors or hazards, including noise, radiation, heat, and vibration. These physical stressors are also the focus of NIOSH research. To study the effects of vibration, for example NIOSH has gone on the road with a van equipped to monitor vibration of such workers as heavy-equipment operators at the job site. In the lab, human volunteers are used as subjects in vibration chambers to determine what frequency vibrations are most harmful to health and performance.

NIOSH is currently attempting to identify better methods for monitoring worker exposure to ionizing, nonionizing, and ultraviolet radiation. Airport workers, the Federal Aviation Administration, and the Airline Transport Association rested easier after a NIOSH study revealed that x-ray hazard to airline employees working with baggage inspection systems was negligible. Now under study is the radiation emitted by several welding processes under various working conditions.

In addition to the typical animal studies on the effects of noise, NIOSH has completed a survey of hearing loss among coal miners. It showed that miners' hearing is much worse than the national average, though not as badly impaired as among some other occupational groups. An investigation of hearing conservation programs in industry produced the conclusion that, while companies are starting such programs, engineering control of noise remains a major problem in many plants. Finally, since no workers are exposed to just one hazard or form of physical stress, NIOSH is now looking into the effects of combined exposures and is proving once again that whole is greater than the sum of its parts.[10]

Psychological stress is another prime concern of NIOSH. Some intriguing research is showing that job hazards attack the mind as well as the body. Studies of job stress indicate that the daily psychological stress imposed on some workers—police officers, air traffic controllers, sales managers, mechanics, public relations specialists—make those people more susceptible to physical and mental illness. Scientists also have uncovered another source of stress that potentially affects more than a quarter of the U.S. work force: shiftwork. NIOSH now is investigating the physical and emotional health, safety records, and job performance of workers in six industries where changing shifts are common.

Although workers are not responsible for nearly the percentage of accidents that some persons claim, the human element in work accidents cannot be denied. Recognizing that machine guards and good housekeeping are not enough, NIOSH is studying the psychological and social factors that contribute to low accident rates in some companies and high rates in others.[11]

In occupational safety and health, as in any field, certain problems seem to demand special attention and special resources. At NIOSH the focus is currently on the following areas:

Occupational cancer Of the 600,000 new cancer cases that occur each year in the United States, some 80 to 90 percent are caused by environmental exposures. NIOSH estimates that anywhere from 4 to 25 percent of those may be directly related to the job. Certainly, work exposures increase the cancer risk for people who smoke or who are exposed to carcinogens elsewhere. And as the daily news makes painfully clear, anyone who breathes, eats, or drinks gets a daily dose of carcinogens outside the workplace.

The Occupational Carcinogenesis Program of NIOSH attempts to identify groups of workers who have an unusually high cancer risk and to pinpoint carcinogens that demand top priority in research and standards development. Studies revealed, for example, a high risk of bladder cancer among leather workers and dairy farmers and genital cancers among hairdressers and cosmetologists. Obviously, further investigation is warranted. NIOSH also has been checking into incidences of "cancer clustering"—such as several cases of brain tumors at a steel mill in Wheeling, West Virginia, and pancreatic cancer at a chemical plant in Massachusetts. Industry-wide studies of cancer risk have been launched in the printing, dairy, uranium-milling and mining, plywood, pulp, and paper, coal gasification, phosphate fertilizer, aluminum, steel, antimony-smelting, beryllium, cadmium-smelting, pesticide-formulation, and lead-smelting industries.

Nonmalignant respiratory disease A war on occupational cancer is little comfort to those workers suffering from such other major killers as black lung, brown lung (caused by cotton dust), asbestosis, or silicosis. A former cotton worker who has only one-third of his lung capacity and can barely walk a block is just as tragic a victim of occupational disease as the lung-cancer patient.

Many occupational diseases strike the respiratory system. More than three million workers are exposed to just a handful of respiratory hazards: asbestos, beryllium, coke-oven emissions, cotton dust, silica, sulfur dioxide, sulfuric acid, and toluene diisocyanate. The consequences of long years of failure to control hazards is becoming evident in the coal industry, where black-lung disability benefits to miners now total $1 billion a year, and in the cotton industry, where machinery modifications needed to meet a new standard may cost more than $800 million. NIOSH has launched a major effort to learn more about the biological effects of noncarcinogenic dusts, fibers, and chemicals and to develop better methods of sampling these substances in the workplace.

Women in the workplace As more and more women move into a wider variety of jobs, an increasing number of unborn children are also coming to work and are being involuntarily exposed to hazardous chemicals that can cross the mother's womb.

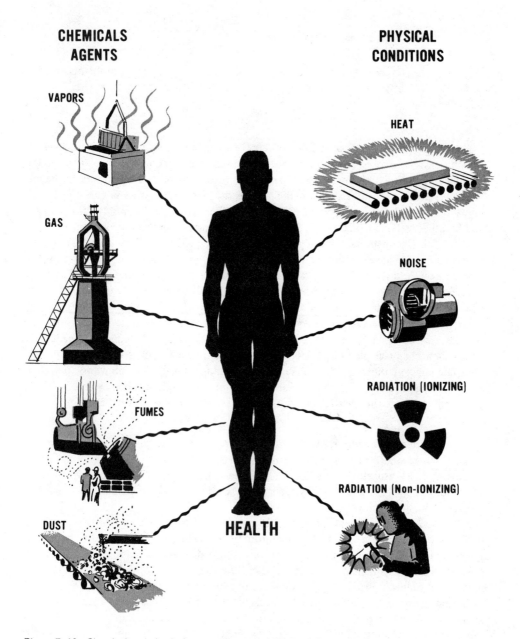

CHEMICALS AGENTS

VAPORS

GAS

FUMES

DUST

PHYSICAL CONDITIONS

HEAT

NOISE

RADIATION (IONIZING)

RADIATION (Non-IONIZING)

HEALTH

Figure 7-10 Chemical and physical agents. Courtesy U.S. Steel Corporation.

Women now account for 40 percent of the nation's work force. NIOSH estimates that one million of the sixteen million working women of child-bearing age are exposed to substances that could cause birth defects or miscarriages. Because very few of the 20,000 chemicals commonly found in the workplace have been tested for their effects on the unborn, NIOSH says only about 20 can be linked to birth defects and miscarriages. Some of the chemicals—such as lead, methyl mercury, and benzene—have been known for some time to damage the fetus. More recent studies have implicated such substances as vinyl chloride and the anesthetic gases that escape into the air in hospital operating rooms. Virtually no substances, even the 400 for which OSHA has specific standards are regulated with the fate of the unborn in mind.

NIOSH is studying the incidence of birth defects and miscarriages among women in certain industries, such as the pharmaceutical industry, the electronics industry, and others where such heavy metals as lead and mercury are used. NIOSH also helped sponsor a three-day Conference on Women and the Workplace, which brought together hundreds of labor, management, scientific, and government experts for the first nationwide meeting on the subject.

The problem of hazards to women workers is especially touchy because it involves the issue of equal employment opportunity. The danger of special requirements for pregnant or fertile women is that they could easily become an excuse for further discrimination against women. Industry nervousness already has resulted in some drastic action. The Lead Industries Association, for example, has recommended against employment of fertile, pregnant, or nursing women in the lead industries "until such time as adequate information has been developed regarding the effect of lead." Such policies can leave working women, many of whom must work to support households, with an incredible choice—their job or their fertility. One Canadian woman already has had herself sterilized so she could keep her job in a General Motors Company lead-battery plant.

Often overlooked is the fact that reproductive hazards are not restricted to women. At least fourteen of the men poisoned by the pesticide kepone are now sterile. Lead has been linked to sexual impotence in men and can alter production of sperm. Recent NIOSH studies have revealed higher rates of miscarriages and birth defects among wives of men exposed to vinyl chloride and anesthetic gases. Thus, while the subject is often referred to as "women in the workplace," the real issue is occupational hazards to the reproductive systems of both men and women. Attention to these hazards could produce some far-reaching results in the area of occupational health.[12]

It is not surprising that more than ten years after the passage of the Occupational Safety and Health Act, there is still much sound and fury, as well as legal action. Hardly anyone is neutral about the law. To some labor activists, it is "the most important piece of legislation for American workers since the Wagner Act," which guaranteed workers the right to organize and to collective bargaining. To some irate business people or corporate executives, the law is "the most dangerous piece of legislation for American business since the Wagner Act."

The effects of this Act have been far-reaching. It has directed the attention of the average citizen and the media to an aspect of public health that had long been ignored. It has prodded labor and industry to launch cooperative programs to improve working conditions in several major industries, including rubber, auto manufacturing, and printing.

In the final analysis, it will not be research, scientific information, or enforcement for that matter, that will truly control hazards. What will make the difference in the long run is a cooperative attitude by both industry and labor in working to achieve this goal.[13]

REVIEW QUESTIONS

1. Describe the nature and extent of the accident problem in the United States.
2. What are the major causes of various fatal and disabling home accidents? Identify host characteristics as they relate to types of home accidents.
3. Identify some of the agencies that promote home safety. Explain the services they provide.
4. What three factors are involved in motor-vehicle accidents? What can be done to decrease the likelihood of accidents in each?
5. What is a public accident? Why have public accidents increased in recent years?
6. Describe the historical events which culminated in the passage of the Occupational Safety and Health Act.
7. What are the major categories of NIOSH research? Give examples of each.

SUGGESTED READINGS

Automobile Facts and Figures. Detroit: Automobile Manufacturers Association, published annually.
"Health Promotion at the Worksite," Special Section, *Public Health Reports,* 95(2) 99–163 1980.

NOTES

[1] *Accident Facts: 1979,* Chicago: The National Safety Council, 1979, p. 11.

[2] *Accident Facts: 1979,* p. 79.

[3] *Accident Facts: 1979,* p. 83.

[4] Ralph Grawunder and Marion Steinman, *Life and Health.* New York: Random House, 1980, p. 467.

[5] *Accident Facts: 1979,* pp. 40–42.

[6] *Accident Facts: 1979,* p. 72.

[7] Marland Strasser, James Aaron, Ralph Bohn, and John Eales, *Fundamentals of Safety Education.* New York: Macmillan, 1973, p. 319.

[8] Marland Strasser, pp. 342–343.

[9] U.S. DHEW, "Part of the Human Condition: Health and Safety Hazards in the Work-Place." Washington, D.C.: U.S. DHEW Pub. No. (NIOSH) 78-137, 1978, p. 11.

[10] "Part of the Human Condition," p. 12.

[11] "Part of the Human Condition," p. 13.

[12] "Part of the Human Condition," pp. 19–22.

[13] "Part of the Human Condition," p. 27.

GLOSSARY

accident an occurrence in a sequence of events that usually produce unintended injury, death, or property damage.

disabling injury an injury causing death, permanent disability, or any degree of temporary total disability.

fatal accident an accident that results in one or more deaths within one year.

home accidents accidents in the home and on home premises to occupants, guests, and trespassers.

motor-vehicle accidents any accidents involving a motor vehicle in motion, in readiness for motion, or on a roadway, but not parked in a designated area.

occupational illness (of an employee) any abnormal condition or disorder, other than one resulting from an occupational injury, caused by exposure to environmental factors associated with employment.

occupational injury any injury, such as a cut, fracture, sprain, or amputation, which results from a work accident or human exposure involving a single incident in the work environment.

public accident accidents in public places or places used in a public way, not involving motor vehicles.

safety-education programs programs dealing with general safety and accident prevention in the schools and in the community.

Threshold Limit Values (TLV) standards which limit the concentration of harmful material in the worker's environment which produce no demonstratable injury or illness.

toxicology the study of existing concentrations of toxic substances in occupational settings, designed to determine environmental exposure risk to workers and possible health hazard.

BIBLIOGRAPHY

Accident Facts: 1979. Chicago: The National Safety Council, 1979.

Bingham, Evla (ed.), *Proceedings Conference on Women and the Workplace.* Washington, D.C.: Society for Occupational and Environmental Health, 1977.

Curran, William, "Preventive Action and Self-Help Under the Occupational Safety and Health Act," *American Journal of Public Health,* 70(9) 1010-1011, 1980.

Goldsmith, Frank, "Job Safety and Health," in Peter M. Lazes (ed.), *The Handbook of Health Education.* Germantown, Md.: Aspen Systems Corporation, 1979.

Malik, Linda, *Sociology of Accidents.* Villanova, Pa.: Villanova University Press, 1970.

Page, Joseph, and Mary-Win O'Brien, *Bitter Wages: Ralph Nader's Study Group Report on Disease and Injury on the Job.* New York: Grossman, 1973.

Peterson, Jack E., *Industrial Health.* Englewood Cliffs, N.J.: Prentice-Hall, 1977.

Shimp, Donna, Alfred Blumrosen, and Stuart B. Finifter, *How to Protect Your Health At Work.* Salem, N.J.: Environmental Improvement Associates, 1976.

Strasser, Marland, James Aaron, Ralph Bohn, and John Eales, *Fundamentals of Safety Education.* New York: Macmillan, 1977.

Thygerson, Alton, *Accidents and Disasters: Causes and Countermeasures.* Englewood Cliffs, N.J.: Prentice-Hall, 1977.

U.S. DHEW, *NIOSH Occupational Safety and Health Symposia: 1977.* Washington, D.C.: U.S. DHEW Pub. No. (NIOSH) 78-169, 1978.

——— "Part of the Human Condition: Health and Safety Hazards in the Workplace." Washington, D.C.: U.S. DHEW Pub. No. (NIOSH) 78-137, 1978.

Williams, Allan and Sharon Goins, "Fatal Falls and Jumps from Motor Vehicles," *American Journal of Public Health,* 70(9), 1010-1011, 1979.

PART

III

health care
delivery

8

HEALTH
PLANNING
IN COMMUNITIES

> Planning for quality health care, or for any other human endeavor, can most simply be defined as "guided change." It is one of our highest, essentially human activities, the attempt—as individuals or as a society— to improve our lot by controlling our future.
>
> *The Honorable Paul G. Rogers*

COMMUNITY DEVELOPMENT AND SOCIAL PLANNING

Community development is a relatively new field designed to improve the total *community* or specific segments of the total population. Even though only one community problem may be dealt with at any one time, theoretically the total community and its improvement is of primary concern. The emphasis in community development is on improving the organization of the community as well as the problem-solving process within the community. The focus on *process* allows a broad systematic approach to many specific problems, whether they be recreational, health-related, or economic.

Community health development programs concern themselves with all the people of the community and with community integration, organization, and the educational problem-solving capabilities of people in a geographic area as they relate to health and health-related problems.[1] This approach, which attempts to foster health among populations through the planning and implementation of programs is what distinguishes community health from medicine and personal health. The major focus of community

206

health development programs is the improvement of health through planning prevention, early intervention, disease control and rehabilitation programs.

A second community development approach used by community health is *technical or social planning.* This approach focuses upon problems rather than processes or goals. It usually involves the organization of resources to tackle problems or tasks, such as building a facility or providing new services, rather than improving the ability of community residents to manage problems. In social planning, a professional health planner or other technical planner assumes a key role. This individual is responsible for gathering and analyzing data relevant to a community problem and implementing a plan to promote solutions. This approach typically involves isolating a *target group,* usually a disadvantaged population, and seeks to solve tangible problems. Programs designed to reduce lead-paint poisoning among impoverished inner-city children is an example of this approach.

Community health efforts designed to foster community development in general or those tackling specific problems such as a reduction of drug abuse fit into a broader philosophical view of the "good community," which is described as

> . . . . one with effective structures and processes which make the community adaptive to its changing environment and the changing needs and desires of its citizens . . . the first goal should be to provide citizens with *opportunity* to obtain food, clothing, shelter, and safety from attack, accident and disease . . . and, a feeling of participating with other people in pursuit of a common goal.[2]

From a community health standpoint, the specialized goals of preventive medicine, access to health care for all people, and environmental protection should be consistent with the broader objective of planning for opportunity within the adaptive community.

Figure 8-1
Community development is a relatively new field.

There are various levels of community improvement. These levels are helpful in evaluating the progress of community improvement programs including health-related programs. The levels are as follows:

1. *Individual Maintenance Level:* This level suggests providing assistance to individuals and families to enable them to meet current needs for the basic necessities of life such as food, clothing, and shelter.

2. *Individual Capacity Level:* Programs designed to improve individuals' capacity help people to improve their ability to sustain themselves and their families. Capacity improvement may be provided through education, health care, mental health programs, family counseling, and so forth.

3. *Community Service Programs:* Rather than providing direct assistance to individuals and families, new or extended programs and services can be provided to assist individuals and families with maintenance and capacity needs. This type of community improvement occurs through the development of new clinics, educational programs, and social service programs.

4. *Community Development:* This type of community improvement is considered the highest level. The emphasis is upon improving the organizational and problem-solving capacities of the community and its residents.

5. *National and State Levels:* At this level, laws, programs, services, and organizations are designed and implemented to promote individual maintenance and capacity, as well as support community service and development programs.[3]

Community development is a process through which individuals can become more competent to cope with and control some of the local aspects of a sometimes frus-

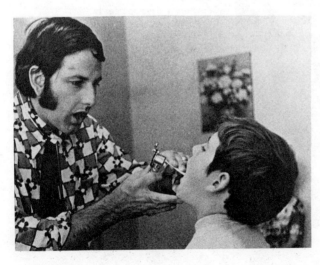

Figure 8-2
Capacity development through dental care. Courtesy Arizona Department of Health Services.

trating and rapidly changing world. "It is a group method [which] involves cooperative study, group decisions and collective action."[4]

The growing body of literature on community development, leadership, and community action has demonstrated at least six basic points. First, modern complex communities are not composed of people with common goals, but individuals and groups with many different interests and goals. Second, it appears that social power or leadership is present and exercised in patterned ways in all social systems including local communities. In addition, certain individuals and groups play key roles in exercising community leadership. Third, community leaders and decision-making groups can be identified by certain techniques. Fourth, only a very small percentage of citizens in a community become actively involved in most community decision-making processes. One researcher has reported that no more than 1 percent of the population is actively involved in most community decisions in the majority of American cities. Fifth, successful community action, depends to a large extent upon finding and involving key community leaders. And, sixth, studies have demonstrated that the professional health planner is much more likely to bring about action toward improving community health programs when he or she involves lay citizens early in the study-planning process.[5]

If the information available concerning community development is accurate, public health officials and others concerned with community improvement will be more successful if they recognize the special-interest and competitive nature of communities, identify key community leaders and groups, and involve community leaders and residents in the study-planning-action process. Therefore, the adaptive community does not exhibit complete harmony and consensus, but rather a willingness and ability on the part of key leaders and other group representatives to recognize that interdependence is required and an organized approach to compromise must be achieved. The needs for an organized leadership structure for controlling competition and community conflict become more important as a community grows larger and more complex.

The Meaning of Health Planning

There is no single acceptable definition of *health planning*. Many different types of activities constitute health planning, all with some justification. However, regardless of the seeming confusion concerning the aims and criteria of health planning,

> . . . . it is clear that health planners must always be able to function despite what will always be considered to be inadequately precise formulation of the problems, limited knowledge of all the alternatives that may be applicable and an insufficiently precise method of assessing the value of each proposed alternative as a solution.[6]

The health planning process has several characteristics. First, planning must be analytical and objective concerning the present. While it does not reject what is good in the present it must successfully sort out deficiencies from adequacies in current programs. Planning seeks to identify unmet needs or inefficient methods, or activities and then correct them. For example, Community X may have very adequate and efficient services

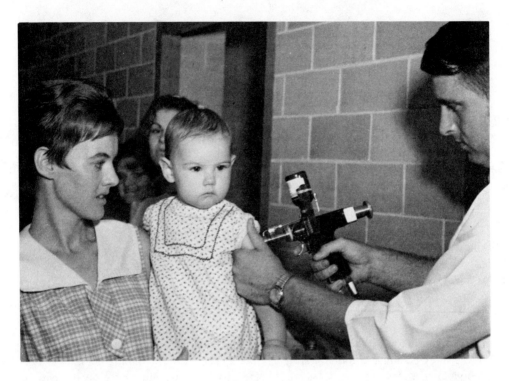

Figure 8-3 Community health planning has involved a system for the control of communicable diseases through immunization. Courtesy Center for Disease Control, Atlanta, Georgia.

and facilities for sexually transmitted disease control yet provide little in the area of poison control. It would be absurd for this community to scrap its sexually transmitted disease-control centers, and replace them with poison-control centers. However, inadequate facilities that provide for poison-control services is a deficiency that should be remedied by Community X.

Health planning is a rational and logical process. "It entails the conscious formulation of future goals, the steps needed to reach these goals, the analysis of available objective data, strategies of change based on goal-oriented analysis and the implementation of such strategies."[7] For example, Community Y must identify its health goals for the future—one year from now, five years from now, and ten years from now. Next, a series of specific steps or tasks are identified which must be achieved in order to reach each goal. Finally, strategies designed to achieve the steps—and, ultimately, goals—are identified and implemented. All of this must be done in light of available resources and constraints.

"Planning is a value-based political activity. Defining goals and objectives for our own future means preferring a good future over a bad one. . . . It is always important to know whose values are being imposed on the future."[8] Those responsible for community health planning in Community Z must be aware of political considerations in the identification of goals and objectives process.

In the past two decades, health care planning has experienced a profound shift in emphasis and scope. Increasingly, health planners are confronted with the task of developing a comprehensive, efficient, and effective health care system to which the entire population has access.

> This broader concern has not diminished the more traditional examination of and response to specific deficiencies in the system and the unmet needs of specific target groups within our population; rather it has begun to incorporate the more traditional concerns into a more holistic framework.[9]

For example, certain environmental conditions, including deteriorating residential structures are indicators of human behavior. And, behavior is determined to a significant degree by peoples' attitudes, knowledge, and values—especially those which are health-related. Behavior, then, also determines to some extent whether environmental conditions lead to disease and injury.

A continuing demographic analysis of a community is essential if health programs are to be relevant to the needs of the people in the community. This is especially the case in instances where health programs have the objective of determining and meeting health needs of groups of people of particular age, sex, race, economic, or occupational characteristics, because the proportion and composition of the population having these characteristics does change.

Figure 8-4
Certain environmental conditions, including deteriorating residential structures are indicators of human health. Courtesy Marc Anderson.

Traditionally, there has been a sharp contrast between the responsibilities of public health agencies representing governmental involvement in health promotion and private medical practice. Today the field is characterized largely by cooperation of private and public sector in promotion of health and fostering quality of life for all people.

In contemporary America another transition has occurred which relates to the way in which health and illness are viewed. It is now accepted that the health status of an individual is based largely upon how and where that individual lives. Such factors as income, educational level or technical training, employment, housing and culture are now recognized as contributory factors in both the attainment of health or susceptibility to illness. Ironically, Edwin Chadwick, the father of modern public health, asserted that disease and poverty were related in 1912 in his paper, "Report on an Inquiry into The Sanitary Condition of The Laboring Population in Great Britain."[10]

Characteristics of the Community

The initial phase of program planning in community health involves an investigation of characteristics related to the population which is to be served and the community setting. Characteristics of the target population include such things as income and socioeconomic status and the predominant cultural or religious beliefs of the group. In community planning, the two most urgent questions about population are its size and its characteristics (age, sex, race, religion, and so on). Of equal importance to the size and characteristics of a given population at a given time are the changes that occur in these features.

Population characteristics Identifying population characteristics is of significance in community health planning and subsequent implementation of successful programs. Those involved in community health analysis should obtain information concerning the number of people within the community in each 5-year age group of socioeconomic status, race and sex, health problems and needs, educational level, and an investigation of any changes which may have recently occurred or which are likely to occur regarding the proportion of individuals in specific age or other target groups.

Population characteristics can significantly effect the type of strategies selected and employed by community health planners. For example, informing a Mexican-American target group about a new health service dealing with childhood immunizations may not be very effective if the infomation pamphlets concerning the program and its importance are not written bilingually. Similarly, developing expanded well-baby and child-health programs in a community tract that has a rapidly aging population and very few young people would be ill-designed to serve the population needs. The more rapidly changes occur in a community regarding proportion and composition of the population the more frequently demographic analyses should be done. The price of not being aware of changes in the characteristics of the population is that efforts are expanded in health

Figure 8-5 The initial phase of planning involves characteristics of target population such as culture and religion.

programs at a time when the need for these programs has changed in one or more important ways.

Characteristics of the setting Knowledge of the physical community as a focus for program planning is also important. An assessment should be made of minority and majority populations within the total community, including their relative size and geographic location. In addition, it is important to determine if the community is in a rural, urban, or suburban setting since this factor as well as population size, and density have a bearing upon public health programs. These factors especially influence the resources available or constraints to program implementation. Additional information that prove valuable in the planning process include such things as *population mobility,* public transportation systems, and other services available such as child care, home health care, and so on. The mobility of a population is important in health planning for two reasons. First, as compared to nonmovers, those who are highly mobile are generally more disorganized personally and socially and therefore require disproportionately more health and other services. Second, migration, be it immigration or emigration, has an effect on the community. Heavy immigration results in increased need for many community services such as housing, schools, and health care facilities. Heavy emigration tends to have the opposite effect. The effect may be a generalized reduction in need for various services and facilities, or it may be highly selective.

Needs Assessment

As is the case with many issues surrounding health planning there is no "right way" to conduct a *needs assessment*. However, there are essentially two types of data which can be gathered to provide the health planner with needed information to design programs which respond to present and future needs.

First, information and data must be collected which relate to the health problems and conditions that exist in a community. Second, data should be collected on the number and types of programs that currently exist in the community to deal with these problems. These two types of assessment although different are complimentary and should be conducted by health planners.

In addition, a needs assessment of problems should identify any unmet needs of a population related to such programs as prenatal care, VD screening, and drug-abuse and alcoholism prevention. It should identify if linkages are established so that a person may move from one type of care to another, depending upon need, with relative ease. It should also take into account personal considerations such as present level of training of various health personnel, including physicians, nurses, and volunteers. The utilization patterns of these professionals in view of their level of training, and any potential maldistribution of health professionals is also important.

1. *Assessment of Existing Programs and Services:* An analysis of currently offered health services is vital to the needs-assessment process. It provides a method by which gaps in service can be identified, such as inadequacies in the services themselves or in the availability of services to those who need them. The first step in this process involves identifying the ideal health program, which represents a full range of desirable services. Then an analysis should focus on the number of facilities available and type of services offered. For example, are provisions made for ambulatory and out-patient care, prevention education, drug addiction, and alcoholism, as well as immunization and sanitation.

Figure 8-6 Needs assessment.

2 Types of Data
  (1) data on problems that exist
  (2) data on types & number of programs that
      exist

6 Data Characteristics
  (1) morbidity data
  (2) mortality data
  (3 indicator data
  (4) psychological or, developmental characteristics
  (5) general social-economic conditions
  (6) utilization data

2. *Assessment of Problems:* This type of assessment attempts to identify community health needs in relation to services available. In terms of service and facility availability, it is important to determine if the residents or target group within a population or community require services, be it family-planning, emergency-care, home health care, or other categorical programs that are not already available. For example, if a significant proportion of the population is elderly, the services should reflect this by providing such things as glaucoma-screening, home health services, hypertension-screening and out-patient arthritis services. Another type of problem assessment might deal with facility needs. For example, what types of facilities might be needed that are not now established in a given geographic area? It may be that residents need a different type of facility than is provided, or its location may be improved to facilitate utilization.

Second, an investigation is conducted to determine the *accessibility* and *availability* of services. These factors are very important in community health planning, since a variety of otherwise valuable services will be of little value if they are not available and accessible to the target population that needs them. For example, family-planning services are of questionable value in a retirement community. And, an out-patient emergency service facility in the middle of a city is of little value to a migrant who needs the service but is in a rural area 100 miles away from the city. In addition, cost of services and *utilization rates* should

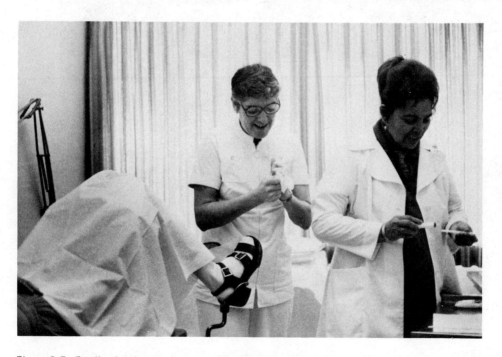

Figure 8-7 Family-planning services are of questionable value in a retirement community. Courtesy Arizona Department of Health Services.

be computed. Utilization refers to the number of persons who use the service on a specified time basis—that is, monthly, yearly, or weekly.

Ideally, a comprehensive health care system should provide health care needs to a population by providing programs that consist of the following elements:

1. Services dealing with acute short-term in-patient needs. This includes special facilities for emergency services, intensive care, and special procedures.
2. Services for ambulatory facilities. This includes all the major settings in which ambulatory medical care is provided.
3. Services in-patients' houses and at the sites of life-threatening occurrences.
4. Long-term in-patient chronic and rehabilitative care.
5. Some area-wide system that provides for linkages among health and welfare agencies. These linkages will coordinate the elements into a total system for treating ill people and helping maintain the health of people.[11]
6. Health education. This is an educational approach designed to foster health in individuals and groups by preventing disease.

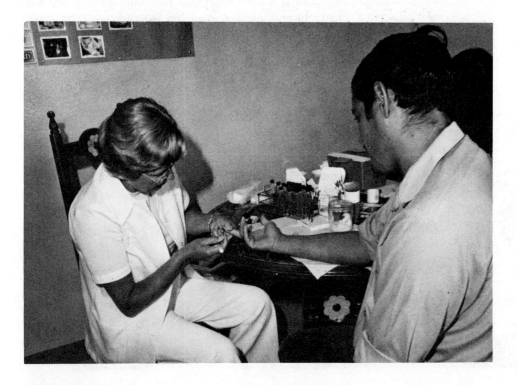

Figure 8-8 Ambulatory care facilities are one aspect of the health care system. Courtesy Arizona Department of Health Services.

| (1) Translate needs assessment data into problem statements that identify the problems that will be addressed. |
| (2) Problem statements are clearly & accurately defined. |
| (3) Problems that can be realistically addressed. |

Figure 8-9 Problem statements.

Goals, Problems, Tasks, and Implementation

The needs assessment provides health professionals with the documentation necessary to generate and support problem statements. In the needs assessment, specific health needs of the population are identified by conducting research and compiling statistics such as morbidity and mortality rates for various health problems, length of hospitalization stays, health-service utilization patterns (see Figure 8-6). The primary task in the initial stages of planning is to translate needs assessment data into problem statements (Figure 8-9) that identify the kinds of problems which need to be addressed.

Problem statements and goals These should be clearly and accurately defined. They represent those problems that can be realistically addressed, given the technology and resources available. There are a number of constraints that may influence the type of problems that can be addressed and the subsequent feasibility of the program including:

1. *Legal Mandates:* Some possible sources of legal mandates include a) enabling legislation, b) directions from a state advisory council or the governor, and c) specific guidelines that accompany the reception of funds.

2. *The State Health Agency Philosophy:* The existing philosophy and policies that the state has developed may limit the problems which can be addressed.

3. *Political Considerations:* In addition to the formal constraints of mandate and policy, there may be numerous informal constraints which limit the problems that can be addressed.

4. *Resources:* The resources available can also limit or influence the problems that can be addressed. The available staff and their skills, the budget and fiscal considerations, and technical capabilities can all influence program feasibility.

Once problem statements have been identified and prioritized, they are translated into goal statements (see Figure 8-10). These statements are the exact reversal of the problem statements. In general, they are expressions of the intended program accomplishments. They state the nature of the change that the program will attempt to effect.

Setting objectives The determination of goals establishes the overall direction of the program. These goals are subsequently reduced into measurable objectives. *Objectives* are statements of specific, measurable outcomes, by which the program can

(1) Reverse problem statement so that you identify a job to be accomplished.

(2) Make sure they represent your agency's committments.

List a goal statement for each problem statement generated.

Do your goal statements now represent overall statement of what needs to be accomplished?

Figure 8-10 Goal statements.

guage its progress. Each objective contributes to the realization of the goal and taken together, the objectives should approximate the accomplishment of the overall goal (see Figure 8-11). Objectives should:

1. Identify the results to be achieved rather than activities to be performed.
2. Be designed to cover a single end result.
3. Be written in quantifiable terms that are easily measurable.
4. Indicate a minimum level of achievement or "standard" that is acceptable.
5. Be consistent with resources available and anticipated.[12]

Program activity/task identification After a set of objectives has been constructed that represents expected outcomes and accomplishments over a period of time, it is necessary to identify specific activities that will be undertaken in the program to meet the objectives. The activities list should be very detailed. During this phase of planning it is still important to consider potential constraints on the program. The *task/activity or steps phase* of planning outlines the actual work that will be undertaken in the project. Activities and tasks necessary in order to achieve the stated objectives are identified. Resources needed to accomplish the tasks should also be determined in this phase. If

BREAK GOALS DOWN INTO MEASURABLE OBJECTIVES

(1) Identify results or conditions to be achieved rather than activites to be performed.

(2) Include time limits-to provide milestones of achievement.

(3) Cover a single end result.

(4) Be realistic & attainable.

(5) Be written in quantifiable terms.

(6) Be consistent with resources available and anticipated.

Figure 8-11 Setting objectives.

discrepancies occur between the resources needed and the resources available, this finding will have an impact on the *feasibility* of the plan. During this phase, if technical or special expertise is needed, it should be noted.

Program implementation When the activities and tasks have been identified, the plan is ready to be put into action. Consumer input should be incorporated into each phase of the planning process. In order to promote desirable levels of health and foster utilization of health services, people in the community must be involved. The health status of people in communities is largely a function of the community environment and its social structure. As a result, community health planning for a population must respond to and involve the people who comprise the social structure. Acceptance of a proposed program by consumers is essential.

Evaluation There are many ways of categorizing research and evaluation efforts as they relate to health programs. However, the major thrust of *evaluation* involves devising effective methods of measuring the degree to which objectives have been achieved. If properly stated, the objectives will define what is to be measured. Thus, the major question is *how* to measure it.

1. *Process evaluation:* This type of evaluation is concerned only with the performance of activities, *not* their usefulness or appropriateness in meeting objectives. Basically, *process evaluation* is designed to measure the efficiency of programs. It assesses such things as whether or not program activities are staying within budget constraints.
2. *Outcome evaluation:* This effort measures the effect of the program. It identifies the extent to which a program has accomplished its intended objectives. The combination of process and *outcome evaluation* can be considered "program evaluation". For example, is the recently established venereal disease clinic achieving high utilization rates by the target population of 14-to-21-year-olds it was designed to help?

Process evaluation :	concerned only with the performance of activities, not their usefulness in meeting objectives.
Outcome evaluation :	measures the effect of the program on desired outcomes. It indicates whether a program has accomplished its intended objectives.
Impact evaluation :	measures the effect of the program on some external variable. Most difficult to perform. Tests the assumptions made. Complex research technology.

Figure 8-12 Evaluation.

3. *Impact evaluation: Impact evaluation* measures the effect of the program on some external variable. This type of evaluation, designed to show causality, is very difficult to perform because it attempts to identify causality between activities and some external variable. It requires complex research to be successful. For example, as a result of home-health-care services, fewer older people are admitted to hospitals. For non-life-threatening problems, length of hospital stays for this group has been reduced for a variety of conditions (see Figure 8-12).

The primary work involved in evaluation is that of: (1) identifying the proper methods for gathering necessary data, and (2) choosing an evaluation design that fits within the technical, human, and financial constraints of the project and agency. Regardless of the program activities, once a program is implemented, it should be evaluated at predetermined intervals—or more frequently if the need arises.

Through evaluation, it is possible to identify those parts of the program that are achieving stated objectives and those that are not. In addition, evaluation is conducted to determine such things as (1) effective personnel training programs, (2) efficient methods of operating program administering, (3) improving the utilization of services, and (4) improving the methods of personnel recruitment and utilization.

In summary, the four elements of program planning—assessment, planning, implementation, and evaluation—are not discrete phases, but interwoven. Assessment concerns data collection and analysis and a statement of conclusions. Planning consists of ordering priorities based on needs, defining objectives, and selecting the appropriate activities designed to effect a solution. Implementation refers to action initiated in a program. And evaluation refers to the measurement of actions and program activities.[13]

MAJOR HEALTH PLANNING FORCES

Government Involvement

The federal government in the past thirty years has shifted its emphasis from fragmented health planning for specific medical needs toward a more holistic effort designed to provide comprehensive services that respond to the total needs of people. The passage of the Hill-Burton Act of 1946 was the first "piece of legislation to specifically require the development of a system of state and areawide planning to guide the expenditure of available resources."[14]

In 1966, Congress enacted the Regional Medical Programs (RMP) Act designed to support and encourage research, education, training and demonstration projects in such areas as cancer, stroke, and heart disease. The RMP reflected an awareness and concern on the part of society that improved access to health care, especially in ghetto and rural areas, could reduce mortality from the leading causes of death. This Act also redirected programming efforts from categorial disease orientation to a more comprehensive service approach.

Included in the priorities established by the Regional Medical Programs Act were:

1. comprehensive and available health care delivery system
2. expansion of health manpower training programs
3. improvement of use and distribution of health professionals
4. provisions for ambulatory and primary-care services. Subsequently, the Department of Health, Education and Welfare added priorities for emergency health services, health maintenance organizations (HMO) and area-wide health education programs.

The Partnership for Health or Comprehensive Health Planning Program (CHP) was enacted in 1967. This Act replaced the authority enacted in 1963 for area-wide health-facilities planning. The Report of the President's Commission on Human Rights outlined four goals for achievement of rights to health as embodied in the Partnership for Health Act:

1. Every person should have maximum protection against disease that need not happen and against illness and injury resulting from the hazards of the modern environment.
2. Every person should have ready access to basic medical care—despite social, economic, geographic or other barriers—and should have the assurance of continuity of quality service through diagnosis, treatment, and rehabilitation.
3. Every person should also have maximum opportunity for developing his capabilities in an environment that is not merely safe but conducive to productive living.
4. All activities conducted in pursuit of health should be carried out with full attention to the dignity and integrity of the individual.[15]

At present, the definition of health care has been broadened to mean more than the treatment of disease.

In 1974, the National Health Planning and Resources Development Act was enacted. This act established a major national health policy for planning a health care system in the United States.

The National Health Planning and Resources Development Act has two principle parts. The first revises and combines existing health planning programs into a single new system of Federal, State, and areawide health planning. The second revises existing programs for health resources development including health facilities construction, and health program development, and ties them more closely to the planning programs specified in the first part of the legislation.[16]

There are ten health policies listed in the National Health Planning and Resources Development Act which under the law deserve "priority consideration" in health planning and resources development. These priorities have been used by the National Council of Health Planning and Development and by Health Systems Agencies and State Health Planning and Development Agencies in formulating health goals and in developing and

Table 8-1. Priorities as Outlined by the National Health Planning and Resources Development Act of 1974 (PL 93-641)

PRIORITIES	EQUAL ACCESS	QUALITY OF CARE	COST CONSTRAINT
1. Primary care for the underserved	x		
2. Coordination of health services		x	x
3. Medical group practices		x	x
4. Physician assistants	x		
5. Sharing of support services			
6. Improved quality		x	
7. Appropriate levels of care	x	x	x
8. Disease prevention	x	x	x
9. Uniform reporting systems			x
10. Health education	x	x	x

carrying out plans and programs. The priorities listed in Table 8-1 are linked to the three overall purposes of the National Health Planning and Resource Development Act, which are equal access, improved quality of health care, and cost constraint.

The role of the federal government in recent years has been to provide initiative for the states to plan and develop health care systems that are comprehensive, of high quality, and efficient.

Consumers

At the state and local levels, there are essentially three key decision-making elements in health planning; consumers, providers and institutions. Consumers of health care are capable of assisting health-care providers and institutions to plan services in a variety of ways. Two of the most important areas for consumers input in health planning are (1) providing input for the identification of perceived health needs, and (2) opening communication lines between consumers, providers and institutions. Consumers have both a right and responsibility to become actively involved in decision making as it relates to health policy. In the present, consumers have not become totally aware of their rights and responsibilities in health planning. However, it is likely that consumers will begin to assume a more active role in the future.

In community health planning, it is imperative to identify key community leaders and recognize the leadership structure or pattern in the community. Community leaders may be the top community influentials (*legitimizers*) whose approval is needed before support at the next level of leadership is obtained. Leaders may also represent those individuals who possess the technical and professional competency in various specialized areas such as education, city planning or public health. These leaders (*effectors*) are more active workers in community decision-making in the planning of community change. Finally, there are those who represent the doers and joiners (*activists*) in a community. These leaders are people who are active workers and office holders in community, civic, and service clubs. These consumers function in such a way as to be involved in minor decisions and they serve as a means through which information is diffused to the community to gain support.

Legitimizers, effectors, and activists do not represent the total leadership structure in a community. Each person or resident has some power and can influence community programs and development. In addition, many people outside the community influence community change and are involved in the network of community decision-making. Since planned community health programs are designed to bring about change, it is important to recognize that all change has its costs, that individuals and groups may either resist or accept the proposed change, and that change in one part of a social system may result in change or adjustment in other parts of the system. The people must be involved in the planning and change process by defining their own problems and attempting to facilitate solutions. *"If government is to be of, by and for the people as our democratic values prescribe . . . it must look to the people to determine its directions and goals."*[17]

Providers

Health planners and physicians constitute the provider element in community health decision-making. Providers have a responsibility to make available the most accurate information they possess regarding health problems and potential solutions to consumers. In like manner, providers have a responsibility to promote informed consumerism by presenting information in a manner that is readily understood by community residents. Finally, providers should have a good understanding of consumers present attitudes regarding health as well as their past efforts to improve health.

Providers must assume responsibility for coordinating and effecting compromise among special interest groups. They should be able to effect an interdisciplinary approach to health promotion that meets the needs of all the people. In addition, providers may utilize the following techniques to overcome difficulties associated with establishing community health programs:

1. *Modify the message:* Providers should be capable of modifying language so that the message is understood by specific groups. Class and ethnic differences within a given community may make it necessary to utilize more than one form of the message.

2. *Involve the people:* Consumers should be accepted as equal partners in health planning. It is important that providers view consumers as competent and valuable resources in the program planning process.

3. *Learn the social networks:* In addition to identifying general and specialized community leaders, it is important to understand social networks at the neighborhood level.

4. *Develop personal contact:* In this age of increasing complexity, specialization, and interdependence, contradictory forces are operating. On the one hand, the increasing division of labor—or specialization—pulls people further apart and decreases their common interests. However, this same specialization makes people more dependent upon other people for the goods and services they need which they do not produce themselves. Community health providers can com-

pete against mass impersonalization and divergent interests and gain consumer involvement and support by employing a personalized, face-to-face approach.[18]

Institutions

In community health, as in many aspects of social planning and community development, the institution plays a major role in controlling much of the system. Whether it is represented by a governmental agency or health facility (hospital, primary-care center, or HMO) the institution has the capacity for controlling financing, facility management, policy making, and legislation. In addition, institutions are responsible for protecting individual human rights.

Institutions have the potential for promoting meaningful change in the future of community health. Perhaps the key to the future of the role of institutions as an element of health program decision making lies in the ability of institutions to identify more open, humane, and efficient organizational patterns.

In the future, each of the local-level components—consumer, provider, and institution—will need to increase its interaction and interrelatedness with other components. And, no doubt, collaborative planning will be nurtured within a framework capable of providing comprehensive services to all people. Expanded consumer input, the use of more humanistic approaches to the planning and delivery of health services, and greater responsiveness to local community needs will all be a part of future program planning efforts. The future may reflect a basic understanding that to be effective,

Figure 8-13 Health institutions have a capacity for controlling financing, facility management, and policy making. Courtesy Marc Anderson.

community health programs and personnel must consider the behavior patterns that predominate in a given group or population, for they mirror community values and beliefs about health and life.

PLANNING EXAMPLES

Two examples of the program planning process follow which illustrate how it occurs in a prevention activity plan and a plan for a new health service in a community.

Example 1: Drug-Abuse Prevention

Suppose that a health planner has been assigned the task of developing a prevention plan for drug abuse in the age group 14-to-20-year-olds. The plan is to be administered by the County X Health Department.

Needs assessment The Drug-Abuse Survey indicates that there has been a 27 percent increase in the use of illicit drugs by 14-to-20-year-olds in County X, compared to a 1979 survey. In prevention programs, a number of assumptions are made before data such as the above can be used to give direction to a program. One of these might be that drug use is neither inherently good nor bad. Drug use becomes a problem when the health of an individual suffers and/or drug use creates a potential threat to other persons. Another assumption could be that the incidence of drug abuse cannot be reduced without the use of effective prevention strategies, such as personal and social growth and communication skills, and knowledge of the existence of alternatives other than substance abuse.

Justification Drug abuse is widespread among 14-to-20-year-olds. Data are cited to indicate the number of 14-to-20-year-olds involved in drug abuse (police records, drug-behavior questionnaires, school records, and so on). Data are cited that indicate the number of 14-to-20-year-olds involved in delinquency, vandalism, school absenteeism, and motor-vehicle operation while under the influence. Studies are cited that indicate that possible effects of substance abuse on adult adjustment and health. Studies are cited to show the effects of drug-prevention and intervention programs on developing responsible patterns of drug use.

Problem statements These are clear statements of what incidence and prevalence data mean. Examples are:

1. Individuals are not sufficiently aware of how drug abuse influences their health.
2. Individuals do not possess adequate skills to cope with and prevail over human problems. Such skills include decision making, communication, problem solving and self-responsibility.

Goals A goal involves the reversal of the problem statement that identifies a task to be accomplished. An example would be:

> To improve knowledge of individuals 14-to-20-years-old concerning how drug abuse influences health. To improve the coping skills of 14-to-20-year-olds in prevailing over human problems. These skills include decision making, communication, problem solving, and self-responsibility.

Objectives These are results and conditions that should be attained during the next year to achieve the goals that are identified. The following list shows some sample objectives.

1. An increase in knowledge concerning the adverse effects of drugs among 14-to-20-year-olds as measured by a drug-knowledge test.
2. A decrease in drug use among 14-to-20-year-olds.
3. An increase in the number of 14-to-20-year-olds who engage in youth clubs and other group activity.
4. A decrease in the number of reported drug-related overdoses, arrests, and motor-vehicle violations among 14-to-20-year-olds.
5. A decrease in school absenteeism among 14-to-20-year-olds.
6. A decrease in suicide rates among 14-to-20-year olds.
7. An increase in the use of effective teaching techniques designed to improve coping, decision making, and communication skills in the junior and senior high schools.
8. A decrease in delinquency rates among 14-to-20-year-olds.
9. An increase in counseling services available to 14-to-20-year-olds in and out of school.
10. An improved self-concept among 14-to-20-year-olds.

These are merely examples. Many other results or conditions could indicate successful goal attainment. Let us examine objectives (1) and (10) more carefully.

1. An increase in drug knowledge among 14-to-20-year-olds as measured by a drug-knowledge test.

If we were to translate objective (1) into a specific measureable objective that meets established criteria, it might now read:

1. By June 1985, 60 percent of tenth, eleventh, and twelfth graders who scored below the mean on the Bedlington Drug Knowledge test will show a 25 percent improvement on that scale. The norm will be determined by administering the test to all tenth, eleventh, and twelfth graders in all County X high schools before September 30, 1984.

Objective (10) reads:

10. An improved self-concept among 14-to-20-year-olds.

Expanded, it might now read:

10. By June 1985, 40 percent of the tenth and eleventh graders in County X high schools who scored below the norm on the Bradford-McClain Self-Concept Scale will show a 25 percent improvement on that scale. The norm will be determined by administering the scale to all tenth and eleventh graders in County X high schools before September 30, 1984.

Identifying tasks/activities One example of the tasks/activities that might be identified to reach Objective (10) follows.

10. Objective: By June 1985, 40 percent of the tenth and eleventh graders in County X high schools who scored below the norm on the Bradford-McClain Self-Concept Scale will show a 25 percent improvement on that scale.

Task Identification

ACTIVITY/TASK	PERSON RESPONSIBLE	COMPLETION DATE	FIT WITHIN ROLE	CONSTRAINTS/ COORDINATION
1. Train 10th- and 11th-grade teachers to provide self-concept-building skills to students	Ron Somers	Aug. 30, 1984	Yes, Training	1. Need to coordinate with local teachers' group, which has on-going in-service teaching commitment from Board of Education.
a. Hire a consultant	Ron Somers	June 30, 1984		
b. Finalize curriculum and schedule	Ron Somers and consultant	July 30, 1984		
c. Run training	Consultant	Aug. 7–8, 1984		2. Need to coordinate with state education agency.

Identifying Resource Needs

ACTIVITY	RESOURCES NEEDED		
	Number of Persons	*Skills*	*Financial*
Train 10th- and 11th-grade teachers to provide self-concept-building skills to students	2	1 coordinator 1 trainer	$1500 for coordinator $1500 for trainer $ 500 for space and materials

Evaluation of plan performance When the plan is adopted, it will go into effect on June 30, 1984. Evaluation is relatively simple for the plan and will consist of administering the Bradford-McClain Self-Concept Scale before September 30, 1984 and again before June 30, 1985. Quantitative reports will be made indicating the degree to which the objective of improved self-concept has been achieved.

Example 2: Mental Health Services and Status

Suppose that the County Y Mental Health Association has expressed interest in identifying the mental health needs, demands (usually estimated by current utilization rates) and services available to older residents in Town Z. This example discusses some possible approaches to a characteristic health planning problem.

Needs assessment Based upon a 1984 one-week survey which used population census data for Town Z and utilization rates for mental health services in hospitals, outpatient clinics, and the like, the number of patient days used by older residents in Town Z was obtained. An underlying assumption is that present utilization rates by older persons of all mental health services in the area is a measure of present demand.

The data show there is a need to be met. The 1984 household interview survey of mental health status of older people suggests that much can be done to improve the mental health status of older persons. In addition, it indicates that 30 percent of older persons are unaware of mental health services available in Town Z. Forty percent of persons interviewed suggested they would have difficulty in utilizing these services because of their location. The information required to identify need can come from such sources as patient-origin studies and household-interview surveys.

A study of present mental health services facilities and other resources in Town Z indicates that there are sufficient hospital beds and in-patient institutionalization services available to older persons. However, there is a deficiency in out-patient mental health services in the community. Underlying assumptions here are that public inventories of medical societies and government licensing agencies are legitimate sources of information concerning available health resources.

A logical approach to this type of planning involves:

1. An estimation of present mental health service utilization rates to measure present demand.
2. An estimation of professionally determined need, which indicates surpluses as well as deficiencies in the present system.
3. An inventory of existing resources and evaluation of how resources need to be altered to provide better services within the constraints of the budget.

Justification In general, there is a scarcity of community mental health services and programs for older people, a group whose needs are great. Data are cited that indicate a large number of older persons are misplaced in institutions, when they could instead return to the community with appropriate services. Data are cited that indicates some older persons remain in their homes who are seriously in need of mental health services. Studies are cited that show that psychopathology in general and depression in particular rise sharply with age. Studies are cited to show that suicide is very high among older people, especially white males. Studies are cited to lend evidence that older people need a social life, good health care, and special housing arrangements to assist them in maintaining mental health.

Problem statements These are clear statements of what needs assessment data mean. Examples are:

1. In general, there are insufficient mental health services and facilities in Community Z for older people.
2. When mental health services are available, frequently they are improperly utilized by older people.
3. Older persons in Community Z suffer psychopathology in general and depression in particular.

Goals Involves the reversal of the problem statement that identifies a task that is to be accomplished:

To improve community mental health services and facilities available to older residents, especially out-patient services. To improve utilization patterns of mental health services and facilities so that people are using services appropriate to the nature and extent of their mental health problems. To reduce the incidence of psychopathology and depression among older people.

Objectives These are results and conditions that should be attained during the next year to achieve the goals that are identified. Sample objectives are:

1. An increase in the number of hospital beds allocated for mental health patients by 25.
2. The creation of a new out-patient mental health center.
3. The development of a mental health facilitator program using older comminity residents as lay advisors.
4. An increase in the proportionate use of out-patient mental health services (ratio), compared to in-patient services.
5. A decrease in the number of suicides among the older population.
6. A reduction in the number of older people diagnosed and treated for depression and other psychopathology.
7. An improvement in the support—recreational, social and other—available to older persons.

8. An increase in the number of older persons who engage in retirement and club activities.
9. An increase in counseling services available to older people in churches and throughout the community.
10. An improved mental health status among older people.

These are merely examples. Many other results or conditions could indicate successful goal attainment. Let us examine objectives (2) and (3) more carefully.

2. The creation of a new out-patient mental health center.

We can translate this into a specific measureable objective that meets established criteria. As such, it might now read:

2. By June, 1985, ground will be broken for the creation of an out-patient mental health center in Catchment Area C. This center will be opened for service to the community by January 1988 with a staff of one psychiatrist, one psychiatric nurse, two counseling psychologists, and one psychiatric social worker.

Objective (3) now reads:

3. The development of a mental health facilitator program using older community residents as lay advisors.

Expanded it might now read:

3. By June 1984, older community residents will be identified and trained to help and support other older people in the community in promoting mental health. The community mental health facilitator staff will include a director-administrator, a health educator, two coordinators, and a secretary.

Identifying tasks/activities   One example of the tasks/activities that might be identified to reach Objective 2 can be found on page 231.

Evaluation of plan performance   The facility will be evaluated annually in terms of the specific objectives set for it. Quantitative and qualitative reports will be made indicating the degree to which objectives are being met. Changes and modifications in operating policy and staff will be made annually, based on feedback information yielded by evaluations. At the end of five years, a major evaluation will be made and the program (services) revised and presented to the County Y Mental Health Association for consideration of whether to continue, seriously modify, or discontinue the project.

Creation of a New Out-Patient Mental Health Center

ACTIVITY/TASK	PERSON RESPONSIBLE	COMPLE—TION DATE	FIT WITHIN ROLE	CONSTRAINTS/ COORDINATION
1. Decide upon location-site for facility	Alta Woodrow, Administrator, Dir., Mental Health Assoc. and Board of Directors.	Jan. 1984	Yes	1. Need to coordinate with area Health Service agency (HSA) 2. Health planner, engineers
2. Break ground for new facility	County Engineer	June 1984	Yes	1. Construction/development company
3. Hire staff for facility	Alta Woodrow, and Board of Directors	Sept. 1987	Yes	1. Affirmative action $35,000, psychiatrist/director $23,000, psychiatric nurse $20,000, psychiatric social worker $18,000 each, 2 counselor/psychologists $9,000, 1 secretary
4. Decide on services to be offered	Alta Woodrow, Board of Directors, Staff	Nov. 1987	Yes	Health Service Agency
5. Open the new facility	Staff	January 1988	Yes	Need to coordinate with area Health Systems Agency

Identifying Resource Needs

ACTIVITY	RESOURCES NEEDED		
	Number of Persons	Skills	Financing
1. Hire staff for facility operation	1	Psychiatrist-director	$35,000
	1	Psychiatric social worker	$20,000
	1	Psychiatric nurse	$23,000
	1	Secretary	$ 9,000
	2	Counseling psychologists	$18,000
2. Buy supplies/equipment			$ 8,500

Summary

Agencies responsible for on-going planning in local areas will undoubtedly seek to complete the cells of a two-way matrix. In the matrix, various types of medical services listed in the first column are expressed in appropriate service units in the total column. Visits, patient days, and other total service units entered on each line are distributed across the various columns to indicate the types of resources that will be needed to meet these service requirements. Such a matrix may be developed for needs or demands and for the difference between the two.

The two program planning examples presented provide illustrations of different types of planning—one is related specifically to prevention activities, and one related to delivery of health services. The approaches described in these examples present a cursory explanation of the health planning process. These exercises were provided for illustrative purposes only. The conclusions presented are not considered valid, but they simplify assumptions to demonstrate the methodology of the planning process.

REVIEW QUESTIONS

1. Differentiate between community development and technical or social planning. Give examples of each.
2. Identify and describe the five levels of community improvement progams.
3. What is meant by the term *adaptive community*?
4. Why are identification of population and community setting characteristics important in health planning?
5. In conducting a needs assessment of existing services and program, what kind of information should be gathered?
6. What are the characteristics of well-written program objectives?
7. Differentiate among process, outcome, and impact evaluation. Why is evaluation so vital in health planning?
8. Describe the historical involvement of the federal government in health program planning.
9. Describe various types of community leaders (legitimizers, activists, and effectors) and the roles they may play in health programs.

SUGGESTED READINGS

Colt, A., "Public Policy and Planning Criteria in Public Health," *American Journal of Public Health*, 59(a) 1678-1685, 1969.

———— "Idealogy, Medical Technology, and Health Care Organization in Modern Nations," *American Journal of Public Health*, 65(3) 241-247, 1975.

Guide to a Community Health Study. New York: American Public Health Association, 1961.

Kast, F. and J. Rosenzwieg, *Organization and Management: A Systems Approach.* New York: McGraw-Hill, 1970.

Kleinman, J.C., *Mortality: Statistical Notes for Health Planners.* Washington, D.C.: National Center for Health Statistics, Health Resources Administration, Dept. HEW No. 3, 1977.

Meredith, Jack, "Program Evaluation Techniques in the Health Services," *American Journal of Public Health,* 66(11) 1069-1073, 1976.

Stoller, Eleanor, "New Roles for Health Care Consumers: A Study of Role Transformation," *Journal of Community Health,* 3(2) 171-177, 1977.

Waters, William, "State Level Comprehensive Health Planning: A Retrospect," *American Journal of Public Health,* 66(2) 139-144, 1976.

NOTES

[1] U.S. DHEW, *The Community and Its Involvement in the Study-Planning-Action Process.* Washington, D.C.: U.S. DHEW Pub. No. (CDC) 78-8355, 1977 pp. 27-29.

[2] Briscoe, M., "Planning for Health Care," *Health in America: 1776-1976.* Washington, D.C.: U.S. DHEW Pub. No. (HRA) 76-616, 1976 p. 30.

[3] U.S. DHEW, *Health in America: 1776-1976.* Washington, D.C.: U.S. DHEW Pub. No. (HRA) 76-616, 1976, pp. 33-34.

[4] Adapted from *The Community Development Process: The Rediscovery of Local Initiative* by William W. Biddle with the collaboration of Loureide J. Biddle. Copyright © 1965 by Holt, Rinehart and Winston, Inc. Reprinted by permission of Holt, Rinehart and Winston.

[5] *The Community and Its Involvement in the Study-Planning-Action Process,* p. 42.

[6] William Shonick, *Elements of Planning for Area-Wide Personal Health Service.* St. Louis: C.V. Mosby, 1976, p. 1.

[7] Paul G. Rogers and Lee S. Hyde, "Planning for Health Care," in U.S. DHEW, *Health in America: 1776-1976.* Washington, D.C.: U.S. DHEW Pub. No. (HRA) 76-616, 1976, p. 108.

[8] Paul G. Rogers and Lee S. Hyde, pp. 108-109.

[9] Paul G. Rogers and Lee S. Hyde, p. 110.

[10] H.D. Chadwick, "The Diseases of the Inhabitants of the Commonwealth," *New England Journal of Medicine,* 216:8, 1937.

[11] William Shonick, p. 7.

[12] *Prevention Planning Workbook.* Washington, D.C.: Center for Human Services, NIDA 271-77-4506.

[13] Carrie Jo Braden and Nancy L. Herban, *Community Health: A Systems Approach.* Englewood Cliffs, N.J.: Prentice-Hall, 1976, p. 59.

[14] Paul G. Rogers and Lee S. Hyde, p. 111.

[15] U.S. Department of State, "For Free Men in a Free World: A Survey of Human Rights in the United States." Washington, D.C.: U.S. DHEW Pub. No. 8434, 1969, pp. 166–168.

[16] Paul G. Rogers and Lee S. Hyde, p. 115.

[17] *The Community and Its Involvement in the Study-Planning-Action Process,* p. 75.

[18] Carrie Jo Braden and Nancy L. Herban, p. 80.

GLOSSARY

accessibility the extent to which health services, facilities, and manpower are able to be used by residents in the community, dependent on geographic location.

activists the doers and joiners; office holders and active workers in a community.

availability the extent to which health services, facilities, and manpower are present in the community.

community population within a well-defined geographic area.

community development activities designed to improve capacity of a community; emphasis is on improving the organization of the community as well as problem solving.

effectors community leaders who possess technical or professional competence in various specialized areas.

evaluation efforts to discover the degree to which the program is successful; measures the extent to which objectives are met.

feasibility the degree to which the program planned is capable of being accomplished or brought about; practicably.

health planning activities designed to identify unmet health needs or inefficient methods or activities and to correct them.

impact evaluation measures the effect of the program on some external variable.

legitimizers community leaders who are top community influentials and whose approval

is needed before support at the next level of leadership is obtained.

needs assessment technique in program planning designed to provide information about health problems, existing programs and facilities, and unmet needs.

objectives statements of specific, measurable outcomes, by which a program may gauge its progress.

outcome evaluation measures the effect of the program; the extent to which the program has accomplished its intended objectives.

population mobility the extent to which the population of concern moves from one residence to another, or in and out of the community.

process evaluation a method concerned with the performance of activities, not their usefulness.

task/activity or steps phase the phase in program planning in which specific activities to be undertaken in the program in order to reach the objectives are outlined.

technical or social planning an approach that involves organizing resources to tackle problems or tasks; focuses on problems rather than process or goals.

utilization rates the extent to which health services, facilities, and manpower are used by residents in the community.

BIBLIOGRAPHY

Bergwall, D., P. Reeves, and R. Woodside, *Introduction to Health Planning.* Washington, D.C.: Information Resources Press, 1974.

Bertrand, A., *Social Organization: A General Systems and Role Theory Perspective.* Philadelphia: Davis, 1972.

Biddle, W. William, and Lourelide J. Biddle, *The Community Process: The Rediscovery of Local Initiative.* New York: Holt, Rinehart and Winston, 1965.

Braden, Carrie Jo, and Nancy L. Herban, *Community Health, A Systems Approach.* Englewood Cliffs, N.J.: Prentice-Hall, 1976.

Buckley, W. (ed.), *Modern Systems Research for the Behavioral Scientist.* Chicago: Aldine, 1968.

Hanlon, J., *Public Health: Administration and Practice,* 6th ed. St. Louis: C.V. Mosby, 1974.

National Commission on Health Services, *Health Is a Community Affair.* Cambridge, Mass.: Harvard University Press, 1967.

Prevention Planning Workbook. Washington, D.C.: Center for Human Services, NIDA 271-77-4506.

Reeves, Phillip, David Bergwall, and Nina Woodside (eds.), *Introduction to Health Planning,* 2nd ed. Washington, D.C.: Information Resources Press, 1979.

Rogers, Paul G., and Lee. S. Hyde, "Planning for Health Care," in U.S. DHEW, *Health in America: 1776–1976.* Washington, D.C.: U.S. DHEW Pub. No. (HRA) 76-616, 1976, pp. 108–121.

Room, Robin, "The Case for a Problem Prevention Approach to Alcohol, Drug and Mental Problems," *Public Health Reports,* 96(1) 26-33, 1981.

U.S. DHEW, *The Community and Its Involvement in the Study-Planning-Action Process.* Washington, D.C.: U.S. DHEW Pub. No. (CDC) 78-8355, 1977.

9

THE UNITED STATES HEALTH CARE SYSTEM

> All our lives we have heard the claim that U.S. citizens are the healthi-
> est, best-cared-for people in the world. For most of us, this is simply
> not true. Health care in this country is both inaccessible and cripplingly
> expensive. Even those of us who can summon up the strength, deter-
> mination, and financial resources required to locate health care find
> that our needs are not being met by the present health care delivery
> system.
>
> *Organizing for Health Care: A Tool for Change*

THE HEALTH CARE DELIVERY
SYSTEM: IN CRISIS?

The health care delivery system in the United States is a complex blend of services, manpower and facilities operating in both the private and public sectors. It is composed of
private practitioners or physicians in solo and group practice, a military network of health
care delivery called *CHAMPUS,* and a variety of publicly funded health facilities that are
administered by federal, state, local, and county public health departments. The financing
of health services is as complex a network as is the actual delivery of care. In its broadest
sense, *health care* refers to any and all activities undertaken in either the public or private
sector that have as their objective improving and maintaining the health of the people.
Health care in America today is indeed a composite of programs, acronyms, and issues.

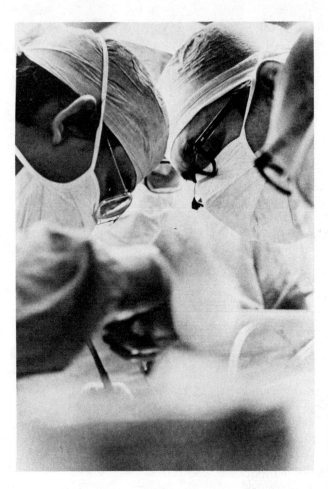

Figure 9-1
The health care delivery system is a complex blend of services, manpower, and facilities. Courtesy U.S. Department of Health, Education and Welfare.

The federal government has been actively involved in planning for health care since 1798, when a medical care system was established for military personnel and native Americans. During the last century, state governments have become more actively involved in planning for quality health care with the enactment of physician licensure laws. However, the funding, publication, and subsequent implementation of the "Flexner Report" by the Carnegie Foundation in 1910 represented the first attempt in the private sector to promote quality medical and health care.[1]

During the past two decades, increased attention has been devoted to developing a comprehensive health care system in the United States that is effective in serving the entire population, is reasonable in cost, and assures a satisfactory level of quality. Indeed, the need to apply a holistic approach to providing health care is now recognized as preferable to attempts at fragmented planning for specific medical needs among specific target populations. Ideally, the health care system should be one which provides high quality care to all people regardless of income, race, or geographic location in an economical and efficient manner, and based on a comprehensive array of services that are linked progressively. Yet the status of American health care as described in 1969 by James Cavanaugh, a former assistant in the U.S. Department of Health, Education and Welfare, is still applicable today:

> The delivery of health services is faltering so badly that we will have to shake the present system literally to its foundations . . . revolutionary changes are needed . . . the nation must have new careers, new professions, new kinds of manpower; and we do not have thousands of years, perhaps not even thousands of days to lose . . . we will have to question every cherished belief about how health care ought to be provided—that the physician must always be the first line of health manpower; that a stay in the hospital at $100 a day is the best way to deal with serious health problems; that prepaid group practice is somehow second-rate medicine.[2]

Despite all of its great technology and resources, the United States is now in a position where a breakdown of its health care system is predicted unless immediate preventive action is taken by government and the private sector of society. The crisis in health care is but one aspect of the complex social and economic problems of contemporary American life. Improving health care will to some extent depend upon solving these other national problems as well.

When examining the health care crisis, the issue of high cost is considered a central concern. Indeed, the issue of cost underlies many of the problems in the health care system. For more than a decade the cost of health care has been climbing more rapidly than all other consumer goods or services (see Table 9-1).

Table 9-1 Consumer Price Index (1967 = 100) for All Items and Selected Items: United States, Selected Years 1950-1978[a]

	ITEM						
YEAR	All Items	Medical Care	Food	Apparel And Upkeep	Housing	Transportation	Personal Care
			Consumer Price Index				
1950	72.1	53.7	74.5	79.0	72.8	68.2	68.3
1955	80.2	64.8	81.6	84.1	82.3	77.4	77.9
1960	88.7	79.1	88.0	89.6	90.2	89.6	90.1
1965	94.5	89.5	94.4	93.7	94.9	95.9	95.2
1970	116.3	120.6	114.9	116.1	118.9	112.7	113.2
1975	161.2	168.6	175.4	142.3	166.8	150.6	150.7
1976	170.5	184.7	180.8	147.6	177.2	165.5	160.5
1977	181.5	202.4	192.2	154.2	189.6	177.2	170.9
1978	195.3	219.4	211.2	159.5	202.6	185.8	182.0

[a]Data are based on reporting by samples of providers and other retail outlets.

Source: Bureau of Labor Statistics, U.S. Department of Labor: *Consumer Price Index;* various releases.

The roots of the problem are complex and intertwined. For example, the multi-billion-dollar-a-year health care industry has been slow in adjusting to the increasing demand by the public for its services. This demand has grown, suddenly and immensely, by the establishment of Medicare and Medicaid. But these programs are not the only explanation for rising management capability. Thus, the demand for health services far exceeds the nation's capability to provide them.[3]

The fact that the demand for health care services has grown far more rapidly than the source of supply is clearly reflected in our nation's health bill, illustrated in Table 9-2. Our country now spends more for this single service than any other country in the world. Health care expenditures are so huge that during 1978 we were spending $863 for every man, woman, and child. And, it is projected that this per-capita figure would be

Table 9-2   National Health Expenditures, According to Source of Funds: United States, Selected Years 1929–1978[a]

YEAR	All Health Expenditures in Billions	Private			Public		
		Amount in Billions	Amount per Capita	Percent of Total	Amount in Billions	Amount per Capita	Percent of Total
1929	$ 3.6	$ 3.2	$ 25.49	86.4	$ 0.5	$ 4.00	13.6
1935	2.9	2.4	18.30	80.8	0.6	4.34	19.2
1940	4.0	3.2	23.61	79.7	0.8	6.03	20.3
1950	12.7	9.2	59.62	72.8	3.4	22.24	27.2
1955	17.7	13.2	78.33	74.3	4.6	27.05	25.7
1960	26.9	20.3	110.20	75.3	6.6	36.10	24.7
1965	43.0	32.3	163.29	75.1	10.7	54.13	24.9
1966	47.3	34.0	169.81	71.8	13.3	66.71	28.2
1967	52.7	33.9	167.61	64.4	18.8	97.74	35.6
1968	58.9	37.1	181.40	63.0	21.8	106.76	37.0
1969	66.2	41.6	201.83	62.9	24.5	118.87	37.1
1970	74.7	47.5	227.71	63.5	27.3	130.93	36.5
1971	82.8	51.4	244.12	62.1	31.4	148.97	37.9
1972	92.7	57.7	271.78	62.3	35.0	164.69	37.7
1973	102.3	63.6	297.17	62.1	38.8	181.22	37.9
1974	115.6	69.0	319.99	59.7	46.6	216.00	40.3
1975	131.5	75.8	348.61	57.7	55.7	255.96	42.3
1976	148.9	86.6	394.73	58.2	62.3	284.06	41.8
1977	170.0	100.7	455.27	59.2	69.3	313.50	40.8
1978[b]	192.4	114.3	512.62	59.4	78.1	350.40	40.6

[a]Data are compiled by the Health Care Financing Administration.

[b]Preliminary estimates.

Sources: Gibson, R. M., "National health expenditures, 1978," *Health Care Financing Review,* 1(1) 1–36, Summer 1979; Office of Research, Demonstrations, and Statistics, Health Care Financing Administration, selected data.

more than $3,000 within ten years.[4] While there are a number of factors that contribute to the spiraling cost of health care, hospital care is the most inflationary component.

The health care industry is one of the largest and most important resources in the United States. Since the early 1960s, there has been a steady increase in health-worker supply. It employs about 6.7 million people, an increase of 60 percent from the number employed in 1970. In 1981, the nation was pouring $252 billion into the health care system.

The word "crisis" aptly describes the severe economic, social, and political problems affecting us in terms of our personal health care. Almost 25 percent of Americans are not receiving adequate health care, particularly in rural areas and in depressed inner city neighborhoods. Older Americans today are paying more in real dollars for medical care than they were prior to the enactment of Medicare in 1965. A 1981 report warned senior citizens that under Medicare, the federal government picks up, on the average, less than one-third of bills for physician services. Hospital costs are now increasing at the rate of $1 million per hour. And the present Medicaid program has become the most rapidly escalating cost item in state budgets.[5] If the health care system remains unchanged, national health costs could skyrocket to $758 billion in 1990. *Allied-health personnel* is poorly distributed within the country. Health services are needlessly duplicated in some areas and unavailable in others. And, until recently, this commercial-sickness industry emphasized cure and treatment over health-promotion and disease-prevention efforts.

In 1981, the Reagan administration pledged to bring the federal health budget under control through budget cuts in entitlement programs such as Medicare and Medicaid. During the last ten years, the disease-prevention–health-promotion idea has gained acceptance in the federal health establishment. Prevention may well continue to be the highest priority of the future.

Figure 9-2
Until recently cure and treatment were emphasized over health promotion and disease prevention.

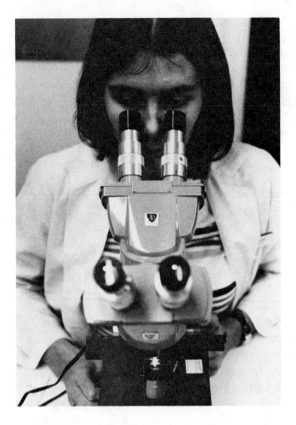

Figure 9-3
At present there are more than 230 recognized health occupations in the United States. Courtesy Arizona Department of Human Services.

WORKERS IN THE HEALTH SYSTEM

Technological advances in medicine and health care in recent years and a host of other factors have resulted in a tremendous proliferation of health occupations. At present, there are more than 230 recognized health occupations in the United States. The health industry employs about 8 percent of the total work force. It includes among many others, physicians, nurses, dental hygienists, x-ray technologists, and physical therapists (see Table 9-3). An important development in recent years has been the emergence of a new allied-health professional—the *physician assistant (PA)*. Physician assistants are trained to perform many of the functions of a primary-care physician, and they have helped ease some problems in the health care delivery system related to maldistribution of physician supply and inadequate supply of primary-care physicians.

Physicians

The supply of active physicians has increased significantly over the past two decades. In 1970, there were approximately 425,000 medical doctors actively delivering health care. Since the population has been increasing at a slower rate than the supply of physicians, there has been an increase in the ratio of active physicians to population.

Table 9–3 Persons 16 Years of Age and Over Employed in Selected Health-Related Occupations: United States, 1970–1978[a]

OCCUPATION	YEAR								
	1970[b]	1971	1972	1973	1974	1975	1976	1977	1978
	Number of Persons in Thousands								
Total, 16 years and over	3,103	3,443	3,621	3,806	3,973	4,169	4,341	4,517	4,753
Physicians, medical and osteopathic	281	309	328	344	346	354	368	403	424
Dentists	91	99	107	105	100	110	107	105	117
Pharmacists	110	113	126	123	127	119	123	138	136
Registered nurses	830	772	801	823	904	935	999	1,063	1,112
Therapists	75	92	115	109	132	157	159	178	189
Health technologists and technicians	260	289	315	330	371	397	436	462	498
Health administrators	84	115	118	137	150	152	162	175	184
Dental assistants	88	90	94	114	107	126	122	123	130
Health aides, excluding nursing	119	144	148	170	186	211	229	234	270
Nursing aides, orderlies, and attendants	718	866	912	942	959	1,001	1,002	1,008	1,037
Practical nurses	237	345	343	358	349	370	381	371	402
Other health-related occupations[c]	210	209	214	251	242	237	253	257	254

[a]Data are based on household interviews of a sample of the civilian noninstitutionalized population.

[b]Based on the 1970 decennial census; all other years are annual average derived from the Current Population Survey.

[c]Includes chiropractors, optometrists, podiatrists, veterinarians, dietitians, embalmers, funeral directors, lens grinders and polishers, dental lab technicians, lay midwives, and health trainees.

Sources: U.S. Bureau of the Census, *Census of Population, 1970, Detailed Characteristics,* Final Report PC1-(D). Washington, D.C.: U.S. Bureau of the Census, Feb. 1973; U.S. Bureau of Labor Statistics, *Employment and Earnings, January 1978,* and *January 1979,* Vol. 25, No. 1 and Vol. 26, No. 1. Washington, D.C.: U.S. Bureau of Labor Statistics, Jan. 1978 and Jan. 1979, and unpublished data.

Table 9-4 Professionally Active Physicians (M.D.s), According to Primary Specialty: United States, Selected Years 1970-1977[a]

PRIMARY SPECIALTY	YEAR					
	1970	1972	1974	1975	1976	1977
	Number of Physicians					
Professionally active physicians	304,926	315,522	325,567	335,608	343,876	359,515
Primary care	115,505	120,876	124,572	128,745	134,051	139,248
General practice[b]	56,804	54,357	53,152	53,714	54,631	54,461
Internal medicine	41,196	47,343	51,143	53,712	57,312	61,278
Pediatrics	17,505	19,176	20,277	21,319	22,108	23,609
Other medical specialties	17,127	16,282	17,220	18,743	18,702	19,656
Dermatology	3,937	4,166	4,414	4,594	4,755	4,844
Pediatric allergy	388	379	423	439	469	485
Pediatric cardiology	471	505	521	527	537	563
Internal medicine subspecialties[c]	12,331	11,232	11,862	13,183	12,941	13,764
Surgical specialties	84,545	89,666	92,123	94,776	97,416	100,059
General surgery	29,216	30,518	30,672	31,173	31,899	32,014
Neurological surgery	2,537	2,716	2,824	2,898	2,959	3,049
Obstetrics and gynecology	18,498	19,820	20,607	21,330	21,908	23,038
Ophthalmology	9,793	10,318	10,621	11,011	11,326	11,483
Orthopedic surgery	9,467	10,216	10,861	11,267	11,689	12,223
Otolaryngology	5,305	5,563	5,509	5,670	5,788	5,910
Plastic surgery	1,583	1,770	2,075	2,224	2,337	2,509
Colon and rectal surgery	663	645	655	655	667	652
Thoracic surgery	1,779	1,899	1,909	1,960	2,020	2,131
Urology	5,704	6,201	6,390	6,588	6,823	7,050
Other specialties	87,749	88,698	91,652	93,344	93,707	100,552
Anesthesiology	10,725	11,740	12,375	12,741	13,074	13,815
Neurology	3,027	3,438	3,791	4,085	4,374	4,577
Pathology	10,135	10,881	11,274	11,603	11,815	12,260
Forensic pathology	193	187	192	186	203	206
Psychiatry	20,901	22,319	23,075	23,683	24,196	24,689
Child psychiatry	2,067	2,242	2,384	2,557	2,618	2,877
Physical medicine and rehabilitation	1,443	1,503	1,557	1,615	1,665	1,742
Radiology	10,380	11,772	11,485	11,417	11,627	12,062
Diagnostic radiology	1,941	2,055	3,054	3,500	3,794	4,236
Therapeutic radiology	855	920	1,060	1,161	1,202	1,305
Miscellaneous[d]	26,082	21,641	21,405	20,796	19,139	22,783

[a]Data are based on reporting by physicians.

[b]Includes general practice and family practice.

[c]Includes gastroenterology, pulmonary diseases, allergy, and cardiovascular diseases.

[d]Includes occupational medicine, general preventive medicine, aerospace medicine, public health, other specialties not listed, and unspecified specialties.

Note: Federal and nonfederal active M.D.s in the 50 States and the District of Columbia are included. Physicians not classified, inactive physicians, and physicians with unknown address in the United States are excluded.

Table 9-4 *(cont.)* Professionally Active Physicians (M.D.s), According to Primary Specialty: United States, Selected Years 1970–1977[a]

For 1977 this includes 17,953 physicians not classified, 28,231 physicians inactive, and 10,946 physicians with unknown address.

Sources: Haug, J. N., G. A. Roback, and B. C. Martin, *Distribution of Physicians in the United States, 1970.* Chicago: American Medical Association, 1971. (Copyright 1971, used with the permission of the American Medical Association.); Roback, G. A., *Distribution of Physicians in the U.S., 1972.* Chicago: American Medical Association, 1973. (Copyright 1973, used with the permission of the American Medical Association.); Roback, G. A., and H. R. Mason, *Physician Distribution and Medical Licensure in the U.S., 1974.* Chicago: American Medical Association, 1975. (Copyright 1975, used with the permission of the American Medical Association.); Goodman, L. J., and H. R. Mason, *Physician Distribution and Medical Licensure in the U.S., 1975.* Chicago: American Medical Association, 1976. (Copyright 1976, used with the permission of the American Medical Association); Goodman, L. J., *Physician Distribution and Medical Licensure in the U.S., 1976.* Chicago: American Medical Association, 1977. (Copyright 1977, used with the permission of the American Medical Association.); Department of Statistical Analysis, *Physician Distribution and Medical Licensure in the U.S., 1977.* Chicago: American Medical Association, 1979. (Copyright 1979, used with the permission of the American Medical Association.)

The 1980 ratio was 199.3 per 100,000 population. According to the AMA Graduate Medical Education Committee, the U.S. will have an over supply of some 30,000 physicians by the year 2000. Yet in spite of increases in physician supply, at present, 138 counties in 26 states with a combined population of nearly a half million people did not have access to physician services. Some rural poverty areas in the United States have only one physician per 10,000 population.[6] The United States Department of Health and Human Services reports that these counties in the Appalachian states where the median disposable income is below $5,000 a year have a doctor-population ratio consistently below 65:100,000 with some as low as 25:100,000.[7] Urban areas, particularly inner-city ghettos and barrios, also suffer from the maldistribution of health worker supply, but depressed rural areas face a more significant problem.

Maldistribution of health workers is a significant problem in the health care delivery system. Physicians, dentists, and other health professionals tend to practice in affluent suburban areas. This is an acute problem, since illness tends to be more prevalent among poverty groups, who tend to live in the inner-city and rural areas of the country. Millions of people live in medically underserved areas in the United States, their access to health care is limited not only by a financial, but a geographic factor.

The Public Health Service has stepped up efforts to correct the geographic maldistribution of health care resources. Over 67 percent of high-priority rural target areas have now been reached through Rural Health Initiative Grants and Health in Underserved Rural Areas grants. Urban health projects now serve about two million people. And, in 1979, an Inner City Health Initiative was developed as part of the President's Urban Strategy to increase the availability of health resources in America's inner cities.

The trend toward specialization in medicine has been very apparent in recent years (see Table 9-4), and has resulted in a shortage of primary-care physicians. As general practitioners, family practitioners and internists, primary-care physicians can manage a majority of the health problems that may affect people. And, generally, these practitioners have lower fees and are more concerned with treating the total human being, as opposed to isolated organs and specific diseases. In 1931, about 75 percent of all physi-

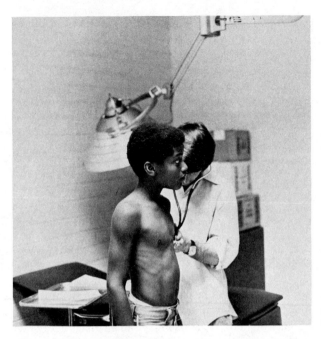

Figure 9–4
Primary-care physicians are essential to an efficient health care system. Courtesy Arizona Department of Health Services.

cians were delivering primary care, but by 1967 this figure had dropped to 39 percent.[8] This proportion of active physicians has remained fairly constant through 1978. Projections by specialty group suggest that from 1980 to 1990, there will be a 49 percent increase in the number of active physicians in primary care. In 1977, the number of active nonfederal physicians per 10,000 population varied from 20.4 in the Northeast region to 14.5 in the North Central region of the country.[9]

Dentists

It is projected that the supply of active dentists will increase much less rapidly in the future as they did during the past decade and a half. Recent increases, due largely to federal support for expansion of dental schools and for new school construction, are approaching a halt, and future enrollments should remain very close to the 1976–77 level. The number of active dentists are projected to rise from 112,000 in 1975 to 141,000 by 1985. The projected increase in the number of dentists will likely result in a small improvement in the nation's dentist to population ratio. The number of specialists has increased rapidly during recent years in dentistry. Over two-fifths of the dental specialists are limited to the practice of orthodontics. At present, only 3 percent of active dentists are women. Minorities account for about 3 percent also.

Nurses

Nurses and related personnel comprise almost half of the total health work force. This total includes registered nurses, licensed practical nurses, and nursing aides, orderlies, and attendants. Two-thirds of the nurses actively working in the field of nursing are employed in hospitals. The total number of nurses registered in practice increased by 80 percent from the 1960 level. However, as is the case with other health professionals, nurses are not evenly distributed throughout the country.

In the coming years, the supply of RNs is expected to continue to rise rapidly, reaching over 1.4 million by 1985. It is projected that the future nursing requirements may be roughly in balance with future supply. However, the consensus appears to be that baccalaureate- and graduate-degree nurses may well be in short supply in the 1980s, while the supply of diploma and associate-degree RNs may be more than adequate.

Allied-Health Personnel

Allied-health personnel are defined by the Health Professions Education Assistance Act as individuals with training and responsibilities for

A. supporting, complementing, or supplementing the professional functions of physicians, dentists, and other health professionals in the delivery of health care to patients or B. assisting environmental engineers and other personnel in environmental health control and preventive medicine activities. Included in categories A and B are such personnel as clinical laboratory technologists and technicians, dietitians, medical records personnel, physical therapist, respiratory therapists, and speech pathologists. More than 100 occupational titles and as many as 250 secondary or alternate titles have been identified within the definitions given in the act.

The current supply of most types of allied health professionals is believed to be relatively adequate. This is largely because of the recent substantial increases in the number of graduates of training programs at the collegiate level. Between 1969 and 1975, the number of formal training programs for allied health professions at the collegiate level nearly doubled, and the number of graduates of such programs more than tripled. Yet there are indications that shortages currently exist among certain types of personnel, including cytotechnologists, medical record administrators, occupational therapists, physical therapists, and respiratory therapists.[10]

And these shortages may continue in the years ahead.

Beyond the general topic of numerical supply figures, there are continuing questions about the geographic distribution of the future supply of health workers. It is clear that there is a highly uneven distribution of physicians and other trained health professionals in the United States, whether the distribution is examined by region, state, county, or health service area. Concern over the maldistribution of practitioners has intensified in the past few years. The total supply of health workers has increased significantly, but improvements in geographic distribution has only been slight.[11]

IN-PATIENT CARE

Hospitals

The hospital industry is a blend of private and public institutions. Most hospitals in the United States are defined as short-stay (see Table 9-5). Short-stay and long-stay hospitals are distinguished by the average length of stay of the patients discharged from them. In *short-stay hospitals,* the average length of stay is less than thirty days; in *long-stay hospitals,* it is thirty days or more. Short-stay general medical hospitals handle over 90 percent of all admissions and employ approximately 77 percent of the hospital industry's total labor force.

Approximately half of the hospitals operating today are sponsored by voluntary, nonprofit agencies and 37 percent are publicly owned. Furthermore, 56 percent of community hospitals are nonprofit institutions, 30 percent are run by state or local governments, and the remainder are *proprietary hospitals* or for-profit.

The growth in the number of community hospital beds was stimulated by the Hospital Survey and Construction Act of 1946 (commonly called the Hill-Burton Act), which initiated planning for health facilities in every state and provided federal funds for the construction of health facilities.

According to the National Guidelines for Health Planning, the number of non-federal short-stay hospital beds (including short-stay psychiatric beds) should be less than 4.0 for every 1,000 persons is a health service area. Too many beds in an area contribute to escalating costs and may encourage improper use of hospital resources.

The number of hospitals offering special services has increased over the last ten years. Open-heart surgery, radioisotope, and renal dialysis units have proliferated in recent years. Expansion of elaborate, expensive, and sophisticated services and facilities has been a significant factor in the rise of the cost of hospital care. For example, a fully equipped x-ray room, with fluoroscopy, costs up to $200,000. An automated blood-cell counter could cost up to $56,000. And models of the CAT scanner cost about $90,000. In England, there are four CAT scanners that service the entire population of the country. In Boston, there are seven CAT scanners, and in Chicago, at least thirty-five. It has been suggested that if hospitals in relatively close geographic proximity would cooperate with each other and pool resources, instead of compete, costs could be significantly controlled. In this way, unnecessary duplication of expensive services could be avoided without reducing the quality of care or its accessibility. In addition, it has been substantiated by research that when elaborate services, such as open-heart surgical rooms and surgical teams, are not used on a regular basis, increased risk is presented to the patient for successful recovery.

During 1980, more than one out of ten Americans were hospitalized. Hospital bills alone accounted for about 40 percent of the entire health bill of the nation. Several factors, in addition to inflation, appear to be responsible for the high cost of medical care delivered in hospitals. One is inappropriate use of hospitals, which contributes to high cost. Many procedures that could safely and more efficiently be performed on an ambulatory or out-patient basis are performed in hospitals on an in-patient basis. Hospitalization

Table 9-5 Short-Stay Hospitals and Beds, According to Type of Hospital and Ownership: United States, 1972 and 1977[a]

YEAR AND TYPE OF OWNERSHIP	ALL SHORT-STAY HOSPITALS	COMMUNITY HOSPITALS			ALL OTHER HOSPITALS			
		Total	General	Specialty	Total	General	Psychiatric	Other
				Number of Hospitals				
1972								
All Ownerships	6,723	6,092	5,948	144	631	492	93	46
Government	2,247	1,787	1,772	15	460	429	22	9
Federal	340	–	–	–	340	336	–	4
State–local	1,907	1,787	1,772	15	120	93	22	5
Proprietary	919	854	808	46	65	–	38	27
Nonprofit	3,557	3,451	3,368	83	106	63	33	10
1977								
All Ownerships	6,637	6,028	5,882	146	609	406	152	51
Government	2,258	1,821	1,801	20	437	385	41	11
Federal	335	–	–	–	335	333	1	1
State–local	1,923	1,821	1,801	20	102	52	40	10
Proprietary	903	808	772	36	95	–	68	27
Nonprofit	3,476	3,399	3,309	90	77	21	43	13
				Number of Beds				
1972								
All Ownerships	1,004,854	905,919	895,217	10,702	98,935	87,986	8,827	2,122
Government	298,875	207,813	205,583	2,230	91,062	86,468	3,732	862
Federal	82,453	–	–	–	82,453	81,908	–	545
State–local	216,422	207,813	205,583	2,230	8,609	4,560	3,732	317
Proprietary	65,499	62,135	60,545	1,590	3,364	–	2,568	796
Nonprofit	640,480	635,971	629,089	6,882	4,509	1,518	2,527	464
1977								
All Ownerships	1,088,348	983,049	969,523	13,526	105,299	88,719	13,653	2,927
Government	307,410	212,365	209,094	3,271	95,045	88,144	5,635	1,266
Federal	85,856	–	–	–	85,856	84,906	409	541
State–local	221,554	212,365	209,094	3,271	9,189	3,238	5,226	725
Proprietary	90,421	84,693	82,880	1,813	5,728	–	4,789	939
Nonprofit	690,517	685,991	677,549	8,442	4,526	575	3,229	722

[a]Data are based on reporting by facilities.

Note: Community hospitals include all nonfederal short-stay hospitals classified by the American Hospital Association to one of the following services: general medical and surgical; obstetrics and gynecology; eye, ear, nose, and throat; rehabilitation; orthopedic; other specialty; children's general; children's eye, ear, nose, and throat; children's rehabilitation; children's orthopedic; and children's other specialty.

Source: Division of Health Manpower and Facilities Statistics, National Center for Health Statistics, data from the Master Facility Inventory.

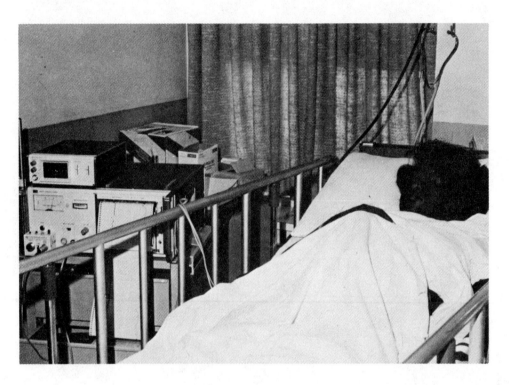

Figure 9-5 Expansion of elaborate equipment like this fetal monitor is a factor in the cost of hospital care. Courtesy U.S. Department of Health, Education and Welfare.

is the most expensive form of medical care, thus unnecessary hospitalization does not improve care, but rather inflates cost. However, there are two factors that promote unnecessary hospitalization—or treatment on an in-patient basis—rather than the more effective and efficient out-patient service. First, many hospitals in the United States are required by law to provide for emergency-room services, yet there is no comparable legal requirement which mandates that these same facilities provide for day-to-day out-patient services that deliver rational and relatively inexpensive primary care. Thus, patients with relatively uncomplicated illnesses or health problems that could be managed on an out-patient, ambulatory basis are hospitalized because the primary-care alternative is not offered by the hospital. Second, *third-party payments* account for almost 70 percent of all medical bills in the U.S. This means that medical-insurance companies, such as Blue Cross, Blue Shield and other commercial health insurance carriers, paid out about $114 billion in 1978. Public sources pay, on the average, over one-third of the nation's health care bill, with the federal government responsible for a much larger share than state and local governments. Thus, the majority of health care providers and facilities are reimbursed by someone other than the individual patient, who receives the services. Most private health-insurance plans reimburse for in-patient care, but exclude payment for ambulatory care. Likewise, publicly funded programs such as Medicaid and Medicare make it possible for medically indigent persons to qualify more easily for in-patient care and services than for out-patient care. Clearly, the incentive is provided to utilize the more costly and inefficient services.

Additional problems related to the utilization of hospitals and high cost of hospital services involve (1) excessive, inappropriate emergency-room utilization, (2) the practice of *defensive medicine,* and (3) unnecessary surgery. It often costs twice as much to be treated in a hospital emergency room than it does in the physician's office. Yet many people continue to use hospital emergency rooms to obtain treatment for non-emergency illnesses and health problems instead of choosing appropriate and less costly services.

One of the major reasons medical costs have risen sharply during the last few years is the threat of lawsuits. Many physicians have begun to practice what has been called "defensive medicine" as they face the possibility of malpractice suits being brought against them. The number of malpractice suits brought against physicians has increased in recent years. An individual orthopedic surgeon, an obstetrician, or neurosurgeon in solo practice may pay between $8,500 and $12,000 a year for professional liability protection. Practicing defensive medicine means that physicians order more lab tests, more x-rays, and schedule more office visits and other expensive procedures—many of which are unnecessary—simply to protect himself or herself against possible liability. These extra procedures are expensive and further inflate the national health bill.

Another contributing factor to the high cost of hospitalization is the perform-ance of unnecessary surgery. Again, because of the manner in which the financing of health care is established by the health-insurance industry, an incentive is provided to perform surgery. Many needless operations are performed on a daily basis at an exces-sively high cost—not to mention at higher risk to the patient. Indeed, the hospital system in the United States is faced with difficult problems, of which curtailing costs is a priority.

Nursing Homes

In the last fifteen years, the number of *nursing homes*—or long-term extended-care facilities—has more than tripled. Increases in the number of older people, changes in treatment patterns of illnesses not requiring hospitalization, and changes in family living arrangements have resulted in a growing demand for such care. It is projected that by the year 2000, an additional 2.2 million nursing-home beds will be needed to meet the growing demand.

Over one million older people spend their last years in nursing homes, at a cost of $3.5 billion per year. Some coverage is provided for certain types of nursing-home care by the government-subsidized programs Medicaid and Medicare. Nursing-home care ex-penditures have showed substantial increases in recent years. The average total monthly charge for nursing-home care rose from $186 in 1964 to $689 in 1977—an average annual increase of 10.6 percent.[12]

Nursing homes are big business in the United States. Unlike hospitals, most of which are either publicly owned or operated, most nursing homes are operated for profit (see Table 9-6). In fact, only about 15 percent of the nation's nursing homes are non-

Table 9-6 Nursing Homes and Beds, According to Selected Characteristics: United States, 1973–1974 and 1977[a]

CHARACTERISTIC	NURSING HOMES 1973-74[b] Number	Percent Distribution	NURSING HOMES 1977 Number	Percent Distribution	NURSING HOME BEDS 1973-74[b] Number	Percent Distribution	NURSING HOME BEDS 1977 Number	Percent Distribution
Total	15,700	100.0	18,900	100.0	1,177,300	100.0	1,402,400	100.0
Ownership								
Proprietary	11,900	75.4	14,500	76.8	832,300	70.7	971,200	69.3
Nonprofit and government	3,900	24.6	4,400	23.2	345,000	29.3	431,200	30.8
Certification[c]								
Skilled nursing facility	5,300	33.5	3,600	19.2	471,900	40.1	294,000	21.0
Skilled nursing and intermediate care facility	2,400	15.4	4,600	24.2	291,600	24.8	549,400	39.2
Intermediate care facility	4,400	28.1	6,000	31.6	253,200	21.5	391,600	27.9
Not certified	3,600	23.1	4,700	25.0	160,600	13.6	167,400	11.9
Bed Size								
Less than 50 beds	6,400	40.8	8,000	42.3	178,800	15.2	182,900	13.0
50–99 beds	5,500	35.0	5,800	30.8	392,500	33.3	417,800	29.8
100–199 beds	3,200	20.4	4,200	22.3	417,900	35.5	546,400	39.0
200 beds or more	600	3.8	900	4.6	188,000	16.0	255,400	18.2
Geographic Region								
Northeast	3,100	19.8	3,900	20.5	250,800	21.3	314,900	22.5
North Central	5,600	35.7	5,900	31.1	408,800	34.7	483,900	34.5
South	4,100	26.1	4,900	26.0	303,700	25.8	381,500	27.2
West	2,900	18.5	4,200	22.4	214,100	18.2	222,100	15.8

[a]Data are based on a sample survey of nursing homes.

[b]Excludes personal care and domiciliary care homes.

[c]Medicare extended-care facilities and Medicaid skilled-nursing homes from the 1973–74 survey were considered to be equivalent to Medicare or Medicaid skilled-nursing facilities in 1977 for the purposes of this comparison.

Note: Numbers are rounded to the nearest hundred. Percents are calculated on the basis of unrounded figures.

Source: Division of Health Resources Utilization Statistics, National Center for Health Statistics, data from the National Nursing Home Survey.

Figure 9-6
Nursing homes are big business in the United States.

profit or publicly owned facilities. Responsibility for supervision of these homes rests largely with state health and welfare departments with some responsibility vested in the federal Department of Health and Human Services. Thus, at a minimum, homes must meet state fire, health, and safety regulations.

Nursing homes have recently come under fire for abuses of public funds and for delivering poor-quality care to older people. Many nursing homes are overcrowded, under-staffed, and offer inadequate medical care and attention to their residents.

Nursing homes operated by churches and other charitable groups are generally more adequate than those which are privately owned and operated. Privately run homes are more prone to attempt to maximize profit by minimizing expenditures. Too often this results in inadequately trained staff, lack of safety and sanitary facilities, and other trimmed services.

AMBULATORY CARE

Ambulatory medical care is gaining importance as a more suitable and less-expensive type of care for many health problems. Since primary care, early detection, routine treatment of health problems, and preventive care all take place in the ambulatory care setting, most people enter the health care system at the ambulatory level. Entry can be made through a variety of institutions, including a physician's office or group practice, a clinic, hospital out-patient department, or a neighborhood health center.

Although preventive-care programs should be a part of the health care system at every level, this is not true for health services in the United States. Some of the few orga-

253

nizations that systematically provide preventive care are the *health maintenance organizations (HMOs),* where comprehensive health services are offered for a fixed monthly fee. Other institutions currently focussing on preventive care include school-health programs, well-baby clinics, and family-planning clinics.

Health Maintenance Organizations (HMOs)

In 1973, Congress passed the Health Maintenance Organization Act, which provided federal funds to develop comprehensive prepaid health maintenance organizations (HMOs) as an alternative to the conventional financing mechanism and the traditional fee-for-service health care delivery system. The fee-for-service arrangement means that payment is made by either a third-party insurer or the individual patient to a provider of health care for services rendered.

A health maintenance organization has four essential characteristics:

1. It is an organized system for providing health care in a geographic area, which assures the delivery of
2. an agreed-upon set of basic and supplemental health maintenance and treatment services to
3. a voluntarily enrolled group of persons, and
4. for which services the HMO is reimbursed through a predetermined, fixed, periodic prepayment made by enrolled persons or families.[13]

An HMO is responsible for providing most health and medical services required by enrolled individuals and families. These services are specified between the HMO and the enrollees. The HMO employs or enters contractual agreements with health care providers and facilities who assume the responsibility of providing services to enrollees.

Recent national interest in health maintenance organizations began in the early 1970s as a result of concern over the rapidly rising cost of health and medical care. Other considerations included the difficulty many Americans encountered in obtaining satisfactory medical services, the fragmentation of those services, and the "crisis and cure" approach of medicine as opposed to maintaining people in good health. In theory, an HMO addresses these problems. The HMO guarantees around-the-clock medical care 365 days a year. The primary-care physician coordinates all of the patients' care, thus fragmentation is replaced by integrated health care, usually provided in a single location. Health care providers in an HMO have a financial incentive to reduce medical costs by providing preventive medical care and health education and, whenever possible, by reduction of hospital utilization and elimination of unnecessary diagnostic work. In return for receiving comprehensive care when needed, the HMO enrollee must use the HMO physician for her or his medical care.

The development of HMOs as an alternative health care delivery plan shows great potential for attacking many of the problems which are a part of the health care delivery system in the United States. They emphasize prevention of disease and prompt care and treatment. They provide incentives for containing costs and for increasing the productivity of resources by encouraging people to stay well and by promoting prompt recovery through the least costly services consistent with maintaining quality. In addition, health maintenance organizations provide opportunities for improving the quality of care, and by mobilizing private capital and managerial talent, they reduce the need for federal funds and direct control. However, the HMO does not adequately serve as a central coordinating force for a comprehensive health care system.

More than 9 million Americans now receive comprehensive care from HMO-type organizations, and about 20 percent of the population lives within their service areas. Research studies show that (1) HMO members are more likely to receive such preventive measures as general checkups and prenatal care, and to seek care within one day of the onset of symptoms of illness and injuries, (2) hospitalization rates are significantly reduced in HMOs through prevention, reducing unnecessary procedures, and by performing minor surgery in the doctors' office; and (3) HMOs lower the total health-care cost to families and individuals, and that premiums cover a greater percentage of total costs.

Neighborhood Health Centers

Neighborhood health centers (NHCs) are designed to provide comprehensive ambulatory care for a target population of poor people. Initially these centers were funded through the Office of Economic Opportunity. In 1972, they moved under the jurisdiction of the Department of Health and Human Services.

Out-patient care has been traditionally demeaning for the poor—impersonal, long waits, and crowded conditions. The neighborhood health center was designed to overcome these demeaning features not only by providing a broad range of primary and secondary ambulatory care services by salaried physicians and other health professionals but also by emphasizing prevention, having available a wide range of supporting non-medical services, and providing these services in the neighborhoods in which the people lived.

Another important feature of these centers is the high priority placed on consumer input in policy and decision making. But the future of these centers is clouded, as government priorities shift and funding is lost.

Primary Health Care Centers

Primary health care centers are like neighborhood health centers, except that they provide a more limited range of services and focus on primary care. The number of primary care centers is increasing rapidly, particulary in underserved rural areas. Like the NHCs, the primary care centers have major financial problems, and the rural centers also have difficulty attracting and retaining professional staffs. Many of these centers have developed with support from one of several federal programs.

The typical federally supported centers have two family practitioners and one dentist. Supporting services beyond nursing vary from center to center. The long-term survival of these centers will depend upon attaining financial stability and retaining professional personnel.

After World War II, psychiatric theory began to shift from institutional care and treatment of mental patients to ambulatory care delivered in the communities. In many of the states during the 1950s, general hospitals, mental hospitals, health departments, and other agencies began to experiment with new types of community-based ambulatory therapeutic programs, and success stories began to be heard with increased frequency.

The Community Mental Health Center Construction Act of 1963 paved the way for the movement toward deinstitutionalization of mental patients. Community mental health centers provide comprehensive services, including

> . . . inpatient, outpatient, day care, and other partial hospitalization services and emergency services; specialized services for the mental health of children; specialized services for the elderly; consultation and education services, assistance to courts and other public agencies . . . ; follow-up care for . . . residents discharged from a mental facility; transitional half-way house services . . . , and specialized programs for the prevention, treatment, rehabilitation of alcohol and drug abusers, alcoholics, and drug addicts.[14]

Despite all the positive contributions these agencies make, financial problems are affecting the comprehensiveness of services these centers can deliver in the present.

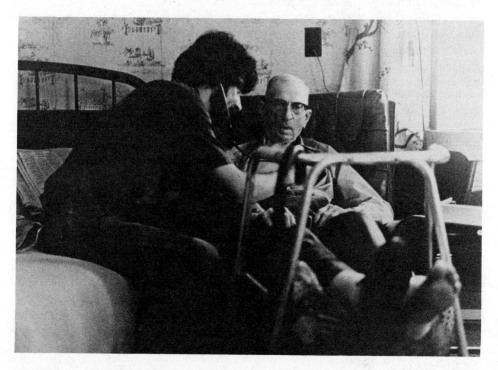

Figure 9-7 Home health care is becoming increasingly important.

Home-Health Agencies

These agencies operate under various names, with varying organizational ties and differing services. Generally, they provide a variety of health and health-supporting services in patient homes. Some home-health agencies, however, offer only one type of service, for example, Meals-on-Wheels. Financial support for these agencies comes from various sources, including Medicare, Medicaid, insurance companies, patients' fees, and charitable contributions.

A visiting nurse association (VNA) is one type of home-health service in which a skilled nurse, usually one with public health training, visits a patient's home and provides some type of nursing care, such as changing a dressing or giving an injection. Many VNAs also provide physical therapy and speech therapy services by qualified personnel.

Some home-health agencies provide needed health aids for the home, such as crutches, walkers, wheelchairs, and other equipment and appliances. Others provide homemaker services: housecleaning, maintenance and repairs, and cooking.

Meals-on-Wheels programs are common in most cities today. In these programs, one hot meal a day is supplied to those confined to their homes. This is typically the noon meal, since it is assumed that someone is at home in the morning and evening to provide the other meals. Meals-on-Wheels agencies usually rely on volunteers to deliver the meals. The meals are provided by various other agencies, including hospitals and schools.[15]

Military Medicine

Military health care is delivered through a dual system that includes (1) an in-house military health-care facility and staffs that serve uniformed personnel on active duty and (2) the Civilian Health and Medical Program of the Uniformed Services (CHAMPUS), which provides civilian health care to eligible dependents of active duty military personnel and retired personnel.

As national health insurance in the United States comes closer to becoming a reality, the military CHAMPUS program is being analyzed carefully by health policy makers and legislators in the nation's capital. For, unlike publicly funded health insurance programs such as Medicare and Medicaid, which serve special clienteles of elderly and the poor, CHAMPUS serves a population that is very close to being a microcosm of the general American public. As such, CHAMPUS and its clientele are viewed as a testing model for any national health insurance program that may ultimately be adopted.

VA hospitals The Veterans Administration continues to act on behalf of the American people to repay their debt of gratitude to men and women whose lives were interrupted or permanently changed as a result of military service. The VA operates a nationwide system of health care delivery, which includes 171 hospitals, 213 out-patient clinics, 84 nursing-home care facilities, and 18 domicilaries. In addition, the VA contracts with approximately 3,400 community nursing homes in 50 states in order to provide care to veterans in or near their own communities.

The Veterans Administration has been regionalizing its nationwide system of health care facilities over the past few years. The goal of this systematic reorganization has been to develop a system that provides high-quality care and avoids costly duplication of services. The program encourages VA hospital cooperation in order to streamline services.

FINANCING HEALTH CARE

The United States has the highest per-capita medical expenditures in the world. In 1978, expenditures for personal health services amounted to some $192 billion. In 1981, the nation was pouring $252 billion annually into a health care system that is unable to control or reduce costs. Over the last several decades, medical-care costs have consistently outpaced prices for all other consumer goods and services.

The nation's total health care bill continues to represent a growing proportion of the *Gross National Product (GNP)*. During the past three decades, the GNP increased at an annual average rate of 7.4 percent. Health care expenditures increased at an average annual rate of 10.2 percent, comprising 9.1 percent of the GNP in 1978. Hospital costs are now increasing at the incredible rate of $1 million a day. By 1978, the cost of a one-day hospital stay had increased by 1,000 percent since 1950. The bill for an average stay of 7.7 days cost more than $1,330. Physicians' fees also increased more rapidly than the Consumer Price Index over the past five years.

In order to understand the health care delivery system in the United States, both financing and planning must be consolidated since they are intimately related. Three major factors account for the rising cost of health care: inflation, inadequate health planning, and other residual factors which include greater health care utilization and improved sophistication and quality of medical technology. As mentioned earlier, the present system of health care promotes inflation of costs through poor utilization of resources and services, incentives for the use of high-cost facilities, and lack of cost-measures. In addition, the delivery of health care has become a market in which, increasingly, one agent sets prices for services (physicians, hospitals), a second receives them (patients), and a third pays for them (health-insurance companies, Medicaid, Medicare). The result is that all too frequently, no one is really concerned about rising costs.

When the Medicare and Medicaid programs went into effect in 1966, public spending began to grow rapidly. In 1978, public funds accounted for over 40 percent of all health expenditures, compared to 25 percent in 1965. Private funds paid some 59 percent of the total health bill in 1978 as compared with 75 percent in 1965.

Third-party payments continue to account for an increasing proportion of personal health care expenditures—67.1 percent in 1978. Public sources paid 38.7 percent of the nation's health care bill in 1978, with the federal government responsible for a much larger share than state and local governments. Within the private sector, the major portion of third-party payments is made by private health-insurance carriers.

The Health-Insurance Industry

The year 1929 is generally credited as marking the birth of modern health insurance. Since that time, the health-insurance industry has become big business in the U.S. and, while the private health-insurance industry claims that its coverage has been broadened considerably in recent years to keep pace with inflation, not everyone agrees with this view.

Over the years both private and public sectors have responded to people's need for protection against unplanned hospital and surgical expenses as well as for other forms of care. However, there appear to be two major problems which face health planners regarding the financing of health care. One relates to financial barriers to the access of care by specific population groups, and the other to inadequate protection. For example, even though employer health-insurance plans cover about 75 percent of the working population, they do not protect all of the working population, especially the working poor. In addition, some employer plans cover workers, but exclude their dependents from protection.

Blue Cross and Blue Shield were created during the Depression. They are technically nonprofit agencies designed to insure the payment of medical bills. Third-party payments, including those by Blue Cross/Blue Shield, now cover nearly two-thirds of personal health expenses, as compared with approximately one-third in 1950. However, third-party payments do not cover all personal health expenses evenly. Nearly 90 percent of hospital expenses are covered by third-party payments, but only 61 percent of physicians services are reimbursable. Dental-expense insurance now covers some thirty-five million people in the U.S. A smaller number of the population is covered for vision-care expenses and prescription drugs. In addition, many of the plans have serious inadequacies in coverage for x-ray and laboratory work done outside the hospital, psychiatric coverage, and some plans cover only about 47 percent of hospital bills and physician bills. This means that the individual patient may incur a tremendous out-of-pocket bill for medical care. The inadequacy of benefits provided by health insurance is a major problem in the current health care delivery system. While most private health insurance does provide good protection against the costs of hospitalization and surgery, out-patient care and prevention services are often excluded. In addition, most private plans either exclude or limit preventive services and maternity care and many Americans are inadequately protected against *catastrophic medical costs.* Catastrophic medical costs refers to large expenses incurred as a result of treating an illness, injury or other medical problem.

Health insurance has become an almost indispensable foundation to the structure of financing medical care. Because of the existence of health insurance the American philosophy and attitude toward seeking medical treatment and paying for care has changed. Health insurance finances America's personal health care expenses—and as such, health insurance has severely distorted the sensitivity of both the patient and the health provider toward the costs of medical treatment.

> Consumer groups haven't criticized hospitals and physicians for charging too much for their services, for building hospitals in areas where they are not needed; and for allowing the costs of health care to skyrocket because they know they will be reimbursed by health insurance programs.[16]

In general, private health insurance encompasses five broad categories: (1) protection against hospital expenses, (2) surgical costs, (3) regular expenses, (4) major medical expenses, and (5) wages lost because of illness or injury.

It is likely that no industry in the U.S. is more aware of the limitations of its product and how far it must progress to overcome its weaknesses than the health-insurance industry. Full, comprehensive coverage is not common, and most nonhospital services call for a substantial deductible and co-insurance payments by the insured. There are many restrictions in health insurance, including age limitations, ineligible illnesses, and eligibility waiting periods. The question that remains is: Is it too late for the health-insurance industry to preserve its place in the health care system?

Medicaid/Medicare

In 1965, Medicaid and Medicare were enacted in the United States to provide financial protection to those who for economic reasons could not obtain health care.

Medicare is a health-insurance program for all people aged 65 and over, regardless of income level. It also covers disabled persons under 65 who have been entitled to Social Security disability benefits for two consecutive years or who suffer from chronic renal disease. In 1972, the under-65 provisions were added to the original Medicare provisions.

The program consists of two parts, A and B. Part A is the hospital-insurance portion of Medicare, which provides coverage for in-hospital care, skilled-nursing facility care, and home-health care. Part A provides:

Up to 90 days of in-patient care for each benefit period. But this coverage does not cover all of the charges. The patient must pay (in 1979) the first $160 of the hospital bill and, after 60 days, the patient must pay $40 a day up to the ninetieth day. If a patient stays in the hospital beyond 90 days, Medicare permits the patient to draw upon a lifetime reserve of 60 extra days, with the patient paying $80 for each day used out of this reserve.

Up to 100 days in a skilled-nursing facility, with Medicare paying the full cost for the first 20 days and the patient (in 1979) paying $20 a day for each day thereafter.

Up to 100 home-health visits for the further treatment of the condition for which the patient was in the hospital or skilled-nursing facility. The visits must include part-time nursing care, physical therapy, or speech therapy.

Part B of Medicare is optional Supplementary Medical Insurance (SMI). Those who opt for Part B coverage must pay for it. Part B coverage provides:

Payment of 80 percent of reasonable physician charges after the subscriber pays the initial $60 annual deductible. Exceptions to coverage include pathology and radiology. Psychiatric-care payments are limited to $250 per year.

Hospital out-patient and emergency-room services.

Up to 100 home-health visits that do not require prior hospitalization or skilled-nursing facility care that are in addition to the 100 visits for posthospital and skilled-nursing facility care under Part A.

A number of other services and supplies, such as out-patient physical and speech therapy, diagnostic x-ray examinations, wheelchairs, artificial limbs, limited chiropractic services, and so on.

The Health Care Financing Administration (HCFA) oversees the Medicare program. While it handles some payments directly, most payments for care are made by fiscal intermediaries for part A and by carriers for part B with whom HCFA contracts. The contractors are mainly Blue Cross, Blue Shield, and commercial insurance companies.

There is little question that Medicare has been more successful than Medicaid in helping to meet the health needs of people, while improving the financing of health care. Many of the problems which face Medicaid were avoided in Medicare by taking the health care of older people out of the welfare system and by not requiring states to finance benefits. However, rising costs of operating the Medicare program has been a problem which has resulted in increasing federal regulations designed to contain costs rather than in improving quality of health care delivered. The Reagan Administration advocated the reform of Medicare to encourage home-base care whenever possible. This reform would contain costs and improve health care delivery for older persons.

Medicaid is a federal-state financed program that pays for health care for the categorically needy and the medically needy (see Table 9-7).

The categorically needy are those receiving public assistance from the Aid For Dependent Children Program (AFDC) and those who receive Supplementary Security Income (SSI) because they are aged, blind, or disabled. The medically needy may be covered under Medicaid if their state has opted to provide coverage for their care. Twenty-eight states have chosen to provide benefits for these low income people. Arizona does not have a Medicaid program.[17]

There is considerable variation in Medicaid benefits from state to state. However, if a state has the Medicaid program it must provide for in-patient and out-patient hospital services, skilled-nursing facility services, physician services, home-health care, family-planning services, and early and periodic screening, diagnosis, and treatment (EPSDT) of children under 21 who are eligible. States have the option of paying for dental care, prescribed drugs, and some other services.

Medicaid is tied to the welfare concept and has not successfully promoted access to health services with dignity. Communities have been relieved of much of their prior responsibility for charity care to improverished persons, but little has been done to improve the quality of health services and promote health maintenance among these groups. Medicaid has indeed not been without its problems. It has been criticized as being unwieldy, inefficient, and unresponsive to the needs of the people, yet expensive. As Rosemary and Robert Stevens observe, "Medicaid, with its uncontrollable budgets and rising costs, has been a reflection of broader deficiencies in the health sector. . . ."[18] Another criticism leveled at the Medicaid program is that individual recipients of Medicaid have had no input in determining program policies or influencing the administration of the program. Conflicts among federal regulations, state administration, and recipients' demands have had little effect on improving the credibility of Medicaid. In addition,

Table 9-7 Medicaid Expenditures[a] and Percent Distribution, According to Type of Service: United States, Fiscal Years 1967–1977[b]

TYPE OF SERVICE	YEAR										
	1967	1968	1969	1970	1971	1972[c]	1973	1974	1975	1976	1977[d]
Expenditure in Millions											
Total	$2,271	$3,451	$4,368	$5,112	$6,476	$7,713	$8,810	$10,149	$12,318	$14,245	$16,300
Percent Distribution											
All Services											
Total	100.0	100.0	100.0	100.0	100.0	100.0	100.0	100.0	100.0	100.0	100.0
In-patient hospital care	40.2	39.4	36.3	36.9	35.3	38.2	35.3	33.5	31.8	31.7	31.5
Physician's services	9.9	11.8	11.8	11.3	11.1	10.4	10.8	10.7	10.0	9.7	9.2
Nursing-home care	33.7	30.8	29.6	25.8	25.8	23.1	21.0	20.0	20.1	18.2	17.2
Intermediate care[e]	–	–	2.2	5.9	8.3	9.6	13.2	15.8	17.7	19.5	22.0
Dental care	3.2	5.5	4.8	3.3	2.8	2.4	2.4	2.6	2.8	2.7	2.5
Prescribed drugs	7.9	6.8	6.9	7.7	7.3	7.1	7.0	7.0	6.6	6.7	6.2
Other services[f]	5.1	6.4	8.4	8.9	9.3	9.2	10.3	10.5	11.0	11.3	11.4

[a]Expenditures from federal, state, and local funds under Medicaid. Excludes per capita payments for Part B of Medicare and administrative costs.

[b]Data are compiled from state and federal government sources.

[c]Does not include Guam.

[d]Data for fiscal year ending September 30; all other data for fiscal year ending June 30.

[e]Payments to intermediate care facilities are included in the total for fiscal years 1969–72 even though they were administered under the cash assistance program until Jan. 1, 1972, when they were switched to Title XIX.

[f]Other services include laboratory and radiological services, home-health, family-planning services, and out-patient hospital services.

Sources: U.S. House of Representatives, Committee on Interstate and Foreign Commerce, *Data on the Medicaid Program, Eligibility, Services, Expenditures, Fiscal Years 1966–77.* Washington, D.C.: U.S. Government Printing Office, March 1977, p. 32; Office of Research, Office of Policy, Planning, and Research, *Medicaid Statistics Fiscal Year 1977.* Washington, D.C.: DHEW Pub. No. (HCFA) 78–03154, April 1978.

while Congress complains about the high cost of operating the program and demands tighter controls, states report a severe financial strain on their resources and charge that strict federal restrictions stifle innovation and initiative. Revision of Medicaid and Medicare entitlement programs are becoming more of a priority. These programs have been considered untouchable in the past, but cost-cutting reform is increasingly viewed as essential. Entitlement programs are designed in Congress, and any changes in entitlement require Congressional action. (See Chapter 12 for a more detailed discussion of Medicaid.)

CONCLUSION

During the past decade or two increased attention has been devoted to developing a health care system in the United States which is comprehensive, effective in serving the total population and reasonable in cost. Most health planners now recognize that fragmented planning for either specific health needs or specific target groups is not the best method of assuring both access and quality care to those in need of services.

It is difficult to predict whether or not comprehensive health planning will be successful in alleviating all of the deficiencies in the present health care system. Recognized problems such as high cost, maldistribution of health professionals and inequitable access to the system are difficult at best to solve. Perhaps we cannot reasonably create a quality, low cost, accessible health care system without also creating a publicly financed, planned and controlled health care system.

REVIEW QUESTIONS

1. Describe trends in health personnel supply and demand that have occurred over the past thirty years. What does the present manpower situation look like?
2. What are some of the problems which have been identified as they relate to health care in the United States?
3. Describe the purpose and organization of a health maintenance organization (HMO). How can these prepaid plans solve some of the current problems in the health care system?
4. How is health care financed in the United States?
5. What are some of the factors involved in causing health care costs to spiral?
6. Speculate into the future and describe what you believe health care in the U.S. will be like in the year 2020.

SUGGESTED READINGS

Carlson, Rick and Robert Cunningham (eds.), *Future Directions in Health Care: A New Public Policy.* Cambridge, Mass.: Ballinger, 1978.

Grossman, Howard, *For Health's Sake: A Critical Analysis of Medical Care in The United States.* Palo Alto: Pacific Books, 1977.

Kotelchuk, David (ed.), *Prognosis Negative: Crisis In The Health Care System,* A Health/ PAC Book. New York: Vintage Books, 1976.

Navarro, Vincente, *Medicine Under Capitalism.* New York: Neale Watson, 1976.

Robbins, Anthony, "Who Should Make Public Policy For Health," *American Journal of Public Health,* 66(5) 431, 1976.

Weaver, Jerry L., *National Health Policy and the Underserved: Ethnic Minorities, Women, and the Elderly.* St. Louis: C.V. Mosby, 1976.

NOTES

[1] Paul G. Rogers and Lee S. Hyde, "Planning for Health Care," in U.S. DHEW, *Health in America: 1776-1976.* Washington, D.C.: U.S. DHEW Pub. No. (HRA) 76-616, 1976, p. 109.

[2] "Medical System Blasted," *The Washington Post,* July 13, 1969, pp. A1–A2.

[3] Jordan Braverman, *Health Care in America: Why It Costs So Much.* Washington, D.C.: Acropolis Books, 1978, p. 8.

[4] Jordan Braverman, "HFCA: Health Costs May Triple in a Decade," *The Nation's Health,* July 1980, p. 5.

[5] Cyril Brickfield, "National Health Insurance: We Need It Now," *American Association of Retired People (AARP) News Bulletin,* 1978, p. 6.

[6] U.S. DHEW, "Assuring a Nation's Health Resources." Washington, D.C.: U.S. DHEW Pub. No. (HRA) 76-630, 1976, p. 4.

[7] *Health in America: 1776-1976,* p. 166.

[8] *Assuring a Nation's Health Resources,* p. 8.

[9] U.S.: DHEW, *Health: United States, 1979.* Washington, D.C.: U.S. DHEW Pub. No. (PHS) 80-1232, p. 151.

[10] Howard V. Stambler, "Health Manpower for the Nation: A Look Ahead at the Supply and the Requirements," *Public Health Reports,* 94, No. 1 (January–February 1979), 9.

[11] Howard V. Stambler, p. 9.

[12] *Health: United States, 1979,* p. 181.

[13] Bureau of Resource Development, *A Guide to Arizona Health Maintenance Organizations.* Tuscon: Arizona Department of Health Services, 1976, p. 1.

[14] Marshall W. Raffel, *The U.S. Health System: Origins and Functions.* New York: John Wiley, 1980, p. 335.

[15] Marshall W. Raffel, p. 336.

[16] Jordan Braverman, *Crisis in Health Care.* Washington, D.C.: Acropolis Books, 1978, p. 183.

[17] Marshall W. Raffel, p. 422.

[18] Jordan Braverman, p. 286.

GLOSSARY

allied-health personnel individuals with training and responsibilities for supporting, complimenting, or supplementing the professional functions of health professionals in the delivery of care to patients and in environmental control.

ambulatory medical care health care, including diagnosis, treatment, and rehabilitation provided to patients on an out-patient basis—that is, without the patient being admitted to a health care institution.

catastrophic medical costs large medical expenses incurred as a result of treating an illness, injury, or other medical problem.

CHAMPUS the Civilian Health and Medical Program of the Uniformed Services, which provides civilian health care to eligible dependents of military personnel.

defensive medicine the practice in which a physician orders more lab tests, x-rays, office visits, and other expensive procedures, many of which are unnecessary, in order to protect himself or herself against possible liability.

Gross National Product (GNP) the most comprehensive measure of a nation's total output of goods and services; represents the dollar value in current prices of all goods and services.

health care any and all activities undertaken in either the public or private sector which have as their objective improving and maintaining health.

health maintenance organization (HMO) group practices in which patients receive their health care in return for a monthly fee that is paid in advance.

long-stay hospitals the average length of stay is thirty days or more.

nursing home the minimum standards and regulations for nursing homes vary among the states, so no uniform definition is possible. Nursing homes are classified according to the level of care they provide.

physician assistant (PA) health professional who works independently under the supervision of a physician and is trained to deliver a broad range of activities and services.

proprietary hospitals hospitals operated on a for-profit basis.

short-stay hospitals the average length of stay is less than thirty days.

third-party payments those payments made for personal health expenditures by insurance companies and/or the government on behalf of individual consumers.

BIBLIOGRAPHY

Aday, Lu Ann, Ronald Anderson, and Gretchen Fleming, *Health Care in the U.S.—Equitable for Whom?* Beverly Hills, Calif.: Sage Publications, 1980.

Anderson, Odin W., *Health Services in a Land Of Pienty.* Chicago: University of Chicago Press, 1968.

Andreano, Ralph and Burton Weisbrod, *American Health Policy: Perspectives and Choices.* Chicago: Rand McNally, 1974.

Braverman, Jordan, *Crisis in Health Care.* Washington, D.C.: Acropolis Books, 1978.

Brown, Jack, *The Health Care Dilemma: The Problems and Technology in Health Care Delivery.* New York: Human Sciences Press, 1978.

Brown, Jack, *The Politics of Health Care.* Cambridge, Mass.: Ballinger, 1978.

Egdahl, Richard, and Paul Gertman (eds.), *Technology and the Quality of Health Care.* Germantown, Md.: Aspen Systems Corp., 1978.

Enos, Darryl, *The Sociology of Health Care: Social, Economic and Political Perspectives.* New York: Praeger, 1977.

Grossman, Howard, *For Health's Sake: A Critical Analysis of Medical Care in the United States.* Palo Alto: Pacific Books, 1977.

Jonas, Steven, *Health Care Delivery in the United States.* New York: Springer, 1977.

MacKintosh, Douglas, *Systems of Health Care.* Boulder, Colo.: Westview Press, 1978.

Morreale, Joseph (ed.), *The U.S. Medical Care Industry: The Economist's Point of View.* Ann Arbor: University of Michigan Press, 1974.

Rabin, David, Kristin Spector, and Patricia Bush, "Ambulatory Care in the Community," *Public Health Reports,* 95(6) 511-519, 1980.

Raffel, Marshall W., *The U.S. Health Care System: Origins and Functions.* New York: John Wiley, 1980.

Romani, John, "Public Health: Notes on the State of Our Union," *American Journal of Public Health,* 70(3) 260-263, 1980.

Rukel, Eugene, "Implementing The National Health Planning And Resources Development Act of 1974," *Public Health Reports* 91(1) 3-9, 1976.

Rushmer, Robert, *National Priorities for Health: Past, Present and Projected.* New York: John Wiley, 1980.

Somers, Anne, and Herman Somers, *Health and Health Care: Policies in Perspective.* Germantown, Md.: Aspen Systems Corp., 1977.

Stambler, Howard V., "Health Manpower for the Nation: A Look Ahead at the Supply and the Requirements," *Public Health Reports,* 94(1) 3-10, 1979.

U.S. DHEW, "Assuring a Nation's Health Resources." Washington, D.C.: U.S. DHEW Pub. No. (HRA) 76-630, 1976.

—————— *Health in America 1776-1976.* Washington, D.C.: U.S. DHEW Pub. No. (HRA) 76-616, 1976.

—————— *Health Planning and Resources Development Act of 1974.* Washington, D.C.: U.S. DHEW Pub. No. (HRA) 76-14015, 1976.

—————— "A Look At Health Care Resources." Washington, D.C. : U.S. DHEW Pub. No. (HRA) 76-617, 1976.

10

REBUILDING THE HEALTH CARE SYSTEM

After nearly a decade of mounting debate, the nation is nearing the point of taking decisive action to remedy the inadequacies of its health-care system. The main question now remaining is which among the many suggested reforms offer the greatest likelihood of proving practical and effective—and at the same time affordable by the nation without a substantial inflationary effect.

The Committee for Economic Development

During the 1970s, there was more discussion about the need for a "national health policy" than at any other time in the history of the United States. The decade of the 1970s was, in fact, a period that reflected growing discontent among consumers, legislators, and health workers with the existing health care system, its policies, cost, quality, and inaccessibility. In the 1980s, it has become increasingly apparent that improving the organization and financing of health care in the U.S. to assure *access* for all people at a reasonable cost will be a difficult but essential task. In the past, the nation has responded to the shortcomings of the health care system in a succession of crises—in facilities, manpower, financing, and social policy. The failure of these patchwork attempts to improve the health care system has lent support to the notion that future efforts must be comprehensive and take into account political, social, and economic factors that operate in the United States. But before we delve deeply into the future reform of the health care system, an analysis of past legislation and its effects on reforming the system is pertinent.

HEALTH LEGISLATION

Until recently, most public planning and legislation for health care focused upon health activities dealing with specific population groups rather than the delivery of health services and medical care to individuals. The free-enterprise system promoted the notion that the delivery of health services and medical care should be managed by the private sector and that government intervention was inappropriate. However, it has become apparent that certain populations and groups of people living in the United States, particularly those who are poor or members of minority groups do not have sufficient access to obtaining health care when it is needed and the rising cost of health care has become such a critical concern that the government has, out of necessity, become more involved in financing health care and formulating health policy. As a result of legislation over the years new rules have been instituted regarding peer-review for physicians, regionalization of health resources including facilities and professionals, and today more people have access to health care than ever before. A 1978 report released by the Robert Wood Johnson Foundation states that: "The population at large—and every subpopulation group studied—has better access to medical services today than in 1970 or 1963." Further it submits that: "Removal of financial barriers appears to have a major impact on whether or not various groups have access to care."[1]

In addition to facilitating improved access to care, legislation over the years has attempted to promote comprehensive health care for all people, as opposed to fragmented delivery of services. However, efforts have been less than successful.

The Hill-Burton Act   The first attempt to promote comprehensive health planning began in 1946 at the federal level with the *Hill-Burton Act*. It provided considerable federal financial assistance to states for the construction of hospital facilities. According to the legislation, each state was to create a hospital planning council responsible for assessing the need for new hospital construction and for assuring that proposals for individual institutions fit into a coordinated statewide hospital service plan.

This was the first legislation which focused on the provision of medical care to the entire United States population, rather than to certain categorical subgroups within the population such as the poor, or aged. The Hill-Burton program assumed that the states would utilize health-facility construction funds in such a way as to fill unmet needs. However, it was necessary to clarify this concept in order to effect efficient *utilization* of federal funds, and in 1964 the Hill-Burton Act was amended. The Amendment strengthened the original mandate for regional or community-based planning of health facilities and hospitals and restated that this planning was the responsibility of both health care providers and consumers in the community.

The Regional Medical Programs (RMP)   This legislation was enacted by Congress in 1965. *Regional Medical Programs* had a health planning component, but focused primarily on resources development. Through this legislation, financial support was provided for "cooperative regional arrangements" of existing medical centers, research centers, and hospitals. The initial scope of RMP called for programs of education, research, training, and demonstration in the areas of heart disease, cancer, stroke, and kidney and related diseases. However, this scope was amended several times. And, although the law basically dealt with categorical diseases, shifts in emphasis extended the program to other areas.

Frequent changes in program objectives created problems, as did the categorical approach itself; after a while, program activities became highly fragmented. Also, there was no requirement to involve State or local government; hence, most of the program responsibility was lodged with academic medical centers, which did not give the RMP objectives their highest priority. The emphasis on a direct federal-regional relationship meant that RMP projects were separate entities, not readily incorporated into or coordinated with existing federal, state and local medical programs. Thus, there were inevitable duplications and gaps in service programs, health manpower education, and training and research.[2]

Comprehensive health planning program (CHP) In 1966, this legislation was passed, which broadened the planning concept to include health services and manpower development, as well as facilities construction and modernization. This Act authorized federal support for new public or private *comprehensive health planning (CHP)* at the local or areawide level. In addition, the Partnership for Health or comprehensive health planning program emphasized the need for eliminating unnecessary duplication of facilities and equipment in the delivery of health care. State and areawide agencies were established by this Act to plan for and promote the rational development of health resources in communities. However, the accomplishment of this Act was minimal.

In 1970, the former Department of Health, Education and Welfare initiated a series of alterations related to the mission and priorities of the Regional Medical Programs. These programs were designed to respond to the needs of medically underserved populations, especially primary care in inner-city and rural areas. This represented a transition from a categorical disease orientation to a comprehensive services approach by the RMPs. In addition, emergency medical services, health maintenance organizations (HMOs) and area-wide health education were identified by the Department of Health, Education, and Welfare as new priorities.

Professional Standards Review Organizations (PSRO) Since the advent of Medicaid and Medicare, government has been assuming an increasing share of medical care costs. In 1972, an Amendment to the Social Security Act was signed into law which called for the establishment of *Professional Standards Review Organizations (PSRO)*. A PSRO is an organization composed of physicians that uses a *peer-review technique* to help assure that the medical services paid for by Medicare, Medicaid, and Maternal and Child Health Care funds are medically necessary, meet professionally recognized standards, and are provided for in the most appropriate setting.

Each PSRO must be a nonprofit, professional organization of licensed physicians. The law mandates that organized groups of physicians monitor institutional care provided for Medicare and Medicaid patients. Basically,

PSROs carry out their responsibilities by reviewing admissions to a health care facility, certifying the necessity for continuing treatment in an inpatient facility, reviewing other extended or costly treatment, conducting medical evaluation studies, regularly reviewing facility, practitioner and health care service profiles of care, and reviewing facility and practitioner records as applicable to a particular review process.[3]

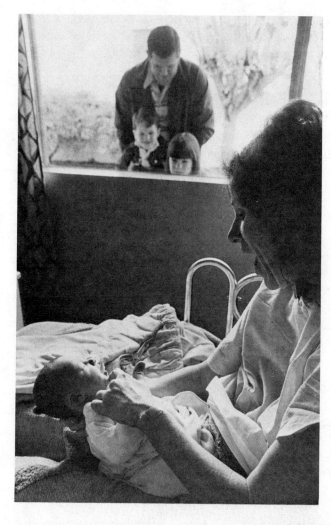

Figure 10-1
PSROs must determine if patient
care is effective and economical.
Courtesy Arizona Republic and
Phoenix Gazette.

The PSRO is responsible for determining whether hospitalization is medically
necessary, is of appropriate duration, and meets recognized professional standards of quality. PSROs also must determine whether patient care could have been given as effectively
or more economically in other types of facilities or on an out-patient basis.[4]

It is still too early to assess the extent to which PSROs have been effectively fulfilling their purposes. It has been suggested that some PSROs have been successful in reducing average length of stay. However, it should be noted that while PSROs have been
minimally effective in reducing costs, they have not contributed to improved quality of
care. The future existence of PSROs is questionable.

During 1973 and 1974 the merits of the various approaches employed by both
the RMPs and CHP to developing a system which provided comprehensive health services
to the American population were debated in both the United States Senate and the House

of Representatives. The National Health Planning and Resources Development Act of 1974 was subsequently developed and signed into law. This legislation attempted to build upon the experience of the three previous programs, incorporating the best feature of each into one new health planning and resources development program.

The National Health Planning and Resources Development Act established a new program for health planning and resources development in the United States. It represented a culmination of experience and was designed to correct many of the problem areas which existed in the health care delivery system.

Highlights of the Act include:

Required HEW to issue guidelines on national health planning policy
Established National Council on Health Planning and Development
Created network of Health Systems Agencies (HSA)s responsible for health planning and development
Authorized planning grants for HSAs
Created statewide Health Coordinating Councils
Established a National Health Planning Information Center
Revised existing Medical Facilities Construction Program.

Health service areas The first step in implementing the law was the establishment of health service areas throughout the United States. These areas were designated by governors according to legislative specifications. These specifications included:

The areas must be a geographic region appropriate for effective development of health services and planning.
Each area must have a population of at least 500,000 and not more than 3 billion.
Area boundaries, to the maximum extent feasible, must be appropriately coordinated with those of Professional Standards Review Organizations, existing regional planning areas, and state planning areas.

Health systems agencies About 200 *health systems agencies (HSAs),* the basic elements of the nationwide health planning effort, were established. An HSA is either a private, nonprofit corporation or a public entity, and is responsible for health planning and development in that area. The HSA is generally responsible for preparing and implementing plans designed to improve the health of the residents in its health services area; to increase the accessibility, acceptability, continuity, and quality of health services in the areas; to restrain increases in the cost of providing health services; and to prevent unnecessary duplication of health resources.

In order to fulfill these responsibilities HSAs were required to gather and analyze data, establish *health systems plans (HSPs)*, provide technical and financial assistance to organizations seeking to implement the plans, and review and either approve or disapprove applications for federal funds for health programs within the health service areas.

The governing board of HSAs are comprised of ten to thirty members, the majority of whom, by law, must be health care consumers. Governing-body members are residents of the health service area and include public elected officials as well as other government representatives who may be either health care consumers or providers.

State health planning and development agencies The governor of each state selected a state health planning and development agency. State health coordinating councils (SHCC) had the major responsibility of reviewing and approving the state health plan by integrating the health plans of the health system agencies into a preliminary state health plan.

Health facilities construction Before the passage of this law, there were few mechanisms in place that could control the costs of health care by limiting construction of health care facilities and capital expenditures. The health planning law required all states to enact *certificate-of-need (C/N)* laws. A certificate-of-need is issued by a governmental body to an individual or organization proposing to construct or modify a health facility or offer a new or different health service, which certifies that such facility or service will be needed.

National council and national guidelines The National Health Planning and Resources Development Act directed the Secretary of the former Department of Health and Human Services to issue guidelines on national health planning policy, provide priorities for health planning goals, and establish a National Council on Health Planning and Development. The Advisory Council and the Secretary of Health, Education and Welfare assumed responsibility for developing national guidelines and implementing the law. The first set of guidelines issued in 1978 included setting standards concerning the appropriate supply distribution and organization of health resources. These guidelines were designed to assist local and state health planning agencies develop their plans, contain costs and achieve a more rational distribution of health care resources.

The National Health Planning and Resources Development Act identified ten priorities. These were:

Primary-care services for medically underserved population, especially in rural or economically depressed areas.

Development of multi-institutional systems for coordinating or consolidating institutional health services.

Developing medical groups practices, health maintenance organizations, and other organized systems for providing health care.

Training and increasing utilization of physician assistants, especially nurse clinicians.

Developing multi-institutional arrangements for sharing support services.

The development by health services institutions of the capacity to provide various levels of care on a geographically integrated basis.

Promoting activities for preventing disease, including studies of nutritional and environmental factors affecting health and the provision of preventive health care services.

Adopting uniform cost accounting and other improved management procedures for health services institutions.

Developing effective methods of educating the general public concerning personal health care and effective use of available health services.[5]

In summary, the National Health Planning and Resources Development Act had two major parts. The first, revised and synthesized all existing health planning programs into a single detailed structure for health planning in the United States. The second, revised existing programs for resources development including health facility construction. The goal of this legislation was the development of an integrated, comprehensive health care system in the United States which met the needs of the entire population. Whether or not this goal will be achieved is uncertain. Many feel that the data needed on which to develop a health systems plan is still unavailable or inadequate. Some believe that the goals of containing health care costs and improving accessibility are conflicting.*

IMPROVING THE SYSTEM

Without question, the United States possesses some of the finest hospitals, physicians, and medical research centers in the world. Spectacular advances have been made in the control of many diseases including cancer, kidney disease, and even heart disease. Life expectancy has increased significantly over the years and is projected to increase by another fifteen years if a major medical breakthrough is achieved in cancer or heart disease. Yet while much is right with the current health care system, the nation can and should do better in rendering health care to its people.

The basic premise underlying the U.S. Public Health Service *Forward Plan For Health* is that there are enormous strengths in the American health care system, and that improvements in the system should be brought about by building on these firm foundations—not by discarding the present system to make way for a radically new structure.

*At the time of this writing, the national health planning program has found itself battling for both its existence and its authority. Numerous administration officials have labeled health planning a place to cut, both to save federal money on a program they claim does not work and to halt what they feel is federal interference in state and local affairs. It seems clear that at the very least the funding of this program will be cut, how severely the cut will be remains a question.

Figure 10-2
Physical fitness testing is one type of
preventive health care service. Courtesy
Arizona Department of Health Services.

According to the *Forward Plan,*

The commitment to individual initiative and freedom has permitted the system to tolerate serious imbalances in the distribution of the nation's health resources. The tendency to focus on purely technological solutions to health care problems has created a climate in which the organizational and system aspects of health care have gone largely neglected. . . . The uncritical enthusiastic acceptance of new technologies into the health care arsenal, in combination with a general absence of attention to planning, has contributed to rising health care costs. . . .

The challenge is clear—to develop the needed improvement while preserving the essential strengths of the system. We must find ways to enhance the planning and regulating abilities of the system without creating a monolith that destroys individual initiative and diversity to pay more attention to problems of organizing and delivering care without undermining the powerful scientific base of the system; and to re-emphasize the human aspects of health care without abandoning the parallel commitment to specialization that enables the health care system to employ complex knowledge effectively.[6]

Ceiling on Health Care Costs

The drive for National Health Insurance (NHI), which began in the early 1970s, was in part related to a belief that NHI could be used to control costs. Yet a related question was—since health care costs were so out of control—could the nation embark on so large an enterprise? Regardless of whether or not the U.S. establishes a national health-insurance system, one thing is clear: actions and mechanisms designed to contain costs can no longer be delayed. If and when a NHI system is developed, the cost-control policies and strategies should already be in place.

The first step in improving the health care system is to establish a firm national ceiling on health care expenditures. Institutional capital expenditures are a major factor in annual health care expenditures, not only because of their initial purchasing cost, but because they are significant determinants of operating costs and utilization. For example, once built, a hospital will be costly to maintain whether or not all its beds are used. And, it is estimated that operating costs for every new piece of equipment will equal the original cost in a period of about two years.[7]

To control costs several suggestions have been put forth. One is to limit expenditures on health care services to some set percentage of the GNP, say 8 percent. It is believed that this national ceiling can be established and met if several related issues are faced. For example, it is recognized that health status is minimally improved by increasing amounts of health care, but maximally improved by improved environmental and living conditions, and higher levels of education and socioeconomic status. So, perhaps the first step in redirecting national efforts to improve health would be to fund programs that attempt to rebuild deteriorating substandard housing, to shape more and better educational programs, and to improve occupational safety and health.

Second, since institutional capital expenditures are such an important factor in

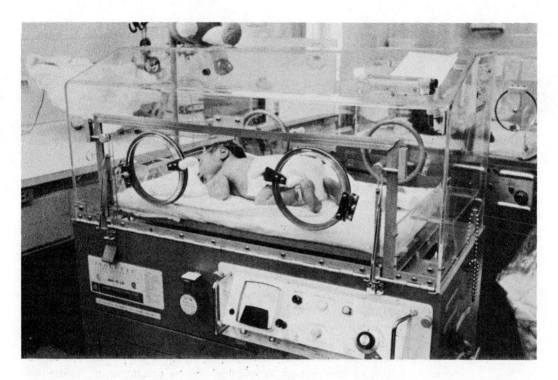

Figure 10-3 The average cost of treating an infant in the intensive care unit is $40,000. Courtesy U.S. Department of Health, Education and Welfare.

spiraling health care costs, a temporary moratorium should be placed on building new or renovating existing acute-care hospital beds, and with certain exceptions on expensive equipment. In addition, there is increasing agreement on the necessity for institutional rate or price controls of some type. This is especially true for hospitals.

Physicians' fees constitute the next-largest segment of the national health bill after capital expenditures. And, physicians play a primary role in determining many other health care costs, including lab and diagnostic work ordered, length of hospital stay, and even whether a patient can be treated on an out-patient as opposed to in-patient basis. Thus, controlling costs in this area is a high priority. Attempts in the past to place a ceiling on physicians' fees, or implementing the concept of "reasonable charges," have been largely unsuccessful. In the future, some other mechanism will need to be developed that accomplishes this cost-containment goal.

The Reagan Administration is committed to controlling the spiraling cost of health care. It is likely that the approach of this Administration to deal with cost control will rely upon competition-based national *health insurance*. In this system, tax laws would be used to encourage the availability of lower-cost health insurance for employees. It is apparent that any legislative program costing large sums of federal money, even in the short term, is not likely to have much chance of passage in the immediate future.

Improved Quality Care

Quality assurance is a pervasive issue in health care in the United States, one that cuts across many of the problems in the system. As the complexity of our medical care system grows, so does the need for a national health policy that focuses the system on producing results—improving the health status of the American people.

Although a generally accepted definition of "quality of health care" does not exist, the following working description was used in the context of the *Forward Plan:*

> Quality health care offers the patient the greatest achievable health benefit, with minimum unnecessary risk and use of resources, in a manner satisfactory to the patient.

> This formulation recognizes that four factors determine the quality of a given episode of health care: effectiveness, safety, cost, and patient satisfaction. The need for effectiveness and safety is obvious. Cost deserves to be considered because health care is necessarily provided from limited funds (personal, government, or third parties). The reduction of expenditures that do not contribute to quality will permit wider and more effective use of funds, thus potentially benefiting more people and producing a greater net improvement in health. . . .

> No one can ensure absolutely that the four determinants of quality—effectiveness, safety, cost, and patient satisfaction—will be present to an appropriate degree in every health care intervention. Nevertheless, it is the shared responsibility of health professionals and government to provide a reasonable basis for confidence that action will be taken both to assess whether services meet professionally recognized standards and to correct any deficiencies that may be found. Quality assurance is thus not a guarantee of performance, much less of satisfactory results, but [a] . . . process that leads to improved health care quality.[8]

One specific issue is apparent when discussing the quality of health care in the U.S. Despite considerable efforts by the government since the enactment of Medicaid and Medicare to make quality health care available to poor persons, the success is relative. There should be no connection between a person's income or socioeconomic status and the extent or quality of care delivered by physicians, other health professionals, and hospitals. Yet the unequivocal fact is that a poor person is less likely to obtain a desirable level of care than his or her more affluent neighbor. Poor people generally have little control over which physician treats them in comparison to their nonpoor counterparts, who have the freedom to select one physician over another and go to yet another physician if the level of care is unsatisfactory.

Equitable Access to Health Care

The problem of providing satisfactory medical service to all the people of the United States at costs which they can meet is a pressing one. At the present time,

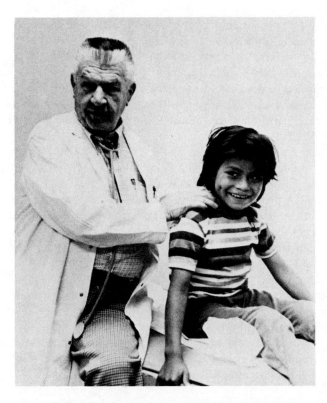

Figure 10–4
Everyone should have access to high quality health care. Courtesy Arizona Department of Health Services.

many persons do not receive service which is adequate either in quantity or in quality, and the costs of service are inequitably distributed. The result is a tremendous amount of preventable physical pain and mental anguish, needless deaths, economic inefficiency, and social waste. Furthermore, these conditions are . . . largely unnecessary. The United States has the economic resources, the organizing ability, and the technical experience to solve this problem.

These opinions were contained in the final report of the Committee on the Costs of Medical Care, published on October 31, 1932. Although significant strides have been made since that time by increasing private and public health insurance, categorical government health care programs, and advancing knowledge and technology, two basic problems remain on which the concern for national health insurance is focused: inadequate coverage, and inappropriate, ineffective, and inefficient organization and utilization of health care resources.[9]

Government financing programs such as Medicaid/Medicare and U.S. Public Health Service centers have been largely unsuccessful in closing the gap between those who require the most health care and receive the least. Ours is a "multi-tiered health care system in which the poor and other minority groups have to rely on clinics and emergency rooms for their health care, while those in higher income categories, whose insurance gives them more health care purchasing power, are able to be much more selective about where, when, and from whom they obtain health care.

Equally troublesome is the fact that most of the insured population has inadequate benefits. Most basic insurance policies exclude preventive care services, *ambulatory care,* prescription drugs and medical devices, and dental care. Many policies still exclude preexisting conditions and congenital defects. Adequate financing for necessary health care services is essential to assure that professional decisions on the kinds, amounts, and types of services delivered are based on health needs.

Another major problem deals with our health care resources. At present, there is both geographic and speciality maldistribution of health field professionals, as well as co-existent proliferation of some resources and scarity of others.[10]

Because state licensure is a precondition for practicing medicine, complete freedom of physicians to practice where they choose does not exist. But while the freedom to practice where one desires is not absolute—it is substantial.[11]

The extent to which this freedom is exercised is reflected in the different ratios of physicians to the population in the urban ghettos vs. the affluent suburbs 20 miles away—the ratios are in the order of 1:50 to 1:100.[12] Attracting competent physicians and other health professionals to medically underserved areas in the U.S. has been difficult. In the future, stronger incentives will need to be utilized to reduce the disparity of supply among states and within states of health providers. Some have even suggested that short of outright coercion, health professionals will never establish nor maintain practices in areas unattractive to them or their families. And, that we will have to mandate the "direction of labor" in a society which considers freedom of job choice and location among its highest values.[13]

Ideally, a comprehensive health care delivery system includes the following components in providing for prevention, early detection, treatment, and rehabilitative care (see Figure 10-5). The model system outlined below emphasizes the health-promotion-disease-prevention orientation, while it also includes treatment and rehabilitation components.

Model Health Care Delivery System

Multiphasic screening Screening represents the entry point into a health delivery system. It includes various types of health and illness testing procedures and diagnostic work. Multiphasic screening can be conducted by trained paramedical personnel who are qualified to administer diagnostic tests, who subsequently compile a medical history on each person who enters the delivery system.

Health care center Prevention of illness and disease is the primary goal of the health care center activities and services. Keeping people well is the goal. It is accomplished by providing activities and services which include immunizations, health education through films, classes and health exhibits, and health counselling. Health care centers can utilize trained paramedical personnel, including nurses, physician assistants, and health educators to perform services under the supervision of medical doctors.

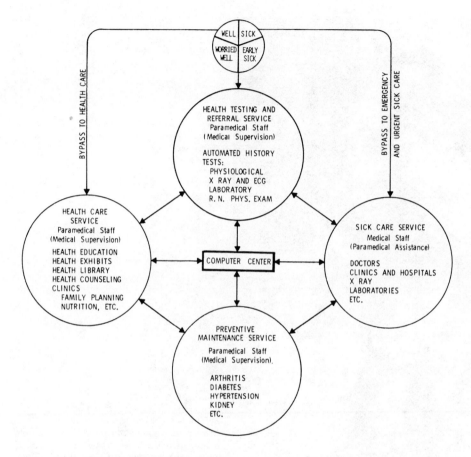

Figure 10-5 Triage system used in Kaiser-Permanente Medical Care Program, Oakland, California.

Preventive-maintenance service Both prevention of disease and the provision of care including rehabilitation for those who suffer chronic disease is the objective of this segment of a comprehensive health care delivery system. Maintenance care is provided to those who are victims of such chronic diseases as arthritis, diabetes, hypertension and obesity. This service would also utilize trained paramedical personnel operating under the supervision of physicians.

Sick-care center This center provides diagnosis and treatment functions. It manages acute episodes resulting from accident emergencies and disease. Diagnostic and treatment functions are performed by physicians who are highly trained health professionals. The sick-care center, as the name suggests, provides services to people who are ill. Its focus is early diagnosis and treatment in order to facilitate rapid recovery. By using physicians in the sick-care center *only*, efficiency of the system is improved and highly trained individuals are called upon to perform only the tasks that other less-trained professionals cannot perform.[14]

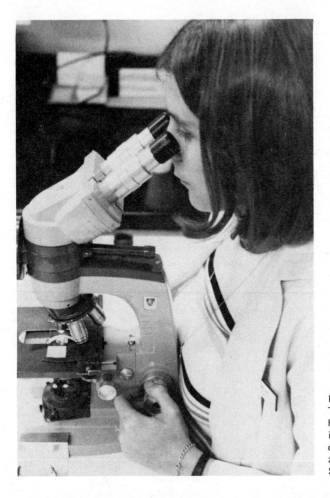

Figure 10-6
The entry level into the model health care delivery system would involve multiphase screenings including lab work. Courtesy Arizona Department of Health Services.

In the future, it is likely that the only long-range satisfactory solution to the problems in our health care system is some form of national health insurance (NHI). At the least, the U.S. will need to develop a decentralized but integrated approach to get health services to the people who need them—that is, decentralized units that reach into neighborhoods and rural areas where the need for service is acute. To assure appropriate utilization of health care, there is now general agreement that ambulatory care will need to be strengthened. The pervasive philosophy of the present centers around an aim to keep people out of health care institutions and to develop more community-based health services such as home care, social services, and mental health clinics. Thus the ambulatory care center could well become the key element in the health care delivery system of tomorrow.

For years the main thrust of the nation's efforts to assure people access to health care has been the elimination of economic impediments to care by means of insurance. This hasn't worked, but the goal is attainable through improvement and extension of the present system.

NATIONAL HEALTH INSURANCE

The United States is the only major industrial nation without a comprehensive national health insurance plan. For years, consumers, legislators, organized labor, and health care providers have debated the question of national health insurance (NHI). There is now general agreement that some form of national health insurance is needed in the United States. Some proponents suggest NHI is essential to ensuring access to health care for all Americans. Others believe it will improve the organization and delivery of health care services, resulting in cost-containment, improved quality of care, and improved health status of Americans.

Some factions support a solution that would involve replacing all private health insurance with public health insurance. This, of course, would mean a complete transformation of the health care delivery system—its organization, financing, and resources development. Complete revision of the system from the private sector to the public sector would no doubt result in significant tax increases. Others support a more moderate change that would preserve the function of private insurance companies, but which would promote active reform in the health care industry to effect solutions to present problems.

The federal goals related to the health care system can be stated in various ways, but the basic aims are to:

> Assure access to quality health care for all Americans, particularly low-income persons;
> Eliminate or reduce inappropriate institutional care and encourage the use of ambulatory and preventive services whenever possible;
> Increase the availability of primary-care services to residents of rural or medically underserved areas;
> Assure the most appropriate, effective, and efficient utilization of existing health care facilities and services; and
> Otherwise promote community health.[15]

Although the exact nature of a national health insurance plan for the United States is still unclear, it does not seem likely that two specific approaches in the immediate future will be abandoned.

> The first is the exclusive reliance on the private, voluntary insurance mechanism for adequate handling of all responsibilities related to costs, controls, and the availability of effective delivery of care. The second is the complete reliance on a public medical service approach, such as Great Britain, the Soviet Union and other large countries employ—in which all costs are financed wholly or largely out of general revenues and reimbursement of physicians is not on a fee-for-service basis.[16]

It is likely that the national health insurance system that is established in the United States will rely on both public and private funds for financial support. Regardless of which proposal is enacted, the cost of medical expenditures will no doubt increase. And, at least initially, private health-insurance companies will no doubt continue to serve as "payment agencies," although it is questionable that they will continue to perform "insuring" functions.

In recent years, over twenty different national health insurance plans have been introduced in Congress. All of these have employed multiple sources of financing, and most support the notion that employers should contribute anywhere from two-thirds to three-fourths of the cost of comprehensive medical-care coverage. One of the key issues that remains to be resolved is whether federal personnel, state personnel, or private insurance carriers will be responsible for providing reimbursements and containing costs. Clearly, one of the most important issues to be resolved before adopting a form of national health insurance is the relative cost of each plan in relation to the benefits it will provide.

Another consideration is the need for the national health insurance system that is adopted to be a powerful force in achieving greater coordination and consolidation of health care services to which every American has access. In this regard, Dr. James G. Haughton proposed guidelines for the adoption of a responsive and responsible national health insurance plan in the United States. These guidelines are:

1. Break the barrier between paying health care and being eligible for the service.
2. Require the employee and the self-employed to pay part of the costs.
3. Require the employer to pay a substantial part of the costs.
4. Require the government to contribute a significant part of the cost.
5. Require that employee and employer contributions to the plan be handled as part of social security contributions.
6. Provide for universal coverage and eligibility to services by federal law solely and simply by virtue of legal residence in the United States.
7. Assure that access to service for all persons throughout the nation would be determined by nationwide rules.
8. Provide for a broad range of medical services with specific arrangements for extending services over a reasonable period of time.
9. Provide for new, innovative, economical and efficient methods of organizing and delivering medical care.
10. Encourage and accelerate plans to increase personnel in the health fields.
11. Provide opportunities for the consumer, as taxpayer and patient to play a significant role in policy formulation and administration of the health system.
12. Assure health personnel reasonable compensation and opportunities for professional practice, advancement, and the exercise of humanitarian and social responsibility.
13. Encourage effective professional participation in the formulation of guidelines, standards, rules, regulations, procedures, and organization.

14. Require state and area health agencies to take affirmative leadership in providing for effective delivery of medical services.

15. Foster a pluralistic and flexible system of administration.[17]

During 1978, the United States Public Health Service conducted a nationwide survey that recorded the medical experiences of citizens to learn how much a national health insurance plan might cost. Some 11,500 families provided information about medical experiences, including treatment received, cost, and time lost from work or school as a result of illness. It is hoped that the data compiled in this study will yield more information on the current status of health care in the United States, as well as a new understanding of the needs that are unmet—thus paving the way for NHI in the future.

Over twenty national health insurance plans were introduced in the 94th Congress. These plans offer a broad range of financial approaches to health care delivery and to the actual organization and delivery of health services. Generally, NHI would provide a uniform range of benefits for all citizens of the United States. Its purpose is to enable all people to secure health care without being deterred due to cost considerations. Beyond this, it is clear that as yet there is no agreement as to the scope of benefits to be provided by NHI, nor how the program should be financed.

National health insurance will exist in the U.S. at some time in the future. However, at present, there is increasing public resistance to further tax increases, which clouds the prospect of NHI for the immediate future. No doubt the benefits, costs, and issues raised by a number of national health insurance proposed plans will be topics of debate for some time.

Specific NHI Proposals

Long-Ribicoff Senators Russel Long and Abraham Ribicoff have proposed a National Health Insurance Plan that has three major parts: (1) *catastrophic coverage* provided through the Social Security Administration to assist all people, (2) a new subsidized plan that would replace Medicaid and cover all basic medical expenses of low-income people, and (3) provisions designed to promote the sale of private health insurance to those who can afford it. Catastrophic illnesses are defined as an illness or illnesses entailing more than sixty days hospitalization or more than $2,000 in medical bills during the period of a year.

In the Long-Ribicoff plan,

. . . . reimbursements to providers follow those of the Medicare program. Hospitals, skilled-nursing facilities, and home-health agencies would be reimbursed on the basis of "reasonable cost" of services. Payments to physicians would be determined on the basis of "reasonable charges." Physicians could either directly bill patients covered under the catastrophic portion or accept assignment of the allowable charge as payment in full; physicians seeing the poor would be required to accept assignment of the payment. Other provisions in the Medicare program which would be applied to the plan include limits on costs for institutional services recognized as reasonable, limitations on payments for services in connection with capital expenditures disapproved by health planning agencies, and limitations on increases in physicians' fees.[18]

The Reagan Administration seems to favor a combination of both a catastrophic program and a fill-in-the-gaps program, aimed at reducing costs.

Comprehensive Health Insurance Plan   This plan was originally introduced during the Nixon Administration and endorsed for a short time by the Ford Administration. It is a mixed public-private approach with a similar range of benefits for all covered persons, but different financing and cost-sharing arrangements. This plan has three basic components: (1) the employee health care insurance plan for working families, (2) the assisted health care insurance plan for the poor, and (3) the federal health care insurance plan to replace Medicare for the elderly. Specifically, this proposal calls for the following:

> States would be given expanded roles to establish reimbursement rates for health care providers. Physicians and other providers who elected to be "full-participating" would receive the state-established rates (including any cost-sharing) as full payments. (All hospitals and nursing homes would be required to be "full-participating.") Providers who elected to be "associate participating" would be permitted to charge more than the state rate for employee-plan patients, but would have to collect the extra charges and cost-sharing amounts from the patients.
>
> Various provisions would require that all families be given the option of enrolling in approved prepaid practice plans.
>
> Regulation of insurance carriers would be conducted by state governments, including approval of premium rates, enforcement of disclosure requirements, annual audit by certified public accountants, and protection against the insolvency of carriers.
>
> State governments would also set standards for participation in the program and approval of proposed capital expenditures.[19]

Given the estimated large cost of beginning this program, and the current political mood in Washington, it seems unlikely that comprehensive national health insurance will have much chance in the near future.

American Hospital Association Plan   Representative Al Ullman introduced the American Hospital Association proposal to Congress. This plan requires that employers purchase standard health-insurance policies for employees and their dependents. Under the provisions of this bill, the federal government would enter into contracts with private health-insurance companies to provide coverage for older persons and the poor. The development of health care corporations would be promoted in this bill and catastrophic coverage is included in the plan.

> A unique feature of the American Hospital Association plan is the development of a new delivery model for health services, called a health care corporation (HCC). These nonprofit or public corporations would furnish comprehensive and coordinated health services through their own facilities or affiliated providers. Enrollment would be open to all residents of a given geographic area. A limited number of corporations would be permitted to serve each area, subject to state approval; priority would be given to an HCC applying for an area not already served. The corporation could charge its enrollees either an annual capitation charge or a separate charge for each service, but a capitation option would eventually be made available to all who wish to enroll. . . .
>
> Administration of the plan would be vested in a Department of Health at the federal level and independent health commissioners at the state level. A national health services advisory council and state advisory councils, with consumer majorities, would participate in policy formulation and review proposed regulations.[20]

Health Care for All Americans Act of 1979   The Health Care for All Americans Act was introduced by Senator Edward Kennedy in May 1979 in the 96th Congress. Every resident in the U.S. would be covered through either mandated health-insurance plans or federal coverage for the poor and aged. The plan would establish comprehensive benefits including in-patient hospital services, physician services, home-health services, x-rays, and lab tests. Costs of catastrophic illness are covered in the plan since no limits are placed on the number of hospital days or physician visits.

Cost control in this plan would be accomplished through prospective budgeting of hospital fees and negotiated physician fees. The program would be administered by a National Health Insurance Board, the members of which shall be a majority of consumers. These members will be appointed by the President.

In the Kennedy plan, most Americans would be insured by an insurer of a health maintenance organization that would be regulated by the federal government. The insurer must be a member of a consortium of (1) insurance companies, (2) Blue-Cross/ Blue Shield plans, (3) federally qualified HMOs, or (4) independent practice associations. Medicare would be upgraded for the aged. The poor would be covered by a national health insurance plan for all benefits except long-term nursing-home care, which would be covered by Medicaid. Every resident of the U.S. would be issued a health insurance card. Thus, every person will have a right to receive medical treatment.

Competition-based national health insurance   The competition-based approach to national health insurance is a popular one. Three bills were introduced in the 96th Congress, and it is nearly certain that similar legislation was reintroduced in the 97th

Congress. These bills included The Health Incentives Reform Act, The National Health Care Reform Act, and The Health Costs Restraint Act. Each of these proposals would use the tax laws to encourage the *availability* of lower cost health insurance programs for employees.

Summary

It appears inevitable that during the next decade Americans will be covered by some form of national health insurance. Each plan that has been proposed to Congress has both merits and weaknesses. No plan offered thus far has proposed to make doctors and other health workers government employees, yet there are still many questions and concerns related to the proposed plans. For example, how much will each plan cost? There is no question that comprehensive national health insurance would result in additional costs, but how much? How would these costs affect income-tax bills? Further, what are the ramifications of either establishing a new government agency to operate a national health program in its entirety, without private insurance companies, or coordinating the efforts of the private health-insurance industry with a government agency? What does seem clear is that the United States needs a national health plan that provides accessible quality health care, at a reasonable price, and is built on consumer and health care provider input.

The concept of national health insurance may well be the most critical domestic issue facing the nation during the 1980s. It is hoped that the net result of current Congressional debates on the question will be a health care delivery system based on a strong theoretical and practical base that will enable it to solve a majority of the problems that have surfaced in the present health care delivery system.

REVIEW QUESTIONS

1. Describe various pieces of legislation that have been enacted over the years to reform the health care system.
2. Explain the purpose of PSROs. On what four basic premises was the PSRO system founded?
3. List and explain the ten priority areas identified in the National Health Planning and Resources Development Act of 1974.
4. Summarize the highlights of the National Health Planning and Development Act. Describe the intent and importance of this legislation.
5. How can the health care delivery system in the U.S. be improved regarding cost, access, and quality?
6. Briefly describe the rationale for National Health Insurance in the United States and compare the major plans thus far proposed.

SUGGESTED READINGS

Carlson, Rick, *The End of Medicine.* New York: John Wiley, 1975.

Braverman, Jordan, *Crisis in Health Care,* Washington, D.C.: Acropolis Books, 1978.

Somers, Anne and Herman Somers, *Health and Health Care: Policies in Perspective.* Germantown, Md: Aspen Systems Corp., 1977.

NOTES

[1] *Access: A Special Report.* Princeton, N.J.: The Johnson Foundation, 1978.

[2] U.S. DHEW, *Regionalization and Health Policy.* Washington, D.C.: U.S. DHEW Pub. No. (HRA) 77-623, p. 21.

[3] U.S. DHEW, "PSRO Factbook." Washington, D.C.: Government Printing Office, May, 1977, p. 2.

[4] Marshall Segal, "A Hard Look at the PSRO Law," *Journal of Legal Medicine.* September-October, 1974, p. 26.

[5] U.S. DHEW, "The Health Planning and Resources Development Act of 1974." Washington, D.C.: U.S. DHEW Publ. No. (HRA) 76-14015.

[6] U.S. DHEW, *Forward Plan for Health: Fiscal Year 1977-1981."* Washington, D.C.: U.S. DHEW, p. 14.

[7] Ann Sommers and Herman Somers, *Health and Health Care.* Germantown, Md: Aspen Systems Corp., p. 455.

[8] *Forward Plan for Health,* pp. 16-17.

[9] *Forward Plan for Health,* p. 18.

[10] *Forward Plan for Health,* pp. 18-19.

[11] *Regionalization and Health Policy,* p. 2.

[12] *Regionalization and Health Policy,* p. 2.

[13] *Regionalization and Health Policy,* p. 3.

[14] Sidney Garfield, "The Delivery of Medical Care," *Scientific American.* 222:15-23, 1970.

[15] *Forward Plan for Health,* p. 47.

[16] James, Haughton, "The Challenge of Equitable Access," in U.S. DHEW, *Health in America: 1776-1976.* Washington, D.C.: U.S. DHEW, Pub. No. (HRA) 76-616, 1976, p. 174.

[17] *Health in America: 1776-1976,* pp. 185-186.

[18] Karen Davis, "Regionalization and National Health Insurance," in U.S. DHEW, *Regionalization and Health Policy.* Washington, D.C.: U.S. DHEW Pub. No. (HRA) 77-623, 1977, p. 182.

[19] Karen Davis, p. 182.

[20] Karen Davis, p. 183.

GLOSSARY

access an individual's (or group's) ability to obtain medical care. Access has geographic, financial, social and ethnic components, and is a function of availability.

ambulatory care all types of health services that are provided on an out-patient basis in contrast to services provided in the home or to in-patients.

availability in terms of type, volume, and location, a measure of the supply of health resources and services relative to the needs or demands of a given individual or community.

catastrophic coverage health insurance that provides protection against the high cost of treating severe or lengthy illnesses or disabilities.

certificate-of-need (C/N) a certificate issued by a governmental body to an individual or organization proposing to construct or modify a health facility, or offer a new or different health service; recognizes that the facility or service will be needed by those for whom it is intended.

comprehensive health planning (CHP) health planning that encompasses all factors and programs which impact on peoples' health.

health insurance insurance against loss by disease or accidental bodily injury. Such insurance covers some of the medical costs of treating the disease or injury.

health systems agency (HSA) a health planning and resources development agency designated under the terms of the National Health Planning and Resources Development Act of 1974.

health systems plan (HSP) a long range health plan prepared by an HSA for its health service area specifying the health goals considered appropriate by the agency for the area.

Hill-Burton Act legislation, and the programs operated under the legislation for federal support of construction and modernization of hospitals and other health facilities.

peer-review technique generally, the evaluation by practicing physicians or other professionals of the effectiveness and efficiency of services ordered or performed by other practicing physicians; refers to the activities of the Professional Standards Review Organization (PSRO).

Professional Standards Review Organization (PSRO) a physician-sponsored organization charged with comprehensive and on-going review of services provided under Medicaid and Medicare.

Regional Medical Program (RMP) a program of federal support for regional organizations, called regional medical programs, which seeks to improve care for heart disease, cancer, strokes and related diseases.

utilization commonly examined in terms of patterns or rates of use of a single service or type of service.

BIBLIOGRAPHY

Aday, Lu Ann, Ronald Anderson, and Odin W. Anderson, "Social Surveys and Health Policy: Implications for National Health Insurance," *Public Health Reports* 92(6) 508-517, 1977.

Berki, S.E., Marie Ashcraft, Roy Penchansky, and Robert Fortus, "Health Concern, HMO Enrollment, and Preventive Care Use," *Journal of Community Health* 3(1) 3-31, 1977.

Blum, Henrik L., *Expanding Health Care Horizons.* Oakland, Calif.: Third Party Associates, 1978.

Building a National Health-Care System, 3rd ed. New York: Committee for Economic Development, 1975.

Davis, Karen, *National Health Insurance: Benefits, Costs, and Consequences.* Washington, D.C.: The Brookings Institute, 1975.

Feder, Judith, John Holahan, and Theodore Marmor (eds.), *National Health Insurance: Conflicting Goals and Policy Choices.* Washington, D.C.: The Urban Institute, 1980.

Goodrich, Thelma Jean and Anthony Gary, "The Process of Ambulatory Care: A Comparison of the Hospital and the Community Health Center," *American Journal of Public Health,* 70(3) 251-255, 1980.

Pennells, Maryland and David Hoover (eds.), *Health Manpower Sourcebook: Section 21 Allied Health Manpower, 1950-1980.* Washington, D.C.: U.S. DHEW, Pub. No. 263, 1980.

_____"National Health Insurance: Which Way to Go," *Consumer Reports,* 40 (2) 118-124, 1975.

Raffel, Marshall W., *The U.S. Health System: Origins and Functions.* New York: John Wiley, 1980.

Roemer, M. I. and S. J. Axelrod, "A National Health Service and Social Security," *American Journal of Public Health,* 67(5) 462-465, 1977.

Rogers, John and Peter Curtis, "The Concept and Measurement of Continuity in Primary Care," *American Journal of Public Health,* 70(2) 122-127, 1980.

Rosen, Harry, J. M. Metsch, and Samuel Levey, *The Consumer and the Health Care System.* New York: John Wiley, 1977.

Segal, Marshall, "A Hard Look at the PSRO Law." *The Journal of Legal Medicine,* 26-37, September-October 1974.

Sheldon, Alan, *Managing Change and Collaboration in the Health System: A Paradigm Approach.* Cambridge, Mass.: Oelgeschlager, Gunn and Hain, 1979.

Terris, M., P. B. Cornely, H. C. Daniels, and L. E. Kerr, "The Cast for National Health Service, Commentary," *American Journal of Public Health,* 67(10) 1183-1185, 1977.

U.S. DHEW, "National Guidelines for Health Planning," Washington, D.C.: U.S. DHEW Pub. No. (HRA) 78-643, 1978.

_____"Conditions for Change in the Health Care System." Washington, D.C.: U.S. DHEW Pub. No. (HRA) 78-642, 1977.

_____ "The Nation's Use of Health Resources: 1979." Washington, D.C.: U.S. DHEW Pub. No. (PHS) 80-1240, 1980.

PART IV

community health:
FOCUS ON TARGET GROUPS

11

PROGRESS IN MATERNAL, INFANT, AND CHILD HEALTH

> The children of America must become the nation's first priority. Our public policies must be changed to favor an environment for children and adults which is socially humane and physically healthy, one which provides children and their parents with the resources and the richness of experience needed for growth.
>
> *Report to the President,*
> *White House Conference on Children, 1970*

In our pluralistic American society, there are mothers and children living in affluence and in poverty. There are children who are black, American Indian, Hispanic, Oriental, and white. Children of America come from various religious, ethnic, and socioeconomic backgrounds. While many American mothers and children suffer from a multitude of different health problems, others are relatively free from abuse, disease, emotional problems, and physical handicaps. It is the conviction of those involved in community health that the children of our society should all have the opportunity to grow and develop in an environment that is free from dangers and conducive to emotional, intellectual and physical growth and *health*. Childhood is a critical state in the life cycle. It significantly influences later development and may make a difference in whether or not a human being reaches full potential in adulthood.

A contemporary misconception is that only the middle-class receives inadequate medical care, since the very wealthy can provide for themselves and their children, and the very poor are provided for by the government. In reality, no social class can obtain health care with great ease, but the poor suffer most. American children who are impoverished and isolated as a result of their racial, cultural, or socioeconomic status receive inadequate medical care. And, many children born in affluence are impoverished in spite of the fact that adequate medical care and physical needs such as proper nutrition are available. There are three ingredients required for successful growth and development during the critical childhood years: (1) nurturance, providing for the basic physical needs of food, shelter, and clothing, (2) guidance, providing direction and discipline for the child's

Figure 11-1
The children of America must
become the nation's first priority.

responsible social and behavioral development, and (3) appreciation, showing the child that he or she is an important, respected, and unique individual. Many children pass through this critical period without knowing that they are appreciated. Others have not been guided and as adults have no conscience, no sense of right and wrong. It is the challenge of this age to restore the value of children in society, to renew and to protect the health and welfare of children.

HISTORY OF CHILD HEALTH

If any of us had been born in America 200 years ago, we would have had only a 50 percent chance of living to celebrate our twenty-first birthday. Times have changed, but progress has been slow in coming. The first Division of Child Hygiene in the United States was established in New York in 1907. At that time, disease prevention and health promotion had no place in public health. Once a disease was contracted, a child was placed in *quarantine.* During the last half of the nineteenth century, the idea that children were individuals in their own right and that they had special health needs emerged. It was also recognized during these years that children represented the future of America. By the mid-1930s, the United States Public Health Service conducted a massive, far-reaching survey of households in the United States and found that "an average of 51 percent of all deaths of children between 1 and 15 years of age were due to infectious and parasitic diseases, pneumonia, and diarrhea and enteritis."[1] The Public Health Service concluded that these deaths measured, in part, the lack of medical care and delay in receiving treatment. By the end of World War II, sulfa drugs and a wide variety of antibiotics, including penicillin, made it possible to treat many of the acute communicable diseases including tuberculosis, pneumonia, and other acute bacterial infections, thereby preventing death. Immunizations for such things as rubella (German measles), smallpox, and measles helped to further brighten the picture of health for children in America.

In retrospect, the greatest and most significant successes of all U.S. community health programs have occurred in the area of protection and promotion of infant, child, and maternal health. We have seen a general decline in the incidence of diseases and death during the first year of life and during childhood. In addition, the successful treatment of childhood diseases, better maternal and *prenatal care,* and the correction of remedial defects such as vision disorders have improved significantly over the past fifty years. But while infants in the United States now get a fairly good start in life compared to children of the past, some of the communicable and chronic diseases that were prevalent in the past continue to be widespread, and the incidence of other diseases and conditions, such as *child abuse, genetic diseases,* have increased. It is likely that the poor, nonwhite child born in the United States is most likely to be affected by ill-health, abuse, generally poor growth and development. Such a child will be the least likely to have access to health care or rehabilitative resources.

Traditional Measures of Maternal and Child Health

The health status of children in the United States cannot be determined simply by recording the incidence of various diseases, since there are many factors that must be taken into consideration in order to get an accurate picture of child health in the United States. In 1930, the White House Conference on Child Health and Protection identified nineteen tenets. They are:

> For every child, full preparation for its birth, his mother receiving prenatal, natal and postnatal care; and the establishment of such protective measures as will make child bearing safer. For every child, health protection from birth through adolescence, including: periodical health examinations, and where needed, care of specialists and hospital treatment; regular dental examinations and care of the teeth; protective and preventive measures against communicable diseases; the insuring of pure food, pure milk, and pure water.[2]

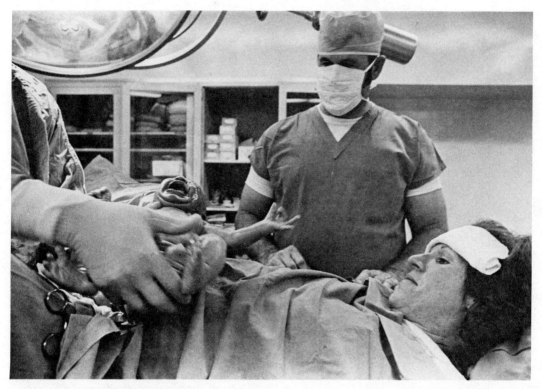

Figure 11-2 Early prenatal care results in less complicated deliveries. Courtesy Arizona Republic and Phoenix Gazette.

Typically, community health has utilized two important measures to assess child health, prenatal care, and *infant mortality rate.* These two indices are the best measures of the general health status of children. The importance of adequate and early prenatal care is related to less-complicated pregnancies and deliveries, which result in a higher rate of live births. In 1977, about 77 percent of white mothers started prenatal care during the first three months of pregnancy, compared to 59 percent of black mothers. Ninety-nine percent of babies in the United States were delivered in hospitals in 1977.[3] But while the number of women receiving prenatal care has increased impressively over the past few decades, there is still a discrepancy between affluent and poor women, between white women and those of other racial groups, and between the highly educated and poorly educated woman. The infant mortality rate is usually accepted as one of the best measure of the health status of a population or country (see Table 11-1 and Figure 11-3). Although infant mortality rate in the United States has dropped from 47.0 per 1,000 live births in 1940 to 14.1 per 1,000 births in 1977, there is much room for improvement. The United States currently ranks seventh in infant mortality, when measured against all other nations.

Although there has been an overall decline in the infant mortality rate in the

299

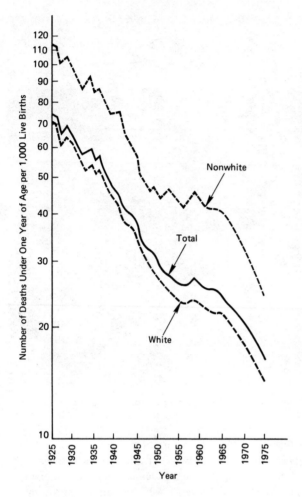

Figure 11-3 Infant mortality rates by color: United States, 1925-1974. Courtesy National Center for Health Statistics, *Vital Statistics Rates in the United States,* 1940-60. PHS Pub. No. 1477; *Monthly Vital Statistics Report,* Provisional Statistics, Annual Summary for the United States, Vol. 23, Number 13, 1974.

United States at an average of 4 percent per year over the last ten years, the mortality rate in 1977 for black infants was 23.6 per 1,000 births, compared to 12.3 for white infants. It is generally accepted that children belonging to segments of the population classified at the poverty level have significantly higher death rates than children from moderate or upper income groups.

It has not yet become clear to community health workers whether higher infant death rates in poverty and minority groups are a consequence of generally poor living conditions, inadequate nutrition, or of difficulty in gaining access to health care. Regard-

Table 11-1 Infant Mortality Rates and Perinatal Mortality Ratios: Selected Countries, Selected Years 1972–1977[a]

COUNTRY	INFANT MORTALITY RATE		AVERAGE ANNUAL PERCENT CHANGE	PERINATAL MORTALITY RATIO[c]		AVERAGE ANNUAL PERCENT CHANGE
	1972	1977[b]		1972	1976[d]	
	Infant Deaths per 1,000 Live Births			Perinatal Deaths per 1,000 Live Births		
Canada	17.1	14.3	-5.8	19.2	14.9	-8.1
United States	18.5	14.1	-5.3	21.9	17.3	-5.7
Sweden	10.8	8.0	-5.8	14.4	–	–
England and Wales	17.2	13.7	-4.4	22.0	17.9	-5.0
Netherlands	11.7	9.5	-4.1	16.7	14.5	-3.5
German Democratic Republic	17.6	13.1	-5.7	19.4	17.6	-3.2
German Federal Republic	22.7	17.4	-6.4	24.1	19.4	-7.0
France	16.0	11.4[e]	-6.6	18.8[e]	17.0[e,f]	-4.9
Switzerland	13.3	10.7	-5.3	16.3	13.2	-5.1
Italy	27.0	17.6	-8.2	29.6	26.5[f]	-5.4
Israel	21.3	22.9	2.4	20.7	20.9	0.2
Japan	11.7	9.3	-5.6	19.0	14.8	-6.1
Australia	16.7	14.3	-5.0	–	–	–

[a]Data are based on national vital registration systems.

[b]Data for Canada, Israel, and Australia refer to 1975; data for German Federal Republic, Switzerland, and Japan refer to 1976; all 1977 data are provisional, except for the United States.

[c]Fetal deaths of 28 weeks or more gestation plus infant deaths within 7 days per 1,000 live births. For all countries, fetal deaths of unknown gestation period are included in the 28 weeks or more gestation. This is not the usual way of calculating the perinatal ratio for the United States, but it was done for the purpose of comparison.

[d]Data for France and Italy refer to 1974; data for Canada, German Democratic and Federal Republics, and Israel refer to 1975.

[e]Excludes infants who have died before registration of birth.

[f]Fetal deaths are of 26 weeks or more gestation.

Source: United Nations *Demographic Yearbook 1973–1974, 1976,* and *1977,* Pub. Nos. ST/STAT/SER.R/2, ST/ESA/STAT/R:3, ST/ESA/STAT/SER.R/4, and ST/ESA/STAT/SER.R/6. New York: United Nations, 1974, 1975, 1977, 1978.

less of the factors involved, community health programs are focusing on the improvement of the health care picture for these groups, as well as attempting to create better living conditions, and implementing nutrition services.

Mortality rates for children in the 1-to-4 age group have shown a larger and more significant decline than for any other age group since the beginning of this century. Mortality rates for children in this group have decreased more than 95 percent.[4] As a result of better nutrition, improved living conditions, the development and utilization of a variety of vaccines, and antibiotic treatment for the respective prevention and control of disease, the likelihood of a child living through the years in which death was once so prevalent has

Table 11-2 Life Expectancy at Birth, According to Sex: Selected Countries, 1970 and 1976[a]

COUNTRY	MALE		AVERAGE ANNUAL CHANGE IN YEARS	FEMALE		AVERAGE ANNUAL CHANGE IN YEARS
	1970[b]	1976[c]		1970[b]	1976[c]	
	Remaining Life Expectancy in Years			*Remaining Life Expectancy in Years*		
Canada	69.3	69.6	0.1	76.2	77.1	0.2
United States	67.0	69.0	0.3	74.6	76.7	0.4
Sweden	72.3	72.2	0.0	77.4	78.1	0.1
England and Wales	68.8	69.7	0.2	75.2	75.8	0.1
Netherlands	70.9	71.6	0.1	76.6	78.1	0.3
German Democratic Republic	68.9	68.9	—	74.2	74.5	0.1
German Federal Republic	67.3	68.1	0.2	73.6	74.7	0.2
France	69.1	69.5	0.1	76.7	77.6	0.2
Switzerland	70.3	71.7	0.2	76.2	78.3	0.4
Italy	68.5	69.9	0.4	74.6	76.1	0.4
Israel[d]	69.9	71.0	0.2	73.4	74.7	0.3
Japan	69.5	72.3	0.5	74.9	77.6	0.5
Australia	67.4	69.3	0.4	74.2	76.4	0.4

[a]Data are based on reporting by countries.

[b]Data for the United States refer to the average for the period 1969–71; data for Switzerland refer to the average for the period 1968–73.

[c]Data for Canada, France, and Italy refer to 1974; data for the German Federal Republic, Israel, and Australia refer to 1975.

[d]Jewish population only.

Sources: World Health Organization, *World Health Statistics, 1970* and *1978,* Vol. 1. Geneva: World Health Organization, 1973 and 1978; United Nations, *Demographic Yearbook 1976,* Pub. No. ST/ESA/STAT/SER.R/4. New York: United Nations, 1977; National Center for Health Statistics, *U.S. Decennial Life Tables for 1969-1971,* Vol. 1, No. 1. Washington, D.C.: U.S. DHEW Pub. No. (HRA) 75-1150, 1975; Final mortality statistics, 1976, *Monthly Vital Statistics Report,* Vol. 26, No. 12, supplement 2, Washington, D.C.: U.S. DHEW Pub. No. (PHS) 78-1120, 1978.

increased significantly (see Table 11-2). Yet in spite of advances in communicable disease control and rapid declines in childhood death rates, minority children are still victims of such things as influenza, pneumonia, and other infectious diseases at a rate about 50 percent higher than for white children.[5]

Since 1979 was the International Year of the Child, disease prevention through immunization of children received special attention. As of mid-1979, 90 percent of children 5 to 14 years of age had been immunized against measles, polio, diptheria, tetanus, and pertussis, and about 84 percent had been immunized against rubella. However, among children 1 to 4 years of age, about 38 percent had not been immunized against rubella, 37 percent had no measles vaccination, and 49 percent were without mumps vaccination (see Table 11-3). In general, white children were more often immunized against these diseases than were children of other races.

Figure 11-4 The greatest public health achievements have been in the area of promoting maternal, infant, and child health. Courtesy Arizona Republic and Phoenix Gazette.

Child Health Today

By far the most common health problems of today's children are acute conditions such as respiratory infections and accidents. In the 1-to-14 age group (see Figure 11-5), death rates from accidents have remained fairly constant, and almost 20 percent of the 10,000 accidental deaths in 1977 resulted from motor-vehicle accidents.[6] In 1977 alone, there were about 25 million accidental injuries incurred by children under the age of 17.

No other preventable cause of death poses such a major threat as accidents which account for 45 percent of total childhood mortality. By itself, a 50 percent reduction in fatal accidents would be enough to achieve the nationally established goal of fewer than 34 deaths per 100,000 by 1990 in this age group.

Eighty-five percent of these children incurring accidental injuries require medical attention. Many of such accidents have resulted in permanent handicaps, with which the

Table 11-3 Immunization and Infection Status of Children 1 to 4 Years of Age: United States, 1970-1978[a]

YEAR	POPULATION, 1-4 YEARS, IN THOUSANDS	HISTORY OF								
		Measles		Rubella		DTP[b] Vaccination		Polio Vaccination		Mumps Vaccination
		Infection	Vaccination	Infection	Vaccination	3 doses or more	0 doses	3 doses or more	0 doses	
		Percent of Population								
1970	14,123	8.1	57.2	14.4	37.2	76.1	7.0	65.9	10.8	(c)
1971	14,112	8.7	61.0	13.9	51.2	78.7	5.8	67.3	8.6	(c)
1972	13,905	7.4	62.2	12.3	56.9	75.6	6.9	62.9	10.7	(c)
1973	13,874	6.3	61.2	12.8	55.6	72.6	6.2	60.4	13.9	34.7
1974	13,210	5.1	64.5	12.2	59.8	73.9	5.2	63.1	11.7	39.4
1975	12,729	4.8	65.5	11.3	61.9	75.2	4.5	64.8	10.3	44.4
1976[d]	12,276	4.3	65.9	10.0	61.7	71.4	3.7	61.6	9.5	48.3
1977	12,071	3.8	63.1	10.0	59.4	69.5	3.3	60.1	8.7	48.1
1978	12,187	3.3	62.8	7.8	61.7	68.0	3.8	61.4	7.9	51.1

[a]Data are based on household interviews of a sample of the civilian noninstitutionalized population.

[b]Diphtheria-tetanus-pertussis.

[c]Mumps vaccination was first reported in 1973.

[d]Beginning in 1976, the category "don't know" was added to response categories. Prior to 1976, the lack of the "don't know" option resulted in some forced positive answers which were particularly apparent for those vaccinations which require multiple dose schedules, i.e., polio and DTP.

Note: The proportions of the population ever infected or vaccinated are not mutually exclusive.

Source: Center for Disease Control, *United States Immunization Survey, 1978.* Atlanta: U.S. DHEW Pub. No. (CDC) 79-8221, 1979.

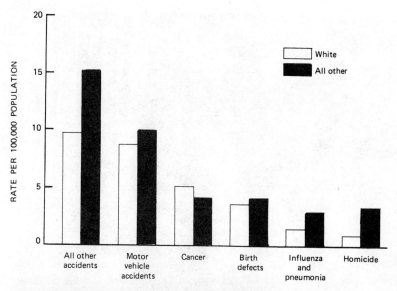

Figure 11-5 Major causes
of death for ages 1–14
years: United States, 1976.
Courtesy National Center
for Health Statistics, Division of Vital Statistics.

Figure 11-6
Children—a resource for America's future. Courtesy Arizona Republic and Phoenix Gazette.

Figure 11-7 One of the most common health problems of children is accidents. Courtesy Arizona Department of Health Services.

child will have to live the remainder of his or her life. Clearly, the prevention of accidents, and disability resulting from these accidents must continue to be a community health priority. In the past, tuberculosis, poliomyelitis, diptheria and measles and other communicable diseases claimed the lives of children. Today, accidents and other acute conditions must become the focus of concern for community health. Although the relative impact of communicable diseases on children is very small in relation to the past, these conditions continue to assume a major role in child health protection. If health problems in childhood—whether they are physical, social, or emotional—are not treated in childhood, it is possible that a short-term disability may well result in a permanent impairment or condition that will be a problem throughout the child's adult life.

Although great strides have been made in infant and child health, there is much more that community health can accomplish. For example, a large number of children suffer from faulty vision. At age 6, the time that most children are entering school for the first time, 17 percent have defective vision, and this number increases by age 11.[7] Many of these children live with vision defects that are remediable. Dental health is yet another area of concern in child health. Over 2 million children in the 6-to-11 age group suffer *malocclusion* problems. "At age 6, one child in eight has one or more decayed permanent teeth, and by age 11 six out of eight children have decayed teeth."[8] Each year, between

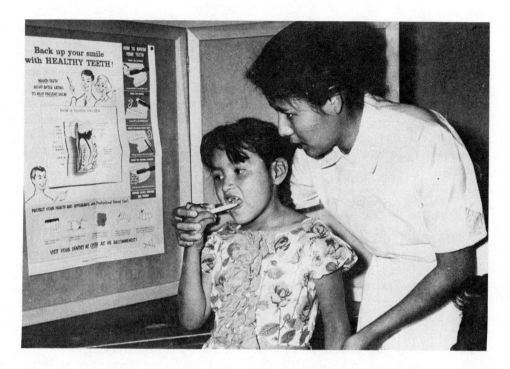

Figure 11-8 Dental health is an area of concern in child health. Courtesy Arizona Department of Health Services.

100,000 and 150,000 live-born infants are affected by congenital malformations, single-gene disorders and chromosomal disorders. The estimated cost of hospitalization resulting from these disorders is more than $800 million annually.[9]

In addition, there are nutritional factors associated with maintaining health. The average daily intake of calories is lower for black children than for white—and for children of poor families than for those of families with incomes above poverty level.[10] A high proportion of children of Spanish-American origin have deficient or low plasma levels and vitamin A values. Low hemoglobin values are significantly more prevalent among black children than among white children and for children below poverty level.

One of the dominant concerns and priorities of community health in the present, and one which will likely continue to be a priority in the future deals with mental health in children and youth. The number of children suffering from mental or emotional disturbances today cannot be ignored. It is estimated that as many as 500,000 children in the United States suffer from psychoses and borderline psychotic conditions and that at least another million are afflicted with personality or character disorders of some type. More than ten percent of school-age children require some type of mental health services for emotional problems. If current projections are accurate, the number of children institutionalized in mental hospitals in the next ten years will triple.

In general, children now living in the United States have a better chance of achieving and maintaining health than ever before in history and the majority are typically classified as falling into either good or excellent categories regarding health. Yet the proportion of children in excellent health is higher in upper- than in lower-income families and is higher for whites than for children of other racial groups. Still, there are many conditions present in today's society that threaten the health of children and the community. New priorities must be adopted to further prevention of child abuse, the identification of the causes of *sudden infant death syndrome* (*SIDS*), and screening for genetic diseases. The traditional community health activities that will continue to serve children include mass innoculations for protection against rubella (German measles), polio, typhoid, and diptheria.

Community Health Services for Mothers and Children

The Maternal and Child Health Program (MCH) authorized under the Social Security Act is responsible for extending and improving health care services for mothers and children through grants to state maternal and child health agencies. The grants support activities such as maternity and infant care, family planning, children and youth dental care, and intensive infant care. The importance of maternal and child health programs is being stressed and effective and equitable care being promoted throughout the Public Health Service through the implementation of systematic state-based child health strategies. Priority areas within this effort include family planning services, prenatal care, perinatal intensive care with special attention given to adolescent pregnancies, well-baby care, and rehabilitative care for handicapped children.

Because of the seriousness of the teenage pregnancy problem—the health risks to mother and child and the socioeconomic consequences of teenage parenthood—the Department of Health and Human Services has launched an adolescent health services initiative. It is designed to help prevent unwanted pregnancies, to provide support services to help pregnant adolescents and adolescent parents become independent contributors to family and community life, and to decrease the likelihood that they will become dependent on welfare.

Reducing infant mortality has received special emphasis through two federal programs: Improved Pregnancy Outcome (IPO) and Improved Child Health (ICH). The IPO program is designed to encourage states to develop a comprehensive statewide system of perinatal care. The purpose of the ICH program is to support health services for high-risk mothers and infants in designated areas with excessive morbidity and mortality.

The Public Health Service has also developed a Child Health Initiative, which is designed to assure underserved mothers and children entrance into the health care system. Attempts are being made to improve school health services, including health assessments, health counseling and health education. Other infant and child health activities identified as priority areas at the national level are reducing birth defects, attempting to learn more about the sudden infant death syndrome, reducing and ultimately eliminating child abuse.

The prescription for child health in the future may well be recognition by those involved with child health that early prevention and recognition of disease and the development of programs aimed at care and child supervision is becoming very important. It is recommended that a National Health Service for Mothers and Children in the United States be developed to include:

Prenatal care;

Obstetric and midwifery services;

Homemaking assistance and mother-craft;

Postnatal care for mother and infant;

Family planning services;

Well-child and developmental check-ups;

Routine immunizations and anticipatory guidance;

Preschool screening and school health services, including a mandate to treat and correct identified defects; and

Sickness care to treat children not reached by private medical care programs even when they are subsidized.[11]

Such a program would not be fragmented, but rather would extend appropriate health services to every child and mother in the United States.

CONTEMPORARY MATERNAL, INFANT, AND CHILD HEALTH CONCERNS

Sudden Infant Death Syndrome: (SIDS)

In the United States, sudden infant death syndrome (SIDS), also known as *crib death,* is the leading cause of death in infants. Among pediatric deaths as a whole, only accidents claim more lives. Although the exact number of deaths resulting from SIDS is unknown, it is estimated that each year approximately 7,500 to 10,000 infants—about 2 infants per 1,000 live births—succumb to this syndrome.[12] The highest incidence is between the second and fourth months of life, with a peak at three months. Sudden infant death syndrome is not a new disease. It has been recognized since Biblical times, yet diagnosis and prevention of SIDS has remained unsolved. A working definition of the syndrome is "the death of an apparently healthy infant, occurring suddenly and unexpectedly and remaining unexplained after an autopsy is performed." In the majority of instances, a seemingly healthy infant is placed in his or her crib to sleep and sometime later is found dead. Post-mortem examinations can identify no specific cause for death, although in a large portion of SIDS victims, tiny hemorrhages have been found in the lungs, indicating that the infant may have had a minor respiratory infection.

During the past ten to fifteen years, a large number of single-factor explanations have been hypothesized to explain the cause of crib death. More recently, epidemiologists have approached the problem using a multicausation model and have proposed that a

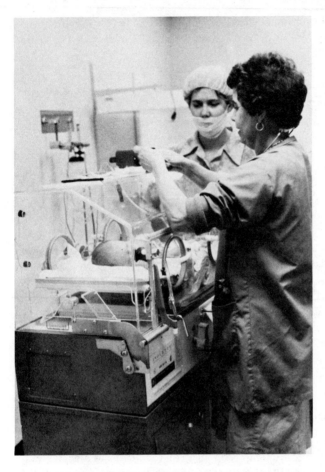

Figure 11-9
Low birth weight and premature infants are particularly prone to SIDS. Courtesy Arizona Department of Health Services.

combination of factors and events precipitate the sudden and unexplained death of infants. These studies have yielded a considerable volume of information with regard to combinations of symptoms after death, but why these babies die is still unknown.

At present, it is known that there is high incidence of SIDS in the low socio-economic groups, where risk appears to be highest in crowded environments. It appears that the high-risk population of SIDS is the same as the high-risk group for a variety of medical and health problems. It occurs more frequently in minorities, with the exception of Oriental groups, and in infants with low-birth weights—particularly those who had gestational ages between 34 and 35 weeks. There is a higher incidence of crib death in boys than in girls, but this male predominance does not exceed that found in infant mortality rates in general in the United States. Twins may be especially vulnerable to SIDS as a consequence of their typically lower birth weight or shortened gestation period. And, babies who have had recent infections may be more susceptable to sudden death, as may be premature infants. Investigations also reveal that the greatest incidence of SIDS occurs in the months between November and March and that most deaths occur between midnight and 8:00 A.M.[13] According to the best available data, SIDS is more likely to occur if the mother is under 20 years old and has had one or more prior live births, or if she is over 40 years old.[14]

Crib death is a worldwide public health problem. It strikes without warning and is probably the result of simultaneous interactions or events in the sleeping infant. These factors may include such things as viral infection, inflammation of the respiratory tract, instability of the central nervous system, and perhaps some environmental conditions. According to Abraham B. Bergman, a noted researcher in SIDS: "It is analogous to a blown fuse on an overloaded electrical circuit—each appliance contributes to the load, some to a greater extent than others, but no single appliance by itself is responsible.[15]

By 1969, following the First and Second International Conferences on Causes in Sudden Infant Death Syndrome, it was possible to identify and establish criteria for the diagnosis of SIDS. Sudden infant death syndrome was accepted as a disease entity, with specific symptoms which were readily definable by autopsy. The limitation is that SIDS could not be diagnosed before death. Therefore, the disease could not be predicted or prevented. This continues to be a major community health and medical concern. At present, the actual mechanism causing sudden infant death syndrome is poorly understood. However, there are some common characteristics related to the unexplained sudden death of infants. Sleep is a necessary component and death always occurs while the infant is sleeping. Apparently, the infant has no suffering and death usually occurs within seconds. Crib death is not contagious in the usual sense, although a viral infection may increase the likelihood of its occurrence. Episodes of *apnea,* or "breath holding," in the infant seems to be associated with SIDS. The 1980 Surgeon General's report, *Healthy People,* identifies SIDS as a priority for future research.

Genetics

The health of each individual is affected at least partially by *heredity.* That is, each person is born with a unique genetic makeup which interacts with various environmental factors. At present, there are over 2,000 known genetic diseases, those diseases which are passed on from generation to generation as a result of inherited traits. Genetic diseases affect a surprisingly large number of people. According to some authorities, five percent of the population is afflicted with such disorders. The National Genetics Foundation estimates that 1 child out of every 5 who are hospitalized suffers from a hereditary condition. In addition, it has been estimated that more than 20 percent of all beds in hospitals and institutions for the handicapped are occupied by people suffering from genetic disorders. Clearly, genetic disease has become a significant community health concern in modern times. These diseases have always been serious medical problems, but they have drawn increasing attention as the communicable diseases have been brought under control by modern drug therapy.

Abnormal cell division, radiation, and spontaneous mutations can lead to errors in the structure of chromosomes which, in turn, contribute to the development of genetic disorders or diseases. In addition, genetic diseases occur as a result of recessive *genes* inherited by offspring from either one or both of the parents.

Birth Defect	Type	Annual Incidence*	Prev- alence†	Cause	Detection‡	Treatment‡	Prevention‡
Down's syndrome (mongol- ism)	func⁺ional/ structural: retardation often associ- ated with physical defects	5,100	44,000	chromosomal abnormality	chromosome analysis, amniocentesis	corrective surgery, special physical training and schooling	genetics services
Low birthweight/ prematurity	structural/ functional	248,000	NA	hereditary and/or environmental: poor prenatal care, maternal disorder	prenatal monitoring, visual inspection at birth	intensive care of newborn, high nutrient diet	proper prenatal care, genetics services
Muscular dystrophy	functional: impaired voluntary muscular function	unknown (late- appear- ing)	200,000	hereditary: often recessive inheritance	apparent at onset	physical therapy	carrier identification, genetics services
Congenital heart mal- formations	structural	24,800	248,000	hereditary and/or environmental	examination at birth and later	corrective surgery, medication	proper prenatal care, genetics services
Clubfoot	structural: misshapen foot	9,300	149,000	hereditary and/or environmental	examination at birth	corrective surgery, corrective splints, physical training	genetics services
Polydactyly	structural: multiple fingers or toes	9,300	184,000	hereditary: dominant inheritance	visual inspection at birth	corrective surgery, physical training	genetics services
Spina bifida and/or hydro- cephalus	structural/ functional: incompletely formed spinal canal; "water on the brain"	6,200	53,000	hereditary and environmental	prenatal X ray, ultrasound, maternal blood test, examination at birth	corrective surgery, prostheses, physical training, special schooling for any mental impairment	genetics services
Cleft lip and/or cleft palate	structural	4,300	71,000	hereditary and/or environmental	visual inspection at birth	corrective surgery	genetics services
Diabetes mellitus	metabolic: inability to metabolize carbohydrates	unknown (late- appear- ing)	90,000	hereditary and/or environmental	appears in childhood or later; blood and urine tests	oral medication, special diet, insulin injections	genetics services
Cystic fibrosis	functional: respiratory and digestive system mal- function	2,000	10,000	hereditary: recessive inheritance	sweat and blood tests	treat respiratory and digestive complications	carrier identification, genetics services

* Incidence: the number of new cases diagnosed within a specific time period. Above statistics based on 1971 data.

† Prevalence: total number living who have been diagnosed as having defect. Above statistics based on number less than 20 years of age.

‡ Last three columns list possible means now known for detection, treatment, and prevention. The techniques may not necessⱔrily be applicable or successful in every case.

Figure 11-10 Selected birth defects, U.S.A. Courtesy National Foundation/March of Dimes.

Sickle-cell anemia In *sickle-cell anemia,* a genetic disease that primarily affects blacks, the red blood cells that transport oxygen through hemoglobin are abnormal. About 10 percent of North American blacks have this disease, and another 10 percent are said to have sickle-cell "trait," or are carriers of the disease. In affected individuals, the red blood cells assume a sickle shape under certain conditions and are unable to transport oxygen to body cells. When this occurs, the individual is said to experience a sickle-cell crisis, an event characterized by severe muscle and joint pain and fever.

For a child to be born with sickle-cell anemia, both parents must transmit the abnormal S gene for producing abnormal hemoglobin. That is, both parents must have sickle-cell trait, and the child must inherit the abnormal hemoglobin gene from each. The

Birth Defect	Type	Annual Incidence*	Prevalence†	Cause	Detection‡	Treatment‡	Prevention‡
Sickle-cell anemia	blood disease: malformed red blood cells	1,200	16,000	hereditary: incomplete dominance—most frequent among Blacks	blood test	medication, transfusions	genetics services
Hemophilia (classic)	blood disease: poor clotting ability	1,200	12,400	hereditary: sex-linked recessive inheritance	blood test	medication, transfusions	genetics services
Congenital syphilis	structural: multiple abnormalities	(newborn only) 313	NA	environmental: acquired from infected mother	blood test, examination at birth	medication	proper prenatal care
Phenyl-ketonuria (PKU)	metabolic: inability to metabolize a specific protein	310	3,100	herdtiary: recessive inheritance	blood test at birth	special diet	carrier identification, genetics services
Tay-Sachs disease	metabolic: inability to metabolize fats in nervous system	30	100	hereditary: recessive inheritance—most frequent among Ashkenazi Jews	blood and tear tests, amniocentesis	none	carrier identification, genetics services
Thalas-semia	blood disease: anemia	70	1,000	hereditary: incomplete dominant inheritance	blood test	transfusions	carrier identification, genetics services
Galacto-semia	metabolic: inability to metabolize milk sugar galactose	70	500	hereditary: recessive inheritance	blood and urine tests, amniocentesis	special diet	carrier identification, genetics services
Erythro-blastosis (Rh disease)	blood disease: destruction of red blood cells	2,600	NA	hereditary and environmental: Rh—mother has Rh+ child	blood tests	transfusion: intrauterine or postnatal	Rh vaccine, blood tests to identify parents at risk, genetics services
Turner syndrome	structural/functional	575	3,100	chromosomal abnormality	chromosome analysis, amniocentesis	corrective surgery, medication	genetics services
Congenital rubella syndrome	structural/functional: multiple defects	varies with occur-rence of disease; less than 50	NA	environmental: maternal infection	antibody tests and viral culture	corrective surgery, prostheses, physical therapy and training	rubella vaccine, good prenatal care

* Incidence: the number of new cases diagnosed within a specific time period. Above statistics based on 1971 data.

† Prevalence: total number living who have been diagnosed as having defect. Above statistics based on number less than 20 years of age.

‡ Last three columns list possible means now known for detection, treatment, and prevention. The techniques may not necessarily be applicable or successful in every case.

The Foundation's experts estimate that among Americans of all ages, birth defects afflict 2.9 million mentally retarded; 4 million with diabetes; 1 million with congenital bone, muscle, or joint disease; 500,000 born completely or partially blind; 750,000 with congenital hearing impairment; 350,000 with heart or circulatory defects; 100,000 with severe speech problems; millions of others with defects of the nervous, digestive, endocrine, urinary, and other body systems. Courtesy The National Foundation/March of Dimes, 1975

trait occurs in about one million individuals, and that is approximately 1 out of every 10 blacks in the U.S.

PKU phenylketonuria PKU is an inherited metabolic disorder, which is linked to mutant genes that prevent the production of a vital liver enzyme or that cause it to be produced in an inappropriate form. This disease is progressive and results in severe mental retardation. It is recessive and occurs only when both parents transmit the abnormal gene.

PKU victims lack phenylalanine hydroxilase, an enzyme normally produced in the liver. Unconverted levels of phenylalanine build up in the blood stream and urine and, if undetected and untreated, can cause irreversable mental retardation. Children with PKU are placed on special diets early in life that reduce phenylalanine intake and this diet is maintained for an extended period of time.

PKU occurs in about 1 of every 15,000 persons in the United States. Diagnosis has become routine in the recent years, and almost every infant born in U.S. hospitals is given a blood test to determine if PKU is present so that dietary management can begin early. Unfortunately, at least 10 percent of patients with PKU are either not screened or are not detected by screening as a result of false negative tests.

Down's Syndrome (mongolism)   About one in every 200 newborns has some kind of chromosomal abnormality, the most common of which is *Down's Syndrome.* In these cases, an abnormality exists in the twenty-first *chromosome,* in which a separation occurs, causing the child to carry an extra chromosome. When such a nondisjunctional cell is fertilized by a normal sperm, the result is an embryo carrying three no. 21 chromosomes, not two. This *Trisomy* causes Down's Syndrome. Individuals with this genetic disease are characterized by physical and mental retardation, poor muscle development, slanted eyes, and a flattened forehead. These children are frequently incapable of taking care of themselves and remain dependent on others throughout their lives.

The chances of producing mongoloid children are far more common if maternal age is 35 or older. The likelihood of a woman producing nondisjunctional eggs increases with the age. The risk is about 1 in 1,500 for the 20-to-30-age group, 1 in 800 for mothers aged 35 to 39, about 1 in 100 for mothers aged 40 to 44, and 1 in 40 for mothers over 45. Down's Syndrome affects about 5,000 newborns each year.

Tay-Sachs Disease   *Tay-Sachs Disease* is one of a group of metabolic disorders which results in serious disorders in brain function and usually death before the age of 4. As yet, there is no cure for this hereditary disease, which affects individuals of Ashkenazi Jewish ancestry. About 90 percent of American Jews trace their origins to this region in Eastern Europe along the Russian border in Northeastern Poland.

A child who inherits two recessive Tay-Sachs genes, one from each parent, will have the disease. A child who inherits only one recessive gene will be a carrier of the disease. If two carriers marry, there is a 25 percent risk with each pregnancy that the child will have the disease. There is another 25 percent chance that the child will neither have the disease or be a carrier. There is a 50 percent risk that each child will be a carrier.

Tay-Sachs occurs when an enzyme in the blood called Hex A is lacking. Hex A is needed as a part of a complex series of chemical reactions in which fats are utilized in the functioning of the body.

As yet, medical science has not been able to provide treatment for children with Tay-Sachs to prevent the disease from running its course. Although it is impossible to cure or treat the disease, it is now possible to diagnose the presence of the disease in an unborn fetus through *amniocentesis,* a procedure that involves an examination of amniotic fluid for the presence of Hex A.

Genetic Screening and Counseling

The incidence of genetic disorders is so high that it is considered to be both a serious medical and public health problem. Every person in the United States silently carries six or more defective genes. It is said that 40 percent of all infant deaths are due to genetic causes and that 3 percent of all infants—or 1 out of 250—are born with some genetic abnormality. Genetic disorders affect at least fifteen million Americans. Of the over 1,500 known genetic diseases affecting the human body, many cannot be cured or treated. But they can be prevented by genetic screening and *genetic counseling.*

Genetic screening and counseling programs can help to reduce the incidence of genetic disease in the U.S., thereby reducing the pain, suffering, and tragedy associated with these diseases, as well as the economic burden on society and the family. In order to diagnose, treat, and help in the prevention of genetic disorders the National Genetics Foundation (NGF) operates a network of Genetic Centers involving forty-seven medical institutions throughout the United States and Canada. The network offers a multi-

Figure 11-11 Genetic counseling can help reduce the incident of genetic disease. Courtesy U.S. Department of Health, Education and Welfare.

disciplinary team approach to the diagnosis, treatment, and counseling of patients with, or at risk for, genetic disease.

It is now possible to diagnose approximately eighty serious genetic problems before birth, and to identify carriers of an even greater number of disorders. In addition, a half-dozen or more techniques for treating a large number of genetic disorders have recently become available, and more are being developed each year. The application of this new knowledge and technology to the community is a high health priority, and community health has an integral part to play in achieving this goal. The profound advances to date in medical genetics represent only a beginning.

The purpose of genetic counseling is to provide advice and guidance to people with genetic disorders and to those who fear that they may produce children with a severe physical or mental defect. The major purpose of genetic counseling is the prevention of genetic defects. Genetic counseling is a communication process that deals with the human problems associated with the occurrence, or the risk of occurrence, of a genetic disorder in a family. One of the techniques used in genetic counseling is amniocentesis. Amniocentesis is an obstetrical procedure usually done in the sixteenth week of pregnancy. A sample of fluid surrounding the fetus is taken by inserting a sterile needle into the amniotic cavity and withdrawing a small amount of fluid (see Figure 11–12). The fluid is derived mostly from fetal urine and secretions, and contains fetal cells. The sample is then *centrifuged* to separate cells from fluid and a variety of tests are conducted. At present, it is possible to detect the presence of over forty genetic diseases through this procedure.

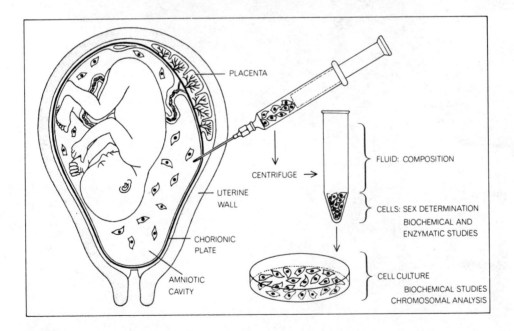

Figure 11–12 Prenatal diagnosis of genetic disease: amniocentesis. From "Parental Diagnosis of Genetic Disease" by Theodore Friedmann. Copyright © 1971 by Scientific American, Inc. All rights reserved.

Genetic counseling must be tailored to the needs of the individual, but usually several facets are present in all counseling activities. First, a detailed family history is taken from the counselors, and a pedigree is constructed. Cultural characteristics of the family, including racial background, religion, occupation, and grandparent's birthplace are recorded. Age and health status of first-, second-, and third-degree relatives are also recorded. The pedigree may reveal a specific pattern of inheritance and make a risk estimate possible. The next step is to project risk estimates based on what is known about the disease and its patterns, with all its implications. The risk may be quite low (less than 5 percent) or high (25 percent to 50 percent, or occasionally 100 percent). The risk is usually presented against the known probability that every child runs a 2 to 3 percent risk of having a major defect of some kind. Finally, a follow-up to the counseling interview is initiated to help the parents further understand the situation and risks.

Genetic counseling is still relatively new and it will no doubt be some time before there is any general agreement on optimal procedures. The need for genetic counseling far exceeds the supply of counselors, facilities, and services. In less than two years, the National Genetics Foundation has received over 13,000 inquiries about genetic diseases.[16] It has been estimated that by the mid-1980s in North America, one person with training in medical genetics will be needed for every 200,000 persons.[17] It is the challenge to the community health field to make people aware of genetic counseling services, to help those who seek counseling to obtain it, and to create accessible and adequate services.

Child Abuse

Within the last decade, a new variety of child health concerns have appeared. They are related, if only indirectly, to the social upheaval and rapid change that began in the early 1960s and 1970s in our society. Some of the health-endangering situations are admittedly related to socioeconomic conditions, but it should be recognized that even for the child who is born with no physical handicaps, to an affluent family, and who grows up not knowing what it is like to be hungry and lives in a safe and modern home, there is still danger of health problems of a new variety. Such is the case with child abuse.

A discussion of child abuse evokes reactions ranging from disbelief to disgust to anger. To most Americans, it seems unbelievable that children could be the target of physical and emotional abuse by their parents and guardians—by those who are supposed to love and care for them. Yet according to the best informed "estimates" in the U.S.— the American Humane Society—if all cases of child abuse and neglect were reported and tabulated nationwide, they might be as high as one million cases annually.[18] This indicates an annual incidence rate for child abuse at 5 per 1,000, and for neglect at 2 per 100. The United States Children's Bureau estimates that from 50,000 to 75,000 incidents of child abuse occur in this country each year. At least 10,000 children are severely battered, 50,000 to 75,000 are sexually abused, 100,000 are emotionally neglected, and another 100,000 are physically, morally, and educationally neglected.[19] It is always difficult to get an accurate picture of the true incidence of a socially disapproved criminal behavior that takes place, typically in the privacy of the home. Yet in a civilized society, even one case per year would be too many.

Child abuse is regarded as a major public health problem affecting the lives of children, infants, and their families. It claims the lives of more children each year than all of the communicable diseases and leukemia combined. Twenty-five percent of all trauma seen in the first three years of a child's life are a result of parental abuse.[20] At least 700 such deaths occur each year—and this is a conservative estimate. Child abuse is not a new problem, nor is it on the increase in comparison to the past. What has changed is that public and professional attention has now focused on this significant form of victimization of children. Today there is better reporting of abuse cases, provisions of immunity for those who report suspected cases, and the development of community programs aimed at the prevention of abuse and at rehabilitating the child abuser.

Child abuse has been defined in many ways by a number of different individuals and groups. The Child Abuse Prevention and Treatment Act of 1973 (PL 93-237) defines abuse as

> . . . . the physical or mental injury, sexual abuse, negligent treatment, or mal-treatment of a child under the age of eighteen by a person who is responsible for the child's welfare under circumstances which indicate that the child's health or welfare is harmed or threatened.[21]

There are six recognized forms of abuse. They include physical abuse, physical neglect, emotional abuse, emotional deprivation, verbal assault, and sexual abuse. Assaults by parents or guardians on children, whether verbal or physical, are considered child abuse. The lasting effect of abuse can take two forms: organic damage (brain damage) and behavioral manifestations (delinquency, mental illness). Child abuse can cause physical and psychological crippling, including retardation, paralysis, and sociopathic behavior—as well as death.

The findings of most research on child abuse indicate the following:

1. From 1966-1970, there was a 500 percent increase in reported cases of child abuse.
2. Boys are more frequently the object of physical abuse, until age 13, when girls are more frequently abused sexually.
3. Abused children were often unwanted, or the result of unplanned pregnancies.
4. New York City has the highest rate of child abuse.
5. There is a 30 percent chance that a child beaten will be beaten again.
6. One-third of abused children are under the age of 3.
7. Ninety percent of child abusers have no history of mental illness.
8. *Everyone* is a potential child abuser.
9. The most common form of abuse is the infliction of head injuries.
10. Many abusive parents have been abused themselves as children.
11. Abusive parents are sometimes disturbed by emotional problems, such as alcoholism or drug dependence.

12. Child abusers do not possess an adequate understanding of child development, and expect perfection.

13. There is typically a series of crisis, or some form of crisis which sets the abusive act in motion and is called the precipitating factor or incident.

14. The disciplining parent usually has the welfare of the child in mind, while the abusing parent is indulging his or her own needs.

15. Factors such as financial difficulty, feelings of inadequacy, immaturity, and inability to cope with stresses seem to be characteristics of the abusive adult.

Prevention of Child Maltreatment

Prevention is the only humane and satisfactory solution to the tragic problem of child abuse. As a society, we have begun to provide legal and civil procedures by which professionals and lay citizens who come in contact with endangered children can take protective action.

In order to prevent child abuse and to reduce the number of child victims, we must learn how to foster the emotional and behavioral well-being of the individual, the family and the community. Child abuse can accurately be seen as a symptom of deeper problems of the family, and of social disorganization. A beginning to the prevention of child abuse might well involve fostering a sense of respect for the life and inherent value of all individuals within the family, as well as a movement away from the violence and aggression and toward love and mutual respect. The more we can learn about what makes a family strong, healthy, and adequate, the more we can improve the lives of children, especially those who are endangered. As is the case with other community health campaigns, the real success comes not in the treatment of health problems, but in their prevention.

In our humanistic attempts to reach potential and actual child abusers, it should be remembered that protecting the child from being victimized is not enough. We must also help the abusive adult. Services must be developed so that many families who need services are not deprived of them. In developing a program to help a family better protect its children, the strengths and resources of the family should serve as a foundation from which the enhancement of child protection, health, and safety can be realized.

Community health programs initiated to protect the health and lives of children in the United States will have to integrate psychological services designed to develop a sense of adequacy in the abusive adult as well as provide nurturance to child victims. In addition, health care services designed to treat the victimized children should provide for emergency care, treatment, hospitalization, and rehabilitation. Crisis centers, and other facilities can be established by community health to provide outlets for abusive parents to relieve stress and tension, without victimizing children.

Until recently, few communities had adequate programs for children in crisis. In 1971, a pilot program called Comprehensive Emergency Services for Children in Crisis was established in Nashville, Tennessee to coordinate the activities of all agencies involved in child protection—social service departments, police, juvenile courts, hospital abuse

Figure 11-13 Crisis nurseries are part of child protective services. Courtesy Arizona Department of Health Services.

teams, and voluntary agencies and organizations. This model program has been most successful and has resulted in impressive expansion of similar programs to over thirty-nine other states. The program includes:

1. a twenty-four-hour answering service, available seven days a week to receive emergency calls
2. a continuous public education campaign to inform the public about the service
3. trained emergency caretakers to go to homes immediately to provide initial care for children, and twenty-four-hour homemakers to take over throughout the emergency situation
4. emergency foster family homes to provide temporary care for children
5. emergency group homes for teenagers who cannot feel at home in a foster family home
6. emergency shelter for the entire family in case of fire
7. immediate access to a hospital child-abuse team for diagnosis and treatment, if needed.

320

Most important to the success of all these components is the availability at all times of an outreach and follow-through team to take quick action in an emergency and to start work immediately with parents and the family in resolving the problem that caused the crisis.[22]

Prevention of child abuse may be based on the traditional public health model of host, agent, and environment. The parents may be viewed as the host, the child as an agent whose presence is necessary but not sufficient for abuse to occur, and the environment of abuse is fraught with change arriving too rapidly for successful adjustment. To prevent the abuse of children we must recognize that this is an interactive system in which both parents, the child, and the physical, social, and cultural environment play a role.[23]

REVIEW QUESTIONS

1. What are the major factors which influence the three aspects of child health— emotional, physical, and social?
2. Compare the health problems of a child living in poverty with those of a child living in affluence.
3. Identify major areas of community health programs necessary for maternal, infant, and child health promotion.
4. What developments in public health and medicine have contributed to reduced mortality during childhood.
5. Discuss the goals and techniques of genetic counseling.
6. Describe the symptoms and effects of sickle-cell anemia, mongolism, and PKU.
7. What are some of the basic facts about SIDS? Synthesize current medical knowledge and implications of the tragedy.
8. Define child abuse and identify at least four of the forms it may take.
9. Analyze the role that children play in American society. What are their rights, responsibilities, and value in comparison to those of adults?

SUGGESTED READINGS

Doctors and Dollars Are Not Enough: How to Improve Health Services for Children and Their Families. Washington, D.C.: Children's Defense Fund of the Washington Research Project, Inc., 1976.

Blair, Justice, and David Duncan, "Child Abuse as a Work-Related Problem," *Corrective and Social Psychiatry*, 23(2) 53-55, 1977.

Callahan, D.; "Ethics Law and Genetic Counseling," *Science*, April 14, 1972, pp. 191-198.

DeMause, Lloyd, "Our Forebearers Made Childhood a Nightmare," *Psychology Today,* April 1975, pp. 85-88.

Duval, Merlin, "Crib Deaths," *Vital Speeches,* April 15, 1972, pp. 396-398.

Haggerty, Robert J., Klaus Roghmann, and Ivan Phess, *Child Health and the Community.* New York: John Wiley, 1975.

Headings, Verle and Jan Fielding, "Guidelines for Counseling Young Adults with Sickle-Cell Trait," *American Journal of Public Health,* 65(8) 819-827, 1975.

Krugman, Saul and Samuel Katz (eds.), *Infectious Diseases of Children,* 7th ed. St. Louis: C. V. Mosby, 1981.

Light, R., "Abused and Neglected Children in America: A Study of Alternative Policies," *Harvard Education Review,* 43(11) 556-598, 1973.

Martin, Harold P., *The Abused Child: A Multidisciplinary Approach to Developmental Issues and Treatment.* Cambridge, Mass.: Ballinger, 1976.

McGough, Elizabeth, "Crib Death: Some Answers to 20,000 Such Tragedies," *Science Digest,* February 1970, pp. 26-30.

Pavenstedt, Eleanor, "An Intervention Program for Infants from High-Risk Homes," *American Journal of Public Health,* 63(5) 393-395, 1973.

Rothwell, Norman V., *Human Genetics.* Englewood Cliffs, N.J.: Prentice-Hall, 1977.

Thorndike, Joseph, "Genetics and the Future of Man," *Horizon,* Autumn 1973, pp. 56-63.

Vernon, Thomas, and others, "An Evaluation of Three Techniques for Improving Immunization Levels in Elementary Schools," *American Journal of Public Health,* 66(5) 457-461, 1976.

NOTES

[1] U.S. DHEW *Child Health in America.* Washington, D.C.: U.S. DHEW Pub. No. (HSA) 76-5015, p. 14.

[2] *Child Health in America,* p. 35.

[3] U.S. DHEW *Health: United States, 1978.* Washington, D.C.: DHEW Pub. No. (HRA) 76-1232, p. 157.

[4] *Health: United States, 1978,* p. 340.

[5] *Health: United States, 1978,* p. 341.

[6] *Health: United States, 1978,* p. 159.

[7] *Health: United States, 1978,* p. 160

[8] *Health: United States, 1978,* p. 160.

[9] *Health: United States, 1978,* p. 374.

[10] *Health: United States, 1978,* p. 378.

[11] C. Arden Miller, "Health Care of Children and Youth in America," *American Journal of Public Health,* 65, No. 4 (April 1975), 356.

[12] "The Sudden Infant Death Syndrome." Washington, D.C.: The National Institute of Health, 1977, p. 1.

[13] "The Sudden Death Syndrome," p. 2.

[14] Jess Kraus, N. O. Borhani, and Charles Franti, "Discriminatory Risk Factors in Post Neonatal Sudden Unexplained Death," *American Journal of Epidemiology,* 96, No. 5 (May 1972), 328-333.

[15] U.S. DHEW, *Summary of the Proceedings of the Second International Conference on the Causes of Sudden Infant Death, Seattle, 1969.* Washington, D.C.: U.S. DHEW Pub. No. (NIH) 75-224, 1975, p. 23.

[16] F. C. Fraser, "Genetic Counseling," *American Journal of Human Genetics,* 26, No. 5 (September 1974), 648.

[17] F.C. Fraser, p. 648.

[18] U.S. DHEW, *National Center of Child Abuse and Neglect.* Washington, D.C.: U.S. DHEW Pub. No. (OHO) 76-30086, p. 2.

[19] David Martin, "The Growing Horror of Child Abuse and the Undeniable Role of the Schools in Putting an End to It," *American School Board Journal,* November 1973, p. 52.

[20] Henry Kempe, "Pediatric Implementations of the Battered Child Syndrome," *Archives of Diseases in Childhood,* 46, No. 3 (March 1971), 28-37.

[21] Bureau of Community Health Services, *Child Abuse/Neglect: A Guide for Detection, Prevention and Treatment in BCHS Programs and Projects.* Rockville, Md.: U.S. DHEW Pub. No. (HSA) 77-5220, 1977, p. 4.

[22] U.S. DHEW, "A Comprehensive Pilot Program," *Child Abuse and Neglect Reports,* June 1975, p. 5.

[23] Justice Blair and David Duncan, "Life Crisis as a Precursor to Child Abuse," *Public Health Reports,* 91, No. 2 (April 1976), 114.

GLOSSARY

amniocentesis an obstetrical procedure usually done in the sixteenth week of pregnancy, designed to detect genetic disease in utero.

apnea breath holding. Infants prone to prolonged apnea show higher incidence of SIDS.

centrifuge a diagnostic device that separates lighter portions of a solution from heavier portions by centrifugal force.

child abuse the physical or mental injury or maltreatment of a child under the age of 18 by a person who is responsible for the child's welfare.

chromosomes the nuclei of cells that control the structure and chemical nature of heredity. In humans, all cells except sex cells contain twenty-three pairs of chromosomes.

congenital malformations diseases and abnormalities or deformities with which a child is born.

crib death a synonym for sudden infant death syndrome (SIDS).

Down's Syndrome a genetic disease characterized by an abnormality in the twenty-first chromosome. Often referred to as mongolism.

genes the basic units of heredity, which are found in the chromosomes. Genes contain DNA, the blueprint of heredity.

genetic counseling activities designed to provide advice and guidance to people with a genetic disease and to those who fear they may produce children with a severe mental or physical genetic disease.

genetic diseases diseases that are passed on from generation to generation as a result of inherited traits.

health quality of life, involving social, mental, and biological fitness on the part of the individual, which results from adaptations to the environment.

heredity genetic defects may be transmitted in varying degree of severity from generation to generation.

infant mortality rate the number of deaths under one year of age per 1,000 live births.

malocclusion improper alignment of the teeth, such as overbite or underbite.

mortality refers to incidence of death as a consequence of a specific illness or sickness.

PKU an inherited metabolic disorder that is progressive and results in severe mental retardation if not controlled through diet.

prenatal care health care of mothers that is related to less-complicated pregnancies and deliveries, resulting in a higher rate of live birth. Prenatal care includes medical exams, proper exercise, nutrition, and rest.

quarantine the detention of a susceptible individual who may have been exposed to a communicable disease.

sickle-cell anemia a genetic disease affecting primarily blacks in which red blood cells take on an abnormal sickle shape.

sudden infant death syndrome (SIDS) the death of an apparently healthy infant, occurring suddenly and unexpectedly and which remains unexplained after an autopsy is performed.

Tay-Sachs Disease one of a group of metabolic genetic disorders that is fatal and affects primarily Jews of Eastern European ancestry.

Trisomy the additional chromosome in Down's Syndrome, usually referred to as Trisomy 21, but actually belongs to the twenty-second group of chromosomes.

BIBLIOGRAPHY

Beckwith, Bruce, "The Sudden Infant Death Syndrome." Washington, D.C.: U.S. DHEW Pub. No. (HSA) 75-5137, 1975.

Bergman, Abraham, "Unexplained Sudden Infant Death," *New England Journal of Medicine,* 287(5) 244-245, 1972.

Blair, Justice and David Duncan, "Life Crisis as a Precursor to Child Abuse," *Public Health Reports,* 91(2) 110-115, 1976.

Change, Albert and others, "Child Abuse and Neglect: Physicians Knowledge, Attitudes and Experiences," *American Journal of Public Health,* 66(12) 1199-1201, 1976.

Chase, Helen (ed.), "A Study of Risks, Medical Care, and Infant Mortality," *American Journal of Public Health,* Supplement, 63: 56, 1973.

Cooper, Theodore, "Implications of Findings from the Amniocentesis Registry for Public Policy," *Public Health Reports,* 91(2) 116-117, 1976.

Fontana, Vincent J., *The Maltreated Child: The Maltreatment Syndrome in Children,* 2nd ed. Springfield, Ill.: Charles C Thomas, 1974.

Fraser, F. C., "Genetic Counseling," *American Journal of Human Genetics,* 26(5) 636-659, 1974.

Gershenson, Charles P., "Child Maltreatment, Family Stress, and Ecological Insult," *American Journal of Public Health,* 67(7) 602-603, 1977.

Helfer, R. E. and C. H. Kempe (eds.), *The Battered Child,* 2nd ed. Chicago: University of Chicago Press, 1974.

Kelley, D. H. and D. C. Shannon, "Epidemiology Clues to the Etiology of SIDS," *American Journal of Public Health,* 70(10) 1047-1048, 1980.

Kempe, Henry and Ray E. Helfer, *Battered Child,* 3rd ed. Chicago: University of Chicago Press, 1980.

Lubs, Herbert A. and Felix de la Crux (eds.), *Genetic Counseling: A Monograph of the National Institute of Child Health and Human Development*. New York: Raven Press, 1977.

Marx, Jean L., "Crib Death: Some Promising Leads But No Solution Yet," *Science*, 189(4200) 1-4, 1975.

Miller, C. Arden, "Health Care of Children and Youth in America," *American Journal of Public Health*, 65(4) 353-358, 1975.

Palmer, James O., *Battered Parent and How Not to be One*. Englewood Cliffs, N.J.: Prentice-Hall, 1980.

Riccardi, Vincent, "Health Care and Disease Prevention through Genetic Counseling: A Regional Approach," *American Journal of Public Health*, 66(3) 268-272, 1976.

——— *Quality of Life: The Early Years*. Acton, Mass.: A.M.A. Publishing Sciences Group, 1974.

Schmidt, William, "The Department of Health Services for Mothers and Children in the U.S.," *American Journal of Public Health*, 63(5) 419-427, 1973.

Stoeffler, Victor and others, "Lessons to be Learned from New Child Health Programs: Where Do We Go From Here," *American Journal of Public Health*, 62(11) 1444-1447, 1972.

Sultz, Harry and others, "An Epidemiologic Justificaton for Genetic Counseling in Family Planning," *American Journal of Public Health*, 62(11) 1489-1492, 1972.

U.S. DHEW, National Institute of Child Health and Human Development, *Summary of Proceedings of the Second International Conference on the Causes of Sudden Infant Death, Seattle, 1969*. Washington, D.C.: U.S. DHEW Pub. No. (NIH) 75-224, 1975.

——— *Child Health in America*. Washington, D.C.: U.S. DHEW Pub. No. (HSA) 76-5015, 1976.

——— Office of Human Development, *Proceedings of the First National Conference on Child Abuse and Neglect, January, 1976*. Washington, D.C.: U.S. DHEW Pub. No. (OHD) 77-30094, 1977.

——— "Behavioral Considerations," and "Epidemiological Research," *Research Planning Workshops on the Sudden Infant Death Syndrome, May 15-16, 1972*. Bethesda, Md.: U.S. DHEW Pub. No. (NIH) 75-577; (NIH) 74-581, 1975, 1974.

Wallace, Helen, Hymen Goldstein, and Allan Oglesky, "The Health and Medical Care of Children Under Title 19 (Medicaid)," *American Journal of Public Health*, 64(5) 501-506, 1974.

12

PUBLIC HEALTH AND MINORITIES

> We are trying to provide medical care and create challenge to the social system which causes these problems. We cannot have good health if we cannot feed our families . . . . Good health does not come out of a bottle of vitamin pills, it comes from food on the table and good working and living conditions.

> *Benito Juarez, People's Health Center*

As information on the health of Americans increases, interest in the health status of the nation's minorities grows. Population size, age and sex structure, socioeconomic composition, and other characteristics differentiate minority groups from the majority white population. Since these characteristics influence health, they must be considered when assessing the health status of minority groups. Groups to be considered in this chapter include black and *Hispanic* minorities; or, Asians, American Indians and Alaskan Natives.

SOCIAL AND ECONOMIC
DETERMINANTS OF HEALTH

Recent efforts by the U.S. Bureau of Census and other agencies have produced a series of information on blacks and Hispanics. Similar data on Asian-Americans and American Indians are still scarce. The largest minority group in the U.S. has been and continues to be the black population. Blacks represent 11 percent of the total population, or an estimated twenty-three million people. Hispanics are the nation's second-largest minority group. Numbering an estimated twelve million, they represent 5.6 percent of the national popu-

TABLE 12-1 Percent of Population with Selected Social and Economic Characteristics, According to Race or Ethnicity: United States, Average Annual 1976–1977

SOCIAL AND ECONOMIC CHARACTERISTIC	RACE OR ETHNICITY			
	Black	Hispanic	Asian or Pacific Islander	White
Family Income	*Percent of Population*			
Less than $5,000	30	19	12	11
$5,000–$9,999	29	33	18	19
$10,000–$14,999	19	24	20	23
$15,000 or more	22	24	51	47
Educational Attainment[a]				
High school graduate or more	50	42	78	70
College graduate	7	5	30	15
Employment Status[b]				
Unemployed	12	9	8	6
Marital Status[a]				
Married, spouse present	47	63	65	67

[a]Persons 17 years and over.

[b]Persons 17 years and over in the labor force.

Note: Racial and ethnic categories are mutually exclusive.

Source: Division of Health Interview Statistics, National Center for Health Statistics, data from the Health Interview Survey.

lation.[1] An estimated three million persons are of Asian origin. And, according to the most reliable recent estimates, American Indians and Alaska natives number 678,000.[2]

Geographically, the black population is concentrated primarily in the South, but less so today than in the past. As a result of migration to other regions, only one-half of the black population now lives in the South. Like other minority groups, blacks are much more urbanized than whites. More than 57 percent of blacks—twice the proportion of whites—live in the inner cities. The Hispanic population including Mexican-Americans, Puerto Ricans, and Cubans, are all more urbanized than the white population that is not of Hispanic origin. Most Asian minorities and Pacific Islanders live in the Western United States and in highly urbanized areas. The American Indian and Alaska native population is, on the other hand, largely rural and residing on federally designated reservation land.

Compared to the white population, minority populations are generally younger, have larger families, higher fertility rates, and lower income levels. Table 12-1 presents a profile of selected socioeconomic characteristics of the principal minority groups. The socioeconomic status of minorities in the U.S. is generally low, with the exception of the Asian group. The proportion of black families with incomes less than $5,000 is about 3 times the proportion of white families; for Hispanics, the proportion is about 2 times that for the white population not of Hispanic origin. On a per-capita basis, levels of family income and other resources are decreased by relatively large families of most minorities. Three of every 10 black and Hispanic families consisted of five or more persons, compared with 2 of every 10 white families.[3] Blacks, Hispanics, and American Indians continue to be generally underrepresented at higher income and educational levels, despite reductions of these inequalities.

The Culture of Poverty

The burdens of poor health, inaccessibility to health care, social stigmatization, inadequate housing and poor education, and *poverty* fall particularly hard on minority groups in our society. Poverty can be defined as a "set of circumstances which prevent employment at a wage sufficient to provide the necessities of life within the context of a particular economy, and a life style subject to resources so limited that hopes and aspirations are destroyed."[4] Poverty is more than lack of money. It is a lifestyle. For those who are chronically impoverished, it is a culture in itself, involving housing, education, health, money, opportunities, and goals—or the lack thereof.

Although poverty affects whites, especially rural residents and the aged, it is much more common among ethnic minority groups. In urban areas, poverty is a prevalent condition of the American Indian, blacks, and Hispanics. In 1969, the Federal Interagency Council adopted the *poverty-level index* to assess the economic status of families. In doing so, it established a poverty line. This index reflects the different composition requirements of families, based on their size, composition, age of the family head, and farm or nonfarm residence. In 1980, some 25.9 million persons in the U.S. fell at or below the poverty line. This represents some 12 percent of all Americans. Another twelve million are classified as near-poor.

Poverty is an economic, social and political stiuation. The Current Population Survey by the Bureau of Census continues to show that the percentage of poverty within groups is greater among the aged and minorities. There are clear relationships between poverty and shortened life span. The predicted *life expectancy* of minorities is five years less than for whites. It is linked to higher maternal and infant *mortality* rates. Racial minorities have an infant mortality rate 2 times higher than the rest of the population and a *maternal mortality rate* 3 times higher. Those who live in poverty are more likely to contract communicable diseases than those whose economic situation is improved. And, unfavorable racial differentials in mortality are noted for all major causes of death except suicide and arteriosclerosis.[5]

Malnutrition is a significant concern in the culture of poverty. It is a contributing factor in the development of many other health problems, including high maternal and *infant mortality rates*. The educational implications of malnutrition are important. It is difficult for a child to learn while he or she is hungry. And, more important, school lunch programs will not help those children who have had inadequate nutrition during their first critical years of life, and who have suffered mental retardation as a result. Inadequate nutrition compounds the economic, educational, and health problems associated with poverty.

Figure 12-1
Poverty is an economic, social, and political condition. Courtesy Arizona Republic and Phoenix Gazette.

Minorities: Health Status

In general, the health status of minorities has improved in recent years. Yet many measures indicate that it is not as good as that of the white majority.

In spite of the fact that Americans spend more money on health care than the people of any other country in the world and have available the most sophisticated medical technology, we still fall below other countries in average life expectancy and have higher infant mortality rates than many other countries (see Tables 12-2 and 12-3). The U.S. ranks eleventh in life expectancy for women and eighteenth for men, compared to other countries. In 1977, the U.S. ranked seventh in infant mortality rates, well behind Sweden, Japan, and many developed nations including England and Wales. It has been suggested that the reason for this apparent incongruity is that poverty breeds health problems. It contributes to increased infant mortality rates and reduced life expectancy. Thus,

Table 12-2 Mortality Ratios[a] According to Race and Age: United States, 1970

| | RACE | | | |
AGE	Black	American Indian	Chinese- American	Japanese- American
	Mortality Ratio			
All ages, crude	1.06	0.76	0.50	0.45
All ages, age adjusted	1.54	1.18	0.73	0.49
Under 5 years	2.00	1.67	0.45	0.61
5–14 years	1.42	1.60	0.78	0.65
15–24 years	1.83	2.69	0.45	0.59
25–34 years	2.94	3.48	0.43	0.40
35–44 years	2.72	2.79	0.53	0.46
45–54 years	2.08	1.67	0.59	0.46
55–64 years	1.63	1.00	0.76	0.43
65–74 years	1.35	0.81	0.93	0.43
75–84 years	0.98	0.70	0.80	0.56
85 years and over	0.67	0.56	0.52	0.64

[a]Excludes deaths of nonresidents of the United States.

Note: Ratios are computed by dividing the age-specific death rate of a specified racial or ethnic group by the death rates of the white population in that age group.

Source: National Center for Health Statistics; data computed by the Division of Analysis from data compiled by the Division of Vital Statistics.

it is not surprising that the U.S. ranks seventh in infant mortality, for the victims of poverty are incorporated into our national statistics.

Tuberculosis, dysentery, and accidents are all more common among the poor than the nonpoor. In addition, more poor people than nonpoor people suffer disability from many of the chronic diseases. A measure of long-term impact of chronic disease is the proportion of the population with limitation of activity resulting from chronic illness. According to data from the Health Interview Survey of 1977, marked differences are observed between poor and nonpoor, with the poor reporting more limitation of activity. However, in general, poor-nonpoor differences in the proportion of those with a limitation of activities within a given racial or ethnic group were greater than racial or ethnic group differences in the proportion within either income category.

Two other measures of the impact of illness, both chronic and acute, are the total number of restricted-activity days per person per year. Black adults reported more restricted-activity days than Hispanic or white adults in the Health Interview Survey. This pattern was true for both poor and nonpoor groups, but the poor reported considerably more days than the nonpoor.

In spite of the federally supported Food Stamp Program, inadequate nutrition continues to be a problem of minority groups. In the Health and Nutrition Examination Study conducted from 1971 to 1974, some minority groups had lower intake than the

Table 12-3 Tenement Preventive Maintenance and Environmental Control: Selected Health and Safety Benefits

ENVIRONMENTAL HEALTH AND/OR SAFETY PROBLEM	POPULATION MOST AFFECTED	RECURRING	SKILL LEVEL[a]	NONRECURRING	SKILL LEVEL[a]
Respiratory infections, pneumonia like illnesses, extreme discomfort	Very young and very old	Boiler maintenance Assuring room humidification	(1) (3)	Major boiler repair Repair of broken windows and leaks	(1) and (2) (1) and (2)
Rat bites, rat-borne infections, flea bites, salmonellosis	Very young	Vector control Garbage removal Stoppage Extermination Education and training	(1) and (2) (1) and (3) (1) (1) and (2) (1), (2), (3)	Stoppage	(1)
Accidents, injuries, falls	All age groups, primarily children and teenagers.	Light bulbs in hallways, corridors	(1)	Installing window guards Repairing broken windows Repairing stair railings Repairing holes in floors	(1) (1) (1) (1)
Burns from fires	All age groups	Training, drills, education	(1), (2)	Installation of extinguishers Fireproofing; fire retardant for high-risk areas Electrical repairs	(1) and (2) (1) and (2)
Carbon monoxide poisoning	All age groups	Boiler maintenance	(1), (3)	Boiler repair	(1) and (2)
Lead poisoning	Preschool age	Removing peeling paint Plumbing repair Education	(1), (3) (1), (2) (3)	Wall covering up to 5 feet; scraping above 5 feet Plumbing repair	(1), (2) (1)
Skin infections from insect bites, poor indoor sanitation practices	Mostly children	Case finding and followup Drainage of pools in yards, cellars Education	(1) (1), (2) (1), (3)		
Asthma from dust, mites, rodent dander	All age groups	Vector and pest control Cockroach control Education Mopping and scrubbing of corridors	(1), (2) (1), (3) (1), (3) (1), (3)		
Waterborne illnesses, diarrhea, including amebic dysentery	All age groups	Plumbing repairs	(1), (2)	Major plumbing repairs	(2)
Animal bites (dogs)	All age groups			Registration	(1), (3)
Physical injuires from violent assaults	All residents	Presence/availability of someone on or near premises with access to police	(1), (3)		
Insecticides: Illness (?) from indiscriminate use	All residents	Education	(3)		

[a]Legend: (1) Service performed by environmental extension agent, (2) service probably requires assistance and/or work performed by backup contracting, municipal or specialist service, (3) service includes education and training component for tenants. Tenants may perform certain services.

Source: Courtney B. Wood and others, "Housing and Health—A New Approach," *American Journal of Public Health,* 63 (10), 1973.

recommended daily allowances for protein, calcium, and vitamins A and C. Calcium intake was lower than recommended for adult black women, regardless of income. Vitamin A intake was below the recommended allowances for young adult women in low income groups and for adolescent black women regardless of income. Protein intake was also below recommended standards for adolescents, adult women, and older men in low-income groups. Deficiencies among Hispanics were noted for three nutrients: vitamin A, iron, and calcium. These deficiencies were found regardless of income level.

In terms of mental health, there are proportionally larger numbers of poor people and minorities who are psychotic, suicidal, or severely emotionally disturbed than the nonpoor in our society. The psychological, social, and environmental stresses associated with poverty can be seen in the emotional and physical problems of this group. Feelings of inferiority and uncertainty about the present and the future are common among poverty groups. It is not surprising then that homicide, suicide, alcoholism, and drug dependence rates are high for low-income individuals. The homicide death rate for blacks is still more than 6 times that for the white population. Suicide and alcoholism are significantly higher for American Indians than for any other group. Between 1950 and 1977, the age-adjusted suicide rate for the black population increased from 4.2 per 100,000 to 7.3 per 100,000. Mexican-Americans living in poverty, while they have very low suicide rates, have exceedingly high rates of heroin addiction and drug abuse.

Findings from the Health and Nutrition Examination Survey indicate that self-perception of general psychological well-being differs between men and women and between blacks and whites. White men reported the highest level of psychological well-being. Black men and white women reported about the same level, with 54 percent and 58 percent respectively. Black women reported the lowest level, with more than half reporting moderate to severe levels of distress. The study concludes that more than half of the black female adult population lives in a condition of psychological distress rather than well-being.

Compared to whites, mortality is much higher for blacks and American Indians, especially for those in the younger and middle years of life. Violent causes of death—accidents and homicide—are especially high for blacks and American Indians. Evidence suggests that differing income distributions may account for part of the race differentials in mortality and infant mortality, differentials that persist despite significant declines in mortality during the past twenty-five years. However, for Asian Americans, mortality is below the national average. Of all minority groups for which data are available, Japanese-American women have the lowest death rate (see Figure 12-2).

A considerably larger proportion of blacks than whites perceive their own health to be "fair" or "poor." Minority children clearly use fewer health services than do white children, but there is no clear pattern of differences among adults. One of the most striking differences between minority populations and the white population is in dental care, with the minorities receiving considerably less dental care, both among the poor and the nonpoor. In addition, while the gaps that existed between the poor and the nonpoor in physician and hospital care have generally been closed over the past decade, they still remain for dental care.

Compared with the white majority, minorities are less likely to have a regular

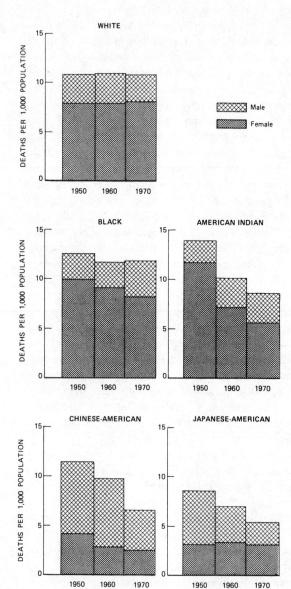

Figure 12-2 Death rates, by sex and race: United States, 1950, 1960, and 1970. Courtesy National Center for Health Statistics, Division of Vital Statistics.

source of medical care, and those who do have a regular source more frequently use hospital out-patient clinics and emergency rooms. The same proportions of the majority and minorities report problems in getting medical care, although a large proportion of the minorities report not getting as much medical care as they need.

In general, the data on the health status of minority populations indicate considerable differences in mortality and *morbidity* when compared to the white population. Differences in health status indication and in utilization of health services are not always

Figure 12–3 Poor people are more likely to have difficulty making necessary arrangements to leave home and seek medical care. Courtesy U.S. Department of Health, Education and Welfare.

as obvious. Some of these differences may be attributed to socioeconomic factors, and others may result from learned patterns of seeking health care.[6]

Health Care and Minority Groups

It is significant, that although the poor have greater needs for health and medical services than any other group within the population until recently they utilized physicians less than any other socioeconomic group. While it is true that there are less physicians available to serve the medically indigent population, it is also true that poverty groups do not use those physicians who are available especially in the area of preventive services. In addition, a trend of utilizing emergency room services and hospital out-patient facilities is much greater among poverty groups than other groups.

The community health field has devoted years to developing a high-quality, comprehensive system of health care delivery from prevention of disease to treatment and cure. Yet in the process of developing this system, which is much improved over that of the past, it was recognized that additional factors had to be considered in order for it to be successful in reaching the target population. At present, the needed changes are being initiated. In the future, no doubt more progress will be made, especially if a system of national health insurance is established in the United States.

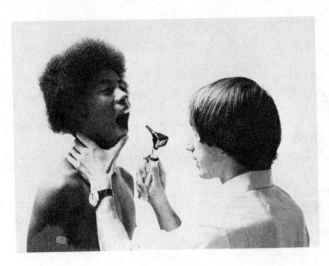

Figure 12-4
Black children visit physicians less
regularly than black adults. Courtesy Arizona Department of
Health Services.

First, it was recognized by those in community health that in dealing with lower-income persons, it is important not only to diagnose and adequately treat health problems, but also to comprehend the social and economic realities of the lives of these people. In addition, it became apparent that generally poor persons tend to place lower priorities on prevention of disease in comparison with the middle and upper classes. For those who live in poverty, survival is a priority—not health per se. The demand for services in this group is greatest in the care and treatment of health problems. Community health professionals began to realize that accessibility to health services would have to be improved in order to meet the needs of poor people without creating significant other problems associated with transportation, child care, and so forth. In other words, as a result of their economic condition, poor people have fewer supportive services available, such as automobiles, and less money for babysitters or preschools than the middle class has. Therefore, they are homebound and have more difficulty in making the necessary arrangements to visit a physician and obtain health care for a member of the family who is ill. Finally, community health professionals became committed to the notion that much would have to be done in order to alter health-damaging behaviors within poverty groups and enhance health-generating behaviors. These suggestions for changes in behavior would necessarily have to respect the cultures, beliefs, and religions of the people of the community.

Medicaid

The creation of *Medicaid* and Medicare, which resulted from the enactment of the Social Security Ammendments of 1965, have contributed significantly to providing health care for both older persons (Medicare) and those who are poor (Medicaid). In addition, this legislation laid the framework for federal involvement in financing health care. Medicaid is a federally assisted state program that is available to low-income persons on public assistance to promote accessibility to health care. The federal government pays between 50 and 78 percent of the.costs of the state Medicaid program, depending upon the per-capita income of the state. Estimates of coverage under Medicaid are not complete because eligibility is determined by a number of factors that differ from state to state. However, under federal guidelines the program is designed to provide medical services and improve access to medical care of certain low income groups. Medicaid is assisting some 23.9 million persons in the U.S. today who are either indigent or medically indigent. Indeed, the impact of the Medicaid legislation in improving the health care outlook for the poor has been significant. But while Medicaid has had many positive effects, it is still not a comprehensive and efficient health care delivery system for the poor in our country. Costs for operating the program have increased dramatically over the years.

Operationally, the program has proved to be unsound. It has been exploited by both providers of health care and recipients alike. And, although Medicaid represents the first major step in recognizing the health needs of poverty groups within the U.S., it continues to be plagued by operational and financial difficulties. As a result of variations within state eligibility requirements, many poor people are not covered.

Medicaid was created with an ambitious goal of providing "the poor with the same access as the rich to mainstream medical care." In attempting to reach this goal, the cost of the program increased seven-fold from $2.3 billion in 1967 to $16.3 billion in 1977.[7] Of significance is the fact that in 1977, 23.9 million people received Medicaid services, as opposed to 9 million in 1967. In addition, medical care costs more in the U.S. now than it did in 1968. Before Medicaid, most poor persons went without medical care, and if care was sought, frequently it was at the expense of food or other essentials for life.

Since the enactment of Medicaid, there have been changes in health service utilization. According to government statistics, between 1964 and 1974, a reversal took place in physician utilization. Prior to 1974, more nonpoor people than poor saw a physician at least once during the year. By 1974, there was a reversal; a trend that continues in the present. In addition, improvements in prenatal care of low-income women was noticeable between 1964 and 1978. More women now than ever before are receiving prenatal care in early pregnancy.

Infant mortality rates have generally been declining. The most remarkable drop occurred for the American Indian population, with a decline from 82.1 deaths per 1,000 live births in 1950 to 15.6 in 1977. The decline among Asian-Americans has almost been as great proportionately. However, the gap between white and black infant mortality rates has actually increased during the past twenty-seven years. Death rates for infants and young children declined substantially, both on the whole and from specific diseases such as pneumonia, influenza, and gastrointestinal diseases. Whether or not these improvements can be attributed to Medicaid is undeterminable. But at the very least, more poor people now have access to health care than before its existence.

In spite of advances in health promotion since Medicaid, the health needs of many poor people in the United States are still not being met. As a result of a complex set of eligibility requirements, many low-income persons are ineligible for Medicaid benefits. Some people who are ineligible include (1) widows under 65 or other nonelderly single persons, (2) most two-parent families which include 70 percent of rural poor families, and (3) about 50 percent of urban poor families with either a working father at a low-paying job or an unemployed father; in twenty-six states. There are a number of other exceptions as well.

Medicaid has represented a financial approach to health care for poor people. Nonhealth considerations, such as the provision of transportation to the health care delivery site, discriminatory practices on the part of health care personnel, and limited expenditures for patient and health education, are all weaknesses in the current approach. These weaknesses must be dealt with aggressively in order to provide comprehensive health services to poverty groups.

Reform of Medicaid is considered vital by many people including those in public health, politics, as well as society in general. The poor by and large remain outcasts to "mainstream medicine" in the U.S. Many poor people still do not have access to health care, this is especially true in rural areas, and physician utilization by poor persons still does not reflect their enormous health needs.

Urban Health Services

The metropolitan freeway, which evolved in the 1960s, produced some ironic paradoxes. In effect, they helped create suburbia, a place where people choose to get away from city life. People who worked in the cities elected to move to suburbia except for the eight-hour working day. Health professionals joined the exodus. And the freeways isolated city residents from the health services they needed in order to survive.

Neighborhood health centers   The first federally funded health centers in the U.S. were administered by the Office of Economic Opportunity (OEO), which was established in 1964. These urban health facilities were called neighborhood health centers. To receive funding neighborhood health centers had to meet certain requirements:

> They had to be a part of the neighborhood, with local residents participating both as workers and board members.
> They had to be accessible and acceptable to the community.
> They had to provide comprehensive and continuous health services.

These early centers were a part of the national effort to wage war on poverty—an effort which began with the enactment of the Economic Opportunity Act of 1964. Neighborhood health centers provided jobs, a focus for social and political action and delivered health services.

In 1966, the effort to provide disadvantaged communities with comprehensive primary health services was stepped up with the passage of the Comprehensive Health Planning and Public Health Services Act. Since the creation of the first neighborhood health center in Los Angeles' Watts, these health facilities now exist in most major cities in the U.S. They are designed to provide efficient, high-quality ambulatory care convenient to urban poor people. Previously funded by the Office of Economic Opportunity, in 1974, these centers became the responsibility of the Public Health Service. The quality of care delivered at these facilities is improving and the availability of services has improved as a result of increasing the number of facilities in the U.S. Yet utilization of the services provided by neighborhood health centers is not optimum. There are many poor, urban residents in need of the services provided by these centers who are not taking advantage of them. Investigations are currently in progress to identify ways in which utilization of the centers can be improved.

In 1975, the Public Health Service Act was amended to cover the planning, development, and operation of community health centers. The newly required services are physicians services, diagnostic laboratory and radiologic services, emergency medical services, and preventive medical and dental services. Provisions must also be made for transportation to the facility to reduce barriers to access—and for the use of personnel who are knowledgeable about the language and culture of the people being served.

The Martin Luther King Health Center is one example of this type of facility. It is located in the South Bronx, N.Y. The center was initially funded by OEO in 1966 and was transferred to HEW (now HHS) in 1973. Its patients are predominantly black (62 percent) and Puerto Rican (36 percent). There are over 90,000 residents in the area served by the clinic, yet the maximum distance to the main health center for any of these residents is thirteen blocks, with 80 percent living within five blocks. The center staff is 90 percent black and Puerto Rican, and 45 percent speak Spanish. The center has negotiated with several hospitals in the area to accept clinic patients on a twenty-four-hour basis when hospitalization is necessary. The center exemplifies how consumer involvement can lead to a health center organized and administered by area residents.[8]

Free clinics   The National Free Clinic Council acts as a funding channel and information disseminator as well as an educational resource for free clinics. In the United States, free clinics are operated by volunteer physicians, nurses and others who assume both allied health professional and staff roles. These clinics are located in most major cities in the country. Although the funds which support the operation of free clinics are earmarked for drug abuse programs, most clinics provide emergency services, venereal disease treatment and problem pregnancy counseling.

Third-world clinics   These programs are initiated and controlled by the residents of the communities in which they exist. Third-world clinics are projects developed by and operated for the people they serve. One example in this category includes the Benito Juarez People's Health Center, which was established to meet the health needs of Chicano people in Chicago. It operates through the voluntary offering of time and services by physicians, nurses, and other allied health professionals. The center provides primary care for the residents in the area. Another example is the George Jackson Free Clinic. In 1971, this clinic opened its doors with the aim of building a comprehensive medical clinic that viewed personal health care and treatment as a part of a human-oriented health care system. The program was endorsed and supported by the San Francisco Black Panther Party.

Rural poverty exists throughout the United States. In fact, the rural poor constitute 40 percent of the nation's poor, although only 30 percent of the total population is classified as rural.

As the United States entered the twentieth century, it changed from a predominantly agrarian nation to an industrial one. This transition resulted in a significant migration of people from rural areas in the U.S. to urban and suburban areas. Today, two-thirds of the population resides on about 10 percent of the land.

As a result of the Industrial Revolution in the United States and the technological change which accompanied it, machines became more efficient than people in operating farms and harvesting crops. Therefore, the need for large numbers of people with farming skills was reduced as machines began replacing people on farms throughout the United States. Modern farm machines have replaced people.

However, some crops cannot be harvested by machines. And, during the planting and harvesting season of many crops, the demand for labor sometimes exceeds the supply of farm workers living in a local area. It is in these instances that migrant or seasonal workers play a major role in the farming industry. The migrant workers in the U.S. are typically Spanish-speaking. By virtue of language differences and the tremendous mobility of this group, the likelihood of economic stability is not good. These people, who work in the fields and orchards in the U.S. picking tomatoes, oranges, and harvesting watermelons, are members of the lowest-paid work force in our country.

In 1978, there were 700,000 migratory workers and their dependents traveling in the U.S., or 8 percent of all farm workers. The group is quite diverse, composed of approximately 82 percent Mexican-American laborers. 12 percent Anglos, 2 percent blacks and 4 percent Orientals and American Indians. Sixty percent of migrants are under 25 years of age. Seventy-two percent are male. The average earnings for eighty-two days of farm work for seasonal workers was $1,807 in 1976.[9] Migrants work the fields six days a week, twelve hours a day.

There are no generalizations that can be made about migrant workers, except that they are a seasonal labor force. Migratory workers vary in income and health status. Migrant camp conditions which serve as temporary housing for these workers, vary from deplorable to adequate. Until the last few years, migrant workers were not protected by any local, state, or federal legislation concerning housing or working conditions. Assistance for migrants became a new and separate section of Title IV as a result of the Economic Opportunity Amendments of 1978 to the Economic Opportunity Act of 1964.

Like other minority groups, many migrants suffer from a variety of health problems. Malnutrition is classified as the most significant health problem affecting this group. The accident rate for migrants is 6 times the rate of the remainder of the U.S. population. And dental problems are a significant concern for these people since proper and adequate dental hygiene is rare among the group when considered as a whole. Working and housing conditions contribute to a high incidence of respiratory diseases including pneumonia, tuberculosis, and bronchitis. An occupational hazard of the migratory worker is skin diseases, which frequently result from contact with various pesticides. Parasitic disorders, including dysentary, are *endemic* to the population. These health problems are intimately related to the fact that many camps still do not provide safe drinking-water supplies. In 1977, 73 percent of the migrant population suffered from parasitic disorders.

Mobility and Migrant Health

The life of a migrant worker is characterized by a large amount of traveling north and south in the United States along the three major migrant streams. Since migrants usually travel as a family, the education of the children frequently suffers. Cesar Chavez, leader of the United Farmworkers of America has said, "I went to thirty-one schools before finishing the seventh grade."[10] A significant amount of migrant time is spent on the roads (see Table 12-4). The result of this mobility is frequently a lack of continuity in the education of migrant children. This deficit usually means that the next generation of migrant workers will also be educationally deprived and will, in all likelihood, lack the necessary skills and education for gainful employment in work other than seasonal labor. Migrant children over the age of 14 are usually out in the fields working with their parents. Even though the United States outlawed child labor in industry over thirty years ago and banned farmers from employing anyone under the age of 16 during school hours, there have been few positive effects on this group as a result of these actions.

Excessive mobility and work demands of seasonal laborers contributes to general

Table 12-4 Migrant Farmworkers: Distribution by Racial/Ethnic Group and Distance Traveled to Do Farmwork, 1976

| MILEAGE TRAVELED | ALL WORKERS | | RACIAL/ETHNIC GROUP | | | | | |
| | | | Whites | | Hispanics | | Blacks and Others | |
	Thou.	Pct.	Thou.	Pct.	Thou.	Pct.	Thou.	Pct.
Under 75	47	22	45	37	2	3	a	b
75–199	29	14	23	19	3	4	3	b
200–399	39	19	24	20	14	18	1	b
400–499	8	4	3	2	5	6	a	b
500–999	24	11	14	11	5	6	6	b
1,000–1,499	12	6	8	7	1	1	3	b
1,500–1,999	28	13	1	1	25	32	2	b
Over 2,000	22	10	3	2	19	25	a	b
Total	213	100	122	100	77	100	15	100

[a]Estimated number less than 500.

[b]Percentages not shown where base is less than 50,000 persons.

Note: Numbers and percentages of workers may not add to totals due to rounding.

Source: Smith, Leslie Whitener and Gene Rowe. *The Hired Farmworking Force of 1976.* Washington, D.C.: U.S. Department of Agriculture, Agriculture Economics Report No. 405, July, 1978, p. 18.

Figure 12-5 Due to mobility, the children of migrants can suffer educationally. Courtesy Arizona Republic and Phoenix Gazette.

discontinuity in the lives of migrant workers. Inadequate prenatal care is common among pregnant migrant women. This in turn can result in complications during childbirth as well as higher infant and maternal mortality rates. The income—and in fact survival—of the migrant depends upon the number of people in the family working in the fields. Frequently, mothers of young infants and children are harvesting the fields while their children remain at camp unsupervised. The combination of unsafe camp conditions and lack of supervision contributes to the high accident rate among migrant children. The excessive amount of traveling migrants do has adversely affected the continuity of the health care and treatment of these people. Migrants frequently do not know where emergency health services are located should they be needed. This is a significant community health concern because of the high accident rate alone. Migrant children may be immunized and protected from the same disease several times, at different health clinics, in different locations, or they may receive no protection under the assumption that the child has already been vaccinated. Clearly, the keeping of accurate medical histories and records for this mobile group is nearly an impossible task.

The Migrant Health Program of the federal government is designed to support centers which provide services to domestic migratory workers and their families, and to persons who perform similar seasonal agricultural services. Migrant health centers provide a number of different services, including:

Primary health services

Access to hospital care in a limited number of areas

Provides referral for supplemental health services

Environmental health services including detection of unhealthful sanitation conditions

Infectious and parasitic disease screening and control measures

Health education

Health services are provided by staff in health centers or through contracts or cooperative arrangements with public or private health professionals and agencies. Nearly two-thirds of the migrant population utilize the Bureau of Community Health Services (BCHS) facilities as their usual source of care. This federal program serves a population of which 88 percent is minority, of which 60 percent is Hispanic. Three-fourths of the patients at BCHS facilities are women, and 82 percent of patients are young.

In 1962, the Migrant Health Act was passed, which provided for project grants for health services to migrants. At that time, health services available to migrants were preventive services such as immunization, health education, and environmental sanitation. These services were provided by local and state public health agencies, and medical services were available through contracts with private physicians. Because of the orien-

Figure 12-6
A migrant health center. Courtesy Arizona Department of Health Services.

tation of the health departments used to attack migrant health problems, emphasis was given to nonpersonal health services for migrants. Since 1962, Congress has extended the Migrant Health Program five times. In each instance the appropriation was increased. Most recently, a provision was added that extended services to the additional two million seasonal farm workers who live in areas where migrants work. This allowed for the provision of health care to the target migrant population without discriminating against their coworkers.

In recent years, delivery of personal health services to migrant and seasonal workers has become a reality. In each succeeding year of the Migrant Health Program, more migrants have received personal health care. In addition, a priority for health care assistance has been placed on high impact areas where 6,000 or more migrants reside for more than two months a year.

At present, there are 125 migrant health projects in thirty-five states and Puerto Rico providing care to some 500,000 people. Nearly 80 of these projects operate on a year-round schedule, providing comprehensive health services with a full-time medical staff. The remainder are seasonal projects with part-time medical staffs. In addition to direct medical care, some projects provide outreach, social services, and transportation to increase access to care and improve utilization of health services available. Other projects coordinate services available from other providers and refer patients to appropriate health resources. Some projects offer limited dental services, rehabilitation, nutrition counseling, home care, outreach, and environmental services. All migrant health projects currently offer treatment, diagnostic, and preventive services.

Approximately 5 percent of the 125 migrant health projects use mobile clinics for delivery of health services. These units, which require utility services, are normally located adjacent to hospitals, health departments, or community centers. The Migrant Health Program also funds a limited hospitalization program in some areas.

To alleviate sanitary problems and address other environmental health problems as mandated by legislation, the Bureau of Community Health Services (BCHS) has begun to expand and intensify existing state migrant labor housing program activities. In conjunction with this effort, standards were developed by the Department of Labor to assess the quality of housing available and to determine the effect of this housing on the health of migratory agricultural workers. The BCHS and Environmental Protection Agency are jointly conducting a pesticide study on the migrant population.[11]

The National Migrant Referral Project (NMRP) was developed to reduce the gap that exists in providing continuity of care to migrants. This system utilizes all migrant health-care clinics and other migrant health providers. By the combined use of the migrant health project directory and a referral form, a migrant health clinic can make direct referrals for its migrant patients as they travel to the out-of-state destinations. Similarly, out-of-state health clinics are encouraged and assisted to initiate referrals back to the migrants' home-base areas at the end of the migrants work season. Consejeros (health workers) stationed in strategic migrant clinics operate and monitor this referral network and act as resource persons to the migrants. The NMRP, which began in 1975, represents the first effort in referral programs for migrants.[12]

Both medical and nonmedical solutions will need to be initiated in order to promote better health among migrant workers. Housing and sanitary conditions are still lacking generally. Educational opportunities for migrant children need improvement. At present, large numbers of children work as seasonal laborers. Most have put in a five-hour day in the fields before noon. California migrant children have a median schooling level of 5.2 years, which is 6.8 years less than the Anglo Californian.[13] In addition, the lack of enforcement of child-labor laws has led to a situation that exploits the children of migrants, who work in the fields from 6:00 A.M.—then, tired and hungry, are bused to school at noon. "A 'day's work' for these unfortunate children is never less than twelve hours between field work, busing, and school."[14] In addition, the situation in the fields, where pregnant women are engaged in hard labor for a twelve-hour period, six days a week, and who as a result of poverty are receiving less than adequate nutrition and pre-natal care, is a significant contributory cause in high infant mortality rates.

Comprehensive health planning for migrant workers will have to incorporate innovative approaches to deal with the economic, educational, and living conditions of these people in order to improve their health status. In addition to nonmedical approaches, several types of specific health services can be offered to aid in the delivery and accessibility of care. Some of these include:

1. *Mobile Clinics:* The establishment of mobil health clinics has been helpful in providing for the acute immediate needs of migrants. However, these clinics are not permanent solutions and cannot provide comprehensive care. Mobile health clinics can take two forms: (1) permanent stations located at prime locations to improve accessibility for migrants, and (2) stations that are truly mobile, providing a service at migrant camps, thus eliminating transportation problems of migrants in utilizing the clinics. These units should provide for as wide a range of services as is feasible, including pharmacy, x-ray units, laboratory diagnostic, and treatment rooms.[15]

2. *Satellite Clinics:* The establishment of clinics during the times in which migrants are in a specific geographic area are also invaluable from a health standpoint. These clinics are set up on a temporary basis by renting buildings in a location which would provide easy access to large numbers of seasonal workers and their families. They should provide a wide variety of services and can help to fill the primary health care needs of this target group.

3. *Night Clinics:* Night clinics can be successfully operated as a temporary function of county hospitals or public health clinics to meet the health needs of migrants during the two or three months in which they are working in a specific area. Since they are operated at night, they can provide services to migrant workers during the hours in which they are off work.

4. *Day-Care Centers:* Utilizing migrant women as auxiliary personnel, day-care

centers can be a first step in improving the health status of migrant children. They can be supervised and spend days in a healthy, safe environment in which they receive adequate nutrition.[16]

Planning Migrant Health Services

There are a number of important factors which must be considered when planning a comprehensive health care delivery system for migrant workers. Such things as the type of crops to be harvested, the amount of mechanization available for harvest, the cultural and ethnic backgrounds of the workers, as well as their religious beliefs, and languages must be taken into account. The type of crop is a concern because it may give some indication as to the amount and types of pesticides used, the position of the workers during the harvest, and types of conditions under which they will be working. The degree of mechanization in harvest cannot be overlooked, because it provides an estimation of the numbers of migrants who will be working and needing health care. Some crops, such as tomatoes, cannot be harvested unless they are hand-picked; therefore, large numbers of migrants will be needed, and this in turn will demand increased availability of health services.

An understanding of and appreciation for the cultural and ethnic backgrounds is of vital importance in planning for health care. Certain patterns of disease are associated with the activities in which these people are engaged. In addition, language, as a part of ethnicity, can provide health planners with information. Mexican-Americans comprise the largest group within the migrant population. Most speak Spanish and health planners must take into account that their language differences may present problems both in relating symptoms to physicians, who are primarily Anglo, and in interpreting physician directions and recommendations for care. Likewise, religion is an important consideration in understanding the utilization of health services by a group of people. This is especially true regarding family planning services. The idea of "curaderismo" or folk medicine has been discussed earlier, and it is a very significant cultural consideration regarding health care delivery to this population.

It is of prime importance that a network be established throughout the U.S. that accumulates and processes information regarding migrant workers, as individuals and/or families. Since these people travel, a national network of medical histories for each person in every family of seasonal workers is necessary.

Although the number of migrants is decreasing in the U.S. yearly as mechanization replaces manual labor in farming, this group of seasonal workers will continue to play a role in agriculture in the U.S. They are an available group that demands less-than-adequate pay and housing. Generally, because the lifestyle of these people is so mobile, they lack educational, health care, and personal-improvement opportunities. Since the seasonal labor force is predominantly Spanish-speaking, language presents yet another barrier to upward mobility out of the culture of poverty.

AMERICAN INDIANS AND
ALASKA NATIVES

There are approximately 700,000 American Indians and Alaska natives in the United States. They are among the most impoverished and isolated of any people in the U.S. Of this population, about 609,000 American Indians reside on or near more than 250 reservations. Sixty-nine thousand of the total are Alaska natives. The states which contain the highest native American populations are Oklahoma, Arizona, and New Mexico respectively. Tribal lands in the United States comprise almost forty million acres, with the Navajo tribe possessing the largest reservation. American Indians are by no means a homogeneous group, except for the fact that they were the first Americans. There are hundreds of different dialects that comprise the six major Indian languages. And physical

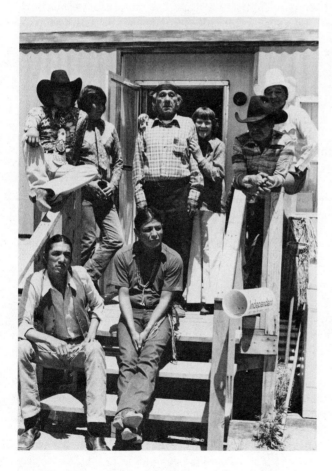

Figure 12-7
American Indians are by no means a homogeneous group. Courtesy Arizona Department of Health Services.

characteristics, somatotyping, cultural beliefs, and traditions are very diverse among the many different tribes which are present in the U.S. Some Indians speak very little or no English, and others speak English only as a second language.

American Indians and Alaska natives have a unique legal-historical relationship with the federal government. This relationship, unlike that of any other group of American citizens, is based on treaties and on laws passed by Congress. After a long history of attempting to exterminate the American Indian during the course of thirty-seven Indian wars, the United States policy toward American Indians has changed dramatically. The current policy attempts to promote both independence and integrity for the many different tribes, in what is termed self-determination. Yet the Indian is in a nearly untenable position. The tribal way of life involves cooperation. It is a communal existence. American society is capitalistic and competitive. The Indian who chooses to leave the reservation is likely to experience considerable culture shock as he or she enters the American mainstream. Yet life on the reservation is difficult at best. The physical environment of the American Indian and Alaska native in most locations throughout the United States is characterized by severe climatic conditions; a rough, often treacherous geographical setting; and extreme isolation. Survival under these conditions attests to the ingenuity, adaptability, and determination of these people. This harsh environment, coupled with decades of economic deprivation and the resulting lack of basic environmental amenities, has contributed greatly to their exceptionally high incidence of disease and premature deaths, particularly among infants. Farming on most reservations is marginal, since reservation lands typically have poor soil and little available water. Less than 7 percent of Indian land is suitable for farming. A 33 percent unemployment rate on reservations is not uncommon.[17]

That poverty is a way of life for American Indians is not surprising. This poverty sets the stage for major health problems among the population. The barriers to wellness and health on the reservations include such things as poor sanitation, crowded living conditions, inadequate diet, and geographic isolation that results in inaccessibility to health services. Yet progress has been made in the recent past to improve health and living conditions for Indians, through federal initiatives and through their self-help efforts.

Health Status of American Indians

The impact of improving the circumstances affecting the health of Indian people through the construction of better health care and sanitation facilities has been remarkable. The infant death rate for Indians and Alaska natives, for example, has been reduced by 74 percent since 1955. The maternal mortality rate has undergone a 91 percent reduction. Yet infant mortality rate for Indians is still about 1.2 times the U.S. rate. The decreases identified above are considered primarily the result of increased emphasis on and availability of maternal and child-health services to American Indians.

The types and nature of major diseases among Indians is largely different from the rest of the nation. Fatal accidents continue to be higher for Indians and Alaska natives than for the total U.S. population (155.5 per 100,000 versus 44.7 in 1977). The accident

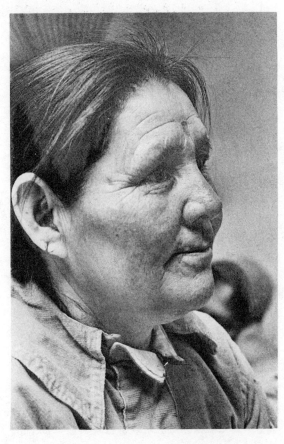

Figure 12-8
Maternal mortality among Indians has undergone a 91% reduction since 1955. Courtesy Arizona Republic and Phoenix Gazette.

death rate for Indians aged 25 to 54 is almost 5 times that of the U.S. population of comparable age. The homicide and suicide death rates are also higher. The suicide rate among native Americans is 2.2 times the national average. Homicide rate was 2.6 times the national average in 1977 (see Table 12-5).

Tuberculosis was once the leading killer of American Indians and Alaska natives. Since 1955, this disease has experienced approximately an 89 percent reduction (see Table 12-6). During the same period, the death rates dropped 65 percent for influenza and pneumonia, 72 percent for certain diseases in early infancy, and 89 percent for gastroenteritis.

Alcoholism continues to pose serious problems for Indians and Alaska natives. It is not only a significant health problem in its own right, but is viewed as a contributory factor in fatal automobile accidents, suicide and homicides. During the past decade, American Indian alcoholism death rates were from 4.3 to 5.6 times as high as the rates for the remainder of the U.S. population.

Several specific illnesses are considered to be special health problems for Indians

Table 12-5 Ten Leading Causes of Death for Indians and Alaska Natives for All Areas and These Causes for Each Area, 1975 to 1977

	ALL AREAS	TUC-SON	ABER-DEEN	BE-MIDJI	ALBU-QUER-QUE	ALAS-KA	BIL-LINGS	OKLA-HOMA CITY	USET	PHOE-NIX	PORT-LAND	NAVAJO
All causes	13,666	344	1,826	814	840	1,386	881	2,527	262	1,559	871	2,356
Accidents	2,908	68	378	124	176	387	209	282	53	336	180	715
Motor vehicle	1,670	51	221	60	121	80	137	175	37	199	115	474
All other	1,238	17	157	64	55	307	72	107	16	137	65	241
Diseases of heart	2,322	34	345	224	73	168	181	704	44	187	171	191
Malignant neoplasms	1,244	29	131	83	67	154	78	346	23	105	68	160
Cirrhosis of liver	814	33	116	39	63	48	65	147	5	129	86	83
Influenza and pneumonia	660	13	90	30	32	61	32	106	4	95	45	152
Cerebrovascular diseases	658	10	67	76	31	51	29	195	22	74	39	64
Suicide	436	11	46	25	39	77	20	30	12	62	36	78
Homicide	391	8	59	24	19	46	25	52	14	61	18	65
Certain causes of mortality in early infancy	390	3	78	11	22	47	28	57	6	41	28	69
Diabetes mellitus	365	8	52	34	21	6	16	102	14	73	14	25
All other causes	3,478	127	464	144	297	341	198	506	65	396	186	754

(Rates per 100,000 Population)

	ALL AREAS	TUC-SON	ABER-DEEN	BE-MIDJI	ALBU-QUER-QUE	ALAS-KA	BIL-LINGS	OKLA-HOMA CITY	USET	PHOE-NIX	PORT-LAND	NAVAJO
All causes	751.2	837.7	1,135.6	918.2	648.1	696.5	869.5	683.6	662.7	751.1	889.2	613.8
Accidents	159.9	165.6	235.1	139.9	135.8	194.5	206.3	76.3	134.1	161.9	183.8	186.3
Motor vehicle	91.8	124.2	137.4	67.7	93.4	40.2	135.2	47.3	93.6	95.9	117.4	123.5
All other	68.1	41.4	97.6	72.2	42.4	154.3	71.1	28.9	40.5	66.0	66.4	62.8
Diseases of heart	127.6	82.8	21.5	252.7	56.3	84.4	178.6	190.4	111.3	90.1	174.6	49.8
Malignant neoplasms	68.4	70.6	81.5	93.6	51.7	77.4	77.0	93.6	58.2	50.6	69.4	41.7
Cirrhosis of liver	44.7	80.4	72.1	44.0	48.6	24.1	64.2	39.8	12.6	62.2	87.8	21.6
Influenza and pneumonia	36.3	31.7	56.0	33.8	24.7	30.7	31.6	28.7	10.1	45.8	45.9	39.6
Cerebrovascular diseases	36.2	24.4	41.7	85.7	23.9	25.6	28.6	52.7	55.6	35.7	39.8	16.7
Suicide	23.9	26.8	28.6	28.2	30.1	38.7	19.7	8.1	30.4	29.9	36.8	20.3
Homicide	21.5	19.5	36.7	27.1	14.7	23.1	24.7	14.1	35.4	29.4	18.4	16.9
Certain causes of mortality in early infancy	21.4	7.3	48.5	12.4	17.0	23.6	27.6	15.4	15.2	19.8	28.6	18.0
Diabetes mellitus	20.1	19.5	32.3	38.4	16.2	3.0	15.8	27.6	35.4	35.2	14.3	6.5

Source: U.S. Department of Health, Education and Welfare, *Selected Vital Statistics for Indian Health Service Areas and Service Units, 1972–1977.* Washington, D.C.: U.S. DHEW Pub. No. (HSA) 79-1005, p. 69.

Figure 12-9 Indians are now living longer than ever before. Courtesy Arizona Republic and Phoenix Gazette.

and Alaska natives (see Table 12-7). One of these is otitis media, or inflammation of the middle ear. This disease affects primarily children and can result in serious hearing disabilities. The rate of this disease was 9,658 per 100,000 in 1978. The concentrated effort of the Indian Health Services to treat and control this disease is credited with decreasing rates of this condition.

Mental illness is a growing concern among Indians. Its increasing prevalence appears to be related to the continuing struggle of the Indian to resolve the conflict between ancient tribal customs and tradition and a modern world with opposing values.

A number of health improvements have been realized by American Indians and Alaska natives since 1955. Tremendous strides have also been made in correcting environmental deficiencies and providing water and sewage disposal facilities for thousands of families. Their health status, however, still lags fifteen to twenty years behind that of the general population.[18]

The Indian Health Service

The Indian Health Service (IHS) is a component of the Department of Health and Human Services, the Public Health Service (PHS), and the Mental Health Administration (HSMHA). During its organizational life of twenty-three years, the IHS has developed

351

Table 12-6 Rates of Reported New Cases of Tuberculosis Among Indians and Alaska Natives[a] and the United States Population by Race, 1955–1978[b]

CALENDAR YEAR	INDIAN AND ALASKA NATIVES	INDIAN	ALASKA NATIVE	U.S. ALL RACES[c]	U.S. WHITE[c]	U.S. ALL OTHERS[c]
1978	66.0	62.8	91.8	13.1	8.6	41.6
1977	62.8	58.2	99.6	13.9	9.2	44.8
1976	69.4	59.2	158.5	15.0	9.9	48.0
1975	102.2	102.4	100.5	15.9	10.7	50.9
1974	79.8	74.5	122.4	14.4	9.7	45.1
1973	107.6	102.4	150.7	14.8	10.2	46.3
1972	100.6	94.3	151.4	15.8	10.8	50.3
1971	157.4	152.0	200.3	17.1	11.7	53.8
1970	154.1	154.1	154.0	18.3	12.4	59.0
1969	140.8	141.6	134.3	19.1	13.7	59.7
1968	133.8	128.0	179.1	21.3	15.3	65.1
1967	155.8	152.7	179.8	23.0	16.6	70.2
1966	141.7	127.8	247.8	24.4	17.9	71.9
1965	201.5	160.5	507.8	25.3	18.6	74.9
1964	237.8	184.1	630.2	26.6	19.9	76.5
1963	234.0	192.3	534.9	28.7	21.7	81.5
1962	257.7	209.4	604.7	28.9	21.9	80.1
1961	318.8	284.8	562.8	37.0	NA	NA
1960	322.4	292.3	547.5	39.4	NA	NA
1959	418.0	338.2	1,048.0	42.6	NA	NA
1958	485.0	421.8	978.7	47.5	NA	NA
1957	565.2	426.9	1,649.7	51.0	NA	NA
1956	680.6	474.3	2,283.8	54.1	NA	NA
1955	758.1	563.2	2,325.7	60.1	NA	NA

[a]Indian and Alaska Native data 1955–1961 include some newly reported inactive cases while the later years include newly reported active cases only.

[b]Rates of new cases per 100,000 population.

[c]*Source:* Center for Disease Control, *Morbidity and Mortality, Volume 27, Number 53, 1978* and *Tuberculosis, States and Cities.* Atlanta: U.S. DHEW Pub. No. 77-8249, 1978, and earlier annual editions.

Note: NA = Not available.

and operated a health services delivery system designed to provide a broad spectrum program of preventive, curative, rehabilitative, and environmental services to approximately 609,000 American Indians who belong to some 250 tribes and to an additional 69,000 Alaska natives. The goal of the IHS is to improve their health status by providing needed health care. The Indian Health Service has three major objectives:

1. To assist Indian tribes in developing their capacity to man and manage their health programs through activities such as health management training, technical assistance, and human resource development and provide every opportunity for tribes to assume administrative authority through contracts and delegation.

Table 12-7 Rank Order of the Rates of Twenty Leading Reported New Cases of Notifiable Diseases in 1978 among Indians and Alaska Natives and These Diseases for Each Year 1970–1978

DISEASE	1978	1977	1976	1975	1974	1973	1972	1971	1970
Acute otitis media	1	1	1	1	1	1	1	1	1
Strep throat	2	3	3	3	3	3	3	2[a]	3[a]
Gastroenteritis	3	2	2	2	2	2	2	3	2
Impetigo	4	4	4	4	4	5	5	NA	NA
Pneumonia	5	5	6	5	5	6	4	5	4
Influenza	6	6	5	6	6	4	6	4	5
Gonococcal infections	7	7	7	7	7	7	7	6	6
Chickenpox	8	8	8	9	9	8	9	8	8
Scabies	9	10	13	17	19	19	20	NA	NA
Bacillary dysentery	10	9	9	8	8	10	10	9	12
Infectious hepatitis	11	11	12	11	11	12	12	10	10
Trachoma	12	12	11	10	10	9	8	7	7
Mumps	13	13	10	14	12	11	11	11	9
Syphilis, all forms	14	14	14	12	13	13	13	12	13
Rheumatic fever	15	15	16	16	16	16	17	16	16
Tuberculosis, new active	16	17	17	15	15	14	15	14	14
Puerperal septicemia	17	18	18	19	17	18	18	17[b]	17[b]
Measles (Rubeola)	18	16	15	13	14	15	14	13	11
Rubella (German measles)	19	19	19	18	18	17	16	15	15
Scarlet fever	20	20	20	20	20	20	19	NA	NA

[a]Strep throat, scarlet fever in 1970 and 1971.

[b]Puerperal septicemia reported January thru June, 1970, and July thru December, 1971.

NA = Not available.

Source: U.S. Department of Health, Education and Welfare, *Illness Among Indians and Alaska Natives, 1970–1978.* Washington, D.C.: U.S. DHEW Pub. No. (HSA) 79-12040, p. 8.

2. To act as the Indians' and Alaska natives' advocate in the health field to generate other interests and resources which can be utilized.

3. To deliver the best possible comprehensive services, including hospital and ambulatory medical care, preventive and rehabilitative services, and to develop or improve community and individual water and sanitation facilities and other environmental factors affecting good health.[19]

A comprehensive health service program has been developed by the Indian Health Service to deal with the health needs of native Americans. The IHS operates a system which

. . . .integrates health services delivered directly through IHS facilities and staff on the one hand, with those purchased by IHS through contractual arrangements on the other, taking into account other health resources to which the Indians have access. To facilitate the operation of the program the system is managed through 88 local administrative units known as Service Units. A service unit is the basic health organization in the Indian Health Service program, just as a county or city health department is the basic health organization in a state. . . .

These are defined areas, usually centered around a single federal reservation in the continental United States, or a population concentration in Alaska. Most service units encompass a hospital or health center, staffed by competent health teams. The service units are grouped into eight larger . . . jurisdictions . . . called IHS areas and four program offices.

. . . Currently 51 hospitals, 99 health centers including 26 school health centers, and over 300 health stations and locations are involved in efforts to deliver direct IHS services.

Contract care is used in those circumstances when direct IHS facilities and staff are not available.[20]

The IHS maintains contracts on over 300 private or community hospitals, and over 500 physicians, dentists, and other health specialists.

The planning and development of all phases of the health services program has insured high consumer input from representatives of local tribal health boards and tribal councils. The service includes Indian recruitment and training programs to facilitate availability of resources so that they can operate and manage their own programs. The law seeks to augment the number of Indian health professionals for Indian communities through the establishment of a Health Professions Scholarship, a Health Professions Preparatory Scholarship, and other opportunity programs. The enactment of the Indian Self-Determination Act of 1975 extended the strength of tribal governments and of Indians themselves to develop the experience and skills needed for self-determination in health affairs. In addition, the enactment of the Health Care Improvement Act in 1976 authorized support for the development of a seven-year program to help close the health gap between the American Indian and Alaska native and the general population of the U.S.

Environmental Health Services

In the total comprehensive program, certain special programs have been initiated in response to significant needs on the part of the Indian population. One of these is environmental health services. These services are provided under the supervision of the Indian Health Service sanitarians and aides and are an integral part of the total health program. They are designed to combat unsanitary environmental conditions such as poor and crowded housing, lack of safe water supplies, and inadequate waste-disposal facilities. With the enactment of the Indian Sanitation Facilities Act in 1959, it became possible to attack energetically the substandard living conditions of the Indian. Provision of sanitation facilities has done much to improve the environment of these people. However, many families still lack basic facilities and are subject to the serious health hazards associated with such environmental deficiencies. During the past twenty years, substantial progress has been made in environmental sanitation. Approximately 92,000 Indian homes have been provided with water supply and sewage disposal facilities. Of this total, 43,600 new and rehabilitated homes were constructed under federal and tribal housing programs.

Other environmental conditions that result from improper sanitation, including insect and wild-rodent vectors, continue to result in sporadic epidemics on Indian reservations. To combat these and other environmentally related problems, the staff of the environmental health program provides a wide range of environmental health services and engineering and technical support to implement sanitation facilities projects, including those undertaken in coordination with federal and tribal housing agencies. A continuing program of consultations and services is made available to Indian and Alaska native families and communities to assist them in implementing a comprehensive environmental health program.

Services of an occupational health and safety nature have also been expanded in recent years. An essential element of these services is the emphasis on community guidance of program activities. This permits the integration of the activities into the total health, social, and economic structure of Indian and Alaska native communities. In addition to the foregoing, the basic environmental health activities incorporate a consultative service to assure that a high level of environmental sanitation is maintained in federal and other facilities serving Indians, particularly those of the Bureau of Indian Affairs and the Indian Health Service.

In the provision of basic sanitation services, Indian and Alaska environmental health aides/technicians are key members of the staff who help to bridge the gap of cultural differences to bring modern environmental health practices to Indian communities and groups.

Indian Health: The Future

In spite of the recent accomplishments in promoting health and improving the situation of native Americans, there are a variety of problems affecting these people that remained unsolved. The solution of some of the problems facing American Indians will be realized when comprehensive health services are available to all Indians. The movement to recruit and train American Indians for health careers is intensifying, yet there remains a critical shortage of health personnel of Indian heritage.

Other problems do not lend themselves to simple solutions. For example, accident rates can be reduced by improving the physical environment on the reservation. But environmental controls or intervention is not enough. Progress has taken place in environmental quality on reservations, yet still the fatal-accident rate is over 6 times the national rate. Mental health maintenance is another area which will need to be energetically supported. Policy makers in the Indian Health Service and the tribal councils will have difficulty in solving this problem. If progress in the next twenty years is comparable to that which took place over the past twenty years, American Indians may well be on the way to achieving a quality of life comparable to every other American.

REVIEW QUESTIONS

1. Describe what is meant by the phrase "culture of poverty." What are the components of poverty?
2. Identify several barriers to providing a comprehensive health care system which possesses continuity for minorities.

3. Describe the progress that has been made in providing for the health care needs of the poor through Medicaid. Identify basic weaknesses in Medicaid.

4. Compare the health problems of American Indians with the general population of the U.S.

5. What are some of the components of a comprehensive health care system for migrant workers?

6. What has been the relative impact of the Indian Health Service, the Migrant Health Program, and the development of community health centers on respective target populations?

SUGGESTED READINGS

Anderson, John and Paul Farseth, "Implementing the Model Medicaid Management Information System," *Public Health Reports,* 92(2) 135-146, 1977.

Ford, Amasa B., *Urban Health in America.* New York: Oxford University Press, 1976.

Leveson, Irving and Jeffrey Weiss, *Analysis of Urban Health Problems.* New York: Spectrum, 1976.

Luft, Harold, *Poverty and Health: Economic Causes and Consequences of Health Problems.* Cambridge, Mass.: Ballinger, 1978.

Organizing for Health Care: A Tool for Change. Source Catalog #3. Boston: Beacon Press, 1974.

Skinner, Thelma and others, "Factors Affecting the Choice of Hospital-based Ambulatory Care by the Urban Poor," *American Journal of Public Health,* 67(5) 439-445, 1977.

Tierney, John, *Sickness and Poverty: A Handbook for Community Workers.* Washington, D.C.: U.S. DHEW Pub. No. (PHS) 2047, 1970.

NOTES

[1] U.S. Bureau of the Census, "Persons of Spanish Origin in the United States, March 1977," *Current Population Reports,* Series P-20, No. 329, 1978.

[2] U.S. DHEW, *Illness among Indians and Alaska Natives, 1970-1978.* Washington, D.C.: U.S. DHEW Pub. No. 79-12040, 1979, p. 3.

[3] U.S. Bureau of the Census, "Population Profile of the United States, 1977," *Current Population Reports,* Series P-20, No. 324, 1978.

[4] Bonnie Bullough and Vern Bullough, *Poverty, Ethnic Identity and Health Care.* Englewood Cliffs, N.J.: Prentice-Hall, 1972, p. 110.

[5] U.S. DHEW, *Health Status of Minorities and Low-Income Groups.* Washington, D.C.: U.S. DHEW Pub. No. (HRA) 230-77-0024, 1977.

[6] U.S. DHEW, *Health: United States, 1979*. Washington, D.C.: U.S. DHEW Pub. No. (PHS) 80-1232, 1980, p. 17.

[7] *Health: United States, 1979*, p. 180.

[8] U.S. DHEW, *Promoting Community Health, 1976*. Washington, D.C.: U.S. Government Printing Office, 1977, p. 4.

[9] Leslie Whitener Smith and Gene Rowe, *The Hired Farmworking Force of 1976*. Washington, D.C.: U.S. Department of Agriculture, Agriculture Economics Report No. 405, 1978, p. 15.

[10] Jose Fuentes, "The Need for Effective and Comprehensive Planning for Migrant Workers," *American Journal of Public Health*, 64(1) 4, January 1974.

[11] U.S. DHEW, *Forward Plan, FY 1979–1983*. Washington, D.C.: U.S. DHEW Pub. No. (HSA) 241-186/1058, 1977, pp. 111-113.

[12] *Promoting Community Health, 1976*, p. 9.

[13] Jose Fuentes, p. 4.

[14] Jose Fuentes, p. 5.

[15] Jose Fuentes, p. 7.

[16] Jose Fuentes, p. 8.

[17] U.S. DHEW, *Indian Poverty and Indian Health*. Washington, D.C.: U.S. Government Printing Office, 1977, p. 28.

[18] *Health: United States, 1979*, p. 16.

[19] U.S. DHEW, *The Indian Health Program of the U.S. Public Health Service*. Washington, D.C.: U.S. DHEW Pub. No. (HSM) 73-12, 003, 1973, p. 5.

[20] U.S. DHEW, *Selected Vital Statistics for Indian Health Service Areas and Service Units, 1972–1977*. Washington, D.C.: U.S. DHEW Pub. No. (HSA) 79-1005, 1978, p. 24.

GLOSSARY

endemic refers to a disease which is markedly localized in a given geographic area or within a specific population group.

Hispanic classification of a person of descent or origin as Mexican, Chicano, Mexican-American, Puerto Rican, Cuban, or other Spanish culture.

infant mortality rate the death of live-born children who have not reached their first birthday; usually expressed as a rate (ratio).

life expectancy the average number of years of life remaining to a person at a particular age, based on a given set of age-specific death rates.

maternal mortality rate the death of mothers from childbirth, usually expressed per 10,000 live births.

Medicaid this program is federally aided, but is state-operated and administered. It provides medical benefits for certain low-income persons in need of medical care.

morbidity sickness or illness, usually expressed in rates.

mortality causes of death, usually expressed in rates.

poverty an economic, social, and political situation.

poverty-level index the official United States poverty line established by the Federal Interagency Council of the Social Security Administration. An index which assesses the economic status of families based on size, composition, age of the family head, and farm or nonfarm status.

BIBLIOGRAPHY

Bullough, Bonnie and Vern Bullough, *Poverty, Ethnic Identity and Health Care.* Englewood Cliffs, N.J.: Prentice-Hall, 1972.

Breyer, Peter, "Neighborhood Health Centers: An Assessment," *American Journal of Public Health,* 67(2), 179-182, 1977.

Davis, Karen, "Achievements and Problems of Medicaid," *Public Health Reports,* 91(4) 309-316, 1976.

Goodwin, Melvin, James Shaw, and Uycle Feldman, "Distribution of Otitis Media Among Four Indian Populations in Arizona," *Public Health Reports,* 95(6) 589-594, 1980.

Kernaghan, Salvanija (ed.), *Delivery of Health Care in Urban Underserved Areas. Report of 1978 Conference in Washington, D.C.* Chicago: American Hospital Association, 1979.

Leveson, Irving and Jeffrey Weiss, *Analysis of Urban Health Problems.* New York: Spectrum, 1976.

Okada, Louise and Thomas Wan, "Impact of Community Health Centers and Medicare on the Use of Health Services," *Public Health Reports,* 95(6) 535-539, 1980.

Roberts, Robert and Eun Sul Lee, "The Health of Mexican Americans: Evidence from the Human Population Laboratory Studies," *American Journal of Public Health,* 70(4) 375-384, 1980.

Smith, Leslie Whitener and Gene Rowe, *The Hired Farmworking Force of 1976.* Washington, D.C.: U.S. Department of Agriculture, Agriculture Economics Report No. 405, July 1978.

U.S. DHEW, *Community Health Representative: A Changing Philosophy of Indian Involvement.* Washington, D.C.: U.S. DHEW Pub. No. 781-495/38, 1972.

————, *Forward Plan, FY 1979-1983.* Washington, D.C.: U.S. DHEW Pub. No. (HSA) 241-186/1058, 1977.

————, *Health Statistics Report Fiscal Year 1978.* Washington, D.C.: U.S. DHEW, 1978.

————, *Health Status of Minorities and Low-Income Groups.* Washington, D.C.: U.S. DHEW Pub. No. (HRA) 230-77-0024, 1977.

————, *Health: United States, 1979.* Washington, D.C.: U.S. DHEW Pub. No. (PHS) 80-1232, 1980.

————, *Investing in Tomorrow: Progress Against Poverty.* Washington, D.C.: U.S. DHEW, 1978.

————, *Selected Vital Statistics for Indian Health Service Areas and Service Units, 1972-1977.* Washington, D.C.: U.S. DHEW Pub. No. (HSA) 79-1005, 1979.

————, *The Indian Health Program of the U.S. Public Health Service.* Washington, D.C.: U.S. DHEW Pub. No. (HSM) 73-12003, 1972.

————, *To the First Americans, Sixth Report on the Indian Health Program of the U.S. Public Health Service.* Washington, D.C.: U.S. DHEW Pub. No. (HSA) 77-1000, 1976.

Weaver, Jerry, "Mexican-American Health Care Behavior: A Critical Review of Literature," *Social Science Quarterly,* 54(1) 85-102, 1973.

Weikel, Keith and Nancy Leamong, "A Decade of Medicaid," *Public Health Reports,* 91(4) 303-308, 1976.

Wood, Courtney B. and others, "An Experiment to Reverse Health-Related Problems in Slim Housing Maintenance," *American Journal of Public Health,* 64(5) 474-476, 1974.

13

PRISON
HEALTH

> The inmates of prisons are not the irretrievable, viscious, and depraved element they are commonly believed to be, but upon the average like ourselves, and it is more often their misfortune than their crime that is responsible for their plight . . . a prison is a cross-section of society in which every human strain is revealed.
>
> *Eugene Debs*

PRISONS, PRISONERS, AND HEALTH

On the average day, there are more than 40,000 men, women, and juveniles behind bars in federal and state prisons and county and local jails in the United States. *Jails* and *prisons* have come to represent not simply an institution in the U.S., but a society in its own right—a society with its own rules, customs, mores, and roles. For the most part, the reality of prison life remains unknown to those who live and work outside of its walls. However, in recent years, the public has become more aware of what daily life behind bars is really like. This awareness has occured largely as a result of the efforts of inmates themselves. The Attica uprising, and, more recently, the New Mexico prison riots, as well as the filing of class action suits by prisoners, has generated community enlightenment regarding the prison environment including those aspects of life behind bars that relate to health care.

Prisons and jails in the United States range from acceptable to deplorable in providing services for health needs and sanitary living conditions for inmates. Correctional institutions by and large are unsanitary, overcrowded, and generally lacking in providing medical services which are acceptable in meeting the health needs of the incarcerated. Very little progress has taken place in the penal system of the United States in its over 200 years history. Many of our nation's inmates either go without medical care entirely or make do with treatment below accepted community standards.

The food that is available in many prisons is often tasteless and nutritionally inadequate. In some jails, even food is considered a privilege for inmates. One of the most controversial issues in prison health relates to experimentation on inmates in scientific research. The use of convicts as subjects in experiments on drugs, pain tolerance, cancer, and fertility has raised difficult ethical questions related to *informed consent* and the

361

Figure 13-1
Prisons and jails in the U.S. range from acceptable to deplorable. Courtesy Arizona Department of Health Services.

extent to which free will is exercised by inmates volunteering for such projects. Cells that are intended to house one person are now housing two. Overcrowding in the institutions continues to pose threats to sanitation and quality of life and privacy for inmates.

In a 1981 prison-crowding case before the Supreme Court, the American Medical Association and the American Public Health Association submitted a brief detailing the health problems caused by overcrowding. The case, *Rhodes vs. Chapman,* arose from the Southern Ohio Correctional Facility. The cells in this facility are 63 square feet and designed for one person. But the prison population has been rising and officials began placing two men in each cell—reducing living space to 30-35 square feet per person. The following is an excerpt from the AMA-APHA brief.

> In the context of overcrowding, the minimum space per person standards are developed by the APHA and other professional organizations. These standards which generally call for at least 60 square feet per person based on the broad consensus of epidemiological, medical and psychological findings that long term overcrowding causes and accelerates the spread of communicable disease and results in increased occurrence of stress-induced mental disorders, tension, aggression, and physical violence. . . .[1]

The Supreme Court decision handed down in this case held that housing two inmates together in a 63 square foot cell is not by itself cruel and unusual punishment. The Court stated, "The Constitution does not mandate comfortable prisons."

The problem of inadequate health care in prisons has many ramifications. The typical prisoner is young (over 50 percent are under the age of 25), usually eligible for bail but cannot pay the amount of money required (4 out of 5 inmates in local jails are eligible), and comes from a slum district (two-thirds of all arrests) where the average life expectancy is ten years less than in other areas of the community.[2] These facts and others have created the belief within many people, both inside and outside the walls of our prisons, that much of what goes on in U.S. prisons may constitute *cruel and unusual punishment,* in which basic needs and rights to adequate shelter and health for the incarcerated are not being met.

A limited number of projects have been undertaken to determine what health conditions in prisons are really like and what health services are available for inmates. The first of these was supported by the National Society of Penal Information in 1929 and was conducted by Frank Rector. The purpose of the study was to investigate the status of public and personal health services in prisons in the United States. At the completion of the project Rector identified standards of medical care that were attainable in 1929. His recommendations included the following;

1. Intake and pre-discharge or parole physical examination of all inmates conducted by a "competent physician."
2. Dental examination, vision screening, blood test for syphillis, urinalysis for all persons over 40 years of age and other laboratory work as might be indicated.
3. One physician per 500 inmates and an additional physician for each extra 1,000 inmates.
4. Daily sick call to be conducted by a physician who would dispense drugs.
5. Complete dental care.
6. Complete optometrical care.[3]

These standards, which were attainable in 1929, have still not been implemented today—over 50 years later—in many prisons and jails in the United States.

In 1976, the American Medical Association (AMA), through a grant from the U.S. Justice Department of Law Enforcement Assistance Administration (LEAA), conducted two studies concerned with health care delivery in prisons and the health status of prisoners.

> In general, the dearth of available health care facilities and services reported in the 1972 AMA survey of 1,159 of the nations jails was mirrored in the thirty pilot sites involved in the AMA program.[4]

In general, there is a correlation between the size of the jail and the number of available services. However, even in the large institutions, only about half of the sixteen most important services were provided, on the average.[5] Clearly, there are many defects in the present system of health care in correctional facilities and these must be improved if punishment in the U.S. is to be considered humane and effective in rehabilitating the offender. It is hoped that the improvement of prison conditions will come out of a spirit of humanism on the part of American society. However, even if it results from self-interest, the improvement will mean better living conditions and health care for the incarcerated.

THE PRISONS

Prisons range from the pace-setting federal institutions like the maximum-security prison in Atlanta to the Alabama State Prisons which have been in the past declared "unfit for human habitation." At the present time, many of the nation's prisons and jails are old, crowded, and unsanitary. Recreational facilities are either absent or grossly inadequate. Prison diets are many times nutritionally inadequate, with milk and meat served sparingly. It is the local and county jails that are typically the worst in providing for health care and with respect to general living conditions. These correctional institutions number about 4,000 in the U.S.

In the 1976 AMA analysis of thirty pilot jails in six states, it was found that 17 percent of the jails provided daily sick call, 67 percent of the jails had some special services available for alcoholics, either in-house or in the community, 37 percent of the pilot sites had similar services for drug abusers, 27 percent of the jails had no emergency equipment at all, and two of these did not have first-aid kits. Of the thirty jails surveyed, one-third provided no mental health services except in extreme emergencies.[6]

For decades, Americans have ignored the situations in prisons. However, today we are in a period of awakening, and Americans are beginning to challenge the institutions that manage criminals in society. There are many unanswered questions concerning health care services and facilities in jails and penitentiaries in the U.S. Clearly, these questions need answers, if health planning and implementation of health services within prisons is to be economical and effective in meeting the needs of the population.

THE PRISONERS

The Department of Justice's Bureau of Prisons identifies the typical inmate who enters our prisons as about 28.5 years old, with a 95 percent chance of needing medical attention and a 66 percent chance that the care he or she receives will be the first contact with professional medical providers. In addition, the individual will have a 50 percent chance of having been involved in drug abuse and a 15 percent chance of suffering from severe emotional problems.[7] For the sake of simplicity, it would be convenient if all prisoners fit the mold of "typical," but they do not. There are those who are not seriously disturbed from an emotional health standpoint, but who may become so before their sentence is served as a consequence of prison conditions. Many prisoners are healthy when they arrive to begin serving their time, but become ill while in prison. Depending upon the institution, they may or may not receive adequate medical care. These individuals may well depart from the prison environment with handicaps, both emotional and physical, which will remain with them throughout their lives if they do not receive quality medical care during the time they serve their sentence. In an effort to eradicate the horrors of prison life, many inmates sniff glue and take pills that have been brought behind the walls by guards, family, or friends. Some would say that most prisoners need psychiatric help. But as yet this fact has not been substantiated. What has been established is that if an inmate needs psychiatric help, he or she had best be incarcerated in a federal

Table 13-1 Most Common Problems of Inmates.[a]

PROBLEMS	NUMBER OF CASES	PERCENTAGE
Drug abuse	97	18.4
(Heroin 35)		
(Alcohol 18)		
(Other 44)		
Anxiety and depression	49	9.3
Phenothiazide-responsive		
emotional disorder	42	9.3
Chronic physical disability	25	4.7
Trauma[b]	25	4.7
Veneral disease[b]		
(nongonorrheal)	25	4.7
Infections of skin and		
subcutaneous tissue	21	3.9
Upper respiratory infection[b]	18	3.4
Peptic ulcer disease	16	3.0
Headaches	14	2.6
Seizure disorder	10	1.9
Hepatitis	10	1.9
Asthma	9	1.7
Diabetes	9	1.7
Backache	7	1.3
Homosexuality	6	1.1
Hypertension	6	1.1
Dental	6	1.1
Acne	6	1.1
External otitis	5	<1.0
Refractive error	5	<1.0
Urinary tract infection	5	<1.0
Tuberculosis	4	<1.0
Otitis media	4	<1.0
Hemorrhoids	4	<1.0
Chronic obstructive		
pulmonary disease	4	<1.0
Contact dermatitis	4	<1.0
Viral warts	4	<1.0
Hernia—inguinal	4	<1.0
Abdominal pain—		
unknown cause	4	<1.0
Other problems with three		
or less cases	80	15.1

[a]In decreasing order of frequency.

[b]True incidence not accurately reflected in table.

Source: Engbretstein Bery and Jane Olson, "Primary Care in a Penal Institution," *Medical Care,* 8(9), 1975, p. 776.

institution, since of the fifty full-time psychiatrists for all American prisons, fifteen of them work in federal institutions, which hold only 4 percent of all prisoners.

The incarcerated, like all people, have certain unique health needs and problems as well as problems that seem typical of the target group. Although it is still difficult to determine whether the health needs of prisoners are significantly different from free Americans, we do have a better picture as to the health problems of specific groups of prisoners at specific institutions. Table 13-1 illustrates the results of a survey which took place at the Dade County Jail in Florida in 1973. The table indicates that many inmates are in need of medical attention, ranging from slight problems to more severe disorders, such as untreated heart and gastric disorders.

The 1976 AMA inmate-patient profile data indicate that the percent of inmates without a single health or physical abnormality was fairly low (about 15 percent). The percent with only one abnormal finding was also low. The majority of the inmates in each state fell in the two-to-four abnormalities category. Over 12 percent of inmates examined had abnormal tuberculosis test results, 5.9 percent had abnormal VDRL tests for syphillis, 30 percent had abnormal hepatitis test results, and 12.4 percent had urine abnormalities.[8]

Freedom of choice exists for other members of the community to change physicians, to drop out of one clinic and enter another which may provide better care and to bring a law-suit for malpractice. The incarcerated lack the options available to those in the free society. However, health is one right that should never be taken away from an individual when he or she loses freedom as a result of committing a crime. Health care in prisons should be at least equivalent to that which exists in the community. According to the AMA report,

> Given the highly communicable nature of some of the diseases identified in this report, the overcrowding that exists in a number of the jails and the fact that the majority of the individuals in jails will be returning to their communities in just a few days, it is inconceivable . . . that even one case of tuberculosis or syphillis or hepatitis should be allowed to go untreated. From a public health standpoint, to continue to ignore the high risk population represented by jail inmates would be sheer folly.[9]

MEDICAL CARE IN PRISONS

There are merits to imprisonment in our society both with regard to preventing crimes and for the purpose of protecting the public from recurrences of socially destructive behavior. In turn, society has the responsibility for the health and welfare of individuals during their term of imprisonment in government supported institutions.

Only a small number of studies have been conducted that are concerned with medical care inside U.S. correctional institutions. These indicate that for the most part, poor conditions generally exist in our jails and prisons, and that they exist due to the low priority attached to medical resources, facilities, and services inside prison walls. The

1976 AMA study of thirty pilot jails in six states found that: 23 percent jails had bed care facilities in house, "37 percent had a medical clinic in house; 13 percent performed routine physical exams on all inmates upon admission; 17 percent of the jails provided daily sick call."[10] The AMA statistics cited in this chapter apply to jails that responded to a self-report survey. In this survey 2,930 questionnaires were mailed out and only 1,159 were returned.

Class Action Suits

One of the agents for bringing about change in prison medical care—both regard to quality and quantity—has been an increased incidence of *class action suits* by inmates in our nation's prisons. In New Orleans, a class action suit *(Louis Hamilton et al. vs. Victor Schiro et al.)* was the first in a series of events that led to the establishment of a new system of medical care at the Orleans Parish Prison. This suit was filed in 1969 against the City of New Orleans, city council, sheriff, and the prison warden by inmates at the prison. The court submitted that the conditions at the prison constituted cruel and unusual punishment, which is in violation of the Eighth Amendment of the Constitution. The judge, in the suit identified several major findings with regard to the prison medical system in the Orleans Parish Prison, including:

1. Danger of an outbreak of contagious disease as a result of unsanitary conditions in the toilets, the kitchen, and sleeping equipment.
2. No medical intake survey was made to detect prisoners with contagious disease.
3. Only sporadic blood tests for syphillis, despite epidemic rates within the prison.
4. There is no room for isolation and quarantine areas for those with contagious disease since the conditions are generally overcrowded.
5. The effects of a fearful environment and crowded, sordid living conditions is severe on psychotic prisoners. Disruptive psychotics were sometimes moved into a hallway by the main gate and shackled to the bars.
6. Hospital facilities and medical attention in general was very inadequate in meeting the needs of the inmates.
7. Medication is carelessly dispensed and often does not reach the inmate in need.[11]

As a consequence of the litigation, a judicial order was issued directing the defendants to immediately correct the deficiencies certified in the suit. A federal court appointed an individual to investigate the deficiencies and formulate a reasonable and effective plan for correcting the situation. The current program for health care at the Orleans Parish Prison is one of the best in the United States.

In 1972, the Alabama State Prisoners brought a class action suit against the state of Alabama to bring attention to the deplorable health care conditions in state penitentiaries. The federal courts acted on the suit and declared that the lack of medical care in Alabama's penal system was "shocking to the conscience" and a violation of the Eighth and Fourteenth Amendments. This case *(Newman vs. Alabama)* was of great significance since it was the first federal case devoted entirely to prison medical care. The opinions cited in the case and affirmed by the courts included

> . . . barbarous abuses; rudimentary laboratory facilities; a lack of standard sanitary procedures; inaccurate and incompleted medical recordkeeping; chronic shortages of medical supplies; inadequate mental health services as well as numerous deaths caused by intentional neglect.[12]

The courts have two responsibilities: to remove the offender from society and to rehabilitate the offender so that he or she will be able to function effectively in their environment once paroled. Clearly, one of the keys to rehabilitation is the correction of medical and dental problems. While under the protection of the court system, medical, emotional and dental needs of the incarcerated must be met.

Constraints in Prison Medicine

Improving the prison health care system is possible, but there are a number of constraints unique to health care delivery in this setting which create additional problems than would be typically encountered in communities outside prison walls. Perhaps one of the most significant difficulties that must be overcome in order to improve prison health is the recruitment of qualified physicians to work in prisons. Physicians must be attracted to work in a situation which has less financial rewards and resources than is offered by private practice in a suburban setting. There are significant physician shortages in federal penitentiaries as well as in state, county, and local prisons and jails.

Recruitment of physicians is difficult even if prisons offer 100 percent malpractice insurance and salary incentives, as many federal prisons do, because many times the physician must work with outdated equipment and limited facilities where working conditions are generally unpleasant. An additional constraint relates to the ever present correctional staff, whose prime concern is security rather than preserving health. Prison physicians are placed in a situation in which they must adhere to prison administration policy yet maintain professional standards. This is difficult since there are times when security considerations may override medical needs. There are many questions which need to be answered in order to balance security and health care considerations in this unique setting. For example, should a person with a record of prison escapes or one who is known to be dangerously violent be transferred to a civilian hospital for open heart surgery or some other procedure that cannot be carried out within prison walls?

Attracting health professionals and allied-health professionals such as nurses, laboratory, and x-ray technicians to work in prisons is also difficult. Many young doctors and nurses who chose to practice behind bars express feelings that before very long they begin to feel like a prisoner themselves. Or equally destructive, is the tendency for prison health professionals to become custodial in their attitudes toward inmates and their health needs. The following example may serve to illustrate this phenomenon:

> After several years the doctor may become hardened to his or her patients. Seldon Williams worked at Attica State Prison during the 1971 uprising in which

43 people died and 80 were wounded. He had been working in this prison system for 22 years and was earning $30,000. Weekday mornings, he and his assistant saw between 100 and 125 inmates from behind a mesh screen that ran from a waist-high counter to the ceiling. On rare occasions, an inmate was led to an examining room. Dr. Williams made no attempt to hide his antagonism toward his patients. According to the New York State Special Commission Report on Attica, inmates claimed that the doctor said things like, "How do you know you have a headache" or "Pain, I don't see any pain." If the inmate objected, he was threatened with placement in the psychiatric ward, a threat that Dr. Williams admits to have carried out occasionally. "The critics should try living with them," Williams said in an interview shortly after the uprising. "These convicts aren't appreciative of anything . . . . I think they got what they deserved. . . . I try to be impartial but I find it hard.[13]

The difficulties associated with attracting recent medical school graduates to penal institutions in the U.S. has resulted in the unfortunate practice of hiring unlicensed physicians and moonlighting senior residents.

Financing is yet another constraint in the delivery of health services behind bars. In most prisons, medical care costs are blended into the total prison budget, and health care expenditures are minimal. It has been estimated that the annual per-capita medical costs for inmates in U.S. penal institutions range from as low as $30 in some prisons to over $2,000 in a small institution where a fully staffed hospital is operated. The salary of physicians should be comparable for those in prison settings and those in the community; yet for the most part they are not. Additional financial appropriation will be needed in order to improve the health care facilities, services, equipment, and personnel available in penal institutions. This will require the support of the public and a commitment on the part of legislators and other elected government officials.

IMPROVEMENT ON THE WAY FOR PRISON HEALTH

There are many individuals and groups who have attempted to transform inferior, disorganized, and haphazard medical care in prisons into up-to-date, comprehensive, sophisticated medical organizations that serve the many needs of wards and inmates. The New Orleans Parish Prison is a good example of the vast improvement that can take place when a project is supported, both financially and philosophically by the community, government officials, and medical professionals. Health care in the prison was totally inadequate until a class action suit was filed. Medical histories were not taken upon imprisonment. No laboratory work was run on any of the inmates. And, although adequate care necessitates that minimal equipment was present, the prison hospital did not possess a scale or examining table. When inmates were treated for disorders or illness, no follow-up was done on the treated patients. About 15 percent of the inmates in Parish Prison were continuously using mood-altering drugs. Prison doctors had no way of knowing if the drugs used in treating patients would produce adverse effects, or had caused adverse reactions. Dental care in the Orleans Parish Prison consisted almost entirely of extractions. On an average, seventeen extractions were performed each week. Psychiatric care was nonexistent, in spite of the fact that many of the prisoners experienced from mild to severe emotional problems. In summary, the Orleans Parish Prison was unable to deliver even minimally acceptable quantity and quality health care to its inmates.

Following the court ruling, which supported the position of the inmates, the situation at the Orleans Parish Prison changed dramatically especially with regard to health care. The prison entered into a contract with a qualified medical group outside the prison to deliver medical services to prisoners. The contractor, Charity Hospital, agreed to perform routine physical examinations upon intake of all inmates into the prison and to conduct routine sick call for inmates on a twenty-four-hour-a-day basis. In addition, the medical group contractor initiated a program which provided comprehensive back-up consultive services including medical, surgical, obstetrical, psychiatric and emergency services. In the program which evolved, the City of New Orleans Health Department became responsible for monitoring the quality of medical care in the Orleans Parish Prison, and Charity Hospital became responsible for delivering the medical care to inmates.

The program in this setting is quite expensive. But, the additional expenditures have provided twenty-four-hour-a-day coverage over the previous eight hours per day, fifty hours of physician time per week over the twelve hours a week, complete laboratory capabilities, as opposed to no laboratory work-ups. In short, a comprehensive, high-quality medical care system for inmates has been created from a previously deplorable one that did not meet even minimally acceptable standards.[14]

The state of Massachusetts has been committed to improving the availability and quality of health services to prisoners. Prison health services developed in Massachusetts in an era of both fiscal and personnel restrictions. The Prison Health Project was developed in response to a survey, the Madoff Report, which had been critical of medical care in state prisons. The Madoff Report recommended, among other things, the establishment of a Division of Prison Medicine under the jurisdiction of the Department of Public Health, separate from the Department of Corrections, but reporting to it.

Since its inception, the Prison Health Project has created the following changes in the correctional system:

1. appointment of physicians in three of the five state prisons,
2. installation of medical assistants (medics) in two prisons,
3. development of standard medical correctional record forms,
4. codification and expansion of the rules governing research on inmates,
5. amplification of the routine sanitary inspections of the Department of Public Health,
6. screening programs for tuberculosis and sickle-cell anemia,
7. establishment of an Inmates' Medical Advisory Committee which meets at least once a month.[15]

At the local level in Kansas City, Kansas, an entirely new medical-dental program was established in Jackson County Jail in 1974. This new unit of operation which is directed by Kansas General Hospital and Medical Center resulted indirectly from the complaints inmates voiced about inadequate food, personal-hygiene facilities, health care, and other matters. A task force was organized to investigate inmates' concerns about health care and to develop recommendations on their findings. The following outlines the changes that have taken place in this local facility:

1. Physician Assistant (PA) utilization on a twenty-four-hour basis to provide health care and attention augmented by physicians services based at the hospital.

2. A partially abandoned section of the jail was renovated into an exemplary health care unit.

3. Construction of a new medical-dental unit.

4. The hospital pharmacy service, one of the keys to success, serves essentially as a medication inventory area. Medications are distributed three times a day by PAs.

5. A modern laboratory and radiology facility has been built for performing routine tests. PAs are trained to perform a full spectrum of routine lab tests; hematology, toxicology, serology, urinalysis, and miscellaneous tests. All inmates are tested for PPD and VDRL. All black inmates are tested for sickle-cell anemia.

6. Medical Record System: In February 1973, a new system was recommended which has since been established, including health education.

7. Dental Care: A four-chair, fully equipped facility that provides comprehensive dentistry services and that is supervised by a full-time faculty member at the University of Missouri School of Dentistry was established.

8. The entire medical unit is provided with twenty-four-hour-back-up-coverage by hospital physicians.[16]

It is of significance to note that this successful program was developed and implemented without the support of federal grant monies. Federal assistance was not sought or obtained, and still this local facility was able to bring organization, efficiency, and expanded health care programing to its inmates. The experience at Jackson should serve as an example to other correctional institutions at the local and state level that it can be done.

THE FUTURE OF PRISON HEALTH

Prison health in U.S. correctional institutions can be improved through support and cooperation. As is the case with all public health programs, innovations, and improvements can be made and changed only within the confines of constraints that are present. There are obviously financial, as well as professional constraints which cause difficulties in setting up adequate prison health facilities that are efficient, effective, and appropriately staffed with knowledgeable and empathetic physicians and other health professionals. But

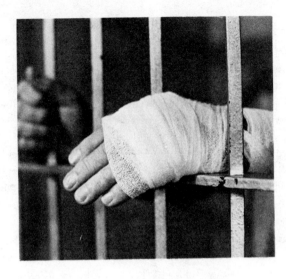

Figure 13–2
One of the agents for bringing about change in prisons is inmates' concerns about medical care. Courtesy American Medical Association.

in view of these constraints, or keeping these constraints in perspective, it is still possible to operate correctional institutions in the U.S. in humane ways, including the provision of adequate health care which can be legitimately expected by imprisoned men and women.

First, the problem of recruiting qualified and concerned professionals will have to be solved. Physicians can be attracted to practice prison medicine if the appropriate incentives are present. Second, a major step in improving the situation of prison medicine would be to transfer responsibility for medical care from the department of corrections to the jurisdiction of the state and local health departments. This would also mean that the hiring of health care professionals to work in prisons would be conducted and processed by the health departments. Finally, it is unlikely that there will never be enough physicians and others on the health care team to serve the U.S. population as a whole. In the future, certain inmates should be trained as allied-health professionals, such as x-ray technicians, paramedics, and LPNs to help supply needed health services for this population. Such training, in which inmates develop marketable skills for health careers, can be used not only while in prison, but also upon release.

In order to improve the status of health behind bars our society must become more committed to the rights of prisoners to health care and must begin to see the incarcerated as people. In speaking to the issue of prison health, the Jails and Prisons Task Force of the American Public Health Association has said:

> The intent of the American Public Health Association is not to promote special treatment for this population, but rather to insure that their incarceration does not compromise their health care.[17]

In conjunction with the policy statement, this national public health association has developed standards for health care in correctional institutions. These include the following principles:

> Each individual committed to an institution of incarceration or detention, should receive a reception health assessment, and no person shall be admitted who is unconscious.
>
> Every correctional institution should make provisions for those persons treated on an ambulatory basis who have special health requirements.
>
> The identification and diagnosis of health problems is only the beginnings of health care.
>
> Any person should be able to seek mental health care.
>
> Full confidentiality of all information obtained in the course of treatment should be maintained at all times with the only exceptions being normal legal and moral obligations to respond to a clear and present danger of grave injury to self or others and the single issue of escape.[18]

Clearly, professionals in public health and medicine are beginning to display the commitment necessary to bringing about improvement in prison health.

REVIEW QUESTIONS

1. Describe the major health problems of prisoners.
2. What were some of the medical care standards for prisons identified in the Rector Report of 1929?
3. What are some of the barriers to developing a high-quality prison medicine system?
4. How can adequate health care delivery in prisons be achieved in the future?

SUGGESTED READINGS

Dole, Vincent, "Medicine and the Criminal Justice System," *Annals of Internal Medicine,* 81 (5) 687-689, 1974.

Goldsmith, Seth B., "The Status of Prison Health Care," *Public Health Reports,* 16 (6) 569-575, 1974.

King, Lambert, Arlen Reynolds, and Quentine Young, "Utilization of Former Military Medical Corpsmen in the Provision of Jail Health Services," *American Journal of Public Health,* 67 (8) 730-734, 1977.

McLean, Elizabeth, "Prison and Humanity," *Lancet,* March 1, 1977, pp. 507-511.

Murton, T., "Prison Doctors," in G. Leinwand (ed.), *Prisons.* New York: Pocket Books, 1972.

NOTES

[1] "Prison Case Before Court," *The Nation's Health,* March 1981, p. 11.

[2] "Medicine," *Time,* July 9, 1973, p. 35.

[3] Seth B. Goldsmith, "The Status of Prison Health Care," *Public Health Reports,* 6, No. 6 (November-December 1974), 569-575.

[4] *Medical Care in U.S. Jails: A 1972 A.M.A. Survey.* Chicago: American Medical Association, 1973.

[5] *Analysis of Jail Pre-Profile Data.* Chicago: American Medical Association, 1977, p. 36.

[6] *Analysis of Jail Pre-Profile Data,* 41-44.

[7] April Koral, "Medicine Behind Bars," *Medical World News,* June 11, 1971, p. 26.

[8] *Analysis of Inmate/Patient Profile Data.* Chicago: American Medical Association, 1977, pp. 76 and 107.

[9] *Analysis of Inmate/Patient Profile Data,* p. 109.

[10] *Analysis of Jail Pre-Profile Data,* pp. 38-41.

[11] Seth B. Goldsmith, "Jailhouse Medicine—Travesty of Justice?" *Health Services Reports,* 87, No. 9, (November 1972), 768.

[12] Seth B. Goldsmith, "Jailhouse Medicine," p. 769.

[13] April Koral, p. 49.

[14] Seth B. Goldsmith, "Jailhouse Medicine," pp. 767-774.

[15] Curtis Prout, "Prison Health Services," *New England Journal of Medicine,* 290, No. 15 (April 1974), 856-857.

[16] E.J. Twin, M.L. Krinsky, and Toby Clark, "Hospital Operates Health Program at Jail," *Hospitals,* July 16, 1975, pp. 51-53.

[17] "Report of the Task Force on Prison Health: Standards for Health Care in Prisons of the American Public Health Association," *The Nation's Health,* November 1976, p. 3.

[18] "Report of the Task Force on Prison Health," p. 3.

GLOSSARY

class action suit a legal action undertaken by one or more plaintiffs on behalf of themselves and all other persons having an identical interest in the alleged wrong.

cruel and unusual punishment a violation of the Eighth Amendment.

informed consent legal statement signed by participants in research studies that are designed to protect the rights and welfare of subjects. These documents support that an individual understands the potential health hazards that may result from serving as a subject in a research study and that he or she is willing to serve as a subject.

jail a holding facility especially for the detention of persons awaiting trial or convicted of minor offenses.

prison building for the confinement of persons accused or convicted of crimes.

BIBLIOGRAPHY

Analysis of Inmate/Patient Profile Data. Chicago: American Medical Association, 1977.

Analysis of Jail Pre-Profile Data. Chicago: American Medical Association, 1977.

Goldsmith, Seth B., "Jailhouse Medicine—Travesty of Justice?" *Health Services Report,* 87(6) 767-774, 1972.

———, "The Status of Prison Health Care," *Public Health Reports,* 16(5) 569-575, 1974.

Jones, David A., *Health Risks of Imprisonment.* Lexington, Mass.: Lexington Books, 1976.

Koral, April, "Medicine Behind Bars," *Medical World News,* June 11, 1971, pp. 25-35.

Medical Care in the U.S. Jails—A 1972 AMA Survey. Chicago: American Medical Association, 1973.

Monahan, John (ed.), *Community Mental Health and the Criminal Justice System.* New York: Pergamon Press, 1976.

Rector, F. L., *Health and Medical Service in American Prisons and Reformatories.* New York: National Society of Penal Information, 1929.

"Report on the Task Force for Prison Health: Standards for Health Care in Prisons of the American Public Health Association," *The Nation's Health,* November 1976, p. 3.

Twin, E. J., M. L. Krinsky, and Toby Clark, "Hospital Operates Health Program at Jail," *Hospitals,* 49(7) 510-513, 1975.

Weisbuch, Jonathan, "Public Health Professionals and Prison Health Care Needs," *American Journal of Public Health,* 67(8) 720-721, 1977.

14

THE
AGED:
fostering quality of life
in the later years

When old people look back on their lives, they regret more often what they did not do rather than what they have done. Medicine should regret its failures to act responsibly in the health care (including mental health care) of the elderly. Physicians, psychotherapists and the public should not assume that nothing can be done for old people. No one should count them out.[1]

Robert Butler, M.D. Director,
National Institute of Aging

THE AGED AND HEALTH

Older people in the United States are frequently the victims of indifference, social abuse, isolation, and discrimination. This occurs in spite of the fact that most people over 65 want to continue to be involved in life, would like to make decisions for themselves, and want to continue to be treated as human beings. In short, the goal of most older people is to approach life affirmatively. However, in our society this is often times difficult as a result of the tremendous impact that ageism exerts. *Ageism* is the systematic stereotyping of and discrimination against older people simply because they are old. Ageism allows younger people to categorize older people as senile, rigid, reactionary, and different from themselves. In community health, ageism plays a significant role, since it may cause health professionals to disregard the value of older persons with whom they are working and eventually this negative view of older persons can result in a failure on the part of health professionals to identify older persons as human beings, and thus they may deliver substandard care.

Concern for the health and welfare of all people—young and old—has been the basis of community health since its beginnings. The emergence of *gerontology,* which is the study of the aging process, including the sociological, physiological, and psychological

Figure 14-1
The goal of most older people is to approach life affirmatively.

dimensions of aging has made significant contributions in helping community health professionals to foster quality of life in the later years. *Geriatrics,* another relatively new discipline, has also contributed significantly. Its purpose is to utilize the information gained from gerontology, to enable older people to live more enjoyably and productively. The focus of community health is to enable older persons to achieve a "quality of life," which is characterized by enjoyment and productivity through improved health status in the later years.

DEMOGRAPHY AND OLDER PEOPLE

Although aging begins at birth, it is customary to think of all individuals 65 and older as aged. It should be noted that this line of demarcation which separates middle age from old age, is an arbitrary one based upon the usual age of compulsory retirement in the United States. Technically, aging begins at 30, when physiological processes first begin to decline. However, perhaps of greater importance when discussing age is differentiating between *chronological age* and *daily functional age*. That is, a person who is 70 chronologically may function physiologically, mentally, and socially as a 45-year-old. Likewise, a 30-year-old may function as the stereotypical 70-year-old.

An investigation of demographic information is quite important in community health planning for older people in the United States. Through gathering and analyzing various statistics, it is possible to project who will be in need of health services, of what type, how they can best be delivered, and how health status can be improved for older people. The proportion of older people in the United States population is growing rapidly. In 1900, when life expectancy was 47 years, the United States population was comprised of only 3.1 million aged, compared to 23 million in 1980. If current low birth rates continue, it is projected that by the year 2020, 1 in every 5 persons will be over 65 (see Table 14-1). The 65-and-older group of the population has increased sixfold since 1900, while the 64-and-under group has increased only 2 times in that same period. The net increase of people joining the ranks of the aged each day numbers 1,000.[2] Today, with improved community health measures, life expectancy is 76 for women, 67 for men, or an average

Table 14-1 Total Population 65 Years Old and Over and 75 Years Old and Over, and Decennial Increase: 1900 to 2020 (Numbers in Thousands; Population Estimated as of July 1, 1975.)[a]

YEAR	POPULATION 65 YEARS AND OVER INCREASE IN PRECEDING DECADE			POPULATION 75 YEARS AND OVER INCREASE IN PRECEDING DECADE		
	Number	*Amount*	*Percent*	*Number*	*Amount*	*Percent*
Estimates						
1900	3,099	(b)	(b)	899	(b)	(b)
1910	3,986	887	28.6	1,170	271	30.1
1920	4,929	943	23.7	1,449	279	23.8
1930	6,705	1,776	36.0	1,945	496	34.2
1940	9,031	2,326	34.7	2,664	719	37.0
1950	12,397	3,366	37.3	3,904	1,240	46.5
1960	16,659	4,262	34.4	5,625	1,721	44.1
1970	20,156	3,497	21.0	7,691	2,066	36.7
Projections						
1980	23,703	3,547	17.6	9,017	1,326	17.2
1990	27,509	3,806	16.1	10,735	1,718	19.1
2000	28,839	1,330	4.8	12,476	1,741	16.2
2010	30,940	2,101	7.3	12,569	93	0.7
2020	40,261	9,321	30.1	13,870	1,301	10.4

[a]More recent estimates, prepared after the compilation of the data in this report, are as follows in thousands: (Current Population Reports, Series P 25, #519).

[b]Not applicable.

Source: U.S. DHEW National Institutes of Health, *Epidemiology of Aging.* U.S. DHEW Pub. No. (NIH) 75-711, 1975.

Figure 14-2
Today with improved community health measures, life expectancy is 73.2 years. Courtesy Arizona Republic and Phoenix Gazette.

of 73.2 years.[3] Clearly, the rapid population increase of this age group is of special significance to community health, in view of the fact that older people need and use health services more than any other group in the population.

Another demographic factor which must be considered relates to the composition of the aging population. There is a marked difference between life expectancy in men and women. According to 1977 statistics, women outnumber men in the over-65 age group by 100 to 70. By age 80, there were only 50 men to every 100 women. By 1990, projections indicate that there will be only 68 men for every 100 women in the over-65 age group. There has been a significant change in sex ratio in this segment of the population, and this trend is expected to continue in the future. On the average, people reaching 65 years of age in 1980 could expect to live an additional 16 years.

There are also differences in the racial composition of older persons in the United States. They account for only 8 percent of the older group. According to 1977 mortality rates, 81 percent of white women, 66 percent of all other women and white men, and 50 percent of all other men will reach age 65 in our country.[4]

One of the most widespread misconceptions concerning the aged is that the vast majority of them live in nursing homes or other institutions. In reality, only 5 percent of the older population is confined to an institution. This means that some 95 percent of the total aged population is living independently in communities. Many of this group live in their own homes, some in apartments, or in homes with relatives or friends. At times, these individuals will need health and social services. It is important that community services are able to provide them with transportation, meals when needed, and recreation and social outlets.

Gathering and analyzing demographic data makes it possible to anticipate problems which might arise in providing and delivering health care to older persons. For example, the concentration of older persons tends to be highest in the states with the greatest overall populations. New York, California, Pennsylvania, and Illinois account for one-third of the over-65 population. It is projected that within twenty-five years, the suburbs will be comprised of predominantly older persons. However, today most live in the inner city and in rural America. Older Americans also appear to be migrating to states which have warmer climates and less industry. In the sun belt, Florida has the highest proportion of older people, but growth has also been experienced in Arizona, Nevada, Hawaii, and New Mexico.[5]

Older Americans, with the exception of psychiatric care, utilize health services more than any other adult age group. Yet the mental health needs of this group are substantial. Both depression and suicide reach a peak in older white men in the later years. The incidence of organic brain disorders increases with age.

About 77 percent of those over 65 have seen a physician in the last year. The short-stay hospital utilization rates for older persons is twice that of the 45–65 age group. Most visits to the hospitals and clinics by the aged are for diseases of the circulatory and respiratory systems. Almost two-thirds of all deaths in this age group are a result of heart disease and stroke. Other major health problems of the older American include digestive disorders and accidents.

In general, the aged tend to use emergency-room care less than do other age groups and use physician's office services more. Out-patient clinics are still a major source of care for older people, especially those who belong to certain minority groups. This service-utilization characteristic is of great significance for community health. Since the enactment of Medicare, the number of poor older persons still report fewer visits to physicians, compared to their nonpoor counterparts, but the differences between poor and nonpoor rates have decreased.[6]

Although the number of older people living in poverty has dropped by 60 percent since 1959, due in large measure to Social Security benefits, still 14 percent of older Americans have incomes below poverty level. Moreover, elderly blacks are affected to a much greater extent. And women are constrained—with median incomes only about half those of men ($3,100 annually versus $5,500 for men in 1977.)

Figure 14-3
Old age can be a satisfying time of
life. Courtesy Arizona Republic
and Phoenix Gazette.

HEALTH STATUS OF OLDER PEOPLE

Old age can be a satisfying time of life with a minimum of physical and mental-emotional impairments, even though there are few who view old age as a time of potential health and growth. Of course the ability of an older person to continue to grow, adapt, and act affirmatively throughout the life cycle is dependent upon physical and emotional health, as well as societal supports such as medical care, shelter, recreation outlets, and opportunities for social interactions. It is significant that until recently, few research studies attempted to identify what healthy aging is like. Interest and support has been evident for research concerned with disease and pathological parameters of old age. Yet old age can be a healthy, fulfilling time of life. At any age, adaptation and flexibility are important to attaining and maintaining health.

There are certain physical changes that do occur with aging, but their presence does not indicate illness, disease, or loss of the ability to function daily at one's potential. Some of these outward signs which are more or less inevitable with aging, include graying of the hair, development of wrinkles, decline in sense acuity (smell, sight, touch, and hearing), and postural changes. Generally speaking, older people have reduced metabolic rates, decreases in the strength and speed of muscular response, and a slowing down in the rates of cell growth and repair. Although 86 percent of older people experience one or more chronic health problems, 95 percent of those who comprise this group are able to live in the community.[7] In spite of the conditions from which they suffer, they are still able to be independent.

Among the most frequent chronic conditions and impairments for older people in the community are: arthritis, which affects 44 percent of the population over 65; reduced vision, 22 percent; hearing impairments, 29 percent; heart conditions, 20 percent; and hypertension, 35 percent.

In the past, physicians have suggested that disease should be considered a basic and inevitable part of aging. Contemporary thought is that it is preventable, and must be challenged early in the life cycle. This is a responsibility of community health. There is also a decline in respiratory, circulatory, and renal functions in older people. The overall effects of these physiologic changes produce important differences in the body composition of the aged person. However, just as the nutritional requirements of older persons are not significantly different from younger individuals, older persons can continue to stay active, increase cardiac efficiency within the confines of their individual potential, as well as respiratory efficiency. Most important is the fact that there is room for improvement in the older persons life with regard to fitness, nutrition, and general health maintenance. Community health educators and outreach workers can help to educate older persons to understand their own responsibility for health maintenance, through activity, good dietary practices, and so forth. In addition, it is the responsibility of community health to make quality services available and accessible to older persons who need them. This includes a positive approach to the provision of many services—out-patient, short-term, and long-term care—as well as health maintenance and rehabilitation.

In addition to the physical changes that occur with aging there can be emotional changes. However, these are not quite as predictable as physical changes and many times are related to either a disease state which is present in the older person or the way the social system and the older person interact. Older persons are sometimes described as forgetful, slow-thinking, and irritable. These psychological states are frequently associated with disease. *Chronic brain syndrome,* resulting from inadequate blood flow to the brain, can cause an older person to be forgetful or slow-thinking. Constant pain, suffered from digestive problems or the pain of *angina pectoris* during mild activity can cause the older person to become irritable.

Like people of every age, older persons exhibit a variety of emotional responses. They feel grief, anxiety, depression, and loneliness. Many of the emotional responses are quite predictable in view of the social situation in which older persons find themselves. Old age is a time when the social conditions present are not the most desirable, especially in American society. Older persons experience loss of spouses, friends, and loved ones—as well as loss of income and wage-earning ability. They must contemplate their own mortality—the realistic appraisal of their own inevitable death. Compulsory retirement can make older people feel useless, out-dated, and no longer of any value or a part of productive society. In many civilizations, older people are respected for their wisdom and their contribution for many years to the society and the community. In some societies, there is no such thing as a nursing home. Too frequently in the United States, the pervasiveness of ageism fosters attitudes among the young, which causes them to treat older people as a burden, as unproductive, and unworthy. It is not surprising that this evokes feelings of anxiety, loss, depression, and isolation within older people.

Generally, American society has provided little support for older persons. It is hoped that in an era when discriminatory practices are looked upon with disfavor—the realization will occur that this is what we do to our aged—and it too will be stopped. In the meantime, older people must continue, for the most part, to provide their own supports, develop their own ego strength, and resist surrendering to those who believe them to be unproductive, senile, and resistant to change.

It is well substantiated that health problems do occur in older persons, but the focus of community health activities, in addition to providing necessary services to care for those aged who have health problems, must be on generating an effective means of disease prevention throughout the life cycle. It is universally agreed that aging is inevitable and some intrinsic changes occur with age, but illness, health problems, and maladaptation are not inevitable. We know, for example, that through genetic make-up, a person is born with biological potential for life. Research suggests that transmitted genetic information provides the individual with greater or lesser resistance to tissue destruction, as well as a greater or lesser ability to overcome challenges and stresses. Other factors such as gender also seem important. However, the relationship is not clear between the biological sex variable and other social factors. Healthy aging and longevity appears to be related to older people making health-generating lifestyle choices, such as obtaining adequate nutrition, keeping physically active, maintaining desired weight, and abstaining from smoking and excess alcohol consumption. The influence of other factors on disease and health problems, such as environmental pollutants, food additives, weather or climatic conditions, and employment and educational status are more complex. Particular dietary habits and their relationship to healthy aging and longevity are still open to some question. Even the relationship between cholesterol intake and heart disease is still surrounded by controversy.

There are a number of social and economic factors related to well-being in aging. In almost all instances, higher socioeconomic status means a greater likelihood of wellness

Table 14-2 Causes of Death: Diseases of the Heart Far Outrank Any Other Cause of Death among Persons 65 and Over. Rates (per 100,000 population) for the 10 Leading Causes of Death Were as Follows:

RANK	CAUSE OF DEATH	RATE
	All causes	6219.7
1.	Diseases of heart	2830.7
2.	Malignant neoplasms	925.2
3.	Cerebrovascular diseases	904.3
4.	Influenza and pneumonia	246.0
5.	Arteriosclerosis	167.3
6.	Accidents	149.3
	Motor vehicle	39.6
	All other	109.8
7.	Diabetes Mellitus	136.5
8.	Bronchitis, emphysema, and asthma	113.4
9.	Cirrhosis of liver	36.3
10.	Infections of kidney	35.1
	All other causes	675.5

Source: U.S. DHEW, National Center for Health Statistics, U.S. Public Health Service.

in old age. In addition, work satisfaction and happiness in life tend to be very predictive of wellness and longevity.

In summary, the activity, diet, personality make-up, educational level, occupational satisfaction and status, as well as genetic factors, are all significant factors in longevity. The relationship between environmental factors and healthy old age is not yet clearly understood. From a community health standpoint, it is important to keep in mind that the focus on longevity is not enough, for quality of life, regardless of how short it may be, is of equal significance. Prevention of disease such as heart disease and cancer has potential for making a real difference in the quality of life as well as its duration. This should be the focus of community health. In the future, the responsibility of community health will be to improve the quality of life by maintaining the function of older people, socially, physiologically, and emotionally. From a health care delivery standpoint, community health will need to develop *multiphasic screening* programs for high-risk older groups. The community health field of the future may be responsible for helping older people develop satisfying new social roles. Regarding community mental health, early instruction must take place in order to reach older individuals who are experiencing bereavement, retirement, and isolation. All these may lead to depression and maladaptive emotional behavior. It is now known that there are certain transition periods in the later part of the life cycle that can lead to maladaptive behavior. Retirement, sickness, and death of a loved one represent such transition stages. Once the effects of these stages on older people are fully understood, intervention will be possible.

Community Health Services and Older People

Community health is responding to the needs of the target population of older people in our contemporary society. Responsiveness by professionals and lay citizens alike is warranted, for at the present time 1 in 10 persons is aged, and within the next fifty years it is projected that 1 in every 5 or 6 persons will be in the ranks of the aged.

The creation of the National Institute on Aging within the National Institutes of Health in 1976 is but one example of evidence that reflects a growing national concern and commitment to improving the quality of life for older persons in our society. In addition, the initiation of the Task Force on Aging of the American Public Health Association and the Task Force on Aging Education in the American School Health Association, suggest the level of current concern. Contemporary society is faced with the responsibility for the aged, a growing nonmilitant population group in our society, for their health, well-being and their continued support. Every person will have some role to play.

The enactment of Medicare, improvements in the Social Security system, and the development of Homemaker–Home Health Aide Services and other programs have all been successful in brightening the picture for older people in the United States. Yet there is much evidence to support the notion that the aged still have many unmet needs. Many of the health problems that affect the aged are related to social isolation, social loss, or the psychological stress which is placed upon them by a society that can be patronizing or insensitive. From an ecological perspective, the aged person interacts with the social, physical, and emotional environment in which he or she lives.

Figure 14–4
Community health can help older people develop satisfying new social roles. Courtesy Arizona Republic and Phoenix Gazette.

A community health approach to generating health and quality of life in the later years will require an appreciation for this ecological perspective and the implementing programs based upon this orientation. A comprehensive community health system for older people should incorporate the interactions of physical health variables in a behavioral and social matrix. It should include the following types of traditional services, which reflect a more comprehensive orientation concerning health promotion:

1. primary-prevention services, including active community health education programs aimed at older persons, adults, and young people,
2. secondary-prevention services, aimed at early detection of health problems and disease,
3. ambulatory and out-patient care,
4. home-care,
5. institutional care to handle acute and serious chronic conditions, and
6. rehabilitation.

In addition to those traditional activities of community health, the adequate and efficient incorporation of physical, social, and emotional health components and their effects on the health of older persons will require that more senior-citizen community services centers be set up. Community health has a significant role to play in the initiation and provision of services at such centers. These should provide the elderly with a wide variety of resources and outlets for recreation, continued growth through learning new skills and crafts, work and volunteer opportunities, and health maintenance and education functions. At a recent Senate Sub-Committee on Health of the Elderly, the idea of universal automated annual health examinations was proposed and gained significant support. These multiphasic screening exams could be conducted under the auspices of community health centers for senior citizens and would detect symptomatic or threatening illness at an early stage, resulting in both reduced cost and suffering to society and to older persons.

Medicare

Enacted in 1966, Medicare was designed to provide health care coverage for the elderly. It is viewed by some as a tremendous accomplishment, and by others as a costly and temporary approach to providing health services to all Americans, not just older people.

Two plans exist within the Medicare program: A. Hospital Insurance, which is available to anyone over 65 who is covered by Social Security; and B. Medical Insurance, to help pay for physicians' services and some medical services not covered by Part A. Both have deductibles. Part B enrollment is voluntary and is financed by monthly premiums shared equally by those who choose this protection and the federal government. Part B of Medicare provides benefits covering 80 percent of medical-surgical charges once the insured individual has paid a $60 deductible on these charges. Insurance companies, Blue Cross/Blue Shield plans, and Group Health Insurance of New York participate in the Medicare program as fiscal intermediaries for the government. Neither plan covers checkups, hearing aids, eyeglasses, dental care, and many home-care services. A recent report from the Health Research Group warned senior citizens that under Medicare the federal government picks up on the average, less than one-third of their bills for physicians' services. The U.S. House of Representatives Select Committee on Aging reported that the Medicare contribution is only about 40 percent of the average older person's health bill.[8]

The 1972 Social Security Amendments also allow the aged who are not eligible for Part A benefits (aliens and some federal civil service employees and annuitants) to enroll in the program by voluntarily paying a monthly premium. The premium is high since it is based on the full cost of hospital care for a high-risk group.

By 1980, more than 26 million persons in the United States, including nearly 2.1 million disabled persons, were entitled to hospital insurance provided by the Medicare program; 24 million persons, including 2.0 million disabled persons, were enrolled for supplementary medical insurance.

The most significant of the achievements of Medicare is that millions of older persons have received health care and services with a reduced financial burden. In addition, the enactment of Medicare carried with it a built-in tangential effort to improve institutional standards, health provider licensure standards, and to some extent regulated the quality standards in the delivery of health care.

As is true with nearly every new program, potential for abuse does exist and such is the case with Medicare. As costs of operating the program mushroomed, federal mechanisms have been implemented in an attempt to restrain skyrocketing costs and establish more acceptable levels of quality care. Ceilings were placed on Medicare reimbursements, which shifted the financial burden once again to older persons and their families.[9]

All institutions who participate in the Medicare program are required to establish utilization review committees, whose responsibility is to monitor service utilization, duration of stay, and admissions. This was the first step in peer review and laid the rudimentary framework for the establishment of Professional Standards Review Organizations (PSROs).

The experience of Medicare suggests that the aged in our society have expansive needs for the services of physicians, hospitals and clinics. As a result of the Medicare experience, we are beginning to recognize that health status of the elderly can be improved by providing them with nearly a full range of hospital and medical services. Since the advent of Medicare, more poor aged persons than nonpoor make use of hospital services, and although physicians services continue to be utilized more by well-to-do aged than the poor, the gap is closing, and there is less disparity in utilization rates than in the past. The Medicare program created a new class of institutions and facilities including the extended-care facility, an expanded program in home-health services, and rehabilitation services.

However, in terms of improving access to health care and quality of care for older persons, many are suggesting that additional revisions in Medicare policy are needed. First is the suggestion that Medicare should be a basic, comprehensive program for all aged persons. This would require an adjustment of eligibility and coverage requirements. Second, there should be no barriers to older persons selecting the combination and sequence of services that are least costly and most effective in any given situation, so that appropriate attention can be given to prevention and rehabilitation. In the future, ways of controlling the high cost of health services must be identified, and the barriers to preventive care must be removed. At present, routine physical examinations, vision and hearing testing, and immunizations require that the older person pay the deductible. It is not justifiable to continue to give lip service to prevention yet lend no motivation for older people to seek preventive health maintenance, much less pose barriers to obtaining these services.[10] Older persons would no doubt have significantly less anxiety about the possibility of becoming ill and needing health services if the Medicare program made preventive services available to them allowing for early diagnosis and treatment of disease and health problems before they become acute and require hospitalization.

Other services and programs that are in need of improvement and expansion to more effectively promote the health and well being of our nation's older people include homemaker services, Meals-on-Wheels services, counseling services, home-health care, and community activity centers or senior-citizen centers, all of which can provide opportunities for older persons to learn new skills and crafts, be socially involved, and continue a fulfilling life.

The net effect of Medicare has been more and better care. Through Medicare it has been possible to foster utilization of services by a segment of the population which too often has been previously denied access. Yet, the job before community health involves both providing better care services to older people who are ill, and generating health promotion and prevention of disease in the first place. Health promotion and disease prevention for older persons must become a priority in community health.

In the future, society will demand that more opportunities be provided for older persons in America. Yet even if the present trend continues, community health can make older people aware that even within the culture, as it now exists, there are opportunities for older persons to continue to grow, and that there are many positive aspects in the postretirement years. In the later years, the individual has the opportunity and responsibility to set his or her own goals, both immediate and long-range. This concept is an important one to incorporate into community mental health programs.

In addition, concerning community mental health, it is important to recognize the special needs of the aged. It is important to be able to make an accurate early diagnosis of high-suicide-risk individuals and drug-sensitivity problems. It is important to recognize early symptoms in people of depression, loneliness and grief, before these individuals become high risk. Dealing with the terminally ill is an additional concern and a focus of the hospice movement. The aged comprise only 10 percent of the population, yet they contribute 25 percent to suicidal deaths. Therapeutic intervention and treatment is vital, as is prevention.

FUTURE COMMUNITY HEALTH PROGRAMS AND OLDER PEOPLE

Clearly, the goals of community health and the role it plays in the health care delivery system is that of promoting both the quality and longevity of human lives.

Approximately 4 out of every 5 older people suffer some chronic condition. About 25 percent of old people have major problems in adapting to some chronic problem. Although health care during acute episodes of disease is very significant to this population, it is primarily in the area of rehabilitation services or helping an older person to solve the problems associated with chronic illness, that are considered most important. The degree of being at risk, of not being able to cope with chronic conditions or needing extra support to adapt, increases after age 75. The 75-and-over age group are significantly more susceptible to mental, physical and environmental anomalies. It is of significance to note that this portion of the aged population is growing most rapidly.

Services will need to be provided for the aged, including community health, social and mental services. These services have been described as being made up of five components: (1) personal care and medical services, (2) supportive medical services, (3) personal maintenance, (4) counseling, and (5) linkages. Personal services refer to those things which are related to personal hygiene and care in the physical sense. Supportive medical services are designed to extend out of the physicians role and are performed by

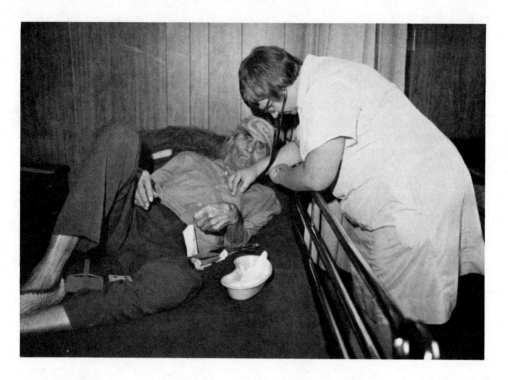

Figure 14-5 Outreach and home-care is an essential health service for older people. Courtesy Arizona Department of Health Services.

others through physician review. Maintenance services include any aspect of activities to the older person maintaining him or herself in a home or apartment. They can include such things as housekeeping, environmental health, home health care, and nutrition services. Counseling services for the older person involve many of the integral functions that counseling a person of any age would involve such as listening skills, providing support, and helping the individual to mobilize and utilize resources. Linkages refer to the important function of a variety of services designed to assure continuity of available health care. Linkages aid older persons in making the connection with the services they need. Outreach and information and referral services, as well as education, and, if necessary the provision of transportation, are all integrated to promote an effective comprehensive system of services for older people.

Health Maintenance Organizations (HMOs) are yet another way in which existing facilities and services may evolve and reflect the needs of the older people. A complete description of HMOs has been provided in Chapter 10, but here let us say that a Health Maintenance Organization is a prepayment type of health plan, which is supported by the federal government and matching organization money. Until 1972, older people were ineligible for coverage by HMOs on a prepaid basis. But the 1972 Amendment to the Social Security Act nullified early legislation and allowed entrance of older people into the plans.[11] It may be that medical care can be obtained by Medicare patients through an HMO better than they have been able to get at a fee-for-service situation under Part A and B of Medicare. A question that remains is whether or not HMOs will be able to deliver not only medical care to the aged, but also social services which can be logically located under the area of health care.[12] The following is a listing of those services which need to be included in a comprehensive program for older people.

Community Mental Health Services and Programs

The two major purposes of community mental health services for older people include promoting mental health in the over-65 age group and providing outreach, emergency, and on-going therapeutic care for those with emotional problems. In addition, community mental health services should include provision of institutional care for those older people whose problems cannot be adequately handled in home care. The mission of community health services is fostering adjustment and emotional well-being in older persons. The programs included are the following:

Mental health promotion These programs are designed to promote emotional-mental well-being and adjustment in older people. This is accomplished through community health education, provision of recreational, social and occupational outlets for older persons.

Early intervention and detection of emotional illness The community mental health team is trained to identify at-risk older individuals who may be candidates for emotional stresses leading to maladaptaion. Such high risk individuals include those who have recently retired and are not making satisfactory adjustment from the work-role; those who have recently lost spouses, friends, or loved ones and are going through bereavement; and those older persons who have grown withdrawn or isolated from social contacts and life.

Outreach and home care Outreach programs are designed to assist the older person who would not be a suitable candidate for institutionalization to attain higher levels of emotional well-being and adjustment. These services include out-patient therapy, home visitations, as well as an integration of other aspects of social services such as occupational therapy and recreation therapy.

Emergency services These services should be provided both in the hospital, clinic and home setting. Physicians should be on call twenty-four hours a day to meet the emergency psychiatric needs of older persons.

Institutional care The provision of institutional care is vital for those older persons who are affected by severe emotional problems such as psychosis or chronic brain syndrome, which make it impossible for them to function in society. Institutional care is utilized when out-patient treatment is not feasible.

Nutritional Services

Among older persons, adequate nutrition is such a major concern that in 1972 the government established a Nutrition Program for the elderly. Through this program hundreds of communities serve one hot meal a day for at least five weekdays to anyone 60 and older. In order to foster adequate nutrition for the elderly, the community should have the following services and programs available:

Meals-on-Wheels Meals-on-Wheels was established to foster adequate nutrition for older people who cannot leave their homes. In this program, hot meals are delivered at lunchtime, with a cold meal left for supper. In addition to improving nutrition, older people are provided with a link to the outside world and social encounters through Meals-on-Wheels.

Nutrition Program for the Elderly As has previously been mentioned, this is a federally supported program. Most communities in the U.S. now provide this service. Nutrition Programs for the Elderly facilitate older persons obtaining adequate nutrition.

Supplemental food and food stamps commodity programs The government food commodity program and food stamps are available to those older persons who exist on a severly limited income. In 1977, 500,000 aged used the surplus commodity program. In the same year, 1.5 million older persons registered for food stamps. Clearly, these two programs are not reaching the large numbers of older persons who are in need of the services the programs provide. There is an education job to do, as well as program revisions which will foster better utilization of these programs.

Poor nutrition can lead to many health programs. Many aged are at or below poverty line and simply cannot afford to purchase adequate food. Psychological conditions such as loneliness and apathy can result in lack of appetite and lead to malnutrition. In addition, physical problems which are frequently the consequence of chronic disease can limit mobility for food shopping and cooking. Nutritional programs, including those with educational and outreach services, should be expanded for older persons. Food, for many older people is a far better prescription for health than drug therapy.

Physical Health Promotion

Not surprisingly, many of the major limitations imposed upon older people occur as a result of physical problems. In most instances the physical health problems of older persons are of the chronic and degenerative category. Such things as heart disease, cancer, arthritis, emphysema, stroke, and diabetes affect many older people. Additional threats to physicial well-being also occur as a result of the communicable and acute conditions. Diseases such as influenza, tuberculosis, and the common cold pose problems for older people. Accidents among older people are very common. The aged, more than any other specific population group, have tremendous needs for physical health preservation, treatment and rehabilitation services. The components of physical health care services for older people should include:

Prevention of acute and chronic disease Programs need to be aimed at promoting well-being and health. Energetic community health education programs must be designed to equip older persons with knowledge concerning the role of lifestyle choices in contributing to health and disease. Included in health education programs designed for the elderly should be:

1. Nutrition education, including weight control.
2. Physical fitness education and the role of relaxation in maintaining health.
3. Drug and alcohol education, including smoking, analysis of over-the-counter drugs and prescription medications.
4. Recreation education, including not only the value of recreation from a social and physical health standpoint, but also in contributing to emotional health.
5. Preservation of the senses and remediation of problems associated with vision, hearing, touch, and taste.

Early detection of acute and chronic disease Although many of the chronic diseases which are prevalent in older people are preventable the simple fact is that too often they are not prevented. Therefore, community health must establish avenues through which early intervention can take place. In this way, suffering, disability and even premature mortality can be reduced for older persons. A program of early detection should include:

1. *Mass Multiphasic Screening Programs:* The provision of health screening for older persons has promoted early detection of such things as hypertension, glaucoma, diabetes, emphysema, enlarged heart, vision and hearing impairments. These community health screening programs can be utilization of mobile screening units, and by conducting health fairs in geographic areas which have a high proportion of older people. Vital to the success of such programs is their accessibility for the target population, active utilization of the services by the group and provision of adequate follow-up of those individuals where a problem is detected.
2. *Periodic Health Maintenance Examinations:* This refers to the yearly physical exam. Unfortunately, obtaining yearly physical exams is not a common practice for most older Americans. Constraints to this include cost, accessibility of services, and insufficient physician time. In addition, Medicare excludes routine physicial exams from its benefit coverage package, which imposes greater financial burdens on older people. In the future, we may well see the practice of yearly multiphasic computer health exams, including laboratory work-ups for every older person in the United States.

Health counseling Health counseling is the cooperative responsibility of all members of the health care team—physicians, nurses, social workers, physicians' assistants, and health educators. Health counseling should perform two functions: (1) health promotion and health maintenance for older persons, and (2) patient education, or helping older patients who suffer either chronic or acute conditions to understand the condition and help them to manage the problem in their lives.

Ambulatory or out-patient care   The majority of health problems which affect older persons are of a chronic nature, many of which can be treated on an out-patient basis or in the home. They are conditions which require maintenance and supervision, but not hospitalization. At present, increasing numbers of chronically ill older persons are receiving treatment in settings such as the home, day hospitals, day-care centers, neighborhood health centers, community health clinics and in hospitals on an out-patient basis. This method of managing those who have chronic disease problems has proved to be a most effective one for ambulatory older persons. Indeed, a key to the effectiveness of out-patient services is the ability of the older person to obtain transportation to the service location. In the future, the provision of transportation services will have to be expanded, if the needs of chronically ill aged are to be met. Poor transportation systems and costly taxis all but immobilize and isolate the aged. Better utilization of volunteer and staff cars to facilitate transportation of older persons from their homes to extended care facilities is needed in the future.

Home-Care

The concept of home-care is not new to medicine. However, "a coordinated home care program is one that is centrally administered and which, through coordinated planning, evaluation and follow-up procedures provides for the medical, nursing, social, and related services in the older persons home."[13] Home-care is vital to older persons who are ill, but do not require the extensive facilities of hospitals.

Unfortunately the number of comprehensive home-care programs in the United States is very small. By expanding this type of service community health could make a significant contribution to the health of older persons. Home-health-care services will no doubt increase in the future. Included in a comprehensive home-care program are the following:

1. *Home Nursing Care:* provision of care to sick or disabled persons under the written directions of a physician. This may include physicial therapy, occupational therapy, speech therapy, and social work.
2. *Homemaker Service:* provision of mature women who are skilled in home management and home-care of the sick, designed to assist older people to remain in the home and out of institutions.
3. *Meals-on-Wheels:* provision of meals for older persons who are unable to do this for themselves. Again, this service allows the older person to remain in the home.
4. *Friendly-Visiting Service:* the objective is one of making regular visits to older people who cannot leave their homes on their own. This service is designed to fulfill companionship and social needs of isolated older people.

Institutional Care

It is not surprising that older people are reluctant to leave their homes and be admitted to institutions. Between the unfavorable reputation of American institutions and the idea of leaving behind familiar surroundings and social contacts, older people resist institutionalization. However, for both physical and emotional reasons older people in the United States are placed in any of a variety of institutions ranging from hospitals, to nursing homes and homes for the aged.

Hospitalization Older persons may be hospitalized during acute stages of chronic and/or communicable illnesses. These short stay hospitalizations, usually between a few days to three months provide professionals with the equipment necessary to diagnose and treat these acute illnesses. During hospitalization, social services should be available to handle home pressures for older persons, such as pets, mail, and watching over the home. In addition, hospitalization may involve long-term care. Unfortunately, often older persons are misplaced in hospitals for chronic care simply because the community has not developed alternate services for helping them.

Nursing homes Almost one million older persons live in nursing homes. These homes have received considerable condemnation from legislators, the press, and the general public. There are good nursing homes, but many have serious deficiencies. Of the five percent of the elderly who are institutionalized the majority resides in nursing homes. Two-fifths of the nursing-home populations are people 85 years old and older. A great proportion of nursing home residents are female rather than male. Nursing homes throughout the United States have been found to be filthy, unsafe, and depressing. Patients are neglected and even abused. Staffs in these homes are often poorly trained, unmotivated and unsupervised. There is much room for improvement in the nursing-home institutions.

Because of the growing feeling that, in general, long-term institutionalization in a nursing home should be avoided, services are being developed to fill the gap between acute care and home-care. These services include out-patient care and extensive day care.

Foster-home care This type of service involves encouraging families to take in healthy older people who are not related to them. At present, foster-home programs have not met with much success. The programs are underfinanced, disorganized, and unregulated. In the future, foster care could be an ideal solution to meeting the needs of older persons who are basically healthy, but require some supervision. However, this will require more financial support and more effective organization. In the past, home placement of older persons was overlooked. In the future, steps must be taken to match older persons to foster families, considering such things as religious beliefs, personal habits and socioeconomic status.

Homes for the aged These facilities provide group living arrangements for older persons. They are usually voluntary, nonprofit institutions. In the past, these

Table 14-3 Nursing Home Residents, According to Selected Characteristics: United States, 1973-74 and 1977[a]

| | RESIDENTS | | | |
| | 1973-74[b] | | 1977 | |
CHARACTERISTIC	Number	Percent Distri-bution	Number	Percent Distri-bution
Total	1,075,800	100.0	1,303,100	100.0
Primary Diagnosis at Last Examination				
Diseases of the Circulatory System[c]	450,300	41.9	516,800	39.7
Congestive heart failure	—	—	52,800	4.1
Heart attack	55,700	5.2	22,500	1.7
Arteriosclerosis	241,800	22.5	264,400	20.3
Hypertension	—	—	47,700	3.7
Stroke	113,400	10.5	103,500	7.9
Mental Disorders and Senility without Psychosis[c]	262,600	24.4	266,100	20.4
Psychosis, including senile	—	—	78,500	6.0
Chronic brain syndrome	—	—	96,400	7.4
Senility without psychosis	146,800	13.6	26,600	2.0
Mental retardation	—	—	42,400	3.3
Other Diagnoses[c,d]	362,900	33.7	520,200	39.9
Diabetes	—	—	71,700	5.5
Fractures	—	—	39,900	3.1
Diseases of the nervous system and sense organs	64,200	6.0	42,500	3.3
Arthritis or rheumatism	—	—	56,200	4.3
Cancer or neoplasm	25,600	2.4	28,900	2.2
Living Arrangement Prior to Admission				
Private residence	402,900	37.5	509,400	39.1
Another health facility[e]	608,400	56.6	706,700	54.2
Boarding home, other place, or unknown	64,500	6.0	87,000	6.7
Length of Stay Since Admission				
Less than 3 months	155,400	14.4	189,300	14.5
3 to less than 6 months	103,800	9.7	122,100	9.4
6 to less than 12 months	155,700	14.5	163,100	12.5
1 to less than 3 years	357,700	33.2	427,800	32.8
3 years or more	303,200	28.2	400,800	30.8
Median Length of Stay in Years Since Admission	1.5	—	1.6	—

[a]Data are based on a sample of nursing homes.

[b]Excludes residents in personal care or domiciliary care homes.

[c]Includes other diagnoses not listed below.

[d]Includes unknown diagnoses. Data for 1977 also includes 56,700 residents who received no physician visits while in facility.

[e]In 1977, 49.4 percent of residents admitted from another health facility had gone to that facility from a private or semiprivate residence.

Note: Numbers are rounded to the nearest hundred. Percents are calculated on basis of unrounded numbers.

Source: Division of Health Resources Utilization Statistics, National Center for Health Statistics; data from the National Nursing Home Survey.

YEAR	AGED POPULATION	%
1900	3 MILLION	4
1978	24 MILLION	11
2000	32 MILLION	14
2030	50 MILLION	17

Figure 14-6
Population of the aged.

facilities have not been totally satisfactory. However, there is a progressive trend which indicates a change is taking place, in the concept of "old-age homes." Homes for aged in the future can follow the example that has been made by the Philadelphia Geriatric Center. In this setting there are facilities for older persons to (1) live independently in apartments on the campus, (2) utilize a hospital which is nearby, should they need short-term or long-term care, (3) participate in day-care center activities, (4) or move in to the nursing home at the facility when their condition warrants such institutionalization.

Hospice   The gathering force of what is referred to as the "hospice movement" has served to focus long-overdue attention on how we as individuals and as a society deal with death. The result has been a more humanistic approach to the care of the terminally ill. There are at least four elements which are crucial to hospice care:

> educating medical, nursing and allied health personnel to be sensitive to the rights, needs, and problems of those in the last few days of life,
>
> discovering new therapies for managing pain and other discomforts of the terminally ill,
>
> providing home care, so that people can remain at home for as long as they desire, and be able to die at home if they wish and if it is possible; and,
>
> attending to both the immediate and long-term needs of grieving survivors.

A real concern of the elderly is the prospect of being exposed to sophisticated technology that prolongs life beyond the time when it is meaningful and enjoyable. The hospice movement calls for society to learn how to help those for whom medical care can offer no more, so that death becomes possible without pain, discomfort, humiliation or financial worries.[14]

There is a trend that will demand in the future that institutions provide care at several levels of need. Without the provision of many different types of services, invariably some older people will be misplaced. The concept of community health in the future in dealing with older people must be one of progressive care through the development of a number of alternatives to institutional care. There are a variety of options which may be investigated and initiated regarding health care for older persons. However, the realization of these alternatives is dependent upon our persistence and commitment to the idea that older persons are valuable human beings and that the best means through which we can fulfill their needs is through a holistic approach to life and health.

Summary

A recent White House Conference on Aging stressed the idea that health care is a basic right. In order to insure that this basic right be fulfilled, a comprehensive system of health care must evolve in the future for older persons. It must incorporate many of the ideas presented in this chapter and progress further. Older people have not been a militant group but they are growing impatient with societies failure to recognize their needs. In the words of Maggie Kuhn, founder of the Gray Panthers, "Our oppressive, paternalistic society wants to keep the elderly out of the way, playing bingo and shuffleboard, but we are challenging it. We are putting our bodies on the line."[15] Alternatives must be developed in the form of adult day-care centers, foster-home programs, homemaker services, programs to check on shut-ins, and any other services which will help older persons to stay healthy and in their homes as long as possible. If we are human, we might be able to feel what older people feel when they are isolated, rejected, patronized, or treated as if they were incompetent burdens to society.

REVIEW QUESTIONS

1. Define ageism. Describe the affects of this stereotyping of older people as it relates to community health and the health care delivery system.
2. Differentiate chronological age from daily functional age.
3. Identify the major demographic characteristics of the aged population. Describe the implication of these characteristics to community health.
4. Identify the physiological changes and emotional responses that are typically associated with the aging process. How do these relate to the health care delivery system and other social support systems?
5. How can community health contribute to "quality of life" in the later years?
6. Describe Medicare. Identify its accomplishments and the improvements which need to be made in Medicare in the future.

SUGGESTED READINGS

Barney, Jane Lockwood, "Community Presence as a Key to Quality of Life in Nursing Homes," *American Journal of Public Health,* 64(3) 265-268, 1974.

Brotman, Herman, "The Fastest-Growing Minority: The Aging," *American Journal of Public Health,* 64(3) 249-252, 1974.

Butler, Robert, *Why Survive? Being Old in America.* New York: Harper and Row, 1975.

Hammerman, Jerome, "Health Services: Their Success and Failure in Reaching Older Adults," *American Journal of Public Health,* 64(3) 253-256, 1974.

Somers, Anne R. and Florence M. Moore, "Homemaker Services—Essential Option for the Elderly," *Public Health Reports,* 96(4) 354-359, 1976.

Weaver, Jerry, *National Health Policy and the Underserved: Ethnic Minorities, Women and the Elderly.* St. Louis: C. V. Mosby, 1976.

NOTES

[1] Robert Butler, "Successful Aging and the Role of Life Review," in Harold Cox (ed)., *Aging,* 2nd ed. Guilford, Conn.: Dushkin Publishing Group, 1980, p. 47.

[2] Herbert Brotman, "The Fastest Growing Minority: The Aging," *American Journal of Public Health,* 64(3), 1974.

[3] U.S. DHEW, *Health: United States, 1979.* Washington, D.C.: U.S. DHEW Pub. No. (PHS) 80-1232, 1980, p. 7.

[4] *Health: United States,* p. 15.

[5] J.S. Siegel and others, "Demographic Aspects of Aging and the Older Population in the United States," *U.S. Bureau of Census, Current Population Reports.* Washington, D.C.: Bureau of Census, Special Studies Series, No. 59, 1976, p. 34.

[6] Arthur Hess, "A Ten Year Perspective on Medicare," *Public Health Reports,* 91(4) 299, 1976.

[7] Robert Butler and Myrna Lewis, *Aging and Mental Health,* 2nd ed. St. Louis: C.V. Mosby, 1977, p. 2.

[8] "Medicare Pays only One-Third of Physicians Bills," *The Nation's Health,* 1980, p. 6.

[9] Arthur Hess, pp. 300-303.

[10] Avedis Donabedian, "Effects of Medicaid and Medicare on Access to and Quality of Health Care," *Public Health Reports,* 91(4) 1976, p. 327.

[11] "Social Security Amendments, Conference Report," *Congressional Record,* 92nd Congress (1st session), October 17, 1972, p. 50483.

[12] Stanley Brody, "Evolving Health Delivery Systems and Older People," *American Journal of Public Health,* 64(3), 1974, p. 246.

[13] Frank Reynolds and Paul Barsam, *Adult Health: Services for the Chronically Ill and Aged.* New York: Macmillan, 1967, p. 2.

[14] U.S. DHEW, *Healthy People: The Surgeon General's Report on Health Promotion and Disease Prevention.* Washington, D.C.: U.S. DHEW Pub. No. (PHS) 79-5509, 1979, p. 79.

[15] Maggie Kuhn, "Health Care and Older People." Unpublished paper. Presented at the American Public Health Association 102nd Annual Convention, October 1974, New Orleans.

GLOSSARY

ageism the systematic stereotyping of and discrimination against older people because they are old.

angina pectoris a condition that occurs as a result of oxygen deprivation to the heart muscle, usually accompanied by atherosclerosis.

chronic brain syndrome atherosclerosis and senile dementia are two patterns of senile brain disease. Senile dementia results in steady and gradual deterioration and wasting away of brain cells. Cerebral arteriosclerosis involves the hardening and narrowing of blood vessels that serve the brain.

chronological age from birth onward, progress through life as tracked by a series of numbers.

daily functional age not the number of years a person accumulates, but a measure of how the person is functioning biologically, psychologically, and socially.

geriatrics a discipline that attempts to facilitate enjoyable and productive living for older people.

gerontology the study of the aging process including the sociological, physiological and psychological dimensions.

multiphasic screening a form of medical diagnostic exam that involves screening the individual or testing for a wide range of conditions and health problems.

BIBLIOGRAPHY

Blazer, Dan, "Life Events, Mental Health Functioning and the use of Health Care Services by the Elderly," *American Journal of Public Health,* 70(11) 1174-1179, 1980.

Brantl, Virginia M. and Sister Marie Raymond Brown (eds.), *Readings in Gerontology.* St. Louis: C. V. Mosby, 1973.

Brody, Stanley, "Evolving Health Delivery Systems and Older People," *American Journal of Public Health,* 64(3) 245-248, 1974.

Donabedian, Avedis, "Effects of Medicare and Medicaid on Access to and Quality of Health Care," *Public Health Reports,* 91(4) 322-331, 1976.

Hess, Arthur, "A Ten Year Perspective on Medicare," *Public Health Reports,* 91(4) 299-302, 1976.

Hess, Beth (ed.), *Growing Old in America.* New Brunswick, N.J.: Transaction Books, 1976.

Kart, Gary S. and Barbara Maynard, *Aging in America: Readings in Social Gerentology.* Port Washington, N.Y.: Alfred Publishing Co., 1976.

Lowy, Louis, *Social Policies and Programs on Aging: What Is and What Should Be in the Later Years.* Lexington, Mass.: D.C. Heath, 1980.

Maddox, G.L. and J. Kransik (eds.), *Planning Services for Older People: Translating National Objectives into Effective Programs.* Chapel Hill, N.C.: Center for the Study of Aging and Human Development, 1976.

McNearney, Walter, "Health Insurance in the Medicare Years," *Public Health Reports,* 91(4) 336-343, 1976.

Ostfeld, Adrian and Don Gibson (eds.), *Epidemiology of Aging.* Washington, D.C.: U.S. DHEW Pub. No. (NIH) 75-711, 1975.

Reif, L. "Expansion and Merger of Home Health Care Agencies," *Home Health Care Quarterly,* 1(3), 1980.

Shanas, Ethel, "Health Status of Older People," *American Journal of Public Health,* 64(3) 361-364, 1974.

Sharma, Rabinder, "Forecasting Need and Demand for Home Health Care: A Selective Review," *Public Health Reports,* 95(6) 572-579, 1980.

U.S. DHEW, *Health: United States, 1979.* Washington, D.C.: U.S. DHEW Pub. No. (PHS) 80-1232, 1980.

INDEX